Dictionary
of British
Housebuilders

A Twentieth Century History

Fred Wellings

Matador
9 Priory Business Park,
Wistow Road, Kibworth Beauchamp,
Leicestershire. LE8 0RX
Tel: (+44) 116 279 2299
Fax: (+44) 116 279 2277
Email: books@troubador.co.uk
Web: www.troubador.co.uk/matador

Web:www.fredwellings.co.uk

ISBN 9781784625399

British Library Cataloguing in Publication Data.
A catalogue record for this book is available from the British Library.

Matador is an imprint of Troubador Publishing Ltd

CONTENTS

PREFACE

The *Dictionary of British Housebuilders* is a companion volume to my *British Housebuilders: History & Analysis*, published by Blackwell. The work was originally started in the late 1990s, when I embarked on what was intended to be a series of mini-corporate histories, and the raw material was then used for the PhD thesis that forms the basis of *History & Analysis*.

The *Dictionary* comprises 141 individual company histories of housebuilding firms spanning the whole of the twentieth century. Whilst the histories provide the corporate source material supporting the analysis in *History & Analysis*, they also provide some fascinating stories in their own right. Within them lie the start of sheltered housing (McCarthy & Stone); partnership housing (Lovell/Rendell); the vanished (Berg, Nash); the bankrupt (Morrell Estates, David Charles, Federated Homes); the over-ambitious (Northern Developments, Beazer); and the abandoned (nearly every contractor you can think of). The majority of the companies are no longer with us but there is also ample coverage of those still extant, from Abbey to Wimpey; they include both the quoted and the private.

As one industry leader put it, `this is a business which just wants to go wrong`, and among the histories can be found almost every conceivable corporate example. Fraud and false accounting; family rows; succession problems; octogenarians who overstayed; naked ambition; diversification into other industries that failed; overseas diversification that also failed; and expansion on borrowed money at the top of the market all feature. Despite this, the Dictionary features success stories – some long gone having sold out at top prices in the early 1970s or late 1980s, and some still enjoying a profitable existence.

All human life is present!

INTRODUCTION

The Preface to *History & Analysis* quoted from Merrett's standard work on owner-occupation, which stated that no systematic treatment of speculative housebuilding has been produced;[1] these two volumes redress that gap in the literature. To date, there have been few substantial corporate histories that cover housebuilders and even where they do exist, they are commissioned histories with the treatment of the housebuilding element of the business languishing besides that of the more glamorous construction side. Apart from that, there are a few corporate brochures or privately circulated mini-histories. Already, well-known names have come and gone with little to remember them by, including 20 companies that have been, at one time or another, among the country's ten largest housebuilders: names such as Broseley, Comben, Costain Homes, Ideal Homes (the largest before the war), William Leech, McLean (the largest in the late 1980s), and Whelmar; not to mention the well-known pre-war names of GT Crouch, Davis Estates, Janes, and Metropolitan Railway Country Estates, or the first quoted housebuilder to fail – Morrell Estates. Neither are there histories of today's industry leaders, such as Barratt, Berkeley, Persimmon or David Wilson. The *Dictionary of British Housebuilders* now provides the first comprehensive coverage of the twentieth century's leading housebuilders.

Criteria for inclusion

The decision as to which housebuilders to include has been determined by a combination of size and quoted status. The size criterion followed that laid out in the league tables in *British Housebuilders: History & Analysis*. There are 72 housebuilders that appear in the league tables comprising all companies thought to have built over 500 units a year in the inter-war and early post-war periods and, as firms became larger, those that built over 1000 units a year from the 1970s; all these firms have been included in the *Dictionary*, subject only to a cut-off date of the year 2000. The one exception is the inclusion of Marc Gregory, a private company that interconnects with more than one of the quoted companies. The second criterion was quoted status. All those housebuilders that have been quoted on the London Stock Exchange (or quoted companies that contained substantial housebuilding entities) have been included, with a similar 2000 cut-off. This does mean that some very small quoted companies, for instance, Eldon R Gorst and WA Hills have been included whereas some larger private firms that did not quite manage the 1000 a year level, for instance English & Continental and Admiral Homes, were excluded. Many other small private housebuilders have also been mentioned *en passant* where they have been the acquisitions or constituent parts of other companies included in their own right.

The extensive interviewing that underpins these two volumes was conducted between 1999 and 2002. As this book is a history rather than contemporary comment, it would have been sustainable to draw a line under each history at the year 2000. However, if there have been major developments since that date, the most obvious being the takeover of the company or a major corporate transaction, the individual stories would have been left hanging unnecessarily. The compromise adopted is that material events post 2000 have been mentioned briefly but not discussed in the same detail as earlier in the histories; in practice, the last ten years or so has been considered too recent to be more than touched on relatively lightly. One final point to mention on cut-off dates: to give a brief idea of the size of each company, its peak annual completions and the year they were achieved are listed immediately under the title name. For consistency,

---

[1] Merrett, *Owner Occupation in Britain*, p.159.

they go no further than 2004 even though 2005 figures are now available for some companies. For contemporary references, the reader is referred to the *Private Housebuilding Annual*.[2]

Source material

Some comment is appropriate on source material for these histories. Many of the companies were already well-known to me as a result of my earlier stockbroking career, particularly since the publication of the *Private Housebuilding Annual* which dates back to 1980. Thus, there was a considerable volume of material available before the start of this project, the most important of which were the regular discussions with senior management on contemporary events and corporate strategy. For the preparation of these histories, I had the additional benefit of interviews with around 140 individuals, either in person or over the telephone. There were also 40 additional written responses. Some 63 firms have built over 1000 units a year at some stage in the twentieth century; for almost all of these there have been one or more interviews. Managing directors or chairmen were interviewed at some 25 of the top 30; in around half of the companies, the founder or a family member was interviewed.

For many of the housebuilders active in the inter-war period, original archive material was made available. Full access to pre- and early post-war minutes was granted for Laing, Taylor Woodrow and Wimpey. Through Persimmon, which acquired a number of old-established housebuilders, the surviving records for Comben, Ideal, Leech and Metropolitan Railway Country Estates could be accessed. Unit Construction minutes were seen at the offices of (the then independent) Beazer. Henry Boot and James Miller have both conducted archive searches to provide data on pre-war unit completions. British American Tobacco provided extracts from the minute books of its Dean Finance subsidiary which had floated, inter alia, Ideal and Taylor Woodrow. On a wider front, many companies (or founding families) have what might be called a 'history file' which contains the occasional relevant item – perhaps some unpublished notes on the company's formation, an article which appeared in the local newspaper, extracts from a house magazine or even a specially assembled fact sheet. Local libraries were an occasional source of useful material. Luton Library has an unpublished memoire of Herbert Janes; Blackburn produced press cuttings on Derek Barnes, founder of Northern Developments; Wakefield had press cuttings on Fell Construction; and Harrow has an invaluable 1933 booklet on T F Nash.

There is a wealth of official documents, particularly for those housebuilders that have been in the public domain. There are, for instance, over 100 prospectuses of companies that floated as housebuilders, and documentation to cover all the major acquisitions. Following on come the company accounts, a massive, and potentially daunting, repository of information. Including unquoted companies, subsidiaries of larger concerns, and a few false trails, some 380 companies have been searched over time periods that, at the extreme, extend back to World War One.

The themes

British Housebuilders: History & Analysis contains the themes that are drawn from the individual company histories, and some modest repetition is in order at the start of this work. *History & Analysis* examines the rationale for growth and the reasons for failure, and the *Dictionary* is instructive in providing fuller background for the examples given in the companion volume. As the majority of housebuilders in this *Dictionary* no longer exist, at least not in their original form, the reasons for failure – or even just long periods of decline – are of especial interest. Failure, both absolute and relative, has been attributed to three overriding causes. Firstly, succession issues: these include those owners, usually founders, who stayed on too long, and Taylor Woodrow's Frank Taylor and Wimpey's Godfrey Mitchell provide archetypal case

---

[2] See www.fredwellings.co.uk for information.

studies. There are more numerous cases where the successor to a dominant individual was unable to replicate his entrepreneurial flair and control: Henry Boot went into a period of long decline after Charles Boot's death in 1945, as did Ideal after Leo Meyer illness in 1959; More recently, Wilson Connolly after Mike Robinson's death in 1990 shows how quickly corporate leadership can translate into failure.

The second decline theme is focus: speculative housebuilding was seemingly unable to prosper either when management diversified, even into seemingly related areas, or when other businesses diversified into housebuilding. The former category includes housebuilders from the 1960s, e.g. Comben and Wakeling, Drury and Fell, that lost their independence as a result of contracting losses. Or one could instance Bovis's acquisition of Twentieth Century Banking ahead of the secondary banking collapse. The histories are also littered with tales of overseas expansion, all of which, excepting only Taylor Woodrow and Wimpey, inevitably ended in failure. For those firms that diversified into housebuilding one can do no better than look at such 1980s contractors as AMEC, BICC and Mowlem, not to mention those like Costain that tried to rebuild what had been a successful inter-war housebuilding business. Alternatively, there are the totally unrelated businesses from such diverse industries as shipping (P&O), food manufacture and distribution (Hillsdown and Whelmar), insurance (Royal Exchange), and china clay (ECC), that have all thought, at one time or another, that they could be housebuilders. Some have done surprisingly well for periods of time but the histories show that none has survived the turn of the cycle with the ownership structure intact..

Finally, the housing cycles of 1974 and 1990 have been extremely efficient at culling those firms that had adopted, for want of a better expression, inappropriate financial strategies, and the histories provide numerous examples. The 1974 recession saw such notable failures as Northern Developments, once second only to Wimpey in size, David Charles, Greaves and Joviel. The support of the banking system meant fewer direct failures in the 1990 recession but it still caused the departure of such specialists as Charles Church, Fairbriar, Federated, Kentish Property and Trencherwood, and the withdrawal from housing of most of the contractors.

The histories provide ample record of the consolidation process that has taken place in the housebuilding industry. *History & Analysis* argues that there was no operational necessity for housebuilders to become national concerns, as small companies, by and large, appeared just as profitable as large ones. Instead, the book and the thesis that preceded it,[3] argue that the consolidation process within the housebuilding industry has been substantially driven by financial opportunity, the influence of the Stock Exchange and personal motivation. The ability to float on the Stock Exchange has provided an incentive for private companies to grow to a size where they can be floated; once there, the ability to issue shares has allowed companies to finance a faster rate of growth and to make acquisitions. Furthermore, they are not allowed to stop: the pressure on quoted company managements is to produce profits growth and consolidate into more marketable entities. With all the quoted housebuilders included, the *Dictionary* provides an even greater range of examples than was possible in *History & Analysis*.

As in all industries, personal ambition amongst the housebuilders remains a strong motive for corporate growth. Although the interviews produced only the occasional honest admission, the behaviour of individual business leaders as set out in the histories provides the strongest supporting evidence of personal ambition; the Beazer, Marc Gregory and Northern Developments histories do not exhaust the case studies. *History & Analysis* also argues that success in an entrepreneurial environment can occur by default, if firms are able to grow merely because they are the ones that avoid firm-threatening mistakes.

[3] 'The Rise of the National House builder', PhD thesis, University of Liverpool, 2005.

Great stress was placed on the judgmental quality of entrepreneurs ahead of major cyclical downturns which enables them to withstand the acute financial pressure that ruins so many of their competitors: by default. This creates a 'pool of survivors' who are able to use the recession to buy land (or competitors) at depressed prices, thereby being best placed to benefit from the cyclical upswing. The 1990 recession provided notable examples of firms who put caution ahead of short term growth, to reap the benefits in the ensuing decade, Bellway, Berkeley and David Wilson for instance among the quoted companies.

Acknowledgments

Acknowledgments were given in *History & Analysis* but if anything deserves repetition in both volumes it is these. I am indebted to the 180 people, frequently founders and invariably senior directors, who granted me interviews or corresponded between 1998 and 2002, some of whom gave extensively of their time. Behind that lie the countless finance and managing directors who have helped me during the course of a stockbroking career. Thanks are also due to the many librarians who helped me track down obscure corporate data.

Several of the individuals mentioned in the book have been knighted during the course of their career, occasionally being raised to the peerage. For simplicity, their original names have been used throughout, except where the individual was already titled at the time of the interview or first mention.

No contents list is provided as, with the exception of a few small quoted companies gathered at the end, the housebuilders are in alphabetical order. However, all are listed in the Index, as are all other housebuilding companies mentioned; peripheral non-housebuilding names have not been included. There is a separate index of people but subjects have not been indexed, as these have been covered in *History & Analysis*.

A–Z OF BRITISH HOUSEBUILDERS

ABBEY DEVELOPMENTS
Peak units: 1027 (1988)

Abbey Homesteads, as it was called for much of its life, was incorporated in 1954 when the Gallagher family, whose roots lay in the pre-war Irish construction industry, made their entry into the English housing market. Four brothers controlled Abbey Homesteads, James, Patrick, Hubert and Charles, with the youngest brother Charles as Managing Director. Soon after, the three older brothers returned to Dublin to concentrate on their Irish contracting business, which later became The Abbey Group. Homesteads concentrated on the London commuter belt, operating off a short land bank and gradually raised its output until by 1962 the 1000th house had been completed, suggesting an annual rate at the start of the 1960s of around 150.

Flotation
By the early 1970s, Abbey consisted of Abbey Homesteads and the M & J plant hire businesses in England, a development operation in Cyprus, and a more diversified property, merchanting, manufacturing and steel fabrication business in Ireland. In 1973, the Gallaghers had decided to float the combined business in both London and Dublin; however, market conditions deteriorated in London, and Abbey acquired a Dublin Stock Exchange listing through the reverse takeover of Torc Manufacturing (producer of carbon paper); it was accompanied in May 1973 by an offer for sale of new shares in the enlarged company. Charles Gallagher was the Group Managing Director with James as Chairman. Charles, still the only brother resident in the UK, was strongly in favour of Abbey concentrating on the English housing market. After a family tussle in which Charles failed to gain control of the company, he left in 1975 and went on to start his own housing company – Matthew Homes.

There had been no indication in the prospectus of the volumes built by the English housing company but a three year land bank totalling 2400 plots suggested an annual build rate of some 800. Abbey Homesteads confined itself to the south east, building from Peterborough to Bournemouth. The UK business had come under substantial pressure shortly after the flotation as the housing market collapsed: there were land write-offs in 1974 and 1976, but the UK remained in profit. UK housing volumes changed little over the decade and were just under 700 in 1980; UK profits gradually recovered and by 1980 they had exceeded the 1973 record for the first time. By then, Ireland was making substantial profits from commercial development. The Group was still chaired by James Gallagher, with Gus McHugh as the Managing Director in Ireland and Ray Davies, who had joined in 1978, as the UK Managing Director.

Gallaghers at war
In March 1983, James Gallagher died and Patrick Gallagher became acting Chairman. 'All of a sudden (there is reason to believe that James, prior to his death had given his approval) a huge rationalisation programme took place in the Irish companies orchestrated by Gus McHugh…Within a matter of days

[the Irish housebuilder] was all but dismantled…While the UK division is performing extremely well, the Irish arm of Abbey is under extreme pressure.'[1] *Irish Business* went on to say that 'All eyes are now on Charles Gallagher, who James thwarted for years when the former attempted to gain control of Abbey'.[2] At the AGM in September, Charles, supported by the James Gallagher family shareholding, stood against Patrick and replaced him as Chairman; Ray Davies was appointed as group Chief Executive. The new team continued to address the Group's loss making Irish activities, closing most of the non-development activities over the next couple of years. They also increased the concentration on housing in the south east of England; UK housing sales, which had fallen to 470 in 1982/83, recovered strongly in the rising market, reaching a peak of just over 1000 in 1988.

In October 1985, French Kier launched a £19m. takeover bid for Abbey, having already received acceptances of 36% of the shares, being the family stakes of the late James Gallagher and the company President, Patrick Gallagher. James' son Seamus was an Abbey director. 'Whatever its intentions, Kier has become involved in a family feud that has spluttered intermittently since Abbey's public listing in 1973'.[3] Although the bid was subsequently increased to £24m, acceptances were only 41%, little more than the family faction had pledged, and the bid lapsed. Following the failed bid, Seamus Gallagher resigned and Charles H Gallagher, Charles' son, joined the board as a non-executive director. Shortly after, the group headquarters was moved from Dublin to Potters Bar, though Abbey's domicile remained in Ireland.

Profits, which had fallen from IR£3m to little more than breakeven in 1984, began to rise sharply, reflecting the benefits of reorganisation, the booming UK housing market and, some suggested, the stimulus of the French Kier bid. By 1988, profits had risen to a record IR£17.2m, most of which had come from Abbey Homesteads which completed over 1000 units that year. Although that profit was just exceeded in 1989, it was helped by the inclusion of £5m profit on land sales. Despite those sales at the top of the market, Abbey had to make substantial provisions against its land holdings and a IR£15m loss was incurred in 1990; unit sales were below 500, half the rate of 1988. Charles H Gallagher began to take a more active role in the company and Ray Davies departed to become Chief Executive of Bellwinch. Charles Gallagher died in 1993 and Charles H Gallagher was appointed Executive Chairman, aged 33.

The recovery in the UK housing company was slow; indeed, unit sales have remained in the 300-500 range since Charles H Gallagher assumed control. However, profitability was steadily restored. and in the year 2000, Abbey Developments earned pre-tax profits of over £13m, exceeding the 1988 record for the first time, going on to reach £20m in 2004. In that year, Abbey delisted from the London and Irish stock exchanges, moving to the London AIM and its Irish equivalent.

[1] Irish Business, July 1983, p.5
[2] Ibid, p.6.
[3] *Financial Times*, 10th October 1985.

ALGREY/DOMINION HOMES
Peak units: 400 (1986)

Algrey Holdings, a quoted company originally known as Albion Greyhounds, was formed in 1927 to acquire tracks in Glasgow and Salford. Around 1960, the Glasgow assets were sold and, with Jessel Securities as controlling shareholder, the Company changed its name and signalled its intention to diversify. Pursuant to this, Cecil Benzecry, then a non-executive Jessel director, was asked to start a property company; Algrey Properties (later called Algrey Homes) was formed with Benzecry as Chairman and sole (albeit part-time) executive. After a couple of successful developments made with outside assistance, there was sufficient capital to enable Algrey to employ its own staff and Peter Sly was recruited from New Ideal Homesteads as Managing Director.

Failed diversification

Algrey Holdings had also begun to purchase unrelated companies, notably a wholesale chemist in 1962 and what proved to be a disastrous purchase of Elizabethan Tape Recorders in 1964. At first, the diversification was successful and group profits, which had been a steady £20,000 from greyhound racing, rose to £80,000 in 1965. However, the severe losses which were subsequently made by Elizabethan forced the parent company to withdraw capital from Homes and Peter Sly left. To sustain its cash flow, Homes formed Algrey Contractors together with a number of housing associations for which it carried out contract work, thereby preserving the nucleus of a development team. However, when Algrey started doing contract work for third parties, notably a 12 storey block of flats in Sutton, a loss of some £100,000 was made, almost eliminating the development profit: 'Oliver Jessel was not pleased.'[1] At that point Derek Brooks was recruited as Managing Director, again from New Ideal Homesteads.

By 1968, Holdings was back in profit, ex-Elizabethan, and then began a succession of ownership changes. Holdings was first merged with another Jessel company, Leeds Fireclay, to form Leeds Assets. Jessel Securities also bought control of the wire manufacturer, Richard Johnson & Nephew and at the end of 1972, RJN bought Leeds Assets before RJN in turn merged with Thos Firth & John Brown, becoming Johnson & Firth Brown. Algrey and Leeds Fireclay thus formed a major part of a JFB property division.

Algrey Homes itself had been expanding through acquisition. In 1972, the remains of the Tame Valley Group was bought to form Algrey Midlands. Tame had been controlled by Edmund Heaton, a surveyor, and George Fisher, an accountant, but when it encountered difficulties it was acquired by another Jessel company, Eastern Produce. Algrey also bought the small Omasetry Developments of Uckfield, Sussex, owned by Clarence Preston, a builder and Ernest Bailey, a coal merchant; Omasetry was acquired for its land bank and became Algrey Homes (Southern). With further finance available from JFB, Algrey was also able to start a property investment company.

From Jessel to Dominion

By 1973/74, Algrey was building nearly 200 houses a year and making profits of over £500,000. A quotation was considered but it was overtaken by external events. Algrey managed to stay in profit through the housing recession and by 1977 was exceeding its earlier level of profit; in 1979, profits reached £1m. However, Jessel Securities had gone into liquidation in 1976 and by 1979 JFB was in trouble and the losses incurred by the steel division forced it to dispose of Algrey. The purchaser was

---

[1] Interview with Cecil Benzecry, Dec. 2001

Max Lewinsohn's Dominion International, another business with a convoluted history.

Dominion started as the Dundee Crematorium in 1935 and stayed that way until Lewinsohn, an accountant, took control in 1975. Three areas were selected for growth – natural resources, property development and financial services. 'the scope is such that there is an argument for concentrating on just one activity. However, it is our policy to strike a balance between activities…such that protection is afforded against any unavoidable downturn in one area.'[2] Property included both commercial and residential and a housing company was formed in Houston in 1982. Brooks resigned as Managing Director of Algrey Homes in 1983 and was succeeded by Roger Horton, formerly Sales Director at Wates. Algrey, now renamed Dominion Homes, increased the number of sites from 10 in 1982 to 17 in 1985, but these were spread over a wide geographical area – the south east, the south west, west midlands and Wales.

Dominion had prided itself on its superior profits record but suffered its first fall in profits in 1987 due to events in the oil industry. By then it had decided to restructure the business to focus more on financial services. In December 1986 Dominion Homes was sold to CALA for £7.2m; it had sold 327 houses in its last financial year and made profits of £1.16m. As a postscript, Dominion International went into administration in January 1990 following 'considerable press speculation about the manner in which the group's affairs were conducted.'[3]

2 Company accounts, 1982.
3 Letter to creditors, 26th March 1990.

ALLEN HOMES
Peak units: 518 (1998)

Samuel and Thomas Allen had worked for their uncle's small civil engineering business before the Second War. In 1946, they used their post-war gratuity to start their own flagging and kerbing business, based at Wigan and trading across Lancashire. They had no trade qualifications and were self-educated; Sam organised the administration of the partnership and Tom led construction. 'In the early 1950s they began to work for the NCB, got well established and, in essence, it was the Coal Board that put them on their feet. From there they branched out doing roads and sewers for local authorities; when the authorities were doing a lot of housing, Allen was doing their roads.[1]

The business was incorporated in 1968 with Samuel and Thomas Allen holding 42% each. The next largest shareholders were Donald Greenhalgh, who had joined as the chief engineer in 1965 from the local authority, Ken Fox in the same year, and Ian Hilton in 1967; all three were professional engineers and all were to play the key roles in expanding the Company. The business remained relatively modest and confined to civil engineering through the early 1970s. In 1973 the first of the shareholding transfers took place between the Allen brothers and Donald Greenhalgh; in 1978 Greenhalgh was made Managing Director and by the early 1980s he was the largest shareholder. The Company was floated in 1989.

Greenhalgh leads the growth

Greenhalgh was responsible for Allen's diversification and its rapid growth, from profits of around £100,000 in the mid-1970s to £5m in 1990. The early 1970s marked the first foray into housebuilding with the purchase of a site in Bury but it was not particularly successful. In 1976, Allen bought a plant hire business, a diversification that was eventually to become the dominant activity and in 1977, Ian Hilton, who had originally started the design and build division, was asked to restart housebuilding. By the mid-1980s, Allen was building around 100 units a year in the Lancashire area. Volumes doubled to 250 in 1987 and its profitability encouraged Allen to move into new areas. 'They had a grand scheme to cover the whole country in the mid-1980s; we had to be a national housebuilder. We had planned out the regions.' In 1986, a manager had been recruited to start an operation in Yorkshire (separate from Hilton's Company) and two new managers were to start building in north Wales and the west Midlands. In the late 1980s, offices in Stoke, Leicester and Nottingham were being opened. 'So we had seven operating companies that were going to do 500 each. Yorkshire and Midlands were a disaster and Wales was only doing 12 a year.'[2] In fact, the addition of these new regions added little more than 10% to the north-west housing volumes, and the total rose to no more than 300 in the year to March 1989 before falling away again; profits, however, continued to rise until 1990/91.

Although the collapse in the construction and development markets brought group profits down from £5.3m in 1991 to £1.5m in 1993, there were no divisional losses and no provisions. At a group level, the subsequent performance was impressive with profits rising every year to a peak of £21m in 1999/2000; throughout this period the driving force was the plant hire division, Speedy Hire, which had been substantially enlarged in 1994 by the acquisition of Kendrick. The attitude to housebuilding, and particularly to the acquisition of land, was cautious. Thus, in the 1994 accounts, land was considered too expensive and there were fears of another cycle of overpaying: 'We never took part in this game before – nor will we this time' Again, in 1996, 'It has proved impossible to maintain our land bank at costs that would give a satisfactory return on capital.' The attitude to capital allocation was spelt out in the March

---

[1] Interview with Ian Hilton, Jan. 2002.
[2] Ibid.

1996 rights issue: 'We have managed our housebuilding activities conservatively through the recession. Land purchases have been held back where we believed that the asking prices were too high and the resources that would otherwise have been deployed in housebuilding have been allocated to other areas of the Group in particular, Hire Services. As Ian Hilton put it: 'Money limitation was a problem; we could not get enough capital to do the numbers. If the returns had been reversed, I would have got the capital.'

Disposal of housing

The net effect was that housing volumes in 1996 were little higher than at the end of the 1980s. Nevertheless, Allen Homes managed to achieve some modest growth in volumes from there, reaching 500 by the end of the decade; profits of £4m in 1999/00 were substantially enhanced by a further £7m profit on the sale of a site at Lymm. That proved to be Allen Homes' swan song. With the release of the March 2000 results, the Chairman announced the intention to dispose of the housing division. 'We have decided to direct future funds and resources to the Hire and Utility Services businesses which provide higher returns on capital than Housebuilding.' The subsidiary explanation that 'as a regional housebuilder we do not have the purchasing advantages of our larger competitors who are also able to achieve higher selling prices for houses similar to those built by Allen Homes' scarcely does justice to other successful regional housebuilders..

The options for Allen Homes included building out the land bank or a trade sale. In August 2000, Allen Homes was sold to Morris Group for £24m. Six months later, in February 2001, Allen announced that its building division had lost £13m. Greenhalgh and Ken Fox (who had become Managing Director in 1995) left the Group to prepare a bid for the building company. In April the building company was sold for £1m to Montpelier (formerly YJ Lovell), leaving Allen concentrating on plant hire; accordingly, the Group was renamed Speedy Hire.

ALLIED LONDON PROPERTIES
Peak units: 500-750? (late 1980s)

The company was incorporated as the Sungei Kruit Rubber Estate Company in 1909 and floated on the Stock Exchange, the name being changed to Allied London Properties in 1958 when it decided to carry on business as a property company; in 1961, the company was merged with Federated and General Investments. In 1969, Allied was providing finance for Galliford Estates with whom they jointly own Sable Homes; the following year, Allied bought 50% of the recently-formed Langstone Homes. The modern history of Allied London starts in 1971 with the acquisition of the privately-owned Sterling Group.

The Sterling Group commenced trading in 1964 under the management of Morris and Geoffrey Leigh. 'Morris Leigh and his son Geoffrey are two entertaining characters who run Allied London Properties. I am convinced that one of the reasons for the Leighs' success is – although they are jovial and introduce humour into their negotiations – father and son retain tight control on all their operations.'[1] Sterling started as a residential developer but had more recently moved into commercial and industrial property development, including shopping centres and offices – it had just made its largest commercial purchase, the MGM Elstree Estate of some 115 acres. At the time of what was a reverse takeover (the Leighs ended up with 64% of the enlarged company) the original Allied London had last earned profits of £90,000 compared with Sterling's £224,000. From the inception of the merger, Allied London enjoyed a steady rise in profits from its initial £432,000 to its 1989 peak of £12.9m. This does not do full justice to the Leigh's achievements for they built up a substantial asset base of commercial properties – £165m in 1988. The growing income from the investment portfolio smoothed out the vagaries of the housing cycle as, for instance, in 1974 – although even then there appeared no need for land write-offs.

In 1980, Allied outbid Starwest in an £11m purchase of the Kent-based housebuilder Gough Cooper. Gough Cooper had reached peak volumes of around 1000 in 1972 but Harry Gough-Cooper had died in 1975 after a long illness and within a couple of years sales were little more than 400. Diversification into contract building was unsuccessful and Gough Cooper incurred a group loss in the first half of 1979/80, signalling the end of Gough Cooper's independence. By 1981 Gough Cooper had been returned to profitability. The residential division, although becoming overshadowed by the growing commercial property portfolio, continued to trade actively through the decade, albeit entirely in the south east. In 1985, Allied acquired Piper Holdings, another Kent housebuilder. Donald Smith who came in with the Gough Cooper acquisition, was appointed Managing Director of Sterling Homes and to the main board. In 1986, Morris Leigh, then aged 79, stood down as Chairman in favour of Geoffrey Leigh, although he stayed on the Board until 1993. Two more acquisitions came in 1988: Cooper Developments (Midlands) trading as Wetenhall Cooper and, for £7m, Blenbury, a Kent and East Sussex housebuilder specialising in the retirement and first time buyer market.

Housing withdrawal
In the face of falling sales, the housebuilding operations were consolidated in 1989 and Peter Burnett (previously Deputy Chairman of Barratt's Midlands Region) became the main Board Director responsible for housebuilding. Although sales were maintained in the year to June 1990, margins were severely eroded and a £2m provision was made against the land bank. The following year saw £10m of provisions against housing land and work in progress, and the group as a whole incurred a £5m pre-tax loss. After yet another £3.5m provision in 1992 the directors decided to retreat from private housing: 'We have therefore

---

1 Erdman, *People & Property*.

decided to suspend the construction of new homes and not to acquire further land for housebuilding.'[2]

Despite the decision to cease housebuilding, in December 1993 Allied made the opportunistic purchase of Pelham Homes, previously owned by Rosehaugh Property, for £3m and the assumption of £14m debt. Pelham was more a developer of land than a builder: it specialised in acquiring white land, obtaining planning permission, providing the infrastructure and selling parcels of serviced land to other builders. At the time of Allied's purchase it had interests in more than 1000 acres of land mainly in the south east, including 66 acres of land with planning permission and other sites with hope value. Pelham turned out to be an exceptionally well timed acquisition. By 1998 it had contributed gross profits of £19m from the sale of 198 acres. In 1999, Allied was still reporting that Pelham controlled more than 1000 acres of land in the home counties with an estimated surplus over book value of £27m.

In June 2001 Allied London Properties accepted a £138m bid from Arrow Property, a company owned, inter alia, by Deutsche Bank Real Estate with Geoffrey Leigh retaining a nine per cent holding.

[2] Group accounts, 1992.

ANGLIA SECURE HOMES
Peak units: 559 (1988)

After McCarthy & Stone, Anglia Secure was the only other quoted sheltered housing specialist; later into the market than McCarthy, it suffered even more than the industry leader in the 1990 recession. The business was founded by Peter Edmondson, an estate agent, and James Moonie, a solicitor, in 1982. Edmondson was the driving force and was Chairman and Chief Executive. Edmondson had joined a firm of Cambridge estate agents in 1963, aged 18, moving to Trowbridge Estate Agents in 1967 to manage their Frinton-on-Sea office, before buying it from them in 1971. Anglia commenced trading in September 1982, some three months after McCarthy & Stone had floated; Edmondson's explanation of his entry into sheltered housing is an interesting example of the random nature of corporate development.

'In 1982 I was made aware of McCarthy & Stone's success in New Milton by an aged client in my estate agency in Frinton-on-Sea. I found it difficult to understand why she had decided at the age of 82 to up-sticks from a bungalow in Walton to buy sheltered accommodation in Hampshire. During our conversations she remarked on many occasions that if only a suitable site were available in the Frinton area, she would have moved there. She felt that a secure environment with people of her own age was an ideal solution to her concerns and anxieties. After visiting New Milton, I went to work on finding a site in my own area. Sometime in 1982 I found that site in Walton-on-the-Naze, 50 yards from the post office and town centre. I offered the site to McCarthy and Stone, who informed me that they were in the process of going to the USM market and had no plans to be developing in Essex in the foreseeable future. By this time I was convinced, through my own market research, that the site was perfect for sheltered housing and with the help of Doug Moonie, Anglia Secure Homes was formed to develop the site.'[1]

Walton was completed in two phases in 1983 and 1984, and additional sites were bought in East Anglia and Cambridge. The capital for the first scheme came from the founder shareholders and bank borrowings; subsequent developments were funded largely by project finance secured on the developments. In June 1985 a private placing of 20% of the equity raised £0.7m and a further £3m was raised when the company floated on the USM in June 1986; the flotation was at an early stage in Anglia's corporate career – it completed little more than 100 units that year and profits were still under £1m

Merger with Retirement Appreciation
Prior to the flotation, Anglia had formed Haven Management Services to take over the important after-sales management of the sheltered developments; Anglia also acquired Edmondson's original Trowbridge Estate Agents. A year after the float, Anglia's market capitalisation had risen from £11m to £70m. It then raised £8m through a rights issue and paid £12m to buy Retirement Appreciation, another developer of sheltered housing. If anything, Retirement Appreciation was larger than Anglia. It had been founded in 1983 in Norwich, and in 1986 had 184 sales compared with Anglia's 107. Together, they sold 576 units in 1987 and profits of the enlarged group were just short of £4m. The Company now had its East Anglia region; a midlands region through Retirement Appreciation; and was buying additional sites in the west country and on the south coast to form the basis of two more regions. Like McCarthy & Stone, Anglia was also planning full nursing care for the elderly and was constructing a pilot scheme at Holland-on-Sea, Essex. The day-to-day management was now in the hands of Richard Clough, an accountant who had joined in June 1987 having been Managing Director of a private textile company.

---

[1] Correspondence with author.

With the housing market now in unrestrained boom, the year to September 1988 saw a small increase in volumes, to 599, and a doubling of profit to £7.5m. Just after the year end, Alfred McAlpine's 130 units-a-year retirement home operation was bought for £4.3m, giving Anglia a south east division; it was described by Peter Edmondson as 'a dream price.'[2] That month was regarded by many as the end of the bull market in housing, but *Building* was describing how Anglia was powering towards a 2500 a year operation over the next three years, with around 1000 units in the current financial year.[3] The reality was different. Unit sales in 1988/89 fell to 455, around half the planned output; profits halved and exceptional charges of £8m meant a £4m pre-tax loss; had interest not been capitalised, the loss would have been doubled. Although Anglia had stopped buying land at the beginning of the year, construction was in progress on 36 sites At the year end, 449 completed units were unsold of which only 125 were reserved; a further 666 units were due for completion in the following year. Following the acquisition of McAlpine's sheltered housing, stock had increased to £60m; without sharp cutbacks stocks would have risen to £100m but even at the date of the Chairman's statement, they were as high as £77m

Reconstruction

Anglia desperately needed a recovery in the housing market but sheltered housing was harder hit than conventional housing and the need to complete the whole development before purchasers could move in tied up capital. Over the next four years sales declined to under 130 units, there were trading losses of £23m and write-offs of a further £26m. The 1993 accounts showed negative shareholders' funds of over £6m and borrowings were still as high as £23m. In March 1994 a restructuring was announced. The sheltered housing business, including stock with a value of £8m plus a shared-equity portfolio of £4m, was transferred with its associated debt into Anglia Secure Homes (South East), a subsidiary, which was then effectively acquired by the banks. The banks also received £3m from share issues by Anglia Secure Homes, now renamed Care UK, in consideration for the release of charges over the remaining assets of the Group. Those remaining assets, the Haven management business and nursing homes, then formed the basis for Care UK which expanded into a successful healthcare company.

Anglia Secure Homes (South East) continued to be run by Paul Edmondson, Peter's younger brother, and the old stock was being sold off until 1998. In May 2000 the Company was acquired by Fairview New Homes. In the meantime, Peter Edmondson had formed a new company, Jaygate Homes.

[2] *Building*, 7th Oct. 1988.
[3] *Building*, 28th Oct. 1988.

ARNCLIFFE HOMES
Peak units: c.300 (late 1970s)

Arncliffe was formed in Leeds in 1971 by Manny Cussins and Ian Fisch. Cussins, who was then aged 65, had a successful business career behind him as a director of Waring & Gillow, many other clothing and furniture companies, and Leeds FC. Ian Fisch was a solicitor. Walter Ratcliffe, a plumber who took over his father's building business, was appointed to the Board in 1973 following the purchase of his company which had previously acted as subcontractor to Arncliffe. Almost immediately Arncliffe had to face the recession of 1974 but, although profits fell, it remained profitable.

Turnover grew steadily to around £4m in 1978 when Arncliffe was floated; the three directors above were all on the Board. No unit sales figures were quoted but the turnover suggests that sales could have approached 300 from sites in Yorkshire, Lincolnshire and Humberside. Profits in1978 were £656,000 and the first annual accounts as a public company reported that the Company was looking at possible acquisitions in the midlands, Lancashire and London. In the event, these ambitions were never realised or, at least, not profitably. Although profits were maintained in 1979, they declined thereafter and, exacerbated by the miners' strike, losses were incurred in 1984 and 1985. By then, sales were probably below 250.

Manny Cussins retired in 1986 leaving Fisch, Chairman and Ratcliffe, Managing Director. A new start was made with a change in the Company's stockbrokers, its solicitors and a proposal to change auditors as well. According to the 1986 Accounts, Arncliffe was now 'actively investigating new areas.' In 1987 commercial property development was started and housebuilding extended into the south west. The following year Arncliffe entered the London market: 'We have invested record sums in new residential land and commercial developments in the year under review.'[1]

Between 1986 and 1989, turnover rose from £6m to £19m, and the property boom enabled the Company to earn operating profits of £4.7m in 1989, or £3.1m after interest. The commercial property commitments were pushing interest charges up rapidly and with sales harder to achieve, Arncliffe was having difficulty in paying its interest bill. In 1990 Arncliffe began negotiations with its bankers; after exceptional charges, Arncliffe lost £2.7m in the year to October 1990. By then, increased cash constraints were affecting the completion of properties. An MBO for the residential side of the business was attempted but there was little interest in the commercial side. In February 1991 a consortium of local businessmen started negotiations for the whole of the Company but these failed in May and a receiver was appointed.

An MBO of the residential side was completed in July 1991. It was led by Michael Stafford, previously the group Finance Director, with Philip Macer and Walter Ratcliffe, previously Managing Director, having equal shares; Ratcliffe retired in 1996 and was bought out along with the venture capital fund. The new Arncliffe Homes continued to build around 100 houses a year, earning modest profits.

---

[1] Company accounts, 1988.

AVONSIDE
Peak units: 262 (1993)

Avonside was established through a series of acquisitions made between 1986 and 1991 by Cannon Street Investments, a City finance house and mini-conglomerate, and floated in 1992. Apart from housebuilding there were a range of building service companies covering such trades as plumbing and roofing. The two housebuilding subsidiaries were separated by England – Parry Homes in Wales and Avonside Homes in Scotland. Parry Homes was incorporated in 1970 by John Emlyn Parry, a building contractor from Rossett in north Wales. It was bought by Cannon Street Investments in 1987 when its last recorded turnover was £2.3m and profits £650,000. Avonside Homes, bought the previous year, had been incorporated in 1972 but there were no dominant shareholders. As well as its housebuilding, Avonside also manufactured timber frames for housing, sold externally and to its sister business.

The peak volumes for the combined housebuilding companies prior to flotation was in 1988 with 225 units; although volumes declined a little in the recession, housebuilding profits had actually risen from £3.3m in 1988 to £4.4m in 1991. The leadership of the Avonside Group was not in the hands of a housebuilder: Gordon Carruth, an accountant who had joined Cannon Street in 1982, was the post-flotation Managing Director but he was succeeded within months of the flotation by Brian Scowcroft, who had founded the heating and plumbing division. There were no housebuilders on the main board.

The intention at the time of the float was to achieve a controlled expansion of the housebuilding division and Parry bought sites in North Shropshire. However, although volumes rose to a peak of 262 in 1993, housing profits declined and, in September 1994, Avonside announced its intention to divest the housebuilding division and focus on building services where it argued that there were significant competitive advantages not existing in the housebuilding division. 'I think it was really then that we realised we were not going to have long to do anything. We saw a very fragmented services industry contracting to housebuilders; and we could see our ability to be a leader in that. We just couldn't see ourselves becoming a leader in housebuilding. It would have taken totally different people. It was just a pragmatic view at the time.'[1]

There was an arrangement with the Parry management whereby they would develop the land with a view to buying the rump of the business by 1997; Avonside Homes was informally put up for sale but to no immediate effect, possibly due to its relationship with the Group's timber frame business. In the event, Parry had to write off some £4.6m from its North Wales land in 1995, a year when the housing market recovery paused. The housing division as a whole lost some £5m and the building services division did no more than break even.

By 1997, unit sales were down to only 68 and the division was still making small trading losses. Scowcroft retired and Craig Slater, previously Finance Director, became Managing Director. The Group was suffering on the Stock Market from investors' disenchantment with small companies and its own lack of focus and in April 1999 Slater led a management buyout. By 1999 Parry Homes had finally built out its land bank and Bob Gillespie led an MBO of Avonside Homes.

---

[1] Interview with Craig Slater, Jan 2002.

BEN BAILEY HOMES
Peak units: 527 (2004)

The company was founded in Mexborough in 1933 by Ben Bailey, then aged 24 and a bricklayer by trade. He had started by building a pair of semi-detached houses, one to live in and the other to rent. However, he sold the pair and the exercise was repeated, to the same effect and he continued building in a small way up to 1939. During the war, the firm did bomb damage work, air raid shelters etc. and was run, after Ben Bailey was called up, by his wife. The business was incorporated in 1946 and confined itself to contracting, including local authority housing, until building controls were removed. Ben Bailey had bought farming land before the war though the intent was not to acquire building land: 'It was just that when farming was in crisis, he always took the view that to buy land was power. He hadn't got any money; I think he bought it all on instalment.'[1] Some of these farms obtained planning permission and those without prospects were sold in 1955. It was this pre-war farming land that gave the Company its base in South Yorkshire.

The Company confined itself to a modest level of private housebuilding in the south Yorkshire area until 1963/64; planning delays in areas affected by proposed coal mining programmes created spare building capacity which Ben Bailey used to undertake local authority housing, a course of action which resulted in lower profits that year. The Company floated in 1967. 'It was the fashion at the time. He had built the business up from nothing and wanted to get some money out.'[2] The profit forecast was £85,000; turnover was only £350,000 which implied an annual output of little more than 100 houses. Ben Bailey remained within the south Yorkshire area until the early 1970s; even then it had no more than a handful of sites in progress at any one time. Profits benefited from the boom conditions, reaching a peak of £400,000 in 1973/74.

Construction losses

One of the responses to the 1974 recession was to form a small public works division and, in view of its early success, Ben Bailey decided to make a fuller entry into the construction market. However, losses on fixed-price contracts were to cause problems and were as much responsible for the fall in group profits to under £100,000 in 1977 as was the weakness in the housing market. The 1970s also saw a more substantial expansion of the builders' merchants (Housecraft) which had been started in the 1950s; a replacement-heating company (Fireparts) was also bought. By 1983, housebuilding was less than half group turnover, though still making over 70% of the profit. What didn't happen was any geographic expansion of the housebuilding. Richard Bailey's explanation was simple: 'One, we probably didn't want to; and two, I'm not sure that we had the ability. We were also involved with general contracting and merchanting right up to the '80s, I think really, we missed a trick. We hadn't got focus.'[3]

Ben Bailey died in January 1983 and his son, Richard Bailey, became Chairman as well as Managing Director. Richard Bailey had joined the company in 1968, after education at the local grammar school and service in the Merchant Navy; been appointed a director in 1970, joint Managing Director, and then Managing Director in 1976. Almost immediately after he became Chairman, the Company was hit by the miners strike, which contributed to losses in 1985 and 1986, but the rapid improvement in market conditions enabled Ben Bailey to substantially increase unit volume to over 300 a year, and profits

---

[1] Interview with Richard Bailey, Jan. 2002.
[2] Ibid.
[3] Ibid.

exceeded £2m in 1989. In that year, Bob Wainright, previously the Finance Director, was appointed Managing Director of the Homes subsidiary.

The 1990 recession, like that of 1974, had a greater impact on the diversified businesses than on the mainstream housebuilding. Firecraft had actually started losing money in 1988 and, after losses of £160,000 in 1990, was closed. The following year Housecraft lost £335,000 and was sold in the 1991/92 financial year, a period when land write-downs contributed to the group loss. Looking back on the distribution business, Richard Bailey stressed the need to focus on the company's strengths: 'We didn't know enough about merchanting. We were OK when it was small but once it got larger with big premises it started to chase us around. I didn't know enough about merchanting – I'm a housebuilder.'[4]

Once Ben Bailey had confined itself to housebuilding, volumes showed a steady, albeit modest, increase exceeding 400 in 1998 with profits recovering to £1.5m, and the group was now expanding its housing into West Yorkshire and Nottinghamshire. By this time, day-to-day control of the business was passing to Paul Russell who had joined the group in 1989 as Finance Director, becoming Managing Director of Homes in 1995 and Group Managing Director in 1997. Russell had to deal with site contamination problems in 1999 when the Group incurred a £750,000 loss but profits recovered to £1.5m in year 2000, and the gradual southwards geographic expansion helped the Company towards a new volume record of over 500 units in 2004, accompanied by profits of £16.5m; Ben Bailey had become a successful regional housebuilder, while managing to keep its independence in the quoted arena.

[4] Ibid.

BANNER HOMES
Peak units: 251 (2004)

Banner Homes originated out of Allied Residential Housing, later Edmond Holdings. Allied Residential had combined the housebuilding interests of Allied Plant Group and the residential development and building financing interests of Thames Investment & Securities in 1981, and floated on the Stock Exchange. Almost immediately, profits collapsed and there were substantial write-offs in 1982. Allied Residential's chosen solution was to sell the southern companies to Stuart Crossley. Crossley had been Thames Investment's company secretary and, according to the Prospectus, was responsible for all aspects of Allied Residential's business other than direct housebuilding; he became joint Managing Director of Allied.

The component part of Allied that was later sold was Ermine Securities, originally a provider of finance to joint venture companies, and this was renamed Banner Homes and based in High Wycombe. The MBO was completed in April 1983 and Crossley began to run down the financing business to concentrate on housebuilding in the south Buckinghamshire and Oxfordshire areas. Numbers were on a modest scale, some 50 a year, rising to 75 in 1986 and 1987. Banner floated in 1987 on forecast profits of £1.25m against under £0.5m the previous year. Once public, Banner moved into commercial property where a 'modest start …was a resounding success.' In 1988, Banner achieved record profits of £1.8m with the help of land sales – only 60 houses were completed.

Banner secured an option on a 400 acre site in Majorca in 1988, pre-selling one third of the development at significant profit. Almost immediately, Banner faced the housing and property recession; despite the sale of the Majorca site, profits collapsed in the extended 1989/90 year and pre-tax losses were incurred in 1991 and 1992. Despite the financial pressures of the recession, Crossley was taking a longer term view and in 1992/93, even while group housing completions fell to a low point of 32, Banner was taking advantage of the depressed land market to increase investment in land. However, the retention of completed commercial property had left gearing at a high level and the balance sheet was strengthened at the end of 1993 by a rights issue. As the housing market recovered, housing sales jumped to around 150 a year and by 1996/97 profits had exceeded £2m.

The different valuations accorded to commercial property assets and housebuilding profits were felt to be adversely affecting the valuation of the Group as a whole. In December 1997 Banner demerged its commercial operations into Comland Commercial to be separately listed on the AIM market, leaving Banner as a pure housebuilder 'with a more focused and ambitious programme for the future.'[1] In its first year as a pure housebuilder, Banner's profits enjoyed the full benefit of rising house prices and, on slightly lower unit sales, profits exceeded £7m. Investors declined to accord the quoted housebuilders the valuations their managements felt they deserved and Banner was one of a handful of housebuilders that sought an MBO.

The MBO was led by Richard Werth, who had joined the company as Finance Director at the flotation. The new vehicle, backed by 3i, made an agreed £23m bid; Crossley, who still owned 66% of the Company, resigned, buying out a 10 acre site in Spain, purchased the previous year, for £5m. In August 2000, Banner opened its first regional office in Winchester, beginning a modest expansion in the southeast, taking volumes up to 250 in 2003 and 2004. A midlands region is planned for 2007.

---

[1] Company accounts, 1998.

BARDOLIN/LONDON & NORTHERN SECURITIES
Peak units: c.1500 (1973)

Bardolin and London & Northern Securities were known in the City as 'Jock Mackenzie companies' and never enjoyed the highest prestige. Bardolin was the vehicle which contained the housebuilding companies, and, as it was eventually taken over by London & Northern, the two companies are best described together. The 'colourful and controversial'[1] John Hugh Munro Mackenzie was born in 1925, the son of Lt Col John Mackenzie, DSO and a former Dublin Gaiety girl. After graduating from Oxford, he was called to the Bar and then moved into industry starting his own company, Grampian Holdings, in 1958. Four years later, he left Scotland and moved south to form London & Northern Securities. There were blue chip names on his Board: Viscount Tenby of Ranks and Associated Portland Cement; Wilfred Sproson, and Frederick Norton (Guardian Assurance and Anglo Israel Bank). L & N went public the following year when profits were only £60,000 but within a decade they had grown to almost £10m. 'How did it come about? By acquisitions and by the application of the much vaunted Mackenzie philosophy…the essence of the philosophy has been to avoid buying outright control of the majority of the subsidiaries…it aims to leave the management with a sizeable minority holding.'[2]

The 1964 shareholders' circular outlined Mackenzie's philosophy: 'In the north of England we own investments in the contracting and construction industries and in short and long distance haulage since we are of the opinion that businesses related to primary constructional activities and bulk haulage form a logical commercial grouping in an expanding sector of the economy.' This was to be extended to other parts of the country with the purchase of interests in quarrying and building products in Cumberland and Ayrshire. 'We attach importance to the retention of an equity stake by the management of companies coming within the group.'[3]

In 1965, the group was structured into three divisions: Northern Land, to hold most of the existing North Eastern interests in contracting plant hire and short distance haulage; Northern Lime and Concrete for lime and concrete; and Consolidated Land for long distance haulage and warehousing and short haul outside the north east. At that stage the construction was mainly earth moving, road surfacing, demolition and scrap. By 1969, the group's interests in contracting and plant hire were widely spread throughout the British Isles and Mackenzie decided it was time to expand overseas. London and Northern bought the majority of the capital of Pauling & Co, once one of the great Victorian contractors and about to benefit from the middle-east oil construction boom. The Building Products Division also owned Weatherseal, the country's largest double glazing company. The final large acquisition before the merger with Bardolin was the 1972 purchase of 75% of J Murphy & Sons, a general civil engineering business, later to have a well-publicised brush with the Inland Revenue. In February 1973, London and Northern announced an agreed bid for Bardolin.

The Bardolin bid
Bardolin Securities was incorporated in 1961 and run by John Eyre Godson Bartholomew, a man with an 'extensive knowledge of property development and negotiation.'[4] (The name came from the 'Bar' of Bartholomew; the 'do' of General Dove, his brother-in-law; and the 'lin' of his solicitor, Margolin.) John Bartholomew describes his start in simple terms: 'I bought a plot of land, found a builder, gave him a

[1] *Building*, 4th Oct. 1974.
[2] Ibid.
[3] Circular to shareholders, June 1964.
[4] Bardolin Prospectus, March 1969.

contract to build the house, and sold the house at a profit. Then I bought two plots and progressed from there.'[5] The plots were usually for two or three houses, occasionally four, and while Bardolin remained private it continued to specialise in providing custom-built houses in rural surroundings, often sold off plan, and financed by stage payments; sales rose to around 20-30 a year in Surrey and Berkshire. Bartholomew worked closely with a John Bishop, a partner in Mann & Co, who found the land and sold the finished product.

In 1966 Bardolin went public via a reverse takeover of the quoted Kent Hop, Fruit & Stock Farms which had sold its last farms during 1964 and was no more than a cash shell. The name of the quoted company was changed to Bardolin Ltd. and at that point the new entity was making around £250,000 profit a year. Two years later, Bartholomew was approached by Jock Mackenzie, his wife's cousin, to explore the possibility of Bardolin being used as a vehicle to buy other housebuilding companies. In 1968, Jock Mackenzie joined Bardolin as Chairman: 'the policy has now been reformulated and we are now in the process of creating a national property investment and housebuilding group.'[6] Three small housebuilders were bought in the summer of 1968; in each case, 25% was left in the ownership or the original proprietors. **Jenkins (Builders)** was a small Birmingham building business, founded in 1898, which started private housing in 1953. William Jenkins and his mother had a controlling stake and their partners were Aubrey Trigg, a caterer and Fred Birch, a plumber; 75% was bought for £450,000. **Alfred Robinson** was incorporated in 1956 by two builders, Derek Hall and Ernest Robinson; a civil engineer, Stanley Bird; and an accountant, Harry Crowe; the company was based in Harrow although it was described as building houses in the lower price range in the west country. The midlands housebuilder **Thomas Langley** had been incorporated in 1961 as Allen and Webster by Alfred Allen, a builder, and Fred Webster, an engineer and joined by the builder Thomas Langley on the acquisition of his companies in 1963.

E. Fletcher Builders

However, it was not until January 1969 that the group achieved substance as a housebuilder, with the purchase of **E. Fletcher Builders;**[7] the different scale is illustrated by the number of employees, 840 at Fletcher compared to Bardolin's 95. The business was founded by Edward Fletcher, then aged 30, in 1935. The business, based at Kingswinford Staffordshire, carried out both contracting and private housing development primarily in the west midlands and Staffordshire. Edward's son Geoffrey joined the firm in 1952 as building controls were being removed, and he became Managing Director in 1960. The company obtained a stock exchange quotation in 1964, by which time it was selling approaching 1000 houses a year. By then, Fletcher was expanding out of the west midlands into Worcester and Gloucester to the south and Cheshire and Lancashire to the north. In January 1969, Bardolin announced that it had bought the Fletcher family's 61% holding and was bidding for the balance, valuing the company at £7¹/₂m. Fletcher was then building over 1200 houses (though it included some for local authorities); the company's profit forecast was £850,000.

To finance the Fletcher acquisition, Bardolin launched a 1-for-1 rights issue in May 1969 to raise £5m; after an over-hospitable lunch for the press and potential investors, some two-thirds of the shares were left with the underwriters: 'the fiasco of the Bardolin rights issue has haunted the Mackenzie empire ever since.'[8] Bartholomew had retired from the main Board late in 1968 but broke completely with Mackenzie

---

5 Interview with John Bartholomew, May 2000.
6 Bardolin Prospectus, March 1969.
7 For the avoidance of confusion, this Fletcher had no connection with the Bruce Fletcher housebuilding business that went into Orme.
8 *Building*, 4th Oct. 1974.

over the rights issue, sold his shares to Mackenzie, and started another small development company. Worse to come was the growing realisation that profits were not going to meet the £1.5m profit forecast, due in part to significant losses at Thomas Langley. In April 1970, Mackenzie resigned on the grounds that the increasing spread of his activities was preventing him from devoting enough time to Bardolin; his colleagues, Herbert Ashworth (Deputy Chairman of the Co-op Building Society) and Stanley Bird also resigned. Mackenzie was succeeded by Robin Brook, Chairman of Ionian Bank, but in effect the business was controlled by Fletcher directors. In the event, profits were only £832,000 and the dividend was cut from 13% to 10%.

.

London & Northern buys Bardolin

Brook had acted as a temporary caretaker, passing the chairmanship to Edward Fletcher; his son Geoffrey asked to be released from his contract which, unusually, involved him paying compensation to the company. In fact, Geoffrey Fletcher appears to have left to join Company Developments, later the owner of housebuilders Monsell Youell. In February 1973, London & Northern announced an agreed bid for Bardolin worth £12m. Langley had returned to profit and the boom in house prices enabled Bardolin to forecast profits of £3m, including £0.7m from land sales; London & Northern was forecasting £6m. The Bardolin board, which that same month had bought C.Price of Abergavenny for £475,000, explained that for some time it had been seeking to reduce its dependence on housebuilding. On the purchase of Bardolin, Edward Fletcher resigned; Ken Riley continued as Bardolin Managing Director but he resigned in 1976. Consistent numbers are not available but it looks as if 1973 represented a peak level of private housing activity for Bardolin/London & Northern. Accounts for 1973 stated that over 3000 housing units were completed or refurbished of which approximately one half were for the public sector, i.e. private new housing and refurbishment was around 1500. Total private and public units fell to 2100 in the 1974 recession year, and it is likely that most of this reduction came in the private sector. In 1975, losses were reported in midlands housing and in 1976 the losses were also in the south as well. By 1982, the group was reporting combined private and public new housing of only 730 and there were press references to private housing being as low as 400; this had probably recovered to around 700 five years later.

As a group, London & Northern continued on its acquisition route, financed by repeated rights issues. Two of the largest purchases were of United Medical Enterprises in 1983 and the American Rockville Crushed Stone in 1985. However, group profits had peaked at £18.4m in 1984, fell to £12.5m in 1985 and in 1986, as a result of problems in overseas construction, London & Northern was heading towards losses of almost £10m. Speculation surrounded its future. A new company, Demerger Two, was formed by fringe investment bankers Ifincorp Earl solely for the purpose of bidding for London & Northern and breaking it up. In December 1986 Demerger Two made its bid; it achieved 64% acceptances but could not reach the 90% necessary to effect a reconstruction and the bid eventually lapsed the following March. Days later, the quarrying group Evered Holdings made successful bid for London & Northern; in 1988 the housing operation was sold to Raine Industries.

As a footnote, a new London and Northern Developments was registered at Companies House in 1996 by two property developers; it is not known whether they had a sense of irony.

BARRATT DEVELOPMENTS
Peak units: 16,500 (1983)

Ask the man in the street to name a housebuilder and it will be either Wimpey or Barratt, both in turn the country's largest housebuilders. Over the years the two companies have provided a marked contrast: Wimpey, the inter-wars creation, construction driven; Barratt, a product of the 1960s, pioneering new marketing techniques. Indeed, the Barratt name has been so high profile over the last thirty years that it may come as a surprise to many to learn that its corporate history starts in 1958 as Greensitt Bros. (Contractors), a Newcastle company formed by Lewis Greensitt, 'a quality builder of the traditional school'[1] and the engineer Henry King. Lawrence (Lawrie) Arthur Barratt was later described as having been 'associated' with the company, but did not become a director until 1962. The following year Henry King had disappeared and Lewis Greensitt and Lawrie Barratt were then in equal partnership, recognised formally by the change in company name to Greensitt & Barratt in 1965. Lawrie Barratt was then 38 and Lewis Greensitt 51. Interestingly, there was another Greensitt, Sid, who worked with Lewis in the early days of the company, and another Barratt – Lawrie's elder brother Bernard who built houses under the name WB Barratt and advertised them as having no connection with Greensitt and Barratt.

'Sir Lawrie Barratt has become something of a legend of our times, yet in his personal bearing he is the antithesis of the dramatic brand image promoted on TV. Softly spoken, still with a trace of Geordie accent, [though born in Yorkshire], he can seem almost diffident at times.'[2] That diffident exterior covered an exceptionally determined character. Lawrie Barratt had left school at 14 to work as a clerk at the local mine, studied accountancy at night school and went on to become a chartered secretary. In 1951, he did not have enough money to buy a house and so decided to build his own. That took him into buying a couple of sites and he sold his first site commercially in 1953, from which eventually developed the partnership with Lewis Greensitt. There seemed a very early determination to achieve sustained long term growth. When Greensitt & Barratt was floated on the stock exchange in 1968, the Prospectus contained the first reference to five year growth plans, the one starting in 1962 having been 'fully achieved.'

Greensitt departs
Lewis Greensitt, now a comparatively wealthy man, stayed with the company only briefly after flotation and moved to the Channel Islands. The story has it that this was not popular with Lawrie, and Lewis Greensitt had to pay the company compensation for breaking his contract – a far cry from modern corporate practice. The name of the company was changed to Barratt Developments in 1973 and Greensitt was not a name to be mentioned again. One of the other key figures in the early history was Harry Thornton, the Deputy Chairman and Finance Director, who was both a lawyer and chartered accountant; he formed a good partnership with Barratt but left the group when the Greensitt name was dropped.

By the end of the 1960s, Greensitt & Barratt had demonstrated a record of steady profits growth, all internally generated; units figures do not survive but the company had probably reached the 500 level; nevertheless, it was still one of many local builders with little hint of what was to come. It was in just one decade, the 1970s, that a wave of acquisitions helped to turn Barratt into a national builder. By the end of the decade, Barratt was selling 10,000 houses a year, and poised to overtake Wimpey as the country's leading housebuilder.

---

1 *The Journal*, 26th Nov. 1997.
2 *Building*, April 1982.

The Acquisition Trail

The acquisitions can be covered together and comprise their own set of mini-histories. Two of them, Arthur Wardle and HC Janes, were major housebuilders in their own right.

Geo Bainbridge *1970/71* The first acquisition was a small Newcastle company, owned by George Bainbridge; it had incorporated in 1954 to acquire his long standing business of builder and contractor. Nothing else is known of it.

Bracken Construction *January 1972* Incorporated in 1965, it was a Leeds based housebuilder founded by two builders, Alfred Spencer and Ronnie Bolton, and two accountants, Norman Binns and Michael Freedman. Norman Stubbs and Trevor Spencer, later to be founders of Tay Homes, were senior figures. By 1970, Ronnie Bolton had become the dominant shareholder. In 1971, Bracken had bought Tony Fawcett's Fairhomes (Yorkshire) and Armley Construction (run by Ted Chipendale) and was building itself up for a flotation when Barratt made its approach. Bracken probably built 200-300 houses a year and its profit in the year prior to acquisition was £122,000

Arthur Wardle [q.v.] *April 1972* Arthur Wardle was one of the larger developers in the north west and was building around 800 a year when acquired. It was a significant acquisition for Barratt, taking it out of the north east for the first time. It also brought men who were to become important figures in the Barratt hierarchy. On the Wardle Board at the time of acquisition were John Cassidy (to become Finance Director and Deputy Chairman) and Alan Rawson (to become Chairman of Barratt Southern).

Sawdon & Simpson *August 1973* The Company, then run by two Simpson brothers, Christopher and David, had been established in the building trade in Yorkshire for over 200 years, The main assets were two very large sites at Haxby and Wetherby and the company became Barratt York. Its profit in the year prior to acquisition was £590,000.

William Bruce *August 1973* Based in Ellon, Aberdeenshire, Bruce was primarily a contracting company with a little local housing. However, it did have a 70-acre land bank. Barratt had begun to develop in Scotland from a base in Falkirk and saw the growth potential in Aberdeen. Bruce's profit in the year prior to acquisition was £108,000. There were three family directors – William Bruce and his two sons Bill and Norman. Bill Bruce joined the main board and became Chairman of Barratt Scotland, eventually becoming Deputy Chairman of the Group. The move to Aberdeen was highly successful during the oil boom, and in its best year, Barratt produced just over 800 houses.

Tom Galloway *August 1973* Tom Galloway was based in Beverley and gave Barratt access to the East Riding. The Company had been incorporated in 1964 by two builders, Tom Galloway and James Jordan; although they had equal shareholdings, control later passed to the Galloway family. Its profit in the year prior to acquisition was £82,000. Tom Galloway himself stayed on and ran the company for a while.

Janes [q.v.] *January 1976* Janes was the biggest UK acquisition (around 1200 units a year), taking Barratt into the south Midlands and the northern Home Counties – at that time Barratt had only Barratt South London (operating out of Wallington) and Barratt Guildford. Ken Janes stayed with the company eventually becoming Deputy Chairman of Barratt's northern region.

James Harrison [q.v.] *March 1978* James Harrison started his construction business in 1953, expanding into private housing in 1971. Barratt had made its first bid for Harrison in 1972, subject to its Chairman buying back the construction operation, which turned out impossible to achieve. A second offer in 1978 brought in a small construction business, some land holdings, and commercial property in Edinburgh; its profit in the year prior to acquisition was around £800,000

Ash Homes *October 1978* Formerly known as Ashworth & Steward [q.v.], it was acquired in 1972 by Ron Shuck's Cornwall Property Holdings and then Argyle Securities. By the time the then Ash Homes was acquired by Barratt it was building around 150 houses a year in the better residential areas of Birmingham.

Scottish Homes Investment Company [q.v.] *February 1980* Scottish Homes had withdrawn from private housing in 1972 and the acquisition was essentially about the purchase of a large land holding at Dalgety Bay plus some commercial property – no management came with the company.

The acquisitions were key to Barratt's geographical expansion. It could not have moved so quickly from Newcastle, down through Yorkshire, across to Manchester and then the midlands and northern home counties without the benefit of ready-made businesses. Largely purchased for shares, they accelerated the expansion of the capital base and added significantly to the profits stream. However, it would be totally wrong to suggest that Barratt's growth was just the product of acquisitions. Where companies were bought in new regions, they provided a base from which Barratt could expand organically. Elsewhere, businesses were started from scratch: Bill Learmonth was involved in creating the original Scottish business, before the Bruce and Scottish Homes acquisition; David Pretty started Central London from scratch; in all there were some dozen new companies started around the country in that decade. In the course of the 1970s, Barratt increased volumes from the low hundreds to 10,000; numbers are not available for all the acquisitions but if the volumes of the acquired companies at the time of their entry into the Barratt group were totalled, then it is doubtful if they were responsible for more than a quarter of Barratt's growth.

A marketing-led business

The character of Barratt as a housebuilding phenomenon fully emerged in the 1970s. The public face of Barratt was its high profile advertising and marketing. There may have been others that advertised on television but for Barratt it was routine: the oak tree, the helicopter and Patrick Allan became so familiar they would even feature in comedians' jokes. Tom Baron: 'I'm always amazed at the way Lawrie Barratt has persuaded the rest of us that we are in a marketing business rather than a building business. He alone convinced the industry that it had to be market orientated.'[3] But marketing was more than just advertising. Sales were predominantly targeted at the first time buyer and everything was done to make the transaction as easy as possible, especially where it affected the buyer's pocket. For those buyers trading up to larger houses, their path was eased by the widespread use of part exchanges, and Barratt would even part exchange the part exchanges. Although Barratt was not immune to downturns in the market, its marketing, innovation and general drive meant it coped better than most; indeed, the company regarded recessions as the times when it could increase market share.

There is no doubt that Sir Lawrie Barratt, as he became in 1982, revolutionised the industry with his marketing approach, the willingness to service the first time buyer and even to the introduction of new product. It is interesting to speculate with all 'breakthroughs' whether it was the ideas that were original, or merely their implementation. He was not the first in the industry to switch the emphasis from production-led to marketing-led development – see the Wates history for Neil Wates' approach to marketing in the 1960s. Without the benefit of an interview with Sir Lawrie, it is hard to know if he developed his ideas independently; ex-colleagues have praised his ability to absorb ideas from elsewhere.

3 *Housebuilder*, Aug. 1986.

What matters is that Wates jettisoned its pilot and declined during the 1970s; Barratt was brilliant in its implementation and became the country's leading housebuilder as a result.

At the start of the 1980s, it seemed little could stop the Barratt machine: it was planning output of about 20,000 houses a year in the UK; developing commercial property and time share; and taking the first steps in creating a Barratt America. John Swanson recalled it as an exciting place to be: 'At that time, I had just joined the main Board as sales and marketing director; the basic structure of the organisation was probably as good as it has ever been in as much as Lawrie was probably at his best, mentally and physically. Alan Rawson was running the Southern division, John Cassidy was deputy Chairman, Bill Bruce was running Scotland. Sitting at a main board meeting were some very experienced operators – it was an operational business.'[4]

One of the driving principles within the Barratt organisation was standardisation, of the product and the development process; there was no doubt that edicts from Newcastle were to be followed. This was both a strength in providing a framework for growth and yet a weakness in that it inhibited local flexibility. John Cassidy reflected on one man who ignored the system: Tony Fawcett was the finest Managing Director I have ever come across in the industry. He didn't like the Barratt philosophy; he liked to run his own business. The philosophy when I became involved was to build 70% for the first time buyer and in Manchester, we were building 1000-1100 houses in the late 1970s and making £3m profit. Tony, over in Yorkshire, ignored the first time buyer market – he did 400 houses a year and he also made £3 million profit. Because he was successful doing it his way, Lawrie was never in a position to challenge it.'[5]

US diversification
Returning to the early 1980s, UK housing completions rose from 11,000 to 16,500 (so far, an all-time peak). The American National Housing Corporation (southern California) was bought for $12m in March 1980; McKeon Construction (northern California) was added a year later for $32m. Between 1980 and 1983 group turnover and profit doubled. At £46m, Barratt's UK housing profit was well ahead of Wimpey's £26m and there were only four other housebuilders that made profits in excess of £10m. The innovation continued and now the striking feature was Barratt's targeting of the single first time buyer with ever smaller flats, complete with kitchen 'white goods' and 100% finance packages. This culminated in the 236 square foot Studio Solo: 'Britain's first fully furnished, fully fitted, mortgageable home for single people.'[6] Interestingly, another housebuilder had tried that route a decade earlier: 'Another alternative is being put forward by the Greaves Organisation which has sent its brochure *Starter Homes* to over 100 local authority planning offices. The brochure contains plans of four small homes ranging from the one-bedroom single-storey Studio home with 330 sq.ft. to the two-storey Prelude house with two bedrooms and 560 sq.ft.'[7] Once again, implementation was everything: two years after its Studio venture, Greaves was in liquidation. Ironically, two years after its Studio Solo, Barratt was also facing its biggest crisis and the name of that crisis was Granada.

World in Action cripples Barratt
On the 27th June 1983, Granada's World in Action broadcast a highly critical programme on timber-framed housing, a construction system increasingly used by the volume builders. Although attacking industry practices, Barratt as the largest housebuilder was given star billing. Almost exactly a year later, World In Action showed 'Your starter for life', a programme specific to Barratt, which suggested that those

4 Interview with John Swanson, Oct. 1999.
5 Fawcett eventually left to form Sketchmead, later joining forces with Duncan Davidson's Persimmon..
6 *Building*, 13th Nov. 1981.
7 *Building*, 21st Sept. 1973.

buying a Barratt starter home stood to lose money. The impact on sales was devastating; the comedians' jokes, so often a reflection of public attitudes, were now an embarrassment. Informal forecasts of volumes for 1984 had been around 18,000; the reality was that UK sales halved in two years – and continued to fall after that. Investigative television programmes are not always noted for their impartiality. The industry's timber framed site practices had probably become a little sloppy but examples of poor workmanship have been instanced in traditional brick and block without the public refusing to buy the product on any scale.

The concerns over starter homes may have been dramatised but they had a more valid rationale and were already being expressed before the Granada programme. *Building* magazine had carried an article in the January headed 'Are First-time Buyers Getting a Poor Start' which referred to the high value of white goods being included in the purchase price and Anglia Building Society valuers' report that mini-homes were not achieving their original value at first resale. A contemporary stockbroking report commented: 'We think that what has actually happened in 1984 was that a general weakness in the market for new small starter homes has emerged. Perhaps the bed-sit for sale market was never as large as originally thought. Certainly, the rapid turnover means that the builder is very quickly competing with his own second hand product. More builders have entered an area once Barratt's exclusive preserve. An oversupply of small starter units would provide a consistent explanation of all that has happened during 1984…at the same time it also explains how there could be resale difficulties for this part of the product range when the general house price indices are rising.'[8] Though not realised then, Barratt's starter home problem was but a foretaste of the negative equity which was to cripple the industry a few years later.

The unit roller coaster: 1972-2004

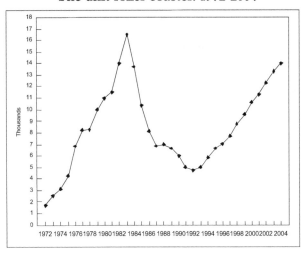

The highly publicised double blow from World in Action, directed at the biggest consumer product that people ever buy, could have finished Barratt. That the company survived and then rebuilt itself is remarkable testament to Sir Lawrie and his team. John Swanson, with some understatement, describes it as 'Not an easy time. We had a lot of support from advisors and people like the NHBC who knew that the Barratt product was not as it was being portrayed. We had to fight our way through it. We gave extra guarantees; we came to an arrangement with the NHBC so we could give a 20 year guarantee; we did a guaranteed buy back scheme – it obviously concerned the institutions and to some extent we were gambling on inflation but at the end of the day we hardly bought a house back, if at all. We just structured the company for survival for the first 12 to 24 months to get it back on its feet again. It took a lot of hard work from each of the

8 Laing & Cruickshank, *Reflections on the Housing Market,* June 1984.

managing directors. We redesigned the house types. Mike Norton did that in a remarkably short period of time given that he had to design around 15 new house types and get planning permissions all over the country. But I don't think any of us ever thought that it would bring the company down. One of the great strengths of the company was its self belief which was generated by Lawrie but he needed our support. And everybody executed what we decided at these board meetings down to the nth degree.'[9]

The cost was high. On the announcement in September 1985 of a collapse in group profits to only £4m, the past year's remedial action was spelt out: 1200 permanent staff out of 5500 had been made redundant; the number of UK housebuilding subsidiaries reduced from 29 to 10; debt reduced from £128m to £59m; timber-framed construction abandoned; the offer to include white goods halted; the new Premier range launched; and the Californian operating divisions reduced from five to three. Despite this, UK volumes continued to fall; still over 10,000 in 1985 they were to fall another third by 1988. However, 70% of sales were now derived from the middle and upper market, i.e. they were substantially larger houses than before and, with house price inflation, group turnover was actually modestly higher than in 1985. Profit, of course, was where house price inflation really counted and for the year to June 1988, the group declared record pre-tax profits of £61.5m, just surpassing those of 1983.

Succession problems
On January 1st 1988 Sir Lawrie, now aged 60, moved from being Chairman and Managing Director to being Executive Chairman and John Swanson was appointed Group Managing Director. A year later, Sir Lawrie retired from the Board to become Life President and John Swanson became Chairman and Chief Executive. He enjoyed the luxury of yet another record year before the recession hit; profits more than halved in 1989/90 but the full extent of the downturn was only realised the following year. On the 29th July 1991, just after the close of the year end, the company announced that losses would approach £100m (they turned out to be £106m). John Swanson resigned and Sir Lawrie came out of retirement to 'rescue' his company. The provisions that produced those losses were attributed to land bought by the group in the previous three years in southern England and the USA.

One must ask how easy it was to succeed the most well known figure in the industry, and one who had ruled the company for thirty years – especially at such a critical time. There is no question that the return of Sir Lawrie was portrayed as a rescue. The author himself was able to ask Sir Lawrie at the time, how much of the land dated back from his own tenure and was left in no doubt that, in his view, he had left the company in perfect health. It was perhaps a harsh judgement on his successor. The totality of UK housing provisions was £65m, less than for Wimpey and well below the £100m provisions seen in four other companies, and as a write-off per plot it was below the average for all medium and large housebuilders.[10]

Looking back, John Swanson did not think the task of following a dominant personality was impossible, but neither was it easy. 'Perhaps if Lawrie had stayed on as Chairman and I had become Chief Executive for a longer period through that transition, that would have helped. There is no doubt at all that I missed Lawrie's counsel when he left the Company; I think in that turmoil and the problems the company had at that time, and they weren't all market driven, it would have helped to have had someone there.' John Cassidy suggested that the recession had perhaps exposed more deep seated problems: 'I have the utmost respect for John and I always saw him as Lawrie's natural successor. If he has a shortcoming he is probably too nice. I think Barratt was out of control when he took it over and too many of the Board were not up to it. We had 25% of the Yorkshire market. Lawrie did genuinely believe that you could take

9 Interview John Swanson.
10 *PHA*, 1994.

25% of any market. The problems came when Lawrie tried to expand too fast.' The distractions of the US operations, which involved frequent visits by UK executives, should not be underestimated.

And the recovery

Whether or not there were deep seated problems or whether it was just the inevitable consequence of buying land in a downturn, remains open to debate. What is incontrovertible is that they were dealt with quickly and effectively. Lawrie Barratt appointed Frank Eaton as Chief Executive under his executive chairmanship; Eaton, a school leaver, had been recruited as a construction director in the Manchester office and had been appointed to the Group Board in 1988 on Sir Lawrie's retirement. With the land written down, profits began a period of sustained recovery; meanwhile reductions in work-in-progress brought borrowings under control. However, UK volumes were still under 5000, less than a third of their peak, and the Group had to create volume growth from those (relatively) low levels. At the beginning of 1993, the company publicly stated that it intended to push UK volumes up from 5000 to 8000 by 1996. It seemed an optimistic target at the time but, although it took an extra year, the target was achieved and then surpassed. The next target was to raise legal completions to 11,000 by year 2000. One of the key strategic decisions was the £90m rights issue to finance expansion in the south east and, in particular the London market. By 1997, Barratt was able to declare record profits as Sir Lawrie retired a second time from the Board. The 11,000 volume target was achieved in 2001, again a year late, but without recourse to the acquisition trail being followed by other industry leaders.

In October 2002 Frank Eaton was killed in a car accident and David Pretty was appointed as the new Chief Executive. Pretty had started his working career as a marketing graduate with Procter and Gamble. He joined Barratt in 1976, started the London operation and, after a spell away from the Group running St George, was appointed to the main board in 1990. Under Pretty, Barratt continued the organic growth that had been so successful under Eaton; by 2004, Barratt's volumes in the UK had exceeded 14,000 and UK trading profits of £366m were earned. Pretty might have been following a well trodden path in the UK but he reversed the overseas strategy by announcing the sale of its US subsidiaries in August 2004. With some £90m available for reinvestment, Pretty commented that 'we only have a 9% market share, so there are significant opportunities for future growth in the UK.'[11]

[11] *Housebuilder* Sept 2004.

BEAZER HOMES
Peak units: 8223 (2000)

Although the 1973 prospectus referred to the sixth generation of Beazers in the building industry, the transformation of a small Bath-based business into an international housing, construction and quarrying company was down to one man – Brian Beazer, variously described as 'a steely individual who is not easily crossed', 'a singular, ascetic and intensely private man' and 'a bull market phenomenon, not an industrial manager.'[1] The original company, CH Beazer, was founded by Cyril Beazer, a stone mason like his father before him. After leaving school in 1921, aged thirteen, he started work for his father, moving to Bath three years later to complete his training. He worked there for several years becoming a contract foreman in 1932. After an enforced break due to polio, Cyril Beazer decided to work on his own and secured a contract to build a couple of houses.

Progress as a contract builder was steady but slow as 'Borrowing was not something which was part of my philosophy',[2] not an attitude that he passed on to his successor. By the start of 1939, Cyril Beazer's finances permitted him to buy his own land although almost immediately he was diverted into war work, first locally and later in London. After the war, Beazer concentrated on reconstruction work, gradually increasing the general construction although with no indication of any speculative housebuilding. In 1956 CH Beazer (Construction) was incorporated to acquire the business; Cyril Beazer's elder son, Ralph, who had worked in the Company since he was 15, became a director and Brian left his job in the City in 1957 to be company secretary, becoming a director in 1960.

The role of the two brothers switched during the 1960s. Ralph left to pursue other interests, although remaining as a non-executive director, and in 1968 Brian Beazer became Managing Director. At that point, Beazer made its first acquisition, **Mortimer & Son**. The Mortimer business had commenced in Bath as jobbing builders in the 1920s and by 1968 it was a general contractor, including local authority housing. The 'Son' was Arthur Mortimer who had died earlier and family trusts owned most of the capital; a minority was held by the Lippiatt family. Beazer was then predominantly a private housebuilder and the Mortimer acquisition gave the group a broader balance. A new holding company was created to buy both companies, with equal board representation from each – three Beazer and three Mortimer directors, including John and Frederick Lippiatt. Also coming with Mortimer was their chief accountant, Alan Chapple, who went on to be Beazer's Finance Director and assistant Managing Director. In 1968, Beazer's turnover was £1.8m, of which Mortimer had contributed over half, and pre-tax profits around £100,000; housing sales were of the order of 150.

European diversification

The business consolidated for a couple of years and then, in 1970, when turnover was still under £2m, the group began to investigate the development possibilities in northern Europe. 'We had been successful in developing property in the UK and felt there were opportunities abroad.'[3] In 1971, Beazer began commercial development in Brussels with a site that made almost £1m profit, followed by developments in Paris, Antwerp, Frankfurt and Hamburg. In June 1973, Beazer obtained its stock exchange quotation. Cyril Beazer remained Chairman, a position he retained until his death ten years later, and Brian Beazer was Managing Director, later succeeding his father as Chairman. Ralph Beazer, by then President of the HBF, was non-executive vice Chairman, Ken Cotton was the Managing Director of developments, and

---

[1] *Management Today,* Oct 1986.

[2] Beazer, *Random Reflections of a West Country Master Craftsman.*

[3] Interview with Alan Chapple, Aug. 2000.

below Board level Terry Upsall, later to be Managing Director of housing, was his deputy. The operational management of housing had its roots in town planning. Cotton had been planning officer to Bath City Council and Upsall, who became a director in 1974, was a chartered surveyor with Wiltshire County Council.

Although house sales at the time of flotation were still below 200, the rise in prices had helped produce profits of over £500,000 in the year to June 1972, and, with the commercial property deals coming to fruition, the 1973 forecast was for £1.35m. The directors' view was that commercial and industrial development in UK and Europe was to be 'the main area for expansion of the future profitability of the Group.'[4] That statement was made as commercial development across Europe was about to move into recession, prompted by the quadrupling of oil prices. Although profits held steady for a while, in 1975/76 they halved to £0.8m and the dividend was cut; borrowings soared and reserves fell by a quarter following write-downs. 'We had to sell properties to survive and only did so by sheer hard work.'[5] Unsurprisingly, the 1970s became a decade of consolidation as Beazer overcame the effects of earlier over-expansion. Some small acquisitions were made, including the Lippiatt's other company, Lippiatt (Bath) in 1977. Having been hurt by the rise in oil prices, Beazer looked to see if it could profit from the oil countries' new-found wealth. They looked at the middle east but instead chose a joint venture with the Nigerian Government to build houses; in the event, this was fairly short lived due to problems repatriating profits.

The acquisition era begins

The next acquisition was far more significant. In April 1979 Beazer bought the Bridgewater-based **RM Smith** group of housebuilding companies for £4.3m. Smith had been incorporated by Robert Smith after the war and had developed into a general contracting, housing and property business. The acquisition more or less doubled Beazer's housing throughput to over 500 a year and, in the year to June 1980, excluding profits on the sale of surplus property, Beazer made profits of £2.3m – just ahead of the 1975 peak. Smith complemented Beazer, which now had good coverage of the west country housing market from Devon to Wiltshire. The business was taken into the home counties the following year when a new office was opened at Yateley on the Hampshire/Surrey border.

The next expansion phase was about to begin. In the 1980 accounts, the Chairman had stated that Beazer was 'now in a position to make larger acquisitions where we feel able to make a contribution to improvement in performance.' Although the acquisitions took Beazer in a new direction, into the brick industry, reinforced plastics and the manufacture of construction plant, the traditional development business was also expanded by the purchase of Monsell Youell, Second City Properties and the commercial property company, M.P. Kent. There were also three unsuccessful bid attempts in this period: in 1982 for R Green Properties; a contested bid for William Leech which left Beazer holding 24% of the shares and another for Bath & Portland, a quarrying and contracting company, based on the shareholding acquired via MP Kent.

The privately-owned **Monsell Youell Group** built from Luton to the west country. Monsell Youell was a merger of two companies under the aegis of Company Developments, an investment company controlled by William Willson, a chartered accountant, and solicitor Peter Southall, and by ex-directors of E. Fletcher, following the latter's takeover by Bardolin. Company Developments bought JK Monsell in 1970/71, and then Youell Developments. Monsell had been in existence for around fifty years and was primarily a housebuilder. Youell Developments, which had extensive land holdings, was owned by Alf Youell who had reached retirement age and was emigrating to New Zealand. In effect, the amalgamation

4 CH Beazer Prospectus, 1973.
5 Interview with Alan Chapple, Aug 2000.

of the two builders saw the Youell land being fed through the Monsell building organisation; in the first year together they had built around 100 houses. Monsell Youell coped well with the recession and, although there were large losses elsewhere in the group, the housebuilder continued to expand with sites ranging from Luton across to the west country; by 1980, housing sales were in excess of 500, although subsequently dropping back to around 400 a year. In 1983, Beazer announced an £8m bid for Monsell Youell: 'We regarded £8m as a full price for the business.'[6]

Second City [q.v.]was a quoted company based in the midlands and in addition to its housing, also brought with it a commercial property portfolio. Monsell Youell and Second City between them had been building some 900 houses a year. MP Kent [q.v.] was based in Bath and had originally been a mixed housebuilding and property business, although by the time of its acquisition was confined to commercial property. An added appeal for Kent was its strategic holding in Bath & Portland for which Beazer later bid; aggregates was an area of the building industry which appealed to Brian Beazer and although he was to be outbid by ARC for this particular company, he was later to return to the sector with unforeseen consequences.

UK housing moves towards national coverage

By 1984 the Beazer housing companies were selling over 2000 houses and contributing just over half the £11m profits; the share capital had trebled since 1979. The speed and diversity of Beazer's acquisitions reflected the temperament of Brian Beazer, a man with an astute eye for an undervalued business and who enjoyed the process of deal-making. In some ways he behaved more like a stock market investor, buying undervalued companies, extracting unrecognised value and, if appropriate, selling assets on at a profit. In the case of Westbrick, for instance, the sale of the building materials division to Tarmac some $2^1/_2$ years after purchase netted a spectacular £20m profit. The Company made more contested takeover bids than any other in this book – perhaps more than all the other companies combined. There was a particularly close relationship with stockbroker Messells (Mike Whittles later becoming a Board member) and County Bank, which provided one executive director and another as a non-executive. 'Beazer and County Bank have had a long, mutually and hugely rewarding relationship, and communication between them is constant. How many Beazer bids were first suggested by County Bank is unlikely ever to be revealed.'[7] Alan Chapple did not think that Brian Beazer was pushed unduly by the City: 'It was a genuine partnership between the company and the financial advisers.' Nevertheless, there is no doubt that Brian Beazer was captivated by the acquisition process; on his own admission to the author at the time, provided the housebuilding companies delivered their financial targets, Brian Beazer had no particular interest in the product.

The next housing acquisition was the second bite at the underperforming William Leech, a north-east housebuilder controlled by a charitable foundation. Having been rebuffed by the trustees in the Autumn of 1984, Beazer acquired the outstanding 76% for £19m in February 1985. Leech had been building just short of 2000 houses a year and its acquisition propelled Beazer to number four in the industry with 4800 houses. Terry Upsall was Chief Executive of the housing division, Alan Chapple as Finance Director and Bob Stephens Managing Director of UK housing. Brian Beazer, Chapple, Upsall and Hugh Rees, the director of strategic planning, constituted the executive that controlled Beazer for most of its quoted existence. By now, however, Beazer's plans were being made on a wider scale. The statement accompanying the May 1985 rights issue said 'Your Board intends to consolidate the Company's position as a national housebuilder.' It duly did that with the purchase of the Yorkshire business of Whelmar (350 houses a year) and further organic growth took Beazer to a 1988 volume peak of 6300. More significantly,

---

[6] Interview with William Willson, July 2000.
[7] *Management Today,* Oct 1986.

the rights issue statement went on to say that the Company 'also intends to expand the group's other activities, particularly in contracting and building-related products.'

Housing Units, 1979-1988

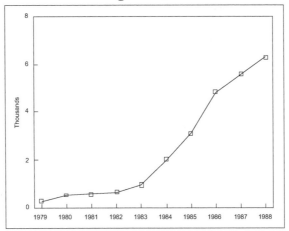

International expansion

In fact, the next move was into US housing with the purchase in August 1985 of Cohn Communities of Atlanta for $6m (300 houses a year); the following April, Randall Phillips of Nashville, completing around 400 units a year, was also bought. 'Brian had a fascination with the US and we had decided that we would go into the US by buying into something we knew best; we wanted to get used in a simple way to what it was like working in the States.' Terry Upsall went out to investigate the market and identified two cities, Tampa and Atlanta, and the Board chose the latter. Jerry Cohn stayed on to run the company (now quoted in its own right); 'it ran well and we had no major problems with it.'[8]

The move into contracting was preceded by a fiercely contested takeover battle for SGB, the country's largest scaffolding business, only failing when Mowlem, which had a family connection, bought SGB. In the following month, November 1985, Beazer did make its contracting move with a £9m agreed bid for the London construction firm, GE Wallis and almost simultaneously bought 26% of French Kier from Trafalgar House for £29m making a hostile bid for the balance. French Kier was a significant domestic and international contractor, and with what was probably an underutilised land bank. French Kier had faced near bankruptcy a decade earlier caused by fixed-price motorway contracts but it had been rescued by John Mott, a tough civil engineer who had taken profits up to £16m and was forecasting £20m for 1985. Mott fought the bid vigorously but Beazer eventually succeeded in the January after increasing the value of the bid from £115m to £145m.

The strategy of making such a substantial diversification into the competitive world of construction was queried by outsiders at the time but Beazer argued that the acquisition would 'provide benefits of synergy and a savings of scale';[9] it fitted in with the general philosophy of making Beazer a large company within the broad envelope of the building industry. However in the rejection document John Mott's response to the concept had been withering: 'he deludes himself if he believes that any one style of management is appropriate at all times. Subsidiary operating units can be neither independent nor autonomous on any definition of the words that I understand. There are economies of scale, but there are also costs

8 Interview with Alan Chapple, Aug 2000.
9 *Building*, 10th Jan 1986.

associated with size. These observations are founded in practical experience and not taken from management text books. In my judgement, the Board of Beazer, largely composed of people with an accounting or merchant banking background, does not possess the depth or breadth of industrial management experience and technological attainment necessary to adapt to the diverse demands of a major international construction business.'

Undaunted, Beazer went on to buy Franki, a Hong Kong contractor, and a stake in Girvan, an Australian contractor. But although they were later to cause their own local problems (Girvan necessitated write-offs of £40m), the scale of the acquisitions in the USA was being significantly increased. In September 1986 Beazer bought the Dallas-based Gifford Hill, the fourth largest cement manufacturer in the US, for £190m, later increasing its aggregates interests with additional acquisitions. Gifford Hill looked like another undervalued asset ripe for the Beazer treatment. Markets were booming around the world; Beazer increased its profits from £16m in the year to June 1985 to £106m in 1987/88. Although gearing now represented 90% of shareholders' funds, but profits were forecast to increase, in June 1988, Beazer made the bid that was to prove its undoing.

Koppers proves Beazers nemesis

Koppers was the second largest aggregates business in the USA; it also had longstanding chemical and wood treatment businesses. The complications of the financial engineering do not concern us here but, initially using an off-balance sheet company and with interest rate caps, Beazer bid $1.8 billion cash for Koppers compared with its published net asset value of only $0.5m. Without an asset revaluation, Beazer would have had a negative net asset value. The Koppers aggregate reserves were duly revalued, both in quantity and price, but the pro-forma 1988 balance sheet still showed the £1.26 billion debt to be 165% of shareholders funds.

Profits for 1988/89 rose to a record £131m with the homes and property division contributing £127m of the £228m trading profit, but the group was structurally vulnerable to the downturn in activity that was now starting to affect both sides of the Atlantic. The Company refused to recognise that the recession had begun. Speaking at a stockbroker's conference, Brian Beazer said: 'From the cradle you are taught that houses are a good investment in this country. While many things you learn from Mummy and Daddy are untrue, this is not!. House prices will not fall because it would be the kiss of death for Mrs Thatcher. People who are even more addicted to self-preservation than I am will have worked that out before me.'[10]

Although Koppers disposed of $875m assets, largely the chemical companies, borrowing remained in excess of £1 billion; the interest rate caps were unwinding; and worst of all, what had been regarded as a relatively small part of the Koppers business, wood treatment, was facing colossal environmental liabilities. The remediation provisions were put in Beazer's 1989 accounts at over $500m compared with the $200m provision in Koppers' last accounts; that provision was to rise further. Looking back on the whole episode, Alan Chapple commented 'The acquisition process was unusual in that normally we had all the borrowing details resolved in advance but in this case, while Citibank were undertaking to provide the finance, such was the pace of the bid that the financial details were not resolved until after the bid was won. Additionally, our plans included a large rights issue at some stage but the double recession meant that this proved to be not possible.'

The Hanson takeover and a new start

The solution Beazer announced in April 1991 was to float off 'Beazer Europe' (primarily UK housing, property and construction), the effect of which would have been to leave the US operations as a separate

10 *Building*, 10th March 1989.

entity. Terry Upsall was Chief Executive and to mark the break with the old regime, Brian Beazer was not a member of the new board but he continued as Chairman of Beazer Homes USA (with Ian McCarthy as Chief Executive, this went on to become one of the top ten US housebuilders, rivalling the UK housing business in size). The UK flotation was scheduled for October 1991; the pathfinder prospectus was circulated and meetings with investors took place. Whether the float would have raised enough finance to solve the old company's financing problems will never be known for, only days after the announcement, Beazer acepted a takeover bid from Hanson which, amongst other things, was one of the largest aggregates producers in the UK. Hindsight is a great asset when reaching a verdict on a corporate enterprise. Brian Beazer undoubtedly stood or fell by his acquisitions: he regarded them as a virtue, telling a seminar that 'expanding a business organically leads to an incestuous organisation without new ideas. Acquisition brings in new ideas and new challenges.'[11]

The Kier construction business was quickly sold to the management. but Hanson had the financial strength to hold Beazer Homes through the worst of the recession, first writing off some £92m in 1992 against the land bank and work-in-progress. It was never intended to be a long term asset for Hanson, however, and the new Beazer Group, now consisting solely of UK housing, was floated in March 1994. Upsall had left the group on the Hanson takeover and the new Chief Executive was Denis Webb, a civil engineer who had come into the group from William Leech. Although it was the intention to run the new Beazer Homes on more conservative lines, acquisitions continued to feature, albeit this time without stretching the balance sheet. The Scottish housebuilder, Walker Homes (owned by Mike Walker), and building around 150 houses a year, had been bought during the last months of Hanson ownership and almost immediately after the flotation Beazer bought the housing interests of Mowlem Homes and land holdings from the liquidator of the small northern firm of Pilcher Homes. This was followed in 1996 by the acquisition of the specialist Charles Church. In the year to June 1995, its first full year as an independent company, Beazer sold a record 6700 houses, with profits of around £55m.

Volumes were increased to around 8000 by the end of the decade, at which point Webb retired, to be replaced by John Low, previously Managing Director of Ideal Homes. However, profits growth did not match other quoted companies in the sector and the share price substantially underperformed its peers. At the same time, Bryant was looking for a solution to its problems and, in December 2000, a 'Merger of Equals' was proposed, to be effected by a new holding company, Domus – a name previously used by a housebuilder that went into receivership in 1990. Although 78% of shareholders voted in favour of the merger, it was overtaken by the bid from Taylor Woodrow for Bryant. This effectively killed the merger and, in February 2001, Beazer was acquired by Persimmon for £610m. The mainstream Beazer business was integrated under the Persimmon name though the Charles Church brand was maintained.

As a footnote, Beazer Homes USA Inc, which had been sold separately by Hanson, went from strength to strength. Brian Beazer remained its Chairman: in 2004 it was USA's sixth largest housebuilder with 16,400 sales.

11 *Contract Journal,* 30th Oct 1986.

BELLWAY
Peak units: 6610 (2004)

Although John T Bell Ltd, the corporate entity that became Bellway, was not formed until 1946, the family involvement with housebuilding dated to before World War I. John T Bell (1878-1965) had worked as a quarryman by day, and first started building houses in 1912 at Newbiggin, outside Newcastle, in his spare time. By the end of the 1920s he had built some 400-500 houses in the area but he was unable to survive the depression as a self-employed builder and returned to working as a manager for another builder, which he did until the outbreak of World War II. By then, his son John was a trainee accountant looking to the building industry as a career, while another son, Russell, was already working with John T Bell.[1]

After the war, Russell Bell began to work on his own account, soon bringing his elder brother John to join him. On the incorporation of the business in 1946, the sons brought their father, then 68, into the firm; the three of them contributed £200 each and named the company after John T Bell. Jack Corscadden, a surveyor, became a key member of the team, joining them in 1951, becoming a director in 1957. Ken Bell, the youngest son, did not join the firm until 1953, aged 21. The firm began doing small-scale building work, particularly for the local authorities, and the first large-scale construction came when the company obtained a contract for some 2000 houses in Newcastle. During the period of post-war controls, the Company also engaged in the conversion of residential properties into flats and the Bells began to purchase development land. By the early 1950s the firm was employing several hundred people..

North British Properties floated

There was always an active interest in developing commercial property. Nine companies were formed between 1953 and 1957 and these were grouped together as North British Properties and floated on the Stock Exchange in 1961 with the three brothers as directors. John T Bell & Sons, still the bigger business, remained private. Two years after its flotation, in 1963, North British acquired John T Bell in a reverse takeover. The offer document gave the first indication of the financial progress that had been made by John T Bell which had increased its profits from £10,000 in 1953 to £314,000 in 1962. Excluded from the flotation was the holding in Le Touquet Syndicate where the Bell family had played a major role in developing the French resort. By 1960, Bell was building around 700 houses a year making it one of the largest housebuilders in the region.

The enlarged North British Properties made steady progress through the 1960s, profits rising to almost £1m by the end of the decade. It is believed that annual output, including local authority housing, reached 2000 a year but the public/private split is not available. Both private housing and commercial property development remained centred on the north-east region until the mid-1960s when the first regional expansion began. Russell Bell, who led the construction programme, recruited local directors to take charge of Yorkshire and Scotland. Their brief was to build and to sell, with everything else controlled by the head office. The housing strategy remained concentrated on large sites serving the first time buyer and a substantial land bank was accumulated, primarily on the outskirts of major conurbations such as Newcastle, Edinburgh and Doncaster. In 1968 Russell Bell decided that he was going to leave the UK and live in Jersey, thereby taking from the Company the family member who had been the driving force behind the day-to-day running of the business. John Bell became Chairman and Ken Bell, then aged 36, Managing Director. Representatives of the next generation, John's son Stephen and Russell's son Michael,

[1] For general background, see *The Sunday Sun*, June 1969: 'Tycoons of Tyne and Tees'.

joined the Board in 1973 but neither stayed more than a few years. The reality was that much of the running of the housebuilding operation was in the hands of Jack Corscadden, while Ken Bell's attention was on diversification. A number of small ancillary businesses were bought in the UK but there were more ambitious moves overseas, as the Group started housing development in Australia in 1969 and in the Paris region of France in 1971.

Group housing sales reached 2000 in 1972 with perhaps 1500 of these coming from the UK. Large sites were a feature of the operation ranging from one to three thousand units apiece; the Chapel House Newcastle site alone accounted for 600 houses a year. John Bell had excellent contacts with the large landowners, particularly Lord Armstrong and the Northumberland Ducal Estates, and these were prime sources of large sites. However, the largest development of all was Cramlington New Town which was started in 1964 jointly with neighbouring Leech; 16,000 houses had been built by 2001. The inflationary house price spiral produced the rapid improvement in financial results common throughout the industry, pre-tax profits rising from £1.1m to £4.7m. By 1973 Bellway was describing itself as active in the north midlands, the north-east of England and the central lowlands of Scotland. Its next strategic move was to buy the south London flat builder A & R A Searle for £3m giving the company its first presence in the south-east market. At the same time the parent company name was changed to the present Bellway. The stated residential policy in the 1973 Accounts was to concentrate in 'specific areas of high demand in the UK where the percentage of home ownership is below the national average and offering the public medium priced dwellings'.

Bellway's domestic housing operation held up relatively well in the recession, the worst year being a £1.9m profit in 1977. Indeed, the group continued to expand regionally in the UK and in 1976 reported new areas including Sussex, York and Lancashire: the 1977 accounts stated that 'We anticipate more than 50% of our housebuilding production will be in areas outside the north-east.' Where the group did suffer was overseas with the two countries losing a cumulative £2.8m between 1975 and 1977, France being the main problem. Despite the fact that rental income was now running at £1m, group pre-tax profits were almost wiped out in 1977 when the decision to withdraw from the overseas markets was taken.

Property demerges

Like other mixed business, Bellway found that the combination of housing trading profits and property assets did not receive its full recognition in the stock market. In 1979, the group reversed its early marriage, separating the two businesses again into Bellway Limited as the housebuilder and North British as the property company.[2] On the de-merger, Ken Bell became Executive Chairman of Bellway and John Bell became President. The senior non-family director by then was John Gibson who had joined the group as a surveyor in 1962 'and assumed responsibility for expanding housebuilding activities.'[3] He was made Deputy Managing Director of the holding company in 1977 and Managing Director of Bellway in 1979. Jack Corscadden, who had been as near to a housing managing director as Bellway had, retired in 1977, though remaining on the Board as a non-executive director. In the demerger year, Bellway sold some 1350 houses, similar to the levels achieved in the previous few years, and these numbers were not significantly exceeded until the late 1980s. However, the 1970s did see a substantial reorientation of Bellway's housing: at the beginning of the decade it was still 70% dependent on the north east, with some 80% of volume coming from starter homes. By the end of the 1970s these percentages were down to 30% and 25% respectively.

[2] In 1984, North British was sold to Sun Life.
[3] Prospectus, 1979.

In 1981 Bellway and Leech announced a possible merger; when the shares were suspended they valued Leech at £13.6m and Bellway at £11.4m The enlarged company would have been number four in the industry with a minimum unit volume of 2500. Although the merger was to take the form of an offer by Leech for Bellway, the new company would be headed by Ken Bell. The announcement that the merger was off came barely 48 hours before the posting of the formal offer document. Under the heading 'Merger Mix-up on the Tyne', *Building* magazine wrote: 'To most construction industry experts in the region, the business lifestyle of the two firms looked to be pretty incompatible.'[4] Bellway appeared to have had the change of mind but the formal announcement merely said that the two boards had discovered a 'fundamental difference in the management philosophies.'

Although the official line was that a period of corporate restructuring followed the collapse of the merger, all was not well. The senior management were not always as one; losses were being incurred in the north-west and Yorkshire, and Ken Bell was still pursuing non-housing investments, the 25% investment in Falmouth Container Terminal being the most public. The day-to-day management of UK housing was increasingly the responsibility of Howard Dawe, then the Technical Director. In 1985, John Gibson retired as Managing Director and Ken Bell became largely non-executive. Howard Dawe became Managing Director with Alan Robson, who had joined in 1983, Finance Director. Although Ashley Bell, Ken's son, represented a new generation the subsequent growth of the Bellway business rested on the non-family duo of Dawe and Robson.

Howard Dawe assumes control

Howard Dawe had joined the Company in 1961 as a site clerk, aged 17, his earlier hopes of becoming a zoologist cut short by the failure of the family business. He later joined the land development team and qualified as a builder via night school, progressing to group Building Director. His most significant achievement before becoming Group Managing Director was the formation in 1984 of two northern subsidiaries specialising in grant-aided inner city redevelopment, a move that was to give Bellway a significant exposure to urban regeneration. 'I was brought up doing slum clearance work for local authority housing in the 1960s.'[5] Howard Dawe was in no doubt of the problems Bellway faced: 'In many ways I don't know how we survived. We had to get rid of all the peripheral businesses. There were losses in the north west, Yorkshire and Scotland. We closed the Chester office and set up in Manchester; we sold the Yorkshire land, split the north east away from the head office. This generated cash which we reinvested in the south. We then took time to rebuild the north using urban renewal where the Government grant money meant it was cash positive.'[6] In 1987 the loss making Scottish business was sold to Tilbury Douglas.[7]

More significant for the long term, Bellway brought in a new generation of operating managing directors and decentralised the businesses. Although approval for land purchases remained under central control, there was no central design or purchasing and all operational decisions were handled at the local level, a strategy which led to the paradoxical slogan 'Bellway, the local national builder.' The new management team continued its regional expansion, usually through opening new offices, though 1987 saw the acquisition of DWF Golding, an Essex firm building around 250 units a year: Nevertheless, volume growth was not dramatic: sales of 1700 at the end of the decade compared with 1500 in 1983, and profits hovered around the £4m level until the second half of the decade when another house price boom helped take profits up to a peak of £17m (1989). As in the previous recession, Bellway withstood the

---

[4] *Building* June 1981.
[5] Interview Howard Dawe.
[6] Ibid..
[7] Sold on again to Persimmon a decade later.

collapse better than most in the industry. Land provisions in 1990 were a modest £7m and the lowest profits fell to was £9m in 1991. Howard Dawe claims to have seen the recession coming a year early: 'We stopped buying land for 12-18 months. We went aggressively for sales via part exchange and sold as hard as we could.' It was in this recession that the foundations were laid for the 1990s, Bellway's most successful decade since the 1960s.

Housing units, 1980-2004

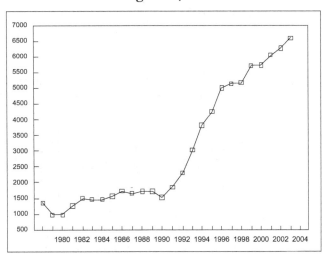

In 1989, as the recession was beginning to bite, Bellway raised £20m through a preference issue and made early selling price reductions to clear stock. This was followed in March 1991 by a £25m rights issue; in total, Bellway raised £79m during the recession using the funds to purchase a substantial land bank at depressed prices; this provided the resources for a medium term target of 4000 house sales, a level which it reached in 1996. Unit sales broke through 5000 by 1997 and reached 6000 in 2002, earning pre-tax profits of £125m. A particular feature of the 1990s was the transfer of Bellway's urban regeneration skills from the north to the London market, the largest project being for 5000 houses at Barking Reach on old National Power land.

The Bell family is no longer connected with the business. Ken Bell, died in 1997 and Ashley Bell died in 1999. Since the mid-1980s the direction of the business has been in non-family hands. Bellway is a rare example of a successful management transition from a founding family. The succession took another step in 1999 with the appointment of John Watson as Chief Executive under Dawe's executive chairmanship. Watson had joined Bellway in 1978 as a surveyor before becoming Managing Director of the north east division and main board Technical Director in 1995. Dawe then became Executive Chairman until 2004 when he became a non-executive director. By then, Bellway had raised its annual profits to over £200m, some three times the level achieved only five years before.

BELLWINCH
Peak units: 602 (1985)

Roger Malcolm was formed in 1932 as a housebuilding company operating in north-west London; its founder was Roger Malcolm Raymond (born 1909). The company initially concentrated on building middle and upper market houses in north-west London. Jackson refers to the Old Rectory Garden and Mill Ridge Estates in 1933-34 with houses selling at over £1000; in 1934, the St Margaret's estate was 'the first house in England fully furnished with built-in furniture.'[1] During the early 1950s the company branched out with projects in Yeovil and Hythe, and by the end of the decade there were also sites in Banbury, Warwick and Oxford.

In 1969 Roger Malcolm was bought by Capital and Counties. Capital & Counties had made its first foray into housing development in 1964 when it bought an 80-acre site at Westminster Park, Chester, building an estate of 650 houses. Under Capital & Counties' ownership, results improved until 1974 when turnover peaked at £4.5m and profits exceeded £500,000. Nevertheless, the business was not well placed to withstand the recession and the next three years saw write-offs totalling £6.7m and overall pre-tax losses of £4m. During 1976 about 700 new homes were completed and the projected figure for 1977 was over 800. However, continued poor trading results led to the resignation of Ron Perriton in 1981 and the appointment of Ron King, previously Chief Executive of John McLean, as a part-time Managing Director, supported from 1982 by George Webb, also ex-McLean.

By then, volumes had fallen to around 400. King halved the staff and started selling an overweight land bank. By 1985 Roger Malcolm was building 500 units but the 1981/82 loss had been transformed into a £1.6m profit. In that year, Ron King led a management buyout of Roger Malcolm under an off-the-shelf company, Bellwinch. The new company also included his own Swindon-based Ronking Homes which he had formed in 1981, and George Webb Homes, a Southampton business formed in 1979. Volumes stayed in the 4-500 a year range but profits rose rapidly to a peak of £7m in 1988, the year after the company's flotation. During 1989, Ron King had expressed a wish to withdraw from day-to-day management and in 1990 he recruited Ray Davies, previously Chief Executive of Abbey, to replace him; King became deputy Chairman before leaving the group at the end of 1991.

Problems in Docklands

Bellwinch was an early exponent of Docklands opportunities and completed a number of successful developments; by 1988 around 30% of it land bank was in Docklands. Its largest site, the 9-acre Millwall Wharf, had been bought in 1986 for £15m, but the site had not gone into production before the crash, and its loss of value and associated debt was the biggest single factor necessitating the group's financial restructuring in January 1992. After £20m of losses in 1990 and 1991, largely due to land provisions, shareholders funds were down to £1m against borrowings of £13m. Key sites, were taken from the group by the appropriate banks; £3m of new money was raised.

From a low point of 130 units in 1992, output moved up to 200-250 a year. A further £6m of new equity was raised in 1993 but the company struggled to make more than nominal profits. In September 1995 Ray Davies died and George Webb took over as Managing Director in the realisation that Bellwinch had little future as an independent quoted housebuilder. The search for a suitable buyer was prolonged, but Kier made an agreed bid of £13m in June 1998.

---

[1] Jackson, *Semi Detached London*, p.209.

E & L BERG
Peak units: 3-400 (1930s)

The brothers Ellis and Lewis Berg began building in 1923 with no previous experience of the industry. They came from a well-off family and built houses in their father's 6-acre garden, unaware of the need to submit plans to the local council. In the first year they built five 4-bedroomed houses.[1] The first estate development was in 1924 at Sunbury-on-Thames and during the 1930s the business expanded to about half a dozen sites in south and south-west London, notably at Hinchley Wood (including the Hinchley Wood Hotel) and Kingston Hill. The two large sites each sold at the rate of two a week and a post-war managing director suggests that the peak rate might have been between 3-400.[2]

Although the family garden had provided the Berg's first land, it was 'Always a tremendous job to be able to find the money to buy an estate.'[3] Before 1939, the development capital was largely drawn from the banks. The Bergs were at the forefront of contemporary housing marketing, 'by what were, at the time, advanced means of publicity.'[4] They advertised in the Daily Mail; exhibited at the Ideal Home Exhibition and paid famous radio stars to visit the sites and be photographed in the nationals. In 1935 they were offering 'Berg's Money Back Mortgages' and Ellis Berg edited a magazine *New Estates Magazine* with a range of general articles. 'Ellis Berg had good land buying skills and his marketing skills were second to none.'[5]

E & L Berg Homes was not incorporated until 1933 and the brothers' estate development business does not seem to have been transferred to the company until 1937. The vendor agreement additionally disclosed that Ellis Berg was also a director of Berg & Dale, where he built houses with Belmont John Dale. During the war, the Company did repair work and some runway construction. Lewis Berg was 'Already middle aged when war broke out and never came back into the fray.'[6] Ellis Berg continued the business after the war, developing further afield – the Waterlooville Estate near Portsmouth being one of the larger estates. Volumes were probably lower than pre-war, at around 200 houses a year during the 1960s.

Kenneth Price moved up from Construction to Managing Director in 1969 but there was no potential family succession and Major Webb, of Alliance Properties (also of Kingston-upon-Thames), persuaded Ellis Berg, then aged around 80, to sell him the Company. In 1972, Alliance Property was sold in turn to Maidenhead Investments, part of Ron Shuck's Cornwall Property group. E & L Berg, still managed by Price, was building around 100-200 houses a year. Maidenhead also owned the midlands developer, Ashworth & Steward, later sold to Barratt. In 1976, control of Cornwall passed to Jimmy Goldsmith's Generale Occidentale SA where there was little interest in housebuilding and the building programme was soon run down. In the 1982 accounts the principal activity was given as housebuilding but the stated policy was to undertake no transactions save those required for realisation of assets and liabilities, and Berg was put into voluntary liquidation in 1986.

1 Drawn from Bundoch interview with Ellis Berg, 1969.
2 Interview with Kenneth Price, Oct. 2002.
3 Bundoch interview with Ellis Berg.
4 Cox, 'Urban Development and Redevelopment in Croydon 1830-1940', p.397.
5 Interview Kenneth Price.
6 Interview with Peter Prowting, Dec. 2000.

BERKELEY
Peak units: 4839 (2004)

Berkeley was formed by Jim Farrer and Tony Pidgley on their departure from Crest, and started trading in February 1976; within 25 years it had (briefly) the largest stock market capitalisation of any housebuilder. The two men were some twenty years apart in age; the elder Farrer had recruited the young Pidgley at Crest and acted as his mentor. Farrer had been an estate agent and then Land Director for Crest. Tony Pidgley had an entirely different, and by now well-publicised, start to life. He was adopted from an orphanage by a family of gypsies at the age of four. The public description of his early life was expressed in the BBC *Back to the Floor* programme in 2000: 'you know gypsies, they're very hard working people, they understand the value of money, and I don't think that sort of upbringing did any harm.' It did not, however, endow him with the same education that most children received in the 1950s leading to the widely accepted story that Tony Pidgley was unable to read or write when he started work. The reality was slightly different.

'I could always read well, reading wasn't a problem – there was a bit more of a problem with writing . You must understand that there is more myth in my life than reality. I don't stop it because it might help other people to see what can be achieved.'[1] Indeed, there was a brief period in his early teens, when he rose to the top of the class. However, what was instilled into him by his upbringing was a trading mentality and an ethic for hard work. 'These people are traders. They buy and sell horses… cars…lorries; we also had a site clearance and demolition business, we cut down trees and turned them into logs. I started on my own account doing whatever I could which was really window cleaning, cleaning your car, which led to mowing your lawn, which led to landscaping and I grew it from there. eventually into demolition.'[2] At his age, there was no access to capital and the first lorry was purchased for £500 cash out of savings. From that developed a fleet of lorries and a ground clearance business that worked for housebuilders.

The Crest relationship

P & J Plant Hire and Haulage was formed in 1965 when Tony Pidgley was 17; the J in the company name stood for Edward James, Pidgley's minority partner. It was started as a conventional tree-felling company and demolition became its second string. 'I had met Roy Wright [Joviel] and we did all of his work, cost plus. We did demolition, sold the bricks to developers, the hard core went into the roads. Roy gave me a road to do and it started from there.'[3] The business was not large (some £325,000 turnover in 1971) but Pidgley had also become a sub-contractor for Crest, even sharing the same office building. Crest bought P & J for Tony Pidgley's building expertise, putting him in charge of their own building programme despite his lack of any formal construction training. 'I just learnt it; I have a retentive memory if it interests me and you don't need a degree to know that the drain has got to go in at the right level. I learnt that the developers just wanted reliability and I gave it to them.'

After a dispute with the Chairman, Pidgley left Crest at the end of 1975 determined to form his own housebuilding company; Jim Farrer joined him shortly after. 'I very much wanted Jim because culturally we worked together very well. He had tremendous skills at land optimisation.'[4] Berkeley Homes was duly formed in February 1976 with Pidgley holding 51% and Farrer 49%. Unlike many in the industry, the founders were

---

[1] Interview with Tony Pidgley, May 2001.
[2] BBC Radio 4 interview January 1993.
[3] Interview Tony Pidgley.
[4] Ibid.

reluctant to use their own names and Berkeley seemed as prestigious a name as they could find. It set a trend for later names including St George, St David, Saint Andrew, St James and Beaufort Homes. Although there was no question that the younger Pidgley was the driving force in the new firm, Jim Farrer provided maturity and balance: 'He was always there for me, he supported me through thick and thin. He took the rough edges off, I suspect.'[5] The early staff were also brought in from Crest – a habit which had not worn out by the 1990s. The philosophy from the beginning was to build on single plots or small sites in the south east, generally in the higher price range sold to upper-income customers from the professions and local businessmen – the leafy lane executive home. As at Crest, there was no attempt to amass a land bank; building started as soon as the site was bought and a high proportion of the houses were sold off plan.

Regional expansion through the 1980s

Based at Weybridge, the early building programme was in Surrey and, after a modest start, sales began to grow quickly with the sale of 13 houses off plan to a Dutch financier; the same financier followed this by purchasing the whole of a 32-house site, a forerunner of the substantial off-plan sales that were to characterise the 1990s. Berkeley soon began to open subsidiaries in other home counties: Chilterns 1979; North London 1980; Kent 1982; and Sussex 1984. In that year, Berkeley obtained its stock exchange quotation. Although not large by number of houses built (85 in its last financial year), it had an excellent profit record and its 1984 pre-tax total of £1.5m was to increase rapidly over the next five years as Berkeley continued its geographic expansion. By the late 1980s, it could be argued that Berkeley had a unique position in the industry. 'There is nothing new in building expensive individual houses – small local builders do so and many of the larger housebuilders can point to expensive houses in their range. What is distinctive about Berkeley is that in comparison with the local man who builds two or three houses, the organisation is professional and committed to growth; and compared with the large developer, the whole management is able to concentrate on its chosen specialisation.'[6]

By 1989, geographical expansion had taken Berkeley into Dorset, Essex, Hampshire, and then out of the home counties through its new South Midlands, Western and East Anglia companies. Clare Homes was bought from Brian Wait to reinforce the southern home counties. Berkeley had also made a modest start in commercial property and St George, the joint venture with Speyhawk, was building in inner London. Despite continuing to operate with most of its sites not exceeding five units, Berkeley sold 657 houses in that last pre-recession year with turnover of £139m and pre-tax profits of £22m. The 1989 annual report contained both a profits warning and a restatement of strategy: this included operating as 'a current trader' without a land bank; concentration on small sites in prime residential locations; and operation through autonomous subsidiaries. Although the principle of autonomy was to survive, the prolonged recession was to change Berkeley's attitude to both a land bank and the size of its sites. Indeed, it was the recession that helped transform Berkeley within a decade from a small, though successful, niche housebuilder into the largest inner-city housebuilder.

Berkeley goes liquid

The story of Tony Pidgley deciding to 'go liquid' as the market peaked has entered into housebuilding folklore. 'Berkeley recognised the weakness of the market at an early date and by February 1989 had already started to turn for home by aggressively converting completed or nearly completed houses back into cash.'[7] The founders' view ten years on was that the signs were clear. Pidgley: 'The reality is that in 1988 it was not difficult to see what was happening. The money we were making was outrageous. Jim and

[5] Ibid.
[6] *PHA*, 1987, p.45.
[7] Group Accounts 1992.

I sat down and decided we would go liquid; we did give up the profit chase to go for cash.'[8] Farrer: 'We think we recognised the same features as occurred in 1973 and if anything AWP was the one to recognise it first.'[9] In practical terms Berkeley found it easier to act on its instincts than some housebuilders by virtue of not having a long land bank; nevertheless, the houses still had to be shifted and here Berkeley had assistance from one of its substantial shareholders, the Saudi Saad Investments. Berkeley sold £10 million of its completed housing stock into a joint company with Saad: 'It gave us £10 million to go back and buy cheaper land; when everybody else was bleeding to death we were going in and buying land at the lower levels.'[10]

The Group did no more than break even for two years; there were other housebuilders that did better than that, but few of substance that were confined to the south-east and Berkeley avoided the substantial losses and write-downs that so damaged many of its competitors. It was 1991, when most of the industry was still writing off land, that marked the turning point for Berkeley. It had cleared out its pre-recession housing stock and a rights issue had left the group cash positive. Berkeley was able to acquire land at depressed and even fire sale prices; it bought from receivers, distressed landowners and the banks. Berkeley argued in its 1992 Accounts that 'we re-entered the land market a trifle early but it is the land acquired at that stage which has formed the backbone of our trading programme in…1992.' It was not just the timing of the land purchases which made 1991 a key year for Berkeley; there were three other strategic moves. Berkeley made its only significant acquisition, the north-west Crosby Homes; Speyhawk's growing financial pressures gave Berkeley the opportunity to buy the other half of St George; and it formed Berkeley Eastoak with Saad Investments. These 1991 decisions all stemmed from a belief that the depressed values represented a once in a lifetime opportunity and provided the opportunity for Tony Pidgley to exploit his undoubted dealing skills.

St George had been formed in 1987 jointly with Trevor Osborne's Speyhawk, following Berkeley's successful development of a Speyhawk site in Twickenham. It was initially run by David Pretty though he soon returned to Barratt (later becoming Managing Director); he was succeeded by the Land Director Tony Carey, who had come with Pretty from Barratt. From the beginning, St George targeted partnership as well as luxury housing and although the high-priced apartment market has dominated St George's growth, the social housing expertise later became of value in the urban regeneration schemes. By 1991, Speyhawk was trying to renegotiate its bank borrowings[11] and Berkeley was able to buy the other 50% for about £4m. In that year St George made pre-tax profits of £3m; by the end of the decade the annual profit was running at over £50m.

The quoted **Crosby Homes** was a long-established builder of executive homes in the Manchester hinterland but its annual volume had fallen to little more than 100 in the recession and, following substantial land write-downs, the interim dividend had been cut. Berkeley bought it for £11m to take the company into the north-west. 'I just thought it was cheap and that Manchester was the next big conurbation for us to go to.'[12] However, it was an old-established company that probably took Berkeley longer to sort out than originally expected. In 1993 Geoff Hutchinson, previously Managing Director of Beazer Central, was appointed Chief Executive and the company was given greater geographic responsibility by absorbing the previous Berkeley Homes midlands company.

---

8 Interview Tony Pidgley.
9 Interview with Jim Farrer, Jan. 2001.
10 Interview Tony Pidgley.
11 Speyhawk went into receivership in May 1993 with debts of £300m.
12 Interview Tony Pidgley.

Berkeley Eastoak was formed in partnership with Saad Investments in March 1991 to invest up to £100m in commercial property; Berkeley contributed 25% of the capital for 40% of the equity; a further £100m was committed eighteen months later though it was never fully invested. A portfolio of investments with strong covenants was acquired to yield almost 11%; some £90m of sales were generated three years later at a substantial profit. 'Eastoak was one of the simplest things that I've ever done, buying 25-year leases on upward-only reviews.'[13]

The rise of urban regeneration

Early in 1993 there was another rights issue, again raising £44m for the group. Jim Farrer had retired as Chairman in 1992, remaining for some years a non-executive director and then Life President. He was succeeded by Graham Roper, who had started his career in Berkeley by opening the Kent office. The new money was now taking Berkeley in a different direction; it was buying larger sites in central London, such as Jacobs Island near Tower Bridge and the partnership with Thames Water to develop the 140-acre Barn Elms reservoir. The successful London experience, carried out by both Berkeley Homes and St George, was then transferred to Crosby. It launched the first new development (Symphony Court) in the centre of Birmingham in 1995 and went on to develop city centre schemes in Manchester, Leeds, Nottingham and Liverpool as well as some of the smaller northern cities. In 1998, Berkeley opened up in Scotland (St Andrew) but, like many English housebuilders, did not find development north of the border as satisfying. The sites were sold on (at a profit) some three years later.

After the initial two years of break even, profits increased rapidly and in 1994, with a record 1400 units sold, they reached £29m, exceeding the pre-recession peak for the first time. By 1998, as these inner city sites increasingly came to fruition, unit sales exceeded 3000 and group profits broke through the £100m mark. The urban development philosophy was then being taken a stage further. Schemes were becoming more complex, increasingly with a mixed use; they were larger, both financially and structurally; they included conversions from other uses, typically older offices; and sites were acquired without clear cut planning. The new generation of sites included Gun Wharf, on the derelict Royal Navy docks at Portsmouth, with over 900 residential units and a £100m plus retail development; the Mailbox in Birmingham, Clarence Dock in Leeds; and in London, a seven-acre site adjacent to the MI5 building; and Imperial Wharf in Hammersmith, a 32 acre disused British Gas site on which 1900 units are planned.

The rapid rate of growth was not without its strains, particularly as the expanding building programme met the growing skills shortage in the building trade. Although St George and Crosby had operated with independent management structures, the original Berkeley Homes had lost its earlier cohesion and different main board executives had responsibility for different Berkeley Homes operating companies. The response in 1998 was to buy Thirlstone Homes, owned and run by Tony K Pidgley, the Berkeley founder's son. TK Pidgley had formed Thirlstone in 1990, aged 22, having previously worked within Berkeley. It specialised in building luxury homes in Surrey in much the same way as Berkeley Homes had in its early days. In its last financial year, Thirlstone had sold 48 houses with a turnover of £21m and operating profit of £2.7m. The business was acquired with the intent of TK Pidgley running the Berkeley Homes subsidiary, and although it was never stated that 'young Tony' would succeed his father as group Managing Director, that was widely assumed to be a long term possibility. However, after reorganising Berkeley Homes, TK Pidgley decided that he wanted move in a different direction and resigned from the group in 2001. 'If I ever made one mistake, it was buying my son's business: nepotism doesn't work.'[14] Two years later (2003), there was a much publicised, albeit brief, flirtation on young Tony's part with bidding for Berkeley.

[13] Ibid.
[14] Ibid.

Housing units, 1984-2004

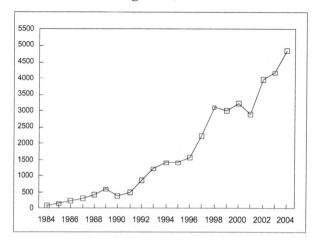

Berkeley was then to develop a different corporate strategy: perhaps it was a consequence of the realisation that family succession was no longer an option; perhaps a view that ever-increasing volumes would become a treadmill; or perhaps that its greatest competitive advantage lay in the London area. For whatever reason, Berkeley began to shrink the size of its business in direct contrast to its quoted peers. Quietly, its traditional small sites in the home counties were gradually being built out, liberating cash, though still allowing the purchase of strategic London sites such as the 76-acre Royal Arsenal at Woolwich or the 2800 unit Beaufort Park at Hendon. More substantial moves were to follow. In August 2003, Berkeley announced the deferred sale of its Crosby subsidiary to its management, structured to return a minimum of £450m. cash to the parent company.(Crosby was sold to Lend Lease in June 2005 for £251m). In June 2004, the results of the full strategic review were announced to the effect that Berkeley would concentrate solely on complex, large-scale, urban regeneration schemes. The run-down in its traditional operations was expected to generate substantial surplus cash and a scheme of arrangement was implemented to return £1.45 billion (£12 a share) to shareholders over a six year period. Subject to those repayments being made, the executive directors were to be rewarded by the allocation of 15% of the equity of the new Berkeley Group Holdings.

BETT BROTHERS
Peak units: 964 (1972)

Andrew Bett originally farmed in Fife, moved to Dundee and, along with his three sons, founded Bett Haulage in 1936. Early work included deliveries to housing sites, creating an interest in the construction industry, and from 1937 Andrew Bett built a few single houses around Dundee, primarily on a bespoke basis. During the war, building was confined to shelters and similar defensive work. The business was incorporated in 1946, with Andrew, his sons John, Albert and Stewart, and two of his daughters, Christine and Helen, on the Board; Christine's husband Jan Szwedowski later became a director. The business was run by the second generation: John, a joiner, led the building work; Stewart the administration; and Albert, a mechanic, ran the plant side.

Between 1946 and 1951 Bett concentrated on building houses and shops for Dundee Corporation and significant volumes were completed. When the first building licences became available, Bett began building houses again in a small way in Dundee and volumes expanded as the controls were totally removed. Capital required for land was not large and came from the profits being earned on local authority contracting. In 1959 Bett started on what was to become their largest estate, Balgillo to the north of Broughty Ferry, bought as agricultural land for £400 an acre. The last houses were built in 2002 making a total of over 2000 houses. In general, Bett's land came from an extensive range of family and local contacts, and it was not until the 1990s that Bett had a formal land buyer.

Bett takes 10% of the Scottish market

After 1960, Bett began to build outside Dundee, spreading across east and central Scotland. The Prospectus issued when the Company floated in 1967 estimated that in 1966 the company was responsible for 10% of the Scottish housing starts, implying sales of some 750-800; of the Scottish-based companies, this was probably similar in size to Miller and well ahead of Mactaggart & Mickel, though less than John Lawrence of Glasgow. Bett also built local authority housing, schools and offices. On the flotation, Bett remained the archetypal family company: the Board included the founder's three sons, daughter, son-in-law and grandson.

Growth continued after the flotation. Completions for 1972 were reported at 964 and this probably represented a peak.[1] Profits rose from under £500,000 in 1967 to £1.9m in 1974; what is unusual for a company operating as a speculative housebuilder and local authority contractor is that profits appeared unaffected by the combination of housing recession and inflation on fixed-price contracts. However, Bett had been considerably helped by its entry into the Aberdeen market at the start of the oil boom. The acquisition of a local firm, Bisset, had given them land and at the peak Aberdeen had contributed up to 300 units a year at rapidly rising selling prices; in a foretaste of what was to happen in London Docklands in the late 1980s, housing contracts were sold on two or three times before the house was completed. Concern over the level of land prices caused Bett to build out its holdings in Aberdeen.

In 1974, John Bett died. Albert, then 71, succeeded as Chairman and Stewart, the youngest brother, became joint Managing Director with Iain Bett, John's son and the only grandson of Andrew. Iain Bett had joined the firm at the age of 16 spending time in each of the departments before joining the Board. 'There was some uncertainty after my father's death on the roles to be played by the directors and about the future of the Company. Albert became Chairman, a position that would now be considered non-executive, and after a while the roles that emerged were that Ronald Mitchell and I became joint Managing

---

[1] *Investors Chronicle,* Feb 1973.

Directors.'[2] Ronald Mitchell was an architect who had been a director since the flotation.

During the second half of the 1970s, Bett's housing volumes fell substantially, to little more than 200. In part, this reflected the decision to withdraw from the Aberdeen market during the boom but there was also a deliberate decision to reallocate capital to commercial property development, where Bett was able to achieve higher returns. Early deals included public houses which led to the formation of Bett Inns in 1977. However, the business as a whole was no longer growing. Turnover stayed constant at around £20m which, in those inflationary times, represented a decline in real terms. Profits began to fall in 1979 and by 1983 they were down to £377,000 largely due to losses in the competitive tendering area of the contracting market.

By 1983 Bett had largely withdrawn from competitive tendering: 'We are now concentrating our energies and resources on private housing development…which offers the best opportunities for profit to an experienced builder with a substantial land bank.'[3] In the event, the concentration on private housing was momentary. Greater emphasis continued to be given to commercial property development where rental income was to be a growing source of profit. In the 1987 accounts, the Chairman was describing a different strategy than four years previous: 'During the past few years we have pursued a policy of reducing our dependence on housebuilding, recognising its limited potential within our geographic area of operations. We will continue to place much more emphasis on the major Group activities of property development and investment, and leisure…We will continue to sell off surplus land.'

Bett turns to non-family management

The 1990 recession treated the company more harshly than did its predecessor. In the late 1980s, Bett had started to develop in the south-east of England and, with its first two schemes making profits, the scale of investment was increased at just the wrong time. Some £23m was written off values, primarily on property in the south east, and the combined group loss in 1991 and 1992 was £13m. Finances were strained 'But we had banked with only the Bank of Scotland since 1946; there was a very good relationship and they supported us.'[4]

Extensive management changes followed: Ronnie Hanna joined from CALA as Chief Executive in February 1992. 'There was no outside pressure but I realised that I required more professional and financial strength and I had known Ronnie for some years.'[5] Ronald Mitchell had left prior to Hanna's appointment and John Calder, previously in charge of housing, was coming up to retirement and stood down. The partnership between family control and non-family executive proved successful. The private housing business was once again expanded. Having been confined to the east of Scotland, sites were acquired further into the central region; by 1994, profits had rebounded to almost £6m of which around half came from the housing company.

A process of expansion south of the border began in the mid-1990s. The first sales were made in Cheshire in 1996 and the first site in the north east was acquired in year 2000. In between (1998) Bett bought the Aberdeen housebuilding business of Hugh MacRae & Co (50 houses a year) for £6m allowing it back into the Aberdeen area.[6] In 2001 the Inns subsidiary (then making profits of £1.7m) was sold to

---

2 Interview with Iain Bett, Jan 2002.

3 Group Accounts, 1983.

4 Interview Iain Bett.

5 Ibid.

6 The business was founded at Beauly, near Inverness, in the 1860s. The founder's grandsons, Charles and Gordon MacRae, decided to sell the business in the absence of any willing succession on reaching 60.

the management for £13m leaving Bett to concentrate entirely on residential and commercial development. By now profits had exceeded £10m although at 640 units, housing volumes were still below the levels of 30 years previous. This, however, was unlikely to last for long. 'The next obvious target areas for us are Yorkshire and Birmingham.'[7] The plans were for units of 850 in 2002 and over 1000 in 2003; housing capacity was estimated at 2000 a year without starting any new regions. Ronnie Hanna set out clearly his belief that Bett could grow organically: 'We intend to continue our growth and therefore to get bigger.'[8] Events were to take a different course. The Bett family still controlled nearly half the equity; there was no immediate family succession; the housing market was arguably approaching its peak; and the memories of the collapse in family wealth in the last recession must have remained. In April 2003 Bett agreed a £92m cash bid from the private Gladedale.

[7] Ronnie Hanna interviewed in *Housebuilder*, Oct. 2001.
[8] Group Accounts, 2001.

PERCY BILTON
Peak units: c.700 (1972)

Although best known as a developer of industrial estates, Percy Bilton was at one time a substantial housebuilder. He began by making lubricating oil in his garden in Ormskirk, Lancashire, cycling round selling the oil to local farmers. He moved south in the late 1920s and established Vigzol Oils (which became a quoted company before being sold to Standard Oil in 1962). In 1928, he formed the London and Provincial Building Company to build houses in Mitcham, Surrey, followed in 1930 by Percy Bilton Properties; in the following year the first industrial land was bought, 260 acres in Perivale. During the 1930s the Company developed both residential and industrial estates; a separate construction company was formed in 1934.

As a private company, no record has survived of the Company's wartime or early post-war activity. From the 1960s, Bilton's industrial development gradually became the more important part of the group but the residential operation still continued to grow. When the Company floated in 1972, the Prospectus reported sales of 496 units in 1971, while the French subsidiary was building 180 units at Versailles. Bilton held 2350 plots at 28 sites across the south east and midlands; these were described as sufficient for 3 years building, numbers that supported press reports that the target for 1972 was 700 units.

The company was run on conservative financial lines. Percy Bilton was quoted at his AGM: 'To pay out dividends from funds that have to be borrowed against paper valuations…seems to me to be fraught with great danger…It is very common for property companies to raid their reserves to pay for the shortfall in profits. In the boom years valuations were made annually and huge items transferred to reserves. Such valuations were fictitious but now when profits fail they are brought back into the profit and loss accounts. This…has never been my company's policy.' Indeed, his attitude to the banking lifeboat was that 'They should have sent the frigates in and shot the lot of them.'[1] That particular quotation came after he had reappointed himself Managing Director at the age of 80.

The housing recession in the early-1970s caused losses in that part of Bilton though they were never quantified and did not prevent group profits from continuing their annual increases. By 1976, the housing division had been reorganised and while it no longer had a long land bank, it continued to build in the midlands and the south. However, Bilton probably built no more than 100-200 houses a year through the 1980s. Percy Bilton died in January 1983 and although the Bilton family retained a significant shareholding, the Company was now in the control of professional managers. Nevertheless, the founder's caution was not abandoned by his successors. The 1987 Chairman's statement warned that the rise in house prices could not continue and substantial profits were made in 1988 from land sales. This did not entirely prevent the housebuilding division from losing money and it emerged from the recession yet smaller, both in absolute size and in relation to the mainstream industrial property business. In 1994 the housebuilding division was reported as trading on 9 sites and, unusually for a small housebuilder, these were spread from Crewe to Peterborough and down to the south coast. In 1998, Percy Bilton was acquired by Slough Estates and the housebuilding division was closed.

---

[1] *The Times*, 28th Jan. 1977.

BLOOR
Peak units: 1870 (2002)

John Bloor has been one of the most successful housebuilders of the late twentieth century. He left school at the age of 15 having spent 'only six months at school between the ages of 12 and 15 due to illness.'[1] He established himself as a self-employed plasterer while in his teens, worked briefly for Clarke Homes and then built a few houses as a sole trader before forming his company, JS Bloor, at Burton-on-Trent, in 1969.

The Company traded on a small scale, though profitably, through the recession of the early 1970s, establishing a solid base in the east midlands, principally housing but also including some commercial development. The early sites were financed by the small merchant bank, Cassel Arenz, and later Midland Bank and First National Finance. By the end of the 1970s, turnover had reached £9m (implying unit sales in excess of 400) and pre-tax profits of £1.3m. The weakness in the market had enabled Bloor to acquire substantial land holdings, including land from FNFC, which provided the basis for expansion not just in the midlands, but also in the south. Financial guidance was provided by Leslie Berry, an accountant who joined the Board in 1972 and was the only other person to hold shares (5%) in the group; these were repurchased by Bloor on Berry's death.

The 1980s saw the emergence of Bloor as one of the larger, and most profitable, housebuilders. By the early 1980s, unit sales were 800-900; turnover trebled in four years to reach £31m by 1983 and pre-tax profits reached £5m. It was in that year that Bloor made one of the more unusual diversifications for a housebuilder, buying the Triumph name following the crash of the Meridian Co-operative. JS Bloor had already bought a motor engineering business in 1978 (C & A Pickering) and the Company set up Triumph Motorcycles to develop a new engine, licensing out the manufacture of the 750cc Triumph Bonneville to Racing Spares of Newton Abbott for a five year period. Bloor subsequently built its own factory in Hinkley Leicestershire and produced a new range of machines from 1990. 'He is no romantic, nor is he a dewy-eyed biking maniac: he could just as easily have invested in washing machines. Bloor simply wanted to get into big-time engineering, and the Triumph name presented him with the perfect opportunity.'[2]

Housing volumes rose steadily through the 1990 recession, rising from 900 in 1989 to 1470 in 1993; remarkably, trading margins never fell below 15% and there were no land write-offs. There was, strangely, a weaker period in the mid-1990s, but volumes continued to grow, albeit modestly, reaching 1870 in 2002 making it then the largest housebuilder to be owned by one man. John Bloor has been described as 'an intensely private man' and an anonymous interviewee attributed his success down to the simple ingredients of ' hard work, common sense, buying the land at the right price at the right time and having the right people around him.'.

[1] *Sunday Express*, 6th Jan. 2002.
[2] *Sunday Times,* May 1997.

HENRY BOOT HOMES
Peak units: 1500-2000 (late 1930s)

Henry Boot was the first quoted housebuilder, floating in 1919 as Henry Boot & Sons (London). Under the leadership of Charles Boot, the company built more houses in the inter-war period than any other housebuilder, and more speculative houses than any but Ideal Homes. It was a major force in social housing, building estates for rental, and became the only housebuilder to own its own building society. Charles Boot was 'a colourful entrepreneur', a social housing pioneer, a Grand Commander of the Redeemer (Greece's highest honour), a director of the early Pinewood Studios and a Justice of the Peace. He was not easy to follow: after a long post war period of decline, it was a fourth generation Boot, Jamie, who led the revival of the speculative housing business.

The original Henry Boot (1851-1931), a farmer's son from Sheffield, served a seven-year joinery apprenticeship and worked for local firms until the age of 35 when he began to work on his own account. 'Progress from initial jobbing work was rapid and he soon successfully moved into larger scale public works and housing projects.'[1] His eldest son, Charles Boot, (1874-1945) joined after leaving school; his building education was secured at nightschool. Henry Boot & Sons registered as a company in 1910 by which time its two addresses were Sheffield and Grosvenor Street, London. It is almost certain that Charles was running the company by then and was probably responsible for taking the company down to London. The Company had become a substantial contractor before and during the war, building army camps (Catterick), Manston Aerodrome, Tees Naval Base and the American hospital at Southampton; in one year alone, a thousand military buildings were completed.

Flotation to Finance Housebuilding

At the end of 1919 the business was floated; by then it was operating out of Sheffield, Birmingham and London. A new company, Henry Boot & Sons (London)[2] was formed with 100,000 £1 ordinary shares issued to the vendors of the old company; a further 100,000 ordinary shares and £200,000 of preference shares were offered to the public; profits of £75-90,000 were forecast. Charles was the Managing Director and brothers William and Edward were on the Board; Henry had retired just before the war. For its Chairman, Henry Boot had Lt. Col. Sir Walrond Sinclair, the wartime director of national service of London and South East Counties and the originator of the Regional System of Recruiting.

Unlike the housebuilding issues of the mid-1930s, there appears to have been no money taken out by the family and the substantial new capital was clearly intended to finance a major housebuilding programme. The 1919 Prospectus recorded that 'During the war period practically no building or constructional work other than for the Government was carried out. It is now imperative in the national interests that the erection of very large numbers of houses and the development of public works generally should be carried out...Provisional arrangements have been made to proceed at once with several large housing contracts involving the building of some thousands of houses under the Ministry of Health scheme and...the Directors ...confidently expect to be able to increase the rate of completion to at least four houses per working day.'

In the 1920s, the larger part of Henry Boot's housing volumes came from local authority contracts. By 1924 the Chairman was reporting that 7886 houses had been handed over; and were being built using the Henry Boot patented concrete system. There were speculative estates as well: Jackson refers to Boot

---

[1] Anon, *Henry Boot A Brief History*.
[2] The 'London' was dropped in 1926.

being 'early on the scene, with houses at Elstree in 1924'[3]. General contracting continued, the Watford by-pass being the best known contract. There was a substantial holding in the brick firm, Flettons. Overseas, Henry Boot had been working in Greece, France and Spain since 1920. By the start of the 1930s the accounts were recording some 20,000 houses having been built since the war; these were predominantly for local authorities but the balance was to change; Henry Boot now became a substantial estate developer, partly for sale, and partly for private rent.

Building for Sale and Rent

Two new companies were formed in 1933 to take specific responsibility for the private housing. Henry Boot (Garden Estates) was to cover speculative development for sale and some £300,000 of housing land and work in progress was transferred from elsewhere in the group. The second company, First National Housing Trust was 'to develop and administer Estates…to let at low rentals. Both these companies are now operating successfully on a large scale.'[4] Jackson, who concentrated solely on London, referred to Boot opening up 'a dozen or so estates in the thirties mostly in west and north west London.'[5] However, a Garden Estates booklet published at the beginning of 1936 showed a wider representation – estates at Hayes (Kent), Northolt and Staines (Middlesex), Litherland (Liverpool), Iver (Bucks) and Garrowhill (Glasgow).

In the same year that Charles Boot was forming his two new housing companies, he became involved in planning to build a film studio at Elstree. Charles Boot bought the land and began building houses for the staff. The project foundered while he was away at length in Greece and he made a second attempt in 1934. On the death of a bankrupt George Morden, he bought Heatherden Hall (where the Irish Free State treaty was signed in 1921) near Iver, Bucks for one tenth of the £300,000 spent by Morden. Charles Boot went to Hollywood and on his return appointed James Sloan as general manager, and work began in November 1935. In 1938, Pinewood merged with Denham Film Studios and Charles Boot became a director on the new Board.

In January 1935, £400,000 in preference stock was issued to finance the expansion of contracting and real estate development. Charles Boot was now Chairman and Managing Director; brother Edward and son Henry Matthews Boot were the other family directors. The other brother, William, had left after 'a bit of friction' to buy an ironmonger's business. The prospectus claimed that the group was 'probably the largest builders of houses in the country, have during the last fifteen years erected approximately 30,000 houses, including those erected for local authorities.' Profits, however, at £56,000, were lower than at the time of the initial flotation. Possibly the largest contract the firm had was a £10m irrigation project for the Greek Government. In February 1935, a month after the preference issue, the Minute Book recorded that owing to the rebellion, ledgers had not been received from Greece for audit.(The contract was finally completed in 1952).

A Social Conscience?

Charles Boot does seem to have had a genuine belief in the social need for housing. His father had been a prominent member of the Plymouth Brethren but who knows whether he inherited or developed a social conscience. 'Grandfather was interested in housing as social policy not just a business.'[6] He was adamant that First National Housing Trust had been established on a no profit basis: 'no profit is made by the parent Company in any shape or way.'[7] He addressed Parliamentary committees and wrote pamphlets advocating lower-cost ways of building new houses. In *A Scheme for the Abolition of Large Slum*

---

[3] Jackson, *Semi-Detached London*, p.109.
[4] Group accounts, 1933.
[5] Jackson, *Semi-detached London*, p.109.
[6] Interview with Ron Baines, March 1999.
[7] Boot, *Post-war Houses*, p.19.

Areas he responded to an LCC proposal to re-house 250,000 with an alternative 'at little more than half the cost.' Charles Boot's proposals came to nothing but First National Housing Trust did build over 8000 houses in some eight estates between 1933 and 1939. The most ambitious was New Addington, outside Croydon. Charles Boot addressed the first tenants in May 1938: 'We have not come to Addington merely to build a dormitory town, but we have come with the very definite purpose of developing a community.'[8] The intention was to build 4500 houses but little more than 1000 had been built before war interrupted production. After the war Croydon council took over the estate and developed it further.

On September 7th 1939 the Board voted 'to discontinue all housebuilding by subsidiaries as soon as the houses now in the course of erection are now completed [and] to tender for and to carry out any government contracts which offer a satisfactory margin of profit'[9] Looking back at the company's housing achievements in that twenty year inter-war period, they rank with any in the industry. However, there is some ambiguity in the numbers. Charles Boot himself quoted different figures at different times. In 1944 he writes 'as a builder of over fifty thousand houses' whereas in 1943: 'my concerns have, during the past twenty years, built over 60,000 houses, some for sale to individual owners, some for local authorities, and the remainder for retention on estates which we own and administer.'[10] Then here was the Company's *A Brief History* : 'During the 1919-39 inter-war period, Henry Boot built in excess of 80,000 houses, significantly more than any other contractor in the UK. Of these, some 50,000 were built for local authorities, over 9,000 for rent…and the balance for sale to the private sector' [i.e.21,000 private]. The company's archives do not provide a complete record but a recent survey by Ronald Baines, identified (with some estimating) around 60,000 houses in total.

World War II saw an extensive range of military construction for all three services and Henry Boot was one of the 24 major contractors working on the Mulberry Harbour.

Succession
Charles Boot died in 1945; it was he who had taken the little family concern of his father and transformed it into a substantial housing and construction business. His successors were less ambitious. He was succeeded first by his brother Edward, until his death in 1953 and then by his only son, Henry Matthews Boot, the largest shareholder.

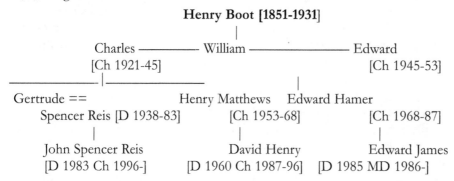

Henry Boot [1851-1931]

Charles ———— William ——————— Edward
[Ch 1921-45]   [Ch 1945-53]

Gertrude ==   Henry Matthews   Edward Hamer
Spencer Reis [D 1938-83]   [Ch 1953-68]   [Ch 1968-87]

John Spencer Reis   David Henry   Edward James
[D 1983 Ch 1996-] [D 1960 Ch 1987-96] [D 1985 MD 1986-]

The construction business continued after the war with a wide variety of work, including Pinewood Studios, local authority housing, and railway engineering. Speculative housebuilding did not resume until after the abolition of controls, and then only in a modest way, especially in view of the large pre-war land

8 *Housebuilder*, July 1938.
9 Company Minute Book
10 Boot, *Post-war Houses*, p.3; *Houses Built by Private Enterprise* 1943, p.6.

holdings – Charles Boot, writing in 1944, claimed 'I have over a thousand acres of land.'[11] The most interesting feature of Boot's housing was actually the approach it took to its stock of rented housing, all subject to rent control. Like others in the same position, Boot pursued a policy of selling to existing tenants but where they differed was that Boot financed the purchase by granting its own mortgages. The tenanted houses were sold for £1000, £50 down and the rest over 30 years. 'This helped cash flow because the interest equalled the rent and the company did not have a repairs cost.'.[12] It did not, however, help the balance sheet as housing assets were gradually replaced by mortgage assets.

The Banner Building Society

The next step was the formation of its own Building society in 1965, Banner Building Society. Prior to this, 'many of the borrowers of First National Housing Trust were being troubled by their local tax inspectors who could not understand the logic of their loan from First National being treated as a building society advance, although this had previously been agreed …with the chief inspector of taxes. The formation of Banner was no easy affair – we were told by many experts that it could not be done.'[13] The mortgages were transferred to Banner Building Society, some 4000 in the first two years, so now Boot's asset was a large deposit with its building society subsidiary. There was also a tax reason for vesting the mortgages in a building society; 'the interest was not included in group profits for 'close company' purposes.'[14] Henry Boot now had to replace its investment in Banner with external funds. The directors had no immediate solution: 'As to the future, who can tell? One day we may become a more normal type of building society, taking investments from the public.'[15] Slowly outside depositors were attracted and Banner even began to undertake conventional lending business but Boot's ownership of a building society was never viewed with favour by the Registrar of Friendly Societies. 'When the close company rules went, the need for Banner was removed; it was getting to be a bit of a thorn in the flesh of the Chairman and it was sold to the Midshires Building Society in 1982.'[16] Henry Boot had finally retrieved its investment in its pre-war rented houses.

Speculative Housing Takes a Back Seat

Speculative housebuilding remained a poor relation and through the 1960s, Boot built around 200 houses a year. In 1968, leadership of the firm had shifted to the other branch of the family and Edward Hamer Boot became Chairman, a position he was to hold for nearly twenty years. Hamer Boot was a contractor, and not overly interested in speculative housing which was run as part of the construction division There was some growth in the 1970s, reaching a peak of 450 in 1977, the year before Henry Boot Homes was incorporated, but by the 1980s it was back down to the 200s again. Under Hamer Boot's Chairmanship, the firm increased its international contracting and its railway engineering specialisation.

Revival and Sale

In 1986, Hamer Boot's son Jamie was appointed Managing Director, one year after the Group had lost £7m, primarily on overseas construction. Jamie Boot gradually changed the emphasis of the Group. Henry Boot Railway Engineering was sold in 1988 and, more relevant to this story, greater emphasis was given to speculative development; private housing was even commented on separately for the first time! Andrew Daly had been appointed a director of Henry Boot Homes in 1986 and succeeded Douglas

[11] Ibid, p.3.
[12] Interview with Derek Glossop.
[13] Anon, *Banner Building Society 'How it Came About'*. Undated Article in Boot archive.
[14] Interview with Derek Glossop.
[15] *How it came About*.
[16] Interview with Derek Glossop, 2000.

Greaves as Managing Director in February 1990. Homes had come through the early 1990s recession with profits unscathed, probably helped by location and low cost land; indeed, group profits were now growing steadily in contrast to the plateau of the 1970s and 1980s. In the late 1990s Henry Boot began to expand its private housing out of its home region, into the Midlands, Scotland, Bristol and Northampton areas. By the year 2001, volumes had increased to 700, though profitability was not yet at the levels achieved by the industry leaders.

During 2002, Henry Boot Homes withdrew from the Scottish market and early in 2003 the housing subsidiary was put up for sale citing competing demands for the group's cash. 'We have property and land management divisions and a plant side and there are cash demands on all those businesses. We don't want to retrench our customer base, so our view was that we would look at offers for the housebuilding business.'[17] In April 2003, Henry Boot announced the sale of its housebuilding business to Wilson Bowden for a total of £48m, including the repayment of inter-company debt.

[17] Jamie Boot, quoted in *Housebuilder*, March 2003.

BOVIS
Peak units: 3500 (1974)

Bovis dates its foundation back to 1885 when Charles William Bovis, a 35-year-old carpenter who had worked in the building industry for twenty years, bought a business founded thirty years earlier by a Mr Sanders on the latter's retirement, changing its name to CW Bovis. From then on, Charles conducted a modest London construction business before ill health forced him to sell the company for £750 in 1908. The company then passed into the hands of the Gluckstein and Samuel families causing incidental confusion with their name changes: the initial buyer was the 20 year old Sidney Gluckstein, the grandson of the founder of the J. Lyons chain, joined shortly after by his cousin Samuel Joseph, both of whom had studied building construction at the Regent Street Polytechnic. After World War I, Sidney's younger brother Vincent joined the firm and it was that triumvirate that developed the Bovis business between the wars, becoming one of the leading London builders with a succession of high-profile contracts.[1]

Bovis was one of the first construction companies to obtain a public quotation, which it did in 1928, having disclosed average annual profits of £40,000. It was about that time that the company developed the 'novel contractual arrangement called the Bovis System'[2] a fee-based relationship which brought Marks & Spencer as its best known client. Development activity also began then with Bovis buying land for retail schemes, later formalised with the formation of Audley Properties. Speculative housebuilding did not start until 1933 but even then Bovis did not engage in the conventional large estate development practised by so many other contractors but confined itself to luxury apartments and houses in central London.

In tracing the history of a family dominated company, name changes can be especially confusing. Fears of anti-Jewish persecution led the Gluckstein family to adopt different names. In the words of the Bovis history: 'Vincent Gluckstein was always known as 'Mr Vincent', so he decided to become Vincent E Vincent in 1937. Sydney Gluckstein opted for the surname 'Glyn', partly because his poor handwriting already made his signature look like 'Glyn.' To complicate matters further, their brother Samuel Gluckstein decided against a change of name, but both his sons took a new surname. Thus Harry, who joined the company in 1931, and Neville Gluckstein became Harry and Neville Vincent respectively.'[3]

War time construction ranged from bomb damage work in London, through factory building (including the move of the Woolwich Arsenal to Staffordshire) to the participation in the biggest construction project of the war, the Mulberry Harbour. Sir Samuel Joseph died in 1944, having been Lord Mayor of London the preceding year. Sidney Glyn took the chair. Sir Samuel's son, Sir Keith Joseph joined Bovis in 1946, later becoming a Cabinet minister (1970-74 and 1979-86).

In the post war period Bovis continued to expand its construction activities although it did not resume its London residential development. By the end of the 1950s, Bovis included such names as Gilbert-Ash, Leslie & Co., and Yeomans and Partners but with profits of around £200,000 it was not yet a major concern. Bovis became involved in speculative housing again in 1962, also through Audley Properties, when the 28-year-old Philip Warner was transferred to work under Harry Vincent; Audley Estates was later formed to concentrate on private housing. Born in 1936, Warner had joined Bovis at the age of 19 and after a 4-year sandwich course at the Brixton School of Building, and National Service, he rejoined the Leslie construction subsidiary. 'I suppose I was acting Managing Director of Audley Estates; it was a

---

1 Cooper, *Building Relationships,* pp.30-46.
2 Ibid, p.48.
3 Ibid, p.62.

very tiny operation. We were buying land all over the place on a very haphazard basis. Harry was an impatient chap and he said, right, we want to build up our land portfolio. There was no one in the business who had worked in spec housing – we were learning as we went.'

Frank Sanderson arrives

Within a couple of years there were some 500 plots with planning permission plus a joint venture with a Middlesex housebuilder, Denham Construction. However, all this was rapidly overtaken by Bovis's association with Frank Sanderson. Malcolm Frank Sanderson was originally an estate agent and developer based in Sidcup. After completing his national service in 1948, Frank Sanderson took a job as a clerk in a local firm of estate agents. After two or three years he opened his own literally one-man practice with the help of a £250 loan from his mother, gaining his business by advertising lower commission rates than the established agents; by 1956 he had three offices and was working closely with a local builder, finding the land, obtaining the planning and selling the houses. There was a separate company for each estate and 'One day he came along and asked if I would like to buy the company. It consisted of 12 half-built houses and enough land for six others…It was a good buy… not only that, I inherited three first rate chaps.'[4]

With excellent profits from that one deal, Sanderson formed **Malcolm Sanderson Developments** in 1955 and was soon building across the Kentish suburbs. The contact that changed Sanderson's future was with Harry Vincent. The Vincent family, and Neville in particular, became shareholders in Sanderson Developments, presumably providing the finance for its growth. The financial success of the company (profits of £240,000 within six years) encouraged Bovis to take a formal interest, purchasing its 30% shareholding in October 1964 from Neville Vincent; in that financial year, Sanderson built around 150 houses. In 1967 the Bovis Board decided that it wanted to make a serious commitment to speculative housing and bought out the remainder of Sanderson Developments, and Frank Sanderson went onto the main board. At the same time, Bovis bought the much larger **RT Warren** from Tom Warren's family. The combined deal cost Bovis £1.8m with £1.1m in cash going to the Warren family. Warren had a low-cost land bank, amounting to some 1500 plots, giving the group a more substantial base for Frank Sanderson. The initial target was for housing sales of some 500 a year.

Frank Sanderson rapidly expanded the housing side of Bovis, with acquisitions playing a significant part. Sales in 1967 were 640 reflecting the consolidation of Sanderson and Warren but by 1973 they had reached 2659, this excluding sales of around 800 in Scotland which then reported separately. Bovis claimed to be the second largest housebuilder in the country, though their unit volumes were probably slightly less than Northern Developments. Sanderson became a key figure at Bovis going on to head the company through turbulent times. 'He had a very fine business sense, there's no doubt of that, because he built a formidable group for the Vincent family. He instinctively understood housing and the housing market but his overall strength was that he was a tremendous motivator, even though you didn't meet him very often, the motivational element lasted months and months. That was his skill.'[5]

More acquisitions

The first two acquisitions were relatively modest. **H W Tily**, in 1967/8, was a west-country housebuilder based at Cheltenham. It owned some 20 sites in Gloucestershire, Somerset, Bristol and South Wales, and was building some 200-300 units a year. **Ron Bell Properties**, bought in 1972 had some 20 sites across Cornwall and West Devon primarily building retirement bungalows; output was around 150 units a year. Bell stayed for around six months before retiring. Like many entrepreneurs acquired by public companies 'He

---

[4] Frank Sanderson, quoted in City Profile, *Sunday Express,* 15th Feb. 1970.
[5] Interview with Bill Gair, Nov. 1998.

found the level of reporting and financial control required by a bigger group totally frustrating.'[6] It was **Page-Johnson** bought in 1971 that gave Bovis scale. It operated from the north east to the south west, and by the time of its acquisition was building around 1250-1500 houses a year in the UK, with development subsidiaries also in France and Australia. Johnnie Johnson stayed only a few months as Managing Director although he remained a non-executive director. The final acquisition, in 1973, was **Varney Holdings** , an English housebuilder with a much more successful Scottish subsidiary. In June 1973, Bovis bid for Varney, wanting only 65%, to leave a public quotation for the minority. Sanderson's intention had been to keep it a Scottish quoted company and put all of Bovis' interests in Scotland into Varney with Bovis holding the majority stake. However, this was never done and the outstanding minority shareholding was acquired.

The abortive P&O bid

On January 1st 1970, Frank Sanderson was appointed Managing Director of Bovis Holdings. In August 1972 Harry Vincent retired aged 60 and Sanderson became Chairman and Chief Executive. Profits were rising fast, led by the housing division: of the £13m being forecast for 1972, half was from housing, £3m from property, £2 1/2m from construction and £1m from banking. In the month that Sanderson became Chairman, he entered talks with the asset-rich P&O., having failed to secure the property giant, MEPC. It was agreed that P&O would make a 'reverse takeover' bid for Bovis which would have seen Sanderson appointed as Managing Director of the enlarged group and given Bovis shareholders 49% of the total shares. However, when it was announced, Lord Inchcape led a rebellion within the P&O board arguing that the terms valued P&O at no more than its properties and cash and ignored the value of its fleet. In November 1972 the P&O shareholders refused to vote through the necessary increase in share capital at the AGM and the bid failed.

If there was turmoil at P&O, it was no more peaceful at Bovis. Sanderson was described as a man who 'appeared distressingly unable to live with his protégés.'[7] Brian Baird, in charge of housing, had been sacked in 1971. Barry Abbott, the property director, quit Bovis early in 1973 after an abortive coup in which he sought to replace Sanderson as Chief Executive. In September 1973, Frank Sanderson in turn was forced out of Bovis.[8] Malcolm Paris, then Finance Director, became Managing Director in his place and Neville Vincent Chairman. Paris was not particularly flattering about his predecessor: 'he had been an estate agent in Sidcup just four years earlier, and really had no idea what he was doing, let alone the management experience to run a big company.'[9] The 'big company' reference may have been fair comment but the tenor of the quotation does not do justice to Sanderson's housing expertise. Cooper himself wrote later in the History: 'It was his strategy that established the future business plan for a decentralised Bovis Homes of the future, a model copied by many other housebuilders.'[10]

A larger problem than management dissension was waiting to hit Bovis. In 1971, Bovis had bought a Section 123 company[11] called Twentieth Century Banking. In 1973 the banking subsidiary was being overtaken by the secondary banking crisis; there was a run on deposits and Bovis had guaranteed £45m. Help from the lifeboat was available 'for a limited period only while Bovis sought an association with a financially stronger partner.'[12] In December, Natwest Bank advised Bovis that it was unable to provide

---

6 Cooper, Peter, *Building Relationships*, p.114.
7 *Building*, 18th Jan. 1974.
8 For Sanderson's later career see McAlpine Homes.
9 Cooper, *Building Relationships*, p.103.
10 Ibid, p.110.
11 Could satisfy the DTI that it could be properly treated …as being persons bona fide carrying on the business of banking
12 Reid, *The Secondary Banking Crisis*, p.92.

continued support. This unrelated outpost of Bovis was now threatening to bring down the whole group. One director remembered how unexpected it was: "'We were having a directors' Christmas lunch, the wine was flowing, and why not? It was Christmas, our last day, and we'd had a successful year." His secretary called him out at the brandy stage to be told by group Chairman, Neville Vincent, that the company could go into liquidation in the next few days. "I could not believe it. The Bank had said 'Get yourself married to another company by 7 January or we'll pull the carpet out from under:' Not the spring, or summer, or sometime, but 7 January.'"[13]

Bovis rescued

The partner Bovis found was again P&O, although the terms were vastly different than before: 'the board went crestfallen to P&O which still held 10% of the capital from the earlier involvement. It had cost £11.7m and was now worth £9m less.'[14] The new terms gave Bovis some 14% of the new entity compared with 49% the first time round. Frank Sanderson now opposed the bid but eventually accepted in respect of his own 5% shareholding. Bovis duly became a P&O subsidiary in March 1974. On Frank Sanderson's elevation to group Managing Director of Bovis, the day-to-day management of the housing business had passed to Brian Baird but when he left, Philip Warner and Ray Whatman were appointed joint Managing Directors. Ray Whatman was Frank Sanderson's half brother who had joined Sanderson Estates in 1956; he left Bovis after Sanderson's departure in 1973 – as did some twenty senior personnel who chose to join up with Sanderson again. Philip Warner was appointed housing Managing Director at this most difficult time and stayed at the helm for a quarter of a century.

In that first year as part of P&O, Bovis completed approximately 3500 houses, with a further 200 in Western Australia. There had also been a brief, though not successful, period of housebuilding in the Paris region. One of the best known sites was New Ash Green, a new village outside Maidstone with consent for 6000 dwellings. It was being developed by Span but after the latter's financial problems, Sanderson had bought it in 1971 and Bovis built some 2000 houses there. One of the unusual features was that over half Bovis Homes' UK output came from only four sites – New Ash Green, Southcott Village near Leighton Buzzard, Amblecote to the west of Birmingham and Elton in Cheshire. In the P&O accounts for 1974, Bovis was described as 'the only national house builder to operate through regionally based, profit responsible, companies, located as far as possible at the centre of the area each serves.'[15] Surprisingly, Bovis managed to sustain its high volumes through 1975, albeit helped by package deals with local authorities. However, from then on sales fell steadily, more than halving by the end of the decade. Warner stressed the level of cancellations at the end of 1973. 'We had heavy work in progress, spread all over the place, because we had had this massive push for volume production. If you're growing at 25 per cent per annum, you have massive construction resources geared up. There is no way that we could have built ourselves out of that recession.'[16]

Despite extensive write-offs at the time of the acquisition, P&O announced in February 1976 that a further £23m was to be written off. A particular problem was the Lower Earley site near Reading, a new town with land for 6000 houses and all that goes with a new town; it had been bought at the top of the market in 1973. A period of rationalisation followed: strategic land sales were made and in 1978 Bovis withdrew from the north east and north west regions although, at the same time, strengthening the midlands by the acquisition of B-Vis Construction for £4.5m. Despite the reduction in volumes during

13 *Building*, 27th March 1987, *Reflections of Bernard Heaphy on his retirement as Bovis Construction President.*
14 *Building*, 1st Jan. 1974.
15 Cooper, *Building Relationships,* p.116.
16 Interview with Philip Warner, June 2001.

the 1970s, Bovis remained one of the top five or six housebuilders in the country and it also finished the decade as one of the most profitable, exceeding the absolute level of profits that had been achieved in the boom conditions of the early 1970s.

Housing abroad

Overseas, Bovis entered the US market for the first time in 1981, forming Bovis-Brunning in Georgia; George Brunning had once been a regional Managing Director of Bovis Homes but was then running another housing company in Georgia. For a UK housebuilder it was a rare case of the chosen managing director having experience of both the UK parent and the overseas market although, as it turned out, to no great avail. Bovis-Brunning also opened in Texas and by 1983 sales were approaching 300 but profits were modest and the Georgia and Texas companies were closed in 1986. Bovis switched to Florida, buying the assets of a small local company, Laurel Homes, in 1987, building sales up to a steady 250 a year. Despite the mixed results of its forays into France and the USA, Bovis also decided to form a German subsidiary in 1992 starting with a 300 plot site south of Berlin but within a couple of years the project was being abandoned.

In the more favourable climate of the 1980s, Bovis began to rebuild its UK volumes, the emphasis being on regional and product expansion. There continued to be little, if any, operational interference by P&O: the constraint from the parent company was financial. 'Our growth aspirations were curbed by what P&O was prepared to invest in the business. As big companies do, we had a five-year plan which set out aspirations and our capital needs. We were always bidding for funds in competition with the other divisions of P&O; it was a very competitive exercise and we were doing that almost from the moment that P&O took us over. It was a thoroughly good form of delegation if you trust your subordinates, you let them get on with it. Nevertheless, we were always bidding for cash: our horizons were always a bit bigger than we are allowed to achieve.'[17]

Housing units, 1971-2004

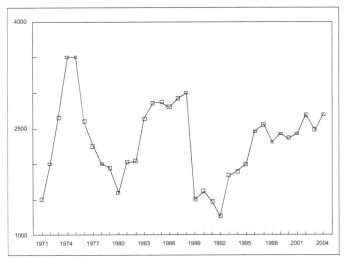

Although Bovis withdrew from Scotland in 1985, a retirement homes division was established in 1986 and Bovis returned to the Manchester area in 1988. That was the year Bovis again reached the 3000 unit level, ironically, it was the last year that Bovis was in the industry's top ten by volume until 2004. Volumes doubled between 1980 and 1988; the general rise in house prices, combined with a policy move to

[17] Ibid.

concentrate on the trade-up market (94% of sales in 1986), lifted turnover from under £50m to over £370m and trading profits rose tenfold from £8m to £87m – the fourth-highest profit earned by a housebuilder in the 1980s.

Once again, when recession hit Bovis the pattern of the 1974 recession was repeated: a halving of volumes, this time immediately, before a gradual recovery back to earlier levels. The trade-up market was particularly severely hit during the recession. 'Clearly we had to think about revising our planning densities from seven or eight to the acre to 12-15 to the acre on sites that had been bought primarily for the trade-up market. So it was a slow recovery for us, partly because we had a large exposure to the south east and a lot of flats, particularly in London, that took us several years to work out.'[18] The low point was in 1992, when sales fell to only 1260 and a trading loss of £34m recorded. There was also a land write down of £5m, although this was the only year in which a provision was made and it was minuscule by the standards of the industry.[19] From then on, Bovis staged a steady recovery, although neither its volumes nor its trading profits recovered to their pre-recession levels. It is not clear to what extent Bovis was constrained by the position of its parent company. Substantial interest charges payable to P&O had actually kept Bovis Homes in a pre-tax loss for four years. The comment in the company history that 'P&O demanded the sale of surplus land to reduce capital employed, but supported the active pursuit of low cost land to dilute the average cost of the land bank'[20] suggested some constraints on exploiting the opportunities in the land market. Nevertheless, in 1996 P&O did support Bovis Homes' £10m purchase of the west-country Britannia Homes (269 units in its last year).

P&O floats Bovis Homes
In 1985, P&O had merged with the property company Sterling Guarantee and its Chairman, Jeffrey Sterling, became group Chairman. By the mid 1990s, pressure was building on P&O to improve its returns, focus its activities more clearly and reduce debt. In November 1997 P&O floated 100% of Bovis Homes on the Stock Exchange.[21] In keeping with the concept of a focused housebuilding company, the US subsidiary and the remnants of the German operation were excluded from the float. Philip Warner had reached retiring age in 1996 completing what must have been the longest period as a non-family director in charge of a major housebuilder. He was succeeded by Malcolm Harris, a management accountant who had joined Bovis in 1974 and had been Managing Director of the south east region since 1978. Volumes changed little after the flotation, reaching no more than 2700 in 2004, barely 100 more than in 1997. However, as management continued the strategy of concentrating on margin improvement Bovis Homes' profit margins were consistently the highest of any of the mainstream quoted housebuilders.

---

[18] Ibid.
[19] However, it is understood that provisions were made elsewhere in the group and in the joint venture companies.
[20] Cooper, *Building Relationships*, p.125.
[21] Two years later Bovis Construction was sold to the Australian Lend Lease Corporation.

BRADLEY OF YORK
Peak units: c.500 (1966)

Bradley Estates, as it was first known, was founded in 1953 by Jack Bradley and Len Wainhouse, both then aged 24. The driving force appeared to be Bradley, who not only lent his name to the enterprise but took the role of Chairman and Managing Director. Bradley left school at 14 to take a job as a plumber's mate. 'I wasn't bright enough for grammar-school', before going to Australia for a couple of years as a labourer where 'I first came in contact with low-price industrialised housing methods.'[1] To begin with, Bradley Estates carried out jobbing work and small contracts but in 1954 the first private housing development was started at Huntingdon near York, offering bungalows at £1995 each which sold rapidly. 'The designs were quite revolutionary and were indeed the forerunners of most of the contemporary types of bungalows that are now widely built in this part of Yorkshire.[2] The bungalow boom was on and by 1957 (the first years for which there is specific detail), production had risen to 300 a year.

The company then began to diversify, acquiring property interests throughout the north east; it also went into retail and wholesale distribution, hotels and catering, the motor industry, hire purchase and farming. Jack Bradley, possibly in a personal capacity, also took control of Slingsby Sailplanes, which manufactured the internationally-famous Slingsby glider, and the factory was also used to produce industrialised housing. In 1960 Bradley Estates moved to bigger premises in Monkgate York with the industrial side being catered for at Osbaldwick. The company then had some 20 sites across Lancashire and Yorkshire and, as was common in the north east, Bradley employed its own labour force, rather than sub-contract; it also had its own joinery factory. When the new office was opened, the press reports suggested that over 4000 properties had been built by Bradley to date, which seems gross exaggeration. Indeed, between 1962 and 1964 unit sales were little more than 200 a year

Jack Bradley is ousted

In 1965, the Company floated as Bradley of York. By then Bradley was also building in Durham and Northumberland, and in Somerset through a subsidiary in Crewkerne. Volumes exceeded 300 in 1965 and reached around 500 in 1966. Bradley then started to expand regionally through acquisition. In 1967 it paid £475,000 for an Edinburgh based firm, Perdovan, bought from James Harrison. This was followed at the start of the 1967/68 financial year by the acquisition of the Lancashire Daleholme Estates from Tom Henderson. When these acquisitions were being made, there were no visible signs of the underlying frailty of the Bradley structure. The 1967/68 interim results gave no warning of what was to happen and even in 1968 the press was extolling the entrepreneurial virtues of the founder. Reading the interview with hindsight, it is possible to see the other side of entrepreneurial leadership: 'Self-made millionaire Jack Bradley looks as beefy and extrovert as a beery rugby league player. Yet I was to discover another side to this 39-year-old egotistical building tycoon and financial manipulator extraordinary. Quick-thinking and decisive, he doesn't suffer fools gladly and been known to be ruthless with employees who do not live up to his expectations. His talent for invective is said to be highly original and quite shattering.'[3]

In March 1969, a £1.1m loss was announced for the year to October 1968, compared with a profit of £462,000 the previous year. Dalehome Estates and Bradley (Scotland) had traded profitably; but there

---

[1] *Yorkshire Evening Press*, 27th May 1968.

[2] Ibid, 13th July.

[3] *Yorkshire Evening Press*, 27th May 1968.

had been substantial trading losses and write-offs in the original Yorkshire business. Jack Bradley was removed from office and the new Chairman, Norman Brown, stated that the losses 'were incurred because Mr Bradley was responsible for over-expansion and assumed tasks which were too large for any man',[4] allegations then hotly denied by Jack Bradley who insisted that the over-expansion was a board decision. The shares fell from 19s to 5s-3d. A Cooper Brothers report blamed weak management controls and incomplete records in the York-based companies. Henderson was granted additional shares 'in consideration of his refraining from taking legal action to cancel the sale [of Daleholme].' Bradley and Wainhouse agreed to waive repayment of loans totalling £100,000 and they and three other directors repaid the £58,000 distributed as interim dividend, now said to have been unjustified.

Interviewed in June 1969, Brown pointed to fundamental weakness in the Bradley organisation: 'We had only a facade of management and without proper management housebuilding is the easiest business to make a mess of. I think the group was operating incorrectly shortly after flotation. Flotation and sudden access to wealth sometimes gives young men very grandiose ideas…Making money in business is a hard tough job. You have to cut out all the flamboyancy.'[5]

Having restored Bradley to modest profitability, Brown resigned as Chairman in November 1970 to be replaced by Henderson, following which the Company's name was changed to Daleholme (Holdings) in recognition of the fact that the bulk of profits now came from the Daleholme Estates subsidiary. It was not long before the Company attracted the attention of predators. The private Cornwallis Estates bought a large stake in November and secured board representation the following April. Their holding was then sold on in February 1972 to Orme which announced its intention of bidding 68p a share. Next month, the Orme offer was withdrawn and its 18% stake sold on to Northern Developments, which made an agreed bid of 81p a share, valuing Daleholme at £4.1m.

[4] *Building*, 14th March 1969.
[5] *Yorkshire Evening Press*, 26th June 1969.

BRITANNIA
Peak units: 355 (1994)

Based in Cheltenham, Britannia was formed in 1960 for the somewhat specialised activity of dismantling gas holders and redeveloping the land. From there it moved on to the independent acquisition of land for industrial and residential development and the sale of serviced plots. The developments appeared to be more commercial than residential, though there was a 250 unit housing site developed outside Cheltenham in the mid-1970s. In 1983 there was an MBO led by Jim Sugrue, Chairman, John Rickards, a quantity surveyor, as Managing Director, and Robert Herrick. In 1987 Britannia was floated; it described itself as concentrating on the development and construction of commercial, industrial, retail and residential property and stressed that a major feature of the Group's business was the interlinking of the development and construction processes – common in residential but less so in commercial work. The construction operation also included third party work..

Profits reached a peak of £3m at the end of the 1980s but by 1991 there was a £0.9m loss. There were changes in the Board structure with Christopher Powell appointed Chairman at the end of 1990 and solicitor Michael Nelmes-Crocker appointed to the Board as Managing Director; Rickards, concentrating on development, and Sugrue remained directors. At the same time, private housing was given new emphasis: 'Board has resolved to expand the activity of the homes division and bought a site for 46 starter homes in the Forest of Dean.'[1] There was also a joint venture on a 70 plot estate with Dowty.

In June 1991, Britannia entered into a management contract and option to buy Clifton Homes, also of Cheltenham. Clifton had been started by Geoff Hester following his resignation as Chief Executive of Westbury in 1981. In 1991, Clifton had completed 96 units from its offices in Cheltenham and Bournemouth; this compared with only 12 sales by Britannia that year. The Clifton option was exercised in April 1993 and the enlarged company had sales of 176 units, though still losing money as a group. Hester joined the Britannia Board, who were now trying to cut back their commitment on commercial property and concentrate on construction and housebuilding.

At the end of 1993, additional equity finance was raised and 1994 saw a record 355 houses sold from 30 sites and group profits of £1.7m. However, the dip in market in 1995 put pressure on sales, which fell to 269. It was argued that the reduced margins on lower priced units made it impossible to justify the working capital necessary to achieve the required volume. The housebuilding division was therefore restructured to operate from fewer sites with a different mix. Although this strategy was publicly supported by Hester it reduced his scope and he left the Group. In June 1996, the housebuilding division, by then loss-making, was sold to Bovis Homes for £10m.

---

[1] Group accounts, 1990.

BROSELEY
Peak units: 4574 (1983)

Owned for most of its history by an insurance company, Broseley will for ever be identified with Danny Horrocks, a Bolton property developer. On leaving grammar school in 1942, Danny Horrocks was apprenticed as a joiner. Some five years later, his brother came out of the navy and the two started an estate agency in Bolton, opening another office in Leigh in 1951. This was an opportune time with building controls then being dismantled and, like many other estate agents, they moved into development. When Danny Horrocks married in 1954, the brothers split the business with Danny taking the Leigh office; in the next couple of years he developed around 80 houses, contracting the work out to builders.

In the early 1950s, Danny Horrocks was introduced to Dunlop Heywood, the leading Manchester chartered surveyors and it was there that he met Tom Baron – another Lancastrian destined to become a leading figure in the housing industry. Tom Baron in turn introduced a local builder, Alf Smith, which led to the formation of joint Horrocks/Smith companies including Wigshaw Properties and Property Investment (Leigh) for housing and Bradshawgate Properties for commercial development. Tom Baron also had an interest through an option arrangement. (Incidentally, the company names, including Broseley itself, were streets in Culcheth, between Leigh and Wigan).[1] The first housebuilding in the joint companies was in 1957-58 and the estates began to be of significant size – 50 at Weststaughton, then 150 at Bolton, and then a similar one in Blackburn.

Enter the Royal Exchange
Commercial development was carried on side by side with housing and the first development had a significance that went well beyond its local interest. When a cinema in Leigh came on the market, Tom Baron used Debenham Tewson & Chinnock to effect an introduction to the Royal Exchange from which developed one of the insurance-developer partnerships that typified the commercial property world: 'The partnerships were unusual as well as profitable combinations of financial sobriety and entrepreneurial verve.'[2] For the record, the ground level of the cinema was converted into a Lennon's supermarket, and the offices above let to the Government on a 21-year lease. Another cinema (in Horwich) was similarly developed and in both cases Royal Exchange provided a letter of intent promising to advance the mortgage money when construction was finished and fully tenanted.

From that point, the relationship with the Royal Exchange became ever closer although the subsequent shareholding history proved somewhat tortuous. In 1960, the three companies mentioned above were consolidated into a new holding company, Broseley Investment Company. Royal Exchange held 26% with the right to take a further 26%; the balance of shares was held by Danny Horrocks, Alf Smith, and Tom Baron (through his option). Royal Exchange continued to provide the end loan to finance the commercial developments, although not for housing.

Followed by MRSL
In September 1961, Metropolitan Railway Surplus Lands (sister company to the Metropolitan Railway Country Estates), entered the story. MRSL was registered in 1933 to acquire the undertaking of the Surplus Lands Committee of Metropolitan Railway Company. The colourful Bernard Docker was

---

[1] One historical footnote from the early 1980s is that Broseley's best known estate was Brookside, which is probably recognised by more television viewers than any other estate in the country.

[2] Supple, The Royal Exchange Assurance, p.527.

Chairman, and the Managing Director of both the Metropolitan Railway companies was 'a courteous and intelligent businessman of the old school, Billy Balch, a distinguished president of the Royal Institute of Chartered Surveyors.'[3] MRSL already had an interest in housing through a joint venture it had with Metropolitan Railway Country Estates, namely the original Whelmar, run by Tom Baron. MRSL bought Tom Baron's option, acquired 20% of Broseley and lent £100,000 to help develop the housing business. The shareholders were thus Royal Exchange, MRSL, Horrocks and Smith, with the latter two still controlling the company. Two years later, in 1963, Alf Smith sold his own building company to Broseley and then sold the whole of his shareholding to Surplus Lands taking the latter's holding up to $49^1/_2$%.

Now the sole entrepreneur left of the original three, Danny Horrocks was asked to run Broseley full time. There then began Broseley's transition from regional to national housebuilder, with expansion into the east midlands and the south west. The south west had another Bolton connection in the form of Frederick Powell who had moved to Devon where he and Danny Horrocks jointly developed a number of small sites, much as Horrocks had done previously with Smith. When Powell died in 1968, the building company was taken into Broseley, when it was further expanded. By the late 1960s, Broseley had become a sizeable developer, building around 1200 to 1500 houses a year, with a significant commercial development programme.

In 1968, Metropolitan Railway Surplus Lands was taken over by the property company MEPC. For whatever reason, MEPC and Guardian Royal Exchange (as it became after the 1969 merger) did not get on – at times they could not even agree where the board meetings should be held. By then, the shareholdings were MRSL $42^1/_4$%, GRE $33^1/_4$% and Horrocks the balance. In March 1970, Horrocks agreed to sell a controlling holding to either MEPC or GRE so that progress could continue. After protracted negotiations, Horrocks was about to sign the sale of his shares to MEPC when GRE cited its 1960 pre-emption agreement. A less-than-amused Danny Horrocks ended up by selling to GRE that same day to give GRE just over 50%. GRE bought out MEPC the following year to achieve 94% ownership. In 1972, GRE made another strategic move, taking over Metropolitan Railway Country Estates, now building around 400 units a year compared with the 2000 a year output when it had controlled Whelmar. The acquisition was without reference to the Broseley management though the rationale was probably the investment properties; after GRE had taken out the properties it wanted, the housebuilding rump was merged into Broseley. At that point, Danny Horrocks sold to Broseley his remaining family interests (Tanway Properties), retaining a $6^1/_2$% interest in Broseley.

Regional expansion
The regional expansion continued in the 1970s taking Broseley into Essex, the north east, and Milton Keynes. By the time the recession came, Broseley was building around 2200 house a year and managed to hold this through the recession, before continuing the regional expansion in the second half of the decade – finishing with Scotland ('a mistake')[4] and then the more successful entry into London Docklands in 1980. Between 1972 and 1979, Broseley's turnover virtually trebled to £51m and trading profits rose from £3m to £8m; throughout the 1974-75 recession, the company remained profitable.

Broseley's growth took place without apparently any guidance or restriction from the parent company. Indeed, between 1979 and 1982, volumes doubled to over 4500 making Broseley the fourth-largest housebuilder in the country. Turnover peaked in 1983 at £130m although there was little further growth in profits. Asked what was the strategy behind the regional expansion and the creation of a national

---

3 Marriott, *The Property Boom*, p.240.
4 Interview with Danny Horrocks, Jan. 1999.

housebuilder, Horrocks said: 'no-one ever decided what to do. There was no basic strategy. We went into new areas because individual people and companies suggested opportunities.' In later years, it often puzzled those in the industry as to what interest an insurance company had in one of the largest housebuilders in the country. However, the roots of the relationship lay in what was originally a risk-free commercial property investment rather than housebuilding, but there was also an appeal in the housing ground rents which gave access to the placing of domestic insurance. There was a brief flirtation with Florida in the first half of the 1980s; Broseley neither made nor lost money.

Although profit margins in the later years never appeared as high as some of its competitors, the accounting was very conservative and the possibility of a flotation lay ahead. However, in 1986 and 1987 Danny Horrocks suffered heart attacks; by then just past 60, he asked GRE what they wanted to do with the business. The association between GRE and Danny Horrocks had lasted over 25 years; without him they felt that there was little sense in owning a business that they did not understand, which they had never managed and which no longer had any common link with the insurance industry. A buyer was to be sought: in December 1986, the housing side of Broseley was sold to Trafalgar House for £71m where it was incorporated into Ideal Homes.

BRYANT
Peak units: 4040 (1997)

Bryant was a long-standing midlands contracting and housing business which turned itself into a national housebuilder in the 1980s and 1990s. The contracting business was founded in 1885 by Christopher Bryant who moved to Birmingham at the age of 20. He trained himself to be a carpenter, as opposed to serving an apprenticeship, and started trading from his home in Smallheath; within a few years was building terraced houses and factories. The business was incorporated as C. Bryant & Son in 1927, acquiring the partnership of the same name for £13,148-16s-11d. The 'Son' of the title was Ebenezer Bryant who had been given a grammar school education before also training as a carpenter.

Chris Bryant died in 1928 leaving Eb to take over 'with the able assistance of Frank Russon', who was then made a director.[1] During the 1930s, Bryant built office blocks, schools, hospitals, industrial buildings and local authority housing throughout the Birmingham area, perhaps as many as 1500 to 2000 council houses a year. For speculative housing, Birmingham Dwellings was incorporated in 1933 although the first sites were not acquired until 1936; the first completed development was of detached houses on the Cedars Estate in Erdington totalling some two or three hundred houses. Apart from that, little private housing was built. During the war, Bryant built munitions factories and military installations and assisted with war damage work. Bryant also incorporated its scaffolding business in 1944 as Kwikform, later to be one of the industry leaders under different ownership.

Frank Russon runs the Company

Eb Bryant was Chairman until his death in 1952. The third generation Bryant, again a Christopher, was then only 28 so Frank Russon took over as Chairman. Russon was an important figure in the Bryant history. He left school aged 14 and served his apprenticeship as a bricklayer before fighting on the Somme in the First War, when he was commissioned in the field. After the war he took an office post in Birmingham to study quantity surveying and estimating, qualifying as a LIOB in 1924, joining Bryant as a surveyor and estimator that year. After becoming a director in 1928 he was appointed joint Managing Director in 1944 (he went on to become President of the Federation of Registered Housebuilders in 1956). Roy Davies' memory of the period when they overlapped was that Russon ran the business for Eb Bryant which is how Russon received 25% of the equity.[2]

The building operations were extended after the war to give a wider spread across the midlands and in 1957 Bryant formed a civil engineering division which soon had contracts for building the Birmingham inner ring road. Frank Russon decided that Bryant should resume speculative housebuilding in the early 1950s. By 1953 the firm was building around 30 houses a year; Bryant Estates was incorporated in 1954, gradually taking over responsibility for private housing from Birmingham Dwellings. In practice, construction and housing were run as one operation and it was not until 1958 that Bryant Estates operated as an independent entity; by then it was building around 350 houses a year. The Company had been receiving financial support from ICFC since 1952 and the latter finance house floated Bryant Holdings on the Birmingham and London Stock Exchanges in 1960, by which time the company was earning pre-tax profits of £247,000 against £63,000 ten years previous. Frank Russon, then 63, was Chairman and Chris Bryant, 36, Managing Director. Chris Bryant was educated at Malvern College and graduated in civil engineering from Birmingham University in 1944. After two years in the Fleet Air Arm he joined the family firm in 1946 working as a contract manager. In 1962 Frank Russon retired; strains

---

[1] *1885-1985 One Hundred Years of Building* [1985 group accounts].
[2] Interview with Roy Davies, Dec. 2000.

were emerging between the two principal shareholders and part of the agreement was that Frank Russon bought Kwikform from the Company; Chris Bryant then became Chairman as well as Managing Director.

Roy Davies develops Bryant Homes
The key figure in the history of Bryant's post-war housing history was Roy Davies, an eccentric but dynamic character, who ran Bryant Estates (later Bryant Homes) from 1958 until he retired in 1987. He had joined the company in 1941 as a trainee surveyor returning after service with the RAF. He was appointed as the group's chief surveyor in 1953, Managing Director of Bryant Homes in 1958, a main board director in 1962 and assistant group Managing Director in 1982. 'The record of the company bears a very adequate witness of his great contribution to our success.'[3] Michael Chapman, later Finance Director, described him as 'a very idiosyncratic but brilliant developer. There was a tremendous partnership between Roy and Chris, both of whom knew their place in the scheme of things. Chris used Roy and let him have his head to run the homes division. The only problem was that if you tried to get them together then they would tend to have a go at each other. But in practice it was a very good working relationship.'

The group expanded steadily in the 1960s off a mixed contracting and private housing base; by the end of the decade, Bryant was making pre-tax profits of £1.4m on £30m turnover. It had, however, experienced considerable problems on its local authority housing contracts when the City of Birmingham halved its housing programme in the late 1960s; fixed-price housing contracts in 1971 and 1972 necessitated provisions of £3m, pushing group profits down to £1m despite record profits from Bryant Homes. Strikes and labour unrest even led Bryant to take its name off its housing developments to avoid irritating the unions. Around 1968, Bryant sought to broaden the base of its business when it 'made a policy decision to use the construction and homes development expertise…to embark on the creation of income producing investments';[4] in the early days this was largely through a joint company with Samuel Properties. Diversification into property was to bring considerable benefit in the 1980s but the earlier move into civil engineering (started in 1957) proved less successful.

Bryant had but one year to show what the private housing market could do for it when it made profits of £4m in 1973, only for the housing recession to hit it the following year. By then it had been selling around 1500 homes a year with plans to increase to 2000. In comparison with many of its competitors, Bryant's housing profits held up reasonably well, supported by an excellent low-cost land bank in the west midlands. But worse was to hit the company later that decade. In 1975 Bryant decided to take its construction overseas and selected Saudi Arabia as being an area that offered the best opportunity. It formed a joint company with a local contractor but in 1978 was forced to make a £2.6m provision against a gunnery contract and the whole of its investment; Bryant's problems had been compounded by the army's insistence on using the gunnery range before it was completed.

Bryant at the Old Bailey
Morale was more deeply affected by events at home. In April 1977 the Chairman had to write to shareholders advising them that summonses had been issued against the Company, C Bryant & Sons, the Chairman himself and others alleging 'a conspiracy to corrupt and corruption'; this followed a case against a former Birmingham city architect, who had been jailed for corruption in 1974. Although Chris Bryant was cleared at the Old Bailey, two directors and one former director of the construction subsidiary

---

[3] Group Accounts, 1987.
[4] Group Accounts, 1980.

were jailed and the company pleaded guilty to corruption charges. 'Let's face it, 1978 has not been our year.'[5] Chapman stressed the legacy of the trial: 'It did affect people and there is no doubt that the threat of being put in prison affected the directors. At times there was a habit of not wanting to keep records; they thought that because they had kept records they had found themselves in court.' The collapse in the share price led to bid speculation; the Finance Director revealed that Alfred McAlpine had been considering opening bid talks with Bryant (it got round to it 22 years later) and Taylor Woodrow also disclosed a share stake – only to wait slightly longer before making its full bid.

It was not until 1976 that Bryant Homes opened its first regional office, at Wokingham, to form the base for a southern division. It was headed by Andrew MacKenzie who had joined Bryant as a management trainee in 1957; he rose to be group Managing Director in 1988 and Chief Executive in 1992. By 1981, around a third of house sales came from the new division. However, group housing volumes showed little change. In 1976, as the southern region was being started, total housing sales reached 2000; in 1986 volumes were no more than 2100. Despite starting the southern region, Roy Davies was not a great believer in regional diversification: 'I couldn't control it at more than an hour and a half away. I realised that staff needed to be supervised by the bloke with the inspiration.'[6]

Perhaps sensing that the company was drifting, ECC (English China Clays that was) launched a £137m takeover bid for Bryant in November 1986. It was fiercely contested, with ECC raising its bid to £187m and Bryant surprising the City with its profit forecasts. 'During the bid, Roy Davies had to disclose all sorts of information on the value of Homes and that shocked everybody; people had not realised how valuable it was!'[7] *Building* magazine also queried the rationale of the bid in its leader. 'To assume an 88 year old housebuilder cum contractor would somehow magically gain additional "strength to compete" through a union with the country's biggest clay quarrier is indeed wishful thinking.'[8] Helped in the final stages by its Pension Fund buying Bryant shares, the company narrowly survived; ECC retained its original 29.9% stake until 1990. The bid appeared to act as a catalyst to the management. Roy Davies reached retiring age in 1987, never having held a Bryant Homes board meeting during his thirty year period in charge 'We didn't need them; I had my team and they stayed with me all the way through.'[9] Andrew MacKenzie took over as Managing Director of Bryant Homes, becoming group Managing Director in 1988, although Chris Bryant remained as Chairman until 1992. The decision was made to launch a much more positive regional expansion policy but the plans were postponed by the onset of recession in 1989. Profits, which had broken through £50m in 1988 on the back of the house price boom (and the need to fight off the ECC bid) fell to £10m in 1991. Apart from its housing, Bryant had also been exposed to the downturn in the commercial property market.

Regional expansion taken seriously
The diversification into property had served Bryant well; it was contributing over 20% of group profits and its Pavilions development had earned £16m in the three years to 1989. But the plans were ambitious: by 1989, either sole or in partnership, Bryant had announced proposals to develop a total of 6.4m sq.ft. with a completion value of over £500m, of which Bryant's share was over £400m. Bryant managed to disengage itself from most of these commitments and contain its losses in the southern housing; it was still making good profits in its housing heartland and with £40m raised from a rights issue in 1990, the

---

5 Chairman's statement, 1978.
6 Interview Roy Davies.
7 Interview with Michael Chapman, April 2001,
8 *Building*, 2nd Jan. 1987.
9 Interview Roy Davies.

regional expansion could start. The new offices were opened in rapid succession: Wetherby for a Yorkshire region in 1990; Warrington for the north west in 1991; and Edinburgh in 1993.

In contrast to most housebuilders who laid stress on finding the right local people to open offices in alien territory, Bryant's policy was to utilise its own senior management, well used to the Bryant philosophy and the trade-up market in which it operated. Taking the decade as a whole, unit volumes doubled, helped by the purchase of Admiral Homes in 1996 (building around 400 units). Profits, however, were slower to recover and when trading conditions became tougher again in 1995 there was a fall in volumes and profits. It was not until 1998 that profits finally exceeded the 1989 peak. At the end of 1998, Bryant conducted a survey of City perceptions of the group which was extremely critical of the policy that Bryant had pursued through the 1994-96 period. 'We had traded through the 1990s downturn very successfully on the basis of value for money, price, no gimmicks and very little use of part exchange. But when that policy was tried again in 1994/95 it got us into all sorts of problems. It comes across as inflexibility – just because it worked once – we didn't have the flexibility to change the second time round.'[10]

Housing units, 1979-2000

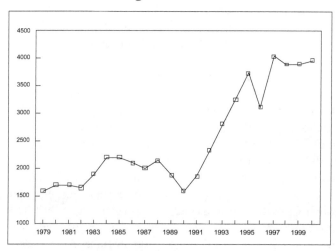

Andrew Mackenzie resigned early in 2000, just short of retirement age. Peter Long, who had joined the Board in 1998 having previously been in charge of Rugby's joinery operations, was appointed Chief Executive. 'Bringing in an outsider has saved the Board the embarrassment of promoting one of the four directors responsible for housebuilding.'[11] The same article also reported Long as 'looking through our competitors to see who would fit best.' At the end of the year the 'merger of equals' was announced between Bryant and Beazer to be called Domus plc. The stated rationale included cost savings, procurement synergies and expertise in off-site fabrication. However, the merger was torpedoed by the hostile bid by Taylor Woodrow. The £539m offer was accepted in February 2001; ironically, the Bryant name stayed on and later replaced Taylor Woodrow Homes as the UK brand name, and Taylor Woodrow also moved its head office to Bryant's Birmingham headquarters.

[10] Interview Michael Chapman.
[11] *Financial Times*, Feb. 2000.

BUDGE BROTHERS
Peak units: c.300 (1973)

The Company's short life as a quoted housebuilder was conducted under several different names. Incorporated in 1911 as The Clovelly Rubber Estate it eventually became one of the many Stock Exchange shells when, in 1958, it bought a number of construction and development companies from Elmer Ellsworth Jones, a Chichester surveyor who became the new Chairman. This produced the first of the name changes, to Ellsworth Estates. Ellsworth had only a modest housebuilding programme – the 1959 accounts reported a land bank of no more than 210 plots.

In 1963 Mark Horowitz and Denis McManus joined the board after buying a controlling interest in Ellsworth. In that year, the new management team bought Orchard House Properties and the plan was always to merge with McManus & Co. This was achieved in 1959 and Denis McManus became Chairman, changing the company's name to McManus Group. McManus Group profits averaged around £70,000 through to the year to June 1968. The following year, the Group incurred losses and McManus resigned in favour of Mark Horowitz who became the largest shareholder. Horowitz argued that 'For some years the profits of the Group have reflected the position of an administrative structure geared to a rate of sales higher than conditions have permitted.'[1]

The company was reorganised, the Potters Bar office let, and the non-development interests sold The Chairman still believed that the anticipated production programme of up to 500 residential units a year could be met – although the later turnover figure suggest that unit sales fell well short of this target. After a brief return to the old level of profits in 1971, there was a small loss in the following year and by 1972, McManus Group was still making no more than £50,000 profit. First it was blaming land shortages and then the failure of its main building contractor.

In 1972 McManus bought the Jubilee Property Company, controlled inter alia by Bairstow Eves partners. Eric Earey and John Bairstow went on the Board of the enlarged company, now renamed Orchard House Property Holdings, although Alan Cherry stood down, going on to lead Countryside. Within a year, there was the more substantial acquisition of the Budge Brothers Group. The four Budge brothers, Peter, Roy, Robert and Leslie, had started their building business in 1963 and soon expanded into residential and commercial development. In 1971 they merged with the private interests of Alex Jacobs; these included motor caravan conversion and hotels as well as property development. A new Prospectus was issued in July 1973 and the forecast was for some 330 houses to be sold, all in London or the south east. Forecast profits were £600,000 from the old Budge Group and £120,000 from Orchard House. However, the new company was highly geared, with the 1973 balance sheet showing debt of over £8m compared with equity of £3m. It was not strong enough to survive the recession and in August it was admitting to liquidity problems; a receiver was appointed in September 1974.

---

[1] AGM, Dec. 1968.

BUNTING ESTATES
Peak units: c.300 (early 1960s)

The business was founded by Angus Bunting, incorporating in 1934 as The Bunting Construction Company; it is not known if Angus Bunting traded before 1934. The firm was based in Edgware and the first directors were Angus Bunting and Douglas Gray, both described as directors of investment companies. From 1934 to 1939 the company developed housing estates and blocks of flats in and around London. However, Bundock refers to Bunting Construction having its head office in Baker St. and building maisonettes through the 1930s.[1] During the war, the company concentrated on Government and local authority contracts – military camps, gun sites, prefabricated houses et al.

No record of Bunting's immediate post war activities survive, other than the appointment of Reginald Guy as building director in 1947; he had 10% of the firm's equity. The company looks as if it had been reasonably successful once building controls ended, profits rising from £17,000 in 1956 to £133,000 in 1960 and it is believed to have been building around 300 houses a year. By then, Angus Bunting was approaching retirement age and, in 1960, he chose to sell his 90% of the Company to the Green family who renamed it Bunting Estates. The only continuity with the past was Guy who remained a director and a minority shareholder. The Green family, for managerial purposes, consisted of three brothers (Joseph, Aubrey and Mark) who, as we will see later, had other building and investment interests.

The Greens instituted what the Prospectus described as 'a programme of reconstruction' and it was not until 1964 that profits exceeded Bunting's 1960 record. By then, Bunting was building in south London and the southern home counties; it also had large sites in north Wales and Buxton. The majority of houses were selling in the £3-6000 price range, suggesting something of the order of 250-300 units. The Company was floated in 1965 with Aubrey Green, aged 58, as Chairman and Mark Green, aged 50, as Managing Director; Reginald Guy remained the building director. Joseph Green, although a large shareholder, was not then on the Board. In the event, the company failed to meet its £230,000 profits forecast: looking back, Joseph Green's son, David, said 'We should never have gone public: the three brothers had different views about the business and it was a way of crystallising cash.'[2]

Reverse takeover of Gas Purification

In May 1967 there was a reverse takeover of Gas Purification and Chemical, which was then chaired by the third brother, Joseph Green, also its largest shareholder. GPI by then comprised the Westminster Construction group of companies, including residential and commercial estate development, double glazing and kitchen units; and an engineering division distributing Grundig radios, etc. Joseph Green was appointed to the Board as Chairman., changing the Company's name to British Industrial Holdings. Bunting Estates was merged with Westminster Construction to form Westminster Bunting and it built around 200 houses a year in the south east and East Anglia. Industrial profits were erratic and the property division again caused problems, losing around £1m in the three years to 1976. In 1977, Greenbrook Securities, Jospeh Green's family investment company, made an agreed bid for British Industrial Holdings. Speculative housing was progressively reduced, sites were sold off, and by 1980 housebuilding had ceased. David Green argued that speculative housing did not sit easily with the group's other interests in view of the much higher borrowing requirement.[3]

---

[1] Bundock, 'Speculative Housebuilding'.
[2] Interview with David Green, Oct. 2001.
[3] Ibid.

BURNS-ANDERSON

The business was founded by William Burns in 1944, then a 33-year-old builder; he appears to have been joined at the end of war by Alan Anderson, a chartered secretary and insurance broker, some 10 years the younger. Burns & Anderson was incorporated in January 1946; Burns and Anderson each had 40% and Ian Black, a cotton merchant, 20%. Later entries in the register suggest a much larger percentage held by Burns. The firm, which was based in Stockport, engaged solely in building and contracting until building controls ended in 1954, when it moved into housing estate and property development. In 1960, the directors formed a south-western company based in Exeter.

The company was floated in 1965 under its new name of Burns-Anderson with Burns as Chairman and joint Managing Director; the other joint Managing Director was Ivor Black, then aged 32 and a graduate of Liverpool School of Building. No indication of volumes or turnover was given but the forecast profits of £105,000 does not suggest a large entity. Although profits exceeded the forecast, they halved in 1966 and the next few years were somewhat erratic.

The disappointments experienced in its private housing led to the directors diversifying. By 1972 Burns-Anderson included plant hire and bulk excavation, vehicle distribution and shop and office fitting plus some rental income; only half the profits came from housing. In the 1974 Accounts, the Chairman said that 'Housing development, which six years ago provided the bulk of the Company's profit, contributed less than 10% to the group result. In the downturn of the private housing sector in the late sixties the Directors decided that its cyclical nature should not in future be of sufficient scale to do severe harm to a steady expansion of profit.'

A year later, the Chairman was reporting that, in the early stages of the recession 'the Board made a policy decision to convert its property and land assets into cash…The property sector…is in the depths of a slump, from which it would appear to have little chance of a recovery to reasonable market conditions for a considerable time ahead…But deeper than that must be the question of whether we will in our generation again experience a viable market.'

In 1981, Ivor Black became Chairman and Managing Director; William Burns resigned as an executive in January 1982. The 1982 accounts recorded that Burns-Anderson had disposed of most of its remaining property assets and the company no longer had any material interest in property. Burns-Anderson formed a financial trust with a deposit taking licence which 'marks a further diversification towards a finance and service oriented Group.'

CALA
Peak units: 1505 (2004)

CALA has the longest history as a quoted company of any of the British housebuilders. Originally known as the City of Aberdeen Land Association, the company was registered in 1875 and quoted shortly after. It 'feued out' or resold much of its land in smaller lots but kept the right to collect fixed ground rents in perpetuity. The Ledingham family were early backers and Sandy Ledingham was Chairman as recently as 1985. The history of the Company's first century can pass with little comment as income remained solely rents and feu duties and only nominal profits were recorded; in 1973, when the modern story begins, the company had a market capitalisation of under £400,000. That was to change dramatically in the 1970s although the corporate relationships were to prove convoluted before CALA emerged as one of Scotland's leading independent housebuilders.

The Greencoat story

Other companies involved in the early 1970s were **Greencoat Properties**, a company with even earlier antecedents than Cala, having been registered as Improved Industrial Dwellings in 1864, and Marc Gregory, a privately owned housebuilder controlled by Malcolm Hawe and Mike Ratcliffe. Greencoat, like Cala, had continued in much the same vein for the best part of a century until 1958 when it acquired Ashley Gardens Properties (of Greencoat Place SW1); a completely new set of directors, led by MF Ferdinando; and a change of name to Greencoat.

In late 1972, a 24% holding in Greencoat was bought by Marc Gregory, whose directors saw the possibility of reversing their business into the quoted company. By August 1973, and after a protracted and acrimonious takeover battle, Marc Gregory controlled the quoted Greencoat, although a significant minority shareholding remained. The Greencoat directors resigned, to be replaced by Malcolm Hawe, Richard Scott (a surveyor), Geoff Ball (chartered accountant) and Tim Razzall (a solicitor and now a Liberal peer), with the exception of Scott, all in their early thirties. In the event, the housing market turned against them before the prospectus for the reverse takeover had been completed. The Greencoat 1973 Accounts reported that the Board 'had embarked on considerable expansion of the Company's development activities.' In addition, the potential of the City of Aberdeen Land Association had been identified. A bid was made for the company and by November 1973 Greencoat held 47% of Cala, later to rise to 55%. In the event, the recession cut short the new Greencoat management's aspirations; a loss was incurred in 1974 and the dividend passed.

In October 1974 a receiver was appointed to Marc Gregory; Guinness Mahon acquired a 47% holding in Greencoat, leaving the receiver holding 39%. This led to the appointment of additional directors, including Martin Landau (then of Guinness Mahon), Peter Goldie and Tony Kelley. Geoff Ball, who had originally identified Greencoat as a suitable quoted vehicle for Marc Gregory, became Greencoat's Managing Director. However, although Greencoat's domestic operations gradually returned to profitability, a fresh crisis was occasioned by its major project at Grancanal Paris. The building permit was revoked by decision of the Conseil d'Etat and write-offs reduced shareholders' funds from £5.5m to £0.7m.[1]

---

[1] As a historical footnote, Greencoat launched a one for one rights issue in 1983 and announced the creation of a new financial services company and a change of name to Abaco Investments. Abaco enjoyed considerable success in the deregulated financial markets before accepting a £134m bid from British and Commonwealth in December 1987.

CALA begins housebuilding

In 1975 CALA began its own housebuilding operations and CALA Homes was formed. Mike Earrey, the ex-quantity surveyor of Marc Gregory, moved to Aberdeen to be Managing Director and the first sales were made in 1976 from the company's prime site in Cults, outside Aberdeen. At the same time, Mike Ratcliffe and Graham Fermor, the ex-Marc Gregory Finance Director, founded Anns Homes. In 1978, Geoff Ball led the negotiations for the purchase of CALA shares from Guinness Mahon; a 55% holding in CALA was acquired for £531,000, 10% by Geoff Ball, 15% by Anns Homes and 30% by Scottish Western Trust, the investment vehicle of the Stenhouse family. Geoff Ball moved up to Edinburgh to be full time Managing Director of CALA with Ratcliffe joining the Board as a non-executive director. Ronnie Hanna joined the board to represent Scottish Western, and take responsibility for strategy and acquisitions, later becoming Finance Director.

By the time of the buyout from Greencoat, much of the old land had been used and CALA entered the land market as a purchaser in its own right. The change in control also signalled the move out of Aberdeen and in 1978 CALA Homes (Lothian) was formed to operate in the Edinburgh area. By the early 1980s CALA was building close on 150 houses a year in its two Scottish regions and had commenced commercial property development, first in Aberdeen and later in the south of England. The next move took CALA back to Geoff Ball's geographic roots when in 1983 it bought Mike Ratcliffe's **Anns Homes**, by then building around 100 houses a year off 13 sites. By 1984, sales were around 250 a year and this was about the last period that Aberdeen accounted for the larger part of profit. Cala's home market had declined as a result of falling oil prices and, with the expansion elsewhere, Aberdeen rapidly lost its importance to the group; this was reflected in the formal abbreviation of name to CALA in 1986. A period of rapid geographic expansion then followed, some organic with a new operation in Cambridge (1987) but acquisitions continued to play a key role.

In April 1986, CALA bought **Tern Residential**, the Hampshire based housebuilding subsidiary of Consolidated Tern Investments ; this was renamed CALA (Wessex), building around 100 units a year. In the December, CALA made the more expensive purchase of Dominion Homes, the housebuilding subsidiary of Dominion International, for £7.2m. **Dominion Homes**, originally called Algrey Developments, had been bought by Dominion in 1979. It had offices in Sussex and Birmingham and by 1986 was selling over 300 houses a year. This expanded Cala's housing interests in the south of England and took the group into the midlands for the first time. This was followed in 1988 by the acquisition of the Somerset based housebuilder **Stanley Stone** (from British and Commonwealth Holdings) which was then amalgamated with the recently formed Western subsidiary. The share consideration gave British & Commonwealth, now the owner of Greencoat/Abaco, a 16% holding in Cala.[2]

CALA Finance

By 1988, unit volumes reached almost 800 compared with only 230 three years earlier. These units included a contribution from CALA Finance, an unusual operation among quoted housebuilders.[3] CALA Finance had been formed in 1985 to provide the finance for schemes where the developer is unable to fund the project; typically, CALA would provide 100% of the finance and take 50% of the profits. Reflecting the enlarged scale of the company a new management structure was established. Tony Kelley and Ronnie Hanna were appointed joint Managing Directors. Stephen Rosier; previously Managing Director of Scottish housing, was appointed to the Board and Alan Downie joined from Wimpey Homes to be Managing Director of the Scottish subsidiaries. Under that new structure, CALA had one more

[2] Sold in 1993
[3] Frogmore, the property associate of Fairview, ran a similar business

good year left: in 1989 unit sales reached 900 and profits just broke though the £10m level.

Group losses in 1991 totalled £7m after land write-downs and losses at CALA Finance of about the same amount. Although mainstream housebuilding roughly broke even, the Scottish operations had continued to make reasonable profits but the south, which now had the larger share of turnover, made substantial losses. As with so many companies, the damage was done furthest from the head office. In coping with the initial impact of the housing recession, CALA had amalgamated four of the southern offices into one office at Basingstoke. The Chairman was frank in his annual report admitting to underestimating the complexities of the Southern merger: 'Recessions generally highlight weakness in controls and in individuals and CALA has not been without its difficulties.' Tony Kelley took active control over the South and for a couple of years the midlands and the south were put under the one management team.

The recovery from the effects of the southern losses duly came but it meant that CALA had marked time for a decade – it was not until 1998 that volumes and profits regained their 1988 levels. By then, a new generation of management had emerged. Ronnie Hanna had left in 1992 to become Chief Executive of Bett Brothers and, following Tony Kelley's retirement in 1995, new managing directors were appointed to each of the housing subsidiaries. Alan Downie was playing a more central role and in January 1997 he became group Managing Director. Restoration of confidence within the group was signalled the following year with the purchase of the Yorkshire housebuilder Victor Homes from Peter Fleming and Frank Willetts, a transaction which involved the Royal Bank of Scotland taking a 9% stake in the group.

Cala's long history as a quoted company came to an end in June 1999 when the management took the company private with a £95m bid, fiercely contested with the neighbouring Miller Group. Management and staff held 54% with Bank of Scotland, which provided the finance, a further 30%. Following the MBO, CALA maintained its volumes in the 800-900 range for several years until 2004, when sales increased to over 1500 units, of which 37% were from the finance subsidiary. CALA continues its regional expansion with plans to open in the north west.

CHARLES CHURCH DEVELOPMENTS
Peak units: 742 (1989)

Charles Church, the son of a farm labourer, studied civil engineering at the Regent Street Polytechnic before joining a construction company in 1961. His entrepreneurial drive was soon evident: 'by the age of eleven he had become a competent electrician and was able to wire his parents' house for electric light;[1] later, he encouraged his father to manufacture breeze blocks on their land. After a post-qualification period as an engineer with Turiff and Laing, he started a small civil engineering partnership, Burke & Church, before building his first house in Camberley Surrey, which was sold in 1967. From this he began to develop the housebuilding business, often turning to sites which other builders regarded as difficult.

Finance to develop the business had not proved easy and the capital to increase its scale in the second half of the 1970s came via joint-venture companies with Martin Grant. Grant, a carpenter by trade with a substantial business as a formwork contractor, was looking for opportunities to invest surplus funds and provided the finance for the purchase of such sites as Lightwater, Surrey (125 plots) in 1975 and a 1000 plot site in Merrow Park, Guildford in 1976 which took annual volumes to around 400. Division of these joint ventures in 1979 halved the number of units to about 200 a year; Grant went on to become a housebuilder in his own right.

Charles Church Developments itself had been incorporated in 1972 with Charles and Susanna Church as equal shareholders; Susanna Church played an active role in the Company's development. Activity was modest through most of the 1970s, with barely any profit, though not all the family companies were consolidated. In 1978, the management was strengthened by the appointment of three new directors, John Duggan (who had joined from Martin Grant a couple of years earlier), Nicholas King, and Clive Harris. The scale of the operation was growing rapidly. The annual reports quoted building rates up from 3 a week in 1978 to 6 in 1980 and 8 in 1981. However, although turnover was growing rapidly, the Chairman warned in the 1981 accounts that it would be hard to maintain margins on housing, and the policy would be to maintain the existing level of construction. Susanna Church later added that 'We could not buy the land we wanted.'[2] Instead, profit was to be increased by commercial work and other new activities; these included the establishment of a subsidiary company in Houston.

Church prepares for growth
By 1982, Church was once again restating its belief that its future lay in housebuilding and was acquiring land in Buckinghamshire and Berkshire; asked what had changed, Susanna Church said 'we had got a team together and we thought we could do it.'[3] By 1984, the Company statements were becoming more positive: the Company had decided 'to prepare for growth.' Two new regions were formed the following year to complement the Camberley office – Southern and Chiltern – and a long term target of 500 units from each division was mentioned. To support that growth, Church recruited 'the strongest land buying team in the South East.'[4] During this period. John Duggan became deputy Managing Director in 1980 and, as Charles began to devote more time to other interests, Managing Director in 1984. However, he left the following year to be replaced by Nicholas King, Finance Director since 1978. In 1987 Charles Church Developments floated with Church as Chairman and King as Managing Director. The loss-

[1] *The Dictionary of National Biography 1986-1990*, pp.71-2.
[2] Interview with Susanna Church, Aug. 2002.
[3] Ibid.
[4] Group accounts, 1985.

making Houston business had been bought back by the family, leaving a pure UK housebuilder with small commercial interests.

Church now had a reputation for its up-market, traditionally-designed housing, on select estates. Its average selling price was twice the national average and 60% above that of the south east. It claimed to be the first housebuilder since the war to reintroduce Tudor and Elizabethan house styles (a 1977 marketing strategy prompted by their estate agent, Roger Carson) and the brick and flint range which had recently been introduced proved an outstanding success. The other exceptional feature of the Prospectus was the land bank quoted at 10,800 plots or some 16 years' supply at its then rate of build. However, only 770 of those plots actually had planning permission. Further regional expansion followed: the 1987 accounts reported the start of Charles Church London; an office was opened in Fareham; and Church bought the loss-making County Homes (Developments), an Essex company owned by Messrs Oxley and Dennis. With the market booming, profits reached a peak £18.5m in 1988 on unit sales of only 560. In February 1989, disenchanted with life as a quoted company, the Chairman proposed an MBO at 120p, 5p above the original flotation price, valuing the company at £104m. 'Charles Church was very unhappy as the Chairman of a public company. Rather like Richard Branson, he just did not like being held accountable to shareholders for his actions. He never really liked the city and it did not like him.'[5]

Charles killed in Spitfire crash
In July 1989 Charles Church, still only 46, was killed when the Spitfire he was piloting crashed. That financial year, volumes reached a record 740, but profits had dipped to £15m; from then it went from bad to worse. Despite the potentially extensive land bank, the amount available to build on was limited; the development of new regions and an increase in volumes had meant the acquisition of considerable land at the top of the market which substantially increased debt. The mezzanine finance element of the MBO was particularly onerous – £33m at 7% over a base rate that peaked at 15%! In 1990, provisions against land holdings of £44m and interest charges of £16m, combined to produce a £56m loss; there were further losses of over £30m in the succeeding four years. The land provisions in 1990 were the largest per plot of any of the quoted housebuilders.[6]

In November, 1990, Susanna Church became Chief Executive; Nicholas King had resigned after 'a difference of opinion with Mrs Church', reportedly relating to an attempted MBO.[7] In August 1991, Stewart Baseley, the new Chief Executive, announced a restructuring. The principal banks converted part of their debt (£78m in February 1991) to preference and equity and agreed deferment of the balance; this left the banks owning 81% of the equity, outside shareholders 8% and the new management team 10%. The refinancing drastically reduced interest charges and by 1995 Charles Church had returned, just, to profit, albeit on unit sales of only 190. Although there was still a negative asset value, the Company's reputation in the executive-home market made it an attractive partner, a fact recognised by Centex Homes, America's largest homebuilder, which formed a UK joint venture with Church in 1995. Church was unofficially put on the market and a deal was agreed with a major housebuilder. However, at the last minute, Royal Bank of Scotland, the Company's principal banker and major shareholder, made a higher offer which became unconditional in March 1996. RBS also bought out the other syndicate banks' debt before selling Church on to Beazer for £36m. Church continued to be run separately within the Beazer Group and, on the latter's acquisition by Persimmon, it was the only part of the organisation to retain its separate identity.

[5] Unattributed city quote in *Building*, 24th Feb. 1989.
[6] *PHA* 1991.
[7] *Building*, 9th Nov. 1990.

CLARKE HOMES
Peak units: 1610 (1988)

Clarke Homes, based at Barton-under-Needwood in Staffordshire, was formed in 1959 by Stan Clarke to carry on his general contracting business. It later became the main housing arm of Balfour Beatty before being sold on to Westbury Homes. Clarke left technical college aged 16, to begin a plumbing apprenticeship, after which he started his own plumbing business. Having saved £125, he bought an acre of farm land, obtained planning permission and sold it for £650.[1] Early capital for the housebuilding business also came from Stan Clarke's brother-in-law, Jim Leavesley, who became a minority shareholder and deputy Chairman. Stan Clarke's early success was based on the acquisition of 'white land.' 'His skill was land assembly. He did some absolutely cracking deals. He bought a lot of land near Burton-on-Trent when it was agricultural and got it through the planning system. That was his strength.'[2]

By the beginning of the 1970s, Clarke was building around 300 houses a year, earning profits of around £100,000 rising to £360,000 in 1973, the top of the housing market. Although profits fell sharply in 1974, no provisions against land values were necessary. In that year, Derek Johnson was made Managing Director of the housing companies. By then, Clarke was also active in commercial property schemes, part of the business that was eventually to emerge as the quoted, and highly successful, St Modwen Properties.

During the 1970s, Clarke Homes 'followed the motorways'[3] expanding through the midlands and into the south, where an office was established at Winchester. Ron Cox had joined after the failure of Greaves, and was able to negotiate a number of southern sites from the receiver. At the end of the 1970s Maurice Payne was appointed group Managing Director, after 10 years with the group. Housing was split into midlands and southern divisions, with four subsidiaries each and Cox was appointed Managing Director of the southern division. In 1980, profits fell from a near £1 million to only £200,000, largely a result of losses in a couple of the midlands subsidiaries; Johnson retired due to ill health and Tony Greasley was appointed Managing Director of the midlands companies. Thus, the group that ran Homes during the last six years of its independent life was Stan Clarke concentrating on land, Maurice Payne as group Managing Director, and Cox and Greasley acting as operational managing directors.

Clarke is sold to BICC

It was not until 1983 that profits recovered to their old peak. In the strong markets that followed, trading profits reached £3m on sales which had consistently averaged some 600-700 a year; trading margins, however, remained in single figures. By 1986, a flotation was under active consideration but it did not take place and Stan Clarke decided to seek an exit route via a trade sale. BICC, through its Balfour Beatty construction subsidiary, had recently diversified into private housing and was looking to enlarge its existing operation. In September 1987 BICC bought Clarke Homes for £51m; Clarke's pre-tax profits in the year to November 1987 were a record £5.6m.

Balfour Beatty was the construction arm of BICC, or British Insulated Callender's Cables as it once was. Back in 1949, BICC had consolidated the long established contract departments of the various companies of the group into one unit. In 1969, BICC acquired Balfour Beatty, a construction company formed in 1909 by George Balfour and Andrew Beatty. Balfour Beatty remained a specialist construction

---

[1] *Daily Telegraph*, 20th Sep. 2004.
[2] Interview with Paul Pedley, Aug. 2000.
[3] *Housebuilder*, May 1987.

company until the 1980s when it began to explore the private housing market, somewhat tentatively to start with: 'they started playing with housing back in 1982.'[4]

The serious commitment came in 1986 when **Balfour Beatty Homes** was created. It started from scratch in Nottingham selling around 100 houses in its first year building up to more than 300 units in the east midlands in 1988. In addition to Nottingham it opened offices in Paisley and Leatherhead. Early in 1987, shortly before the Clarke acquisition, Balfour Beatty bought the Derbyshire housebuilder David M Adams; father and son resigned on the acquisition. Adams had turnover of under £5m on acquisition and profits in excess of £300,000. Together, they gave Balfour Beatty an annualised rate of house sales of around 700 which was then doubled by the acquisition of Clarke Homes. Stan Clarke had not joined the enlarged group, staying with his property and racecourse interests; Ron Cox was appointed Managing Director of Balfour Beatty Homes.

And sold to Westbury

In 1988, completions reached a record 1610 but from then on the size of the business was substantially reduced. By 1991, unit sales were down to 1000 and to only 500 by the mid 1990s. No financial information was ever published but BICC's housing was widely understood to have been a heavy loss maker, particularly the Balfour Beatty joint ventures in London with property companies. In a process of rationalisation within BICC, Balfour Beatty Homes was renamed Clarke Homes and then sold to Westbury in December 1995 for £61m; the acquisition document showed that Clarke Homes had been loss-making for the previous three years

[4] Ibid, Oct. 1987.

COMBEN HOMES
Peak units: 2064 (1979)

Comben and Wakeling was one of the larger London housebuilders in the inter-war period but its post-war history never matched its earlier success until the reverse takeover of the private Carlton Homes injected fresh management and took Comben into the industry's top ten. There was, not surprisingly, a Mr Comben and a Mr Wakeling; James White Comben (1864–1931) and his brother in law, William Henry Wakeling (1874–1951). James Comben's family had for generations been involved with quarrying of Portland stone and he began his career with a five-year master mason apprenticeship before moving to London where he worked as a mason on the large Italianate villas being built in Fulham. According to Stanley Comben, James 'saw the waste on the jobs and studied site management',[1] perhaps the first recorded case of a housebuilder studying his subject before practising it. James Comben also developed an insurance agency and, as building work became scarce at the end of the 1880s, started a provisioning business. This increased to three shops, one of which was run by his brother-in-law Will Wakeling, a carpenter by trade. He must have been reasonably successful as a tradesman for, around the turn of the century, 'Frequently passing a row of unsold speculative houses, he negotiated with the builder, bought them, plastered and decorated one as a show house and sold the lot.'[2] This developed into a partnership in 1904 between James Comben and the builder, with the latter building exclusively for the former.

Houses were built in Richmond for the working class containing, unusually, fitted sinks and baths. When these sold successfully, James Comben and now Will Wakeling as well, 'cycled around the new areas of Golders Green, Worcester Park and Wembley' looking for suitable building land, and a site was chosen in the Harrow Road (the Stanley Park Estate) Wembley.[3] It was that step in 1904 that marked the start of the Comben and Wakeling partnership, based on two of the fundamental building skills and James Comben's proven commercial and entrepreneurial ability. One assumes that the capital was more likely to have come from Comben, 12 years the senior, but an unnamed wealthy friend bought the sites, his interest being the subsequent flow of ground rents. With the insurance agency being used to provide mortgages and the land being purchased by an independent financier, Comben & Wakeling had provided an early solution to the housebuilders' financing problems.

The London expansion

A steady expansion was concentrated on the Wembley area, taking advantage of the opening of new commuter railway stations. The largest single purchase of land was made early in 1914 – the Manor Farm Estate at Wembley Park which was only partly built when war broke out. After the war, the practice of selling houses on leasehold declined in favour of freehold sale and the private investor pulled out, seemingly precipitately, as 'Barclays Bank stepped in and saved the day for the partners.'[4] By then, the next generation was ready to join the firm. After serving in the Royal Naval Air Service, Horace Comben qualified as a civil engineer at London University, going on to lead the laboratory research at the newly formed Building Research Station. He was persuaded to join the family firm in 1924 along with his cousin Eric Wakeling. That led to the incorporation of the previous partnership with the older generation sharing two–thirds of the business and the two sons sharing the remaining third. Stanley Comben, the younger son and a chartered architect, joined the firm in 1932. Despite the new corporate structure, the founders retained the land in their ownership, using the proceeds to invest in houses to rent, backed by

---

[1] Comben, *Comben through the Ages*.

[2] Ibid.

[3] Ibid.

[4] Ibid.

bank finance; only gradually did the building firm begin to buy land in its own right. In a later aside, Horace Comben revealed that they recouped the whole of the purchase price of some of the estates by stripping and selling the turf.

Still confining itself to its local area, output steadily increased, reaching 500 a year by 1931, the year that James Comben died By the early 1930s the firm had built some 6000 houses in the Wembley area. Geographic diversification then consisted of developing estates no further away than Eastcote, Hatch End, Finchley and Pinner, and by 1938 it had extended its operations to cover most of North London; it was probably building at an annual rate of 600. During the Second World War, the company built airfields – 12 in East Anglia at one time – air raid shelters and engaged in war damage repair work. Contracting continued after the war, including the running track for the Olympic Games, banks, churches and a bus station. From 1951, estate development gradually resumed: the number of houses increased steadily from 88 in 1953 to 493 in 1962 – respectable but no more than had been achieved twenty years previously. Green belt restrictions in the London area had also encouraged the company to look further afield to the homes counties, East Anglia, Hampshire, Dorset and south midlands.

In March 1964, the company floated on the Stock Exchange. Horace and Stanley Comben, aged 67 and 55 respectively, led the Board, and there were representatives of the next Comben generation on the staff. Housebuilding turnover was around £2m and stayed so for the rest of the decade. Contracting turnover, in contrast, was expanding rapidly, though not profitably. Group profits fell in almost every year after flotation and substantial losses on one contract in 1969 caused a group loss. It was then just a question of who bought the company. At the end of 1970 there were two bid approaches – Galliford Estates, offering 8s–6d a share, and Carlton Industries, offering 7s–6d. However, Carlton had the advantage of 51% irrevocable acceptances and Comben and Wakeling became an 80%-owned part of the London and Merchant Securities group of companies. Comben retained its stock exchange quotation and, following the subsequent merger with Carlton Homes, the 20% minority was increased to 30%.

Leon Roydon and Carlton Homes

The history of Carlton and its wider involvement within London Merchant Securities now becomes relevant. It involves two cousins, Leon Roydon and Max (later Lord) Rayne, whose grandfather, then Rubinstein, had been part of the Russian Jewish emigration in the late nineteenth century, trekking across Europe until finally reaching England. Their sons changed their names, one to Rayne, the other Roydon but it was the next generation which made its name in the property world. Max Rayne, then aged 34, did his first big property deal in 1952 making an £850,000 profit on a £2m office development in Wigmore St. He went on to build one of the larger post-war property empires and became a leading figure in the arts world. His role in the Carlton story emerges later.

Leon Roydon was born in 1923 in East London. During the blitz the family moved its tailoring business to the Bristol area (they made uniforms for the army in the war, went into manufacturing and then retailing). After Grammar School he began to train for the medical profession but 'I was too squeamish' and war time army service followed instead.[5] After the war, Leon Roydon went into his father's business but did not like it. His own choice was house conversion work. 'You could buy these old Victorian houses, beautiful houses, usually about four stories high, absolutely made for conversion; you could pick up houses for very little money and therefore could enter this business without a lot of capital.' Asked if he had any experience: 'No, not at all – well, one learns! I was involved in it. I didn't employ contractors, I employed people. And worked on it that way.' Capital came from his father and the banks: 'in those days,

5 Interview with Leon Roydon, Oct. 1998.

money was very cheap and banks were not terribly difficult.'[6]

The progression from renovation to new build came at the end of the 1950s when, with Max Rayne's help, he bought a disused greyhound racetrack in the Knowle district of Bristol, building the best part of 300 houses over a three year period. With that initial success, Max Rayne suggested expanding the business and Carlton Homes was formed in 1961, London Merchant Securities taking 51% to Leon Roydon's 49%. Why only 49%? 'Let us say that in hindsight it was probably not one of my best decisions but basically Max felt that as a public company they ought to have nominal control and, during the period that we ran the 49–51 company, things went very smoothly.'[7] By the end of the 1960s Carlton Homes was building around 300 units a year, mainly in the south-west region; and through the acquisition of Ames & Peacock (itself a merger of W Ames and CA Peacock), another 200 a year in East Anglia. Its holding company, Carlton Investments, also acquired some other construction interests in the form of Bristol Plant Hire and Gardiner builders' merchants.

Formation of Carlton Industries

At the same time as London Merchant Securities was developing its commercial property empire, it was also spreading its net more widely into industrial ventures. These included Sanitas pharmaceuticals, Rimmel cosmetics, Invergordon Distillers and Haddon batteries. They were not uniformly successful and, by the end of the 1960s, LMS had decided to return to the simplicity of commercial property and sought a way out of its industrial empire. The solution was to group them into a new holding company, to be called Carlton Industries, under the direction of Leon Roydon; the jointly owned Carlton Homes was then fully acquired. LMS retained 72% of Carlton Industries, Leon Roydon held a significant minority stake, and the remainder was in public hands. Thus, in 1970, Carlton Homes became one of a number of businesses in an industrial conglomerate whose majority shareholding was controlled by Max Rayne's London Merchant Securities and whose rationale was the extrication of LMS from industrial investments it no longer wanted.

With Leon Roydon's wider involvement, management control of Carlton Homes passed to his son, Terry Roydon – prepared for his role by a degree in Estate Management and a Pittsburgh MBA. He joined Carlton Homes in 1968 aged 22 and was made Managing Director the following year. Despite the relevance of his academic qualifications, it was an early age to take control. Leon Roydon: 'I suppose nepotism is something but he was brought up in the atmosphere of housebuilding – mealtime was always talking business.'[8] By the time of the Carlton Industries consolidation, turnover at Carlton Homes had reached £4m and profits approached the half million pound level. Terry Roydon's plan was to create a national housebuilding company, a strategy which had the support of both the Carlton and LMS boards: 'We strongly believe that within a few years Carlton Homes will be the second biggest housebuilder in England.'[9] The most substantial move in this plan was the acquisition of Comben and Wakeling, just recovering from its contracting losses, which is where we pick up the story again. The merger of the two businesses gave geographical coverage across the south of England and building at a rate of around 1000 houses a year. The next step was in 1972 with the £600,000 acquisition of Ryedale which built around 300 houses a year in Yorkshire and Scotland. (Ryedale was owned by Duncan Davidson who went on to found Persimmon). Comben's output reached 1370 in 1973 and the following year turnover reached £13m and profits a record £3.3m.

---

[6] Ibid.

[7] Ibid.

[8] Ibid.

[9] Carlton Homes Newsletter, Dec. 1969.

In addition to moving north, Comben had also begun to develop in Europe – subsidiaries were formed in France and Portugal in 1972. The Portuguese operation was based on a belief that there would be a growth in resort areas and that proved successful. In France, Comben tried to play the role of a conventional housebuilder, developing in the Paris area, and was never able to make adequate returns – though it never lost money. 'There was a big change going on in the French housing market at the time, going towards more developments than one-offs. It seemed a wonderful opportunity to give English estate development skills, which didn't exist very much in Paris at that time. We never lost money in France. What got us was that we could never get our hands on sufficient land to make a go of it.'[10] However, it was in the UK that the greatest ambitions lay as the management built up a national organisation suitable for 2500–3000 a year – at which point the crash came. Comben avoided losses; the business was restructured to build around 1000 houses a year, and profits hovered around the million pound level. Two small deals were done at the end of 1976 – the purchase of the rump of Greaves from the receivers, and of Downglade, a South Wales company selling around 200 houses a year, owned by Alf Gooding (of Catnic fame).

Hawker takes control

In 1978, Hawker Siddeley purchased 52% of Carlton Industries' shares, largely from London Merchant Securities; with an obligation to make a second bid in 1981. Max Rayne had thus achieved his objective of divesting his non–property interests. The attraction to Hawker lay in Carlton's battery business and Hawker, in turn would dispose of businesses it regarded as peripheral. After the second bid, Leon Roydon emigrated to the West Indies where he became 'the father of Anguillan tourism' by developing its Malliouhana hotel – though he remained non–executive Chairman of Comben. Hawker was supportive of Comben's long term strategy and almost immediately after it had taken control, Comben bought Orme Group; the issue of shares reduced Hawker's stake to just below 50%. Orme had been formed in 1970 by two entrepreneurs, Whitfield and Tanner, who proceeded to build up a housebuilding company by acquisition. Orme included such names as Bruce Fletcher, (Leicester) Tudor Jenkins, (South Wales) and Norman Ashton; it was building around 1000 houses a year with a land bank of 6000 plots. The contact with Orme had been Bram Davies, Tudor Jenkins' old partner. On leaving Jenkins after its takeover by Orme, Davies had formed a joint venture with Comben in South Wales, and later suggested Orme as a suitable target for Comben. After the highly controversial involvement of St Piran, Comben eventually succeeded with its bid. This immediately took Comben's production to over 2000 units in 1979 making it the fifth largest housebuilder in the country, though more difficult trading conditions and a consolidation of the land bank subsequently took output down to around 1500 a year.

Sold to Trafalgar House

Following the Orme acquisition, Comben began building in Texas but its overseas profits were largely derived from Portugal. In 1983, Comben made an agreed £8.3m bid for the Midlands developer, William Whittingham, selling the latter's photographic processing subsidiary for £3.2m. That was to be Comben's last corporate move. Although Hawker Siddeley had been supportive of the Comben management, it was always viewed as a potential seller of the business. When Trafalgar House approached Hawker in August 1984, the controlling interest was sold without reference to the Comben Board and the full takeover, valuing the Company at £44m, was then a fait accompli.

---

[10] Interview with Terry Roydon, Jan. 2000.

COSTAIN HOMES
Peak units: 2212 (1987)

The business was founded by Richard Costain (1839-1902). He was a joiner who moved in 1865 from the family farm in Colby, Isle of Man, together with his future brother-in-law, Richard Kneen, to Liverpool where they set up in partnership as a local jobbing builder. The partnership lasted for 22 years before Richard Kneen launched out on his own in 1888: Richard Costain was then joined by three of his five sons, Richard Arthur, William Percy and John Kneen Costain. Between Richard Costain's death and the First War, the sons spread into north Wales and the Isle of Man as well as Lancashire. The firm built some of the first blocks of artisans flats in Liverpool and during the war built houses for steel workers in Redcar and for munitions workers in South Wales. Speculative housebuilding started in Liverpool after the First War, the rationale being a means of counterbalancing fluctuations in the local authority workload: 'Progressive firms were anxious to offer continuity of employment...but when engaged to work for a local authority continuity...had to depend on successful tendering...To overcome this problem, Costain decided to purchase land and to develop their own estates'[1]

From Liverpool to London
As building sites became scarcer in Liverpool, the Costains, like others, were drawn to the south east. William Costain moved south in 1922; his initial intention was to buy a plot for himself on land owned by Walton Heath Land but seeing their lack of progress, William Costain decided to buy the Walton Heath company, supported by the Liverpool timber merchant, Trevor Roberts. Indeed, the centenary edition of the *Bulletin* states that 'the directors acquired various interests in estates around London in which they were joined by Lord Clwyd and his brother D Trevor Roberts'; both men were on the Costain Board and it seems likely that they provided financial assistance for the expansion of Costain's housing. Costain's first large London estate at Kingswood was started in 1923 and Richard Costain & Sons Limited was formed; the Liverpool company remained a separate entity. In contrast to other large estate developers, the houses were expensive, ranging up to £4000. Kingswood was followed by other estates in and around the Croydon area – at Selsdon (1925), Addington (1925), Caterham (1926), Croham Heights (1927), 'Even when thick fog abounds in Croydon or the City, Croham Heights is usually bathed in sunshine',[2] and one estate north of the Thames at Brent Water (1927).

William died in 1929 aged 55; the other two brothers remained in the north and William's eldest son, Richard Rylands Costain (1902-1966), then aged 27 and acting as a general foreman on the Brent Water Estate, became manager of the London branch. He had been educated at Merchant Taylors' School, Crosby and then Rydal School in Colwyn Bay which did not stop him training as a bricklayer and joiner. After a short architectural course in Rome he joined the firm in 1920. He was supported by George Peachey, who had developed the early Liverpool houses and was a major influence on the business in the 1930s. William's younger son Albert left the College of Estate Management where he was training to be a quantity surveyor and tool over at Brent Water, later becoming director of production. Under R.R. Costain, the estates spread further around London and by the 1930s included ones for 1400 houses at Sudbury, 1600 at Dagenham and the largest of them all, for 7500 houses at South Hornchurch, started in 1934. Of course, the building for which Costain will always be remembered is Dolphin Square. In 1933 Richard Costain bought seven acres of land on the Embankment at Pimlico from an American, Frederick French. The block of 1250 serviced flats was finished in October 1937, but war and rent restrictions reduced the profitability of the project and in 1959 the flats were sold to Maxwell Joseph for £2.5m, a

[1] Costain, *Reflections*, pp.24-5.
[2] Contemporary sales brochure.

profit to the company of £1m. Costain's London housebuilding business diversified into construction in the 1930s. Bertie Bonn, a distant cousin by marriage, worked as a civil engineer responsible for the estate roads; he then started to bid for civil engineering jobs in the south east. Projects included a Glaxo laboratory (built on Sudbury Hill land), blocks of flats and a sewage works at Beckton (needed for the Elm Park estate).

Flotation in 1933

In April 1933, Richard Costain floated on the stock exchange, the new company incorporating the London assets of Richard Costain and the Walton Heath Land Company, but not the Liverpool business. The largest individual shareholder was John Kneen Costain, one of the original Richard Costain's three sons, and still living at Blundellsands. Profits in 1932 were recorded as £90,000, down from £103,000 in 1929, but the only unit numbers stated that upwards of 4000 houses had been sold 'in the immediate vicinity of London.' This suggests a rate of over 500 a year, although by the flotation it was probably in excess of this. Geoff Wheatcroft, who joined in 1956, estimates that from his knowledge of the pre-war sites, and the contemporary comments of colleagues, the annual sales from the early 1930s probably exceeded 1000, though not by a significant margin. Following the flotation, Costain recruited a qualified civil engineer with overseas experience – Lawrence Beck.. Costain won one of the sections on the Trans-Iranian Railway but 'It only became evident after the award of the contract that this was one of the most difficult sections'[3] However, it did lead on to work on Abadan township for BP from 1938 and Costain had established its middle east credentials long before its post-war rivals, Laing, Taylor Woodrow and Wimpey. Unfortunately, group finances were stretched by the losses on the Trans-Iranian Railway, Beckton and the costs of Dolphin Square. Barclays declined to renew the overdraft facilities and Costain switched to Lloyds; Costain even had to suffer an investigation of its finances by Peat Marwick.

During World War II, Costain carried out extensive military work. 'There seems to be no doubt that the war set the company on its feet in the contracting business and that but for the contracts carried out in the mid-thirties the company would not have been on the War Office list. For the greater part of the war, Richard Costain was at the Ministry of Works as Director of Emergency Works. The Company was engaged primarily in the construction of airfields….They also built ordnance factories and finally they were the first to complete their quota of twelve Mulberry units…By the end of the war they were thoroughly experienced contractors and, together with other major contractors, had built up a strong position in the latest contracting plant.'[4]

In 1945 R.R. Costain became Chairman as well as Managing Director with Albert as joint Managing Director; John Whiter, Albert's brother-in-law, became an additional Managing Director in the 1950s. It was during this period that the first attempt was made to delegate authority outside the family. Fred Catherwood, later Director General of NEDC and Chief Executive of John Laing, had joined Costain in 1954 as Secretary and financial controller. Catherwood gave his interpretation of his appointment: 'The Company, though public, was family-run by two brothers and two brothers-in-law. It was overtrading and at the point where it needed professional management. In this delicate transition, the thought of someone younger who would not be inclined to throw his weight around too much, evidently appealed to Dick Costain and he offered me the job at twice my current salary.'[5] The following year, aged 30, Catherwood was appointed Chief Executive but his tenure was not long. 'Fred Catherwood was very influential; he stirred things up and diagnosed Costain's problems. Richard Costain believed in him and

[3] Costain, *Reflections*.

[4] Catherwood, 'Development and Organisation of Richard Costain Ltd', p.274.

[5] Catherwood, *At the Cutting Edge*, p.52.

made him Chief Executive to implement the recommendations. However, he couldn't do it and only stayed three or four years.'[6]

In the face of building controls at home and a weak economy, Costain was determined to move overseas, and by 1957 as much as 60% of group turnover was overseas. There was little attempt made to restart private development until the mid 1950s. Costain was more active in the post-war drive for system-built housing for local authorities and the company built nearly 30,000 pre-fabricated houses. There was also an early move into housing overseas. In contrast, there was no mention of UK housebuilding until the 1955 report: 'We have purchased a number of estates on which to build houses for sale and this has made a small contribution to your company's activities during the year.' Like John Laing, Costain appeared reluctant to have its name associated with speculative housing; instead, it was carried out by the Dolphin Development Co. which had been incorporated in 1954; its name was not changed to Richard Costain Homes until 1966.

Acquisition of Rostance

When speculative housing did begin it was on a modest scale. Richard Costain had recruited Eric Adams, the General Manager of Harlow Development Corporation who in turn brought in Les Flowers, a finance man from the local authority world, who later took over from Adams as Managing Director. In a *Housebuilder* interview in 1992, Geoff Wheatcroft remembered Costain selling 150 units a year in 1956 with the headquarters still in Dolphin Square. Although volumes stayed around that level, the sites were spread widely including Teeside, Exeter, Birmingham, Kent and South Wales, and it was not a business that had strong direction. Around 1960 the Costain Board decided to expand housing through acquisition. In 1961, Costain bought Moorhouse & Barker of Thornaby, Yorkshire, an old established firm also building around 150 houses a year. However, the key acquisition was the following year – the **Rostance Group** of Nottingham. This provided operational management more familiar with the housing market; among others, it brought in Tony Greasley (later the Homes Managing Director) and Roy Cresswell, later construction director.

Rostance had been formed immediately after the war by Alf Rostance who had been a carpenter with Simms Son and Cooke. So the story goes, Alf Rostance won a large sum of money on dog racing in Nottingham and, with that financial backing, started building council houses for the local authority. By the time Costain was looking for acquisitions, Rostance was building around 150 speculative houses a year and looking to leave the business. Two other small acquisitions were CH Chaston of Clacton, Essex in 1964; and The Summerley Estates Ltd of Bognor Regis. In 1966, the five housebuilding companies were amalgamated into one, under the new Richard Costain Homes name, with the Rostance office in Nottingham being the new Homes head office. In 1969 Costain bought R Fielding and Son of Blackpool, which had been building around 300 houses a year, and it was integrated with the existing Costain developments in Lancashire and Cheshire; its office was closed and a new regional office opened at Preston. By the late 1960s to early 1970s, Costain Homes was probably building around 1000 houses a year. There were two more acquisitions before the housing recession, this time in the south. In 1970/71 Costain bought Smith & Lacey based at Corsham in the south west; the two principals were Frank Smith and Barrie Howell, and the company was building around 200 units a year. This was followed in 1973 by Parkland Homes of Finchley, whose output was also around 200 a year. Parkland was owned by Ben and Ike Bobroff, with their sons Paul (later Chairman of Tottenham Football Club) and Robert. Both the offices in Corsham and Finchley became regional offices.

The expansion of speculative housing was being undertaken within a group that was undergoing significant

[6] Interview with Peter Costain, Nov. 2001.

change. During the 1960s, the family hold on the business weakened. Serious illness had kept Richard Costain away from the firm for lengthy periods while Albert Costain was spending an increasing amount of time on his political career (he had been elected MP for Folkestone and Hythe in 1959). In 1966 Richard Costain died; the natural succession would have been Albert but he stood down as joint Managing Director to become non-executive Chairman. 'The brothers were very different in personality. Father would have been happy being a Methodist minister in the East End and he was more interested in politics by this time.'[7] Costain went outside the Group for the second time, appointing Sir Robert Taylor, previously of Standard Bank and a Rhodesian civil servant, as Chief Executive, a position he held until 1969. However, the group profit performance in the 1960s was not impressive and the management consultant McKinsey was brought in to review the group's strategy. Taylor had reached retirement age and he was replaced by John Sowden; a civil engineer who had joined Costain in 1947 and worked extensively overseas.

Hanson, Jim Slater and Al-Fayed

Despite the reorganisation and a substantial profits increase in 1970, Costain was coming under considerable pressure from external shareholders. After the build-up of strategic holdings, Hanson Trust launched a hostile takeover bid in February 1972. Although that failed, Jim Slater joined the Board in 1973 holding 21% of the equity. In 1975 he sold his shares to 'undisclosed Arab buyers' and Mohammed Al-Fayed was appointed a director. The relevance of this to Costain Homes was the parent company's wish to show a strong balance sheet and Greasley remembers being instructed by Sowden to sell land; as a result, Homes had little good land to build on in the boom of the early 1970s, doing little more than breakeven in 1971 and 1972.[8] There was just the one good trading result in 1973 before the recession. At that critical point in the housing market, Greasley took over as Homes Managing Director; Flowers retired in 1976 and then Greasley himself resigned later that year to join David Wilson; he was succeeded by Ian Rutherford, previously in charge of David Charles' construction division. For the rest of that decade, speculative housing lay in the shadow of the hugely successful international contracting business. 'Homes was rather neglected.'[9]

The increased revenues accruing to the oil states led to a middle-east construction boom, and Costain exploited the opportunities to the full, particularly in the Emirates. Group turnover rose from £95m in 1969 to over £500m in 1979 and profits from little more than £1m to £47m. When such profitable contracts could be obtained in the middle east, perhaps it was inevitable that Costain Homes, operating in the difficult markets of the 1970s, would take second place. In the aftermath of the recession, UK housing numbers were substantially reduced, down to around 300-400 on sites scattered around the country. In 1977 Costain Homes withdrew from the north of England to concentrate on the midlands, south west and the home counties; the head office was moved from Nottingham to Marlow. Although there had been a partial recovery in profits to around £1m in 1979, by 1981 Costain Homes was losing money again.

The end of the 1970s saw further changes at the top. As John Sowden reached retirement age, Tyrell Wyatt was appointed Executive Chairman in 1980. A quietly spoken, contemplative individual, Wyatt had joined Costain in 1954, had been responsible for the international expansion in the 1970s, and was appointed group Chief Executive in 1975. One of his first moves as Chairman was to bring a reluctant Peter Costain (Albert's son) back from Australia where he had been successfully running the mining-dominated business, to become group Chief Executive. Recognising that middle-east contracting profits would inevitably reduce, Wyatt set about securing new streams of income. Cash balances of over £100m

[7] Interview Peter Costain.
[8] Interview with Tony Greasley, May 2001.
[9] Interview with John Wells, Aug. 2001.

were redeployed into coal mining, housing and property, and five-year forecasts of doubled turnover and profits were offered to those who enquired.

Speculative housing expanded again

Brian Hewitt was recruited from Davis Estates in 1981 to be Managing Director of Costain Homes. UK sales rose from 400 in 1982 to 2200 in 1987, a phenomenal rate of growth in just a five year period; the medium term target was 3000. UK housing profits recovered rapidly though at £8m, the return on £163m of turnover was low by industry standards. As well as UK housing, Costain was also developing in Spain, Canada, California, Australia and, through a joint venture, in Germany. Although unit sales fell in 1988, profits doubled to £17m but from then on the recession appeared to hit Costain quicker, and harder, than virtually any of the larger housebuilders. Unit sales fell from 1870 to under 700 and after provisions, a loss of £37m was recorded. Similar, if not greater, losses were made in each of the next three years and a total of £176m was lost by Costain Homes.

Ironically, an internal report in 1986 had predicted problems in the housing market and Costain reduced its land purchases with the effect that it was short of land at the peak of the market. 'With the market already heading for the severest recession anyone could remember, we were buying land. Some were very large and expensive sites bought through the open tender method and not all were capable of being brought on stream in a reasonable time. It could be argued that if you were buying land in this manner you were inevitably paying top price. In one particular case[10] the gap between first and second in the tender list was frightening.'[11] Hewitt was critical of the City's influence on strategy: 'Costain was very sensitive to City views and analysts were criticising the company because it had no land bank. We felt we were being pushed into building a land bank at the wrong time.'[12] Fear of hostile takeover was another stimulus to short term decision making. Peter Costain had a more strategic view of the land problem, reflecting on the place of a housebuilding business within a publicly-quoted contractor: at the bottom of the cycle there were usually other commitments for the funds and at the top of the cycle they would be short of land and have to buy it in at the wrong price.[13] However, it is hard to think of a stronger reason for losses of this magnitude other than poor land buying followed by forced sales.

And the collapse

Costain was also experiencing financial pressure elsewhere in the group. Commercial property had been increased following the acquisition of County & District in 1981 and the mining expanded by the purchase of deep coal mines in the USA, helping group profits to a new peak of £89m in 1988. In July 1989, just as its main markets were turning down, Costain spent $193m on the purchase of Pyro Energy, its US coal joint venture partner, pushing gearing up to virtually 100% of shareholders funds. Within three months of the purchase a fatal accident led to the closure of the mine for six months and it never again operated as profitably. The group pre-tax loss reached £92m in 1991 and £205m in 1992; debt was 400% of shareholders' funds. Asset disposals were inevitable and UK housing was one of a number. It had already been reduced in size (sales were down to 400 houses) to release capital and in July 1993, Costain Homes was sold to Redrow for £17m giving the latter company a ready-made southern division at the bottom of the cycle, plus substantial tax losses.

[10] An asbestos-contaminated Royal Navy site costing over £20m.
[11] Interview with Geoff Wheatcroft, July 2001.
[12] Interview with Brian Hewitt, Oct. 1998.
[13] Conversation with author 1991.

COUNTRYSIDE
Peak units: 2201 (1995)

The central characters behind the formation of the businesses which became the quoted Countryside Properties were Solomon 'Bob' Bobroff, Alan Cherry and Dudley Anderson; however, from the mid 1970s, the company was run by Alan Cherry alone and he has been regarded as synonymous with Countryside. Alan Cherry, born in 1933, had early ambitions to follow his brother into architecture. He was offered a job in the architects' department of Ilford Borough Council after leaving school at 15 but they were not able to take him for six months so he found a temporary job as junior clerk with a one-office firm of estate agents in the Ilford area, called C. Eves and Son. The work appealed; he stayed, and qualified as a chartered surveyor aged only 20. After national service, he returned to Eves but by 1958 determined to go his own way. With John Bairstow, the son of the Eves founder, he started the estate agency firm of Bairstow Eves & Son, and within a few years they had offices throughout Essex. As with many other estate agents, Cherry was drawn more directly into private housing. 'I had always enjoyed the nitty-gritty of surveying, valuing, selling houses. I think Bairstow Eves became the first estate agency in Britain to really adopt commercial marketing techniques to selling homes.'[1]

In 1959 the four Bairstow Eves partners formed Copthorn as a development business, with Alan Cherry running it on a part-time basis. In a comment reminiscent of Tom Baron's formation of Whelmar , Cherry said: 'I was the partner who specialised in planning and development and was getting frustrated giving advice to developer-clients and thought I would love to do this myself. On one occasion, I had a big client, Swift Brothers, and I tried to get them to buy a particularly good site — I would have bought that site, and that's what really led me into development.'[2]

Bobroff introduces Countryside

The different Copthorn companies were only building around 10 to 20 houses a year — though still making more than the estate agency at one point. This changed in 1965 when 'Bob' Bobroff wrote to Alan Cherry out of the blue, expressing an interest in residential development. Born in 1908, Bobroff was originally a furniture manufacturer in north London. After the war, he went into property development; Countryside Properties was formed in 1958 but run as a part-time business relative to his mainstream commercial property operation. Alan Cherry, as an estate agent, found him sites and project managed them. In 1968, three years after their first meeting, Countryside Properties formed two new subsidiaries, Countryside Developments with Cherry having a third of the equity and Countryside Properties (Southern) where Dudley Anderson had a quarter of the shares; Anderson was a building contractor who had been associated with the group since 1967.

The various housebuilding operations were consolidated: in 1970, Cherry and Anderson were bought out for shares in the Countryside parent company; next year, Copthorn Homes acquired the other companies then forming the Copthorn Group, and Countryside bought out Copthorn in exchange for shares. By 1972, the new grouping was selling 300 houses. Countryside was floated in the November of that year with Bobroff as Chairman and Cherry and Anderson joint Managing Directors. The objective of the flotation was to provide liquidity for the partners should it prove necessary but also to access additional capital to reduce gearing and expand the business. In the event, Countryside's public debut was not a success; with 83% being left with the underwriters, it was the start of Countryside being 'misunderstood' by City investors. 'Unfortunately, the stock market has never proven for me to be as rewarding as I think

---

[1] Interview with Alan Cherry, Jan 1999.
[2] Ibid.

it should have been in terms of the ability to raise money.'[3]

The recession hit Countryside hard. Profits collapsed in 1974 and, after provisions against land values, Countryside lost £1.3m in 1975 and passed the final dividend; the share price fell to a low of 7p. To make matters worse, Dudley Anderson's contracting business was facing its own problems (it was eventually forced into liquidation) and it was thought best for him to leave Countryside. Bobroff stood down as Chairman in 1974 and Alan Cherry was now in sole control. His experiences in the recession, combined with what seemed the reduced size of the new housing market, changed his approach to development. 'Once the housing shortage had been closed, I realised that we had to produce housing that is much better designed, that has qualities that the second-hand market does not offer. I suppose it was from then on that I began to concentrate our business on much better design standards. We became a design and marketing-led business.' Housing remained concentrated in the eastern home counties, particularly Essex with volumes ranging between 300 and 500 a year through the 1970s and most of the 1980s. Countryside was also expanding its commercial property division, which had completed its first commercial development in 1973; a series of attractive developments around the M25 followed. Although housing volumes did not increase significantly (the peak in 1989 was 600), a combination of price inflation, a move up-market and the commercial property activity took turnover from £16m in 1981 to £96m in 1988 while profits peaked a year later at £20m against £1.3m in 1981.

Chelmer takes Countryside into large sites

As well as changing its attitude to the quality and design of its end product, Countryside made another significant move in the 1970s. In 1970, Countryside paid £40,000 for an option to buy 127 acres in Chelmsford at market value. In 1974, the company was granted outline planning permission for a scheme to cover more than 250 acres with 3000 new homes, shopping centres, schools and industrial development. This was a large project for the Company's size: 'Most people thought we were too small to handle Chelmer Village… I suppose I have always had personal ambitions beyond the size of the company and I thought, "we can handle that if we structure the land purchase right". It was planned for up to 3000 homes and I was able to enter into contracts which controlled two-thirds of that. We did the master plan of the whole project.'[4] Chelmer was to provide the model for a string of other very large sites in the Essex area, plus Chatham Maritime, optioned or secured through the 1980s and 1990s. By the mid-1990s, Countryside had a land bank amounting to 10-15 years' sales.

Notwithstanding the experience of 1974, Countryside went into the 1990 recession with high gearing (debt of around twice equity at the peak) partly a product of financing its long land bank and partly because it had increasingly been retaining the commercial properties it had developed. Around £100m was raised by rights issues in 1991 and 1993 and by the disposal of the investment property portfolio in 1994. Operationally, Countryside's response to the pressures in speculative development was to increase its social housing: from a standing start in 1989, social housing units rose to 1600 in 1995, whereas speculative units remained the same at 600; the combined total of 2200 was substantially in excess of the previous peak. However, social housing was operated more as a contracting than a development business and problems with fixed-price contracts were a contributor to group losses in 1995. Countryside was slow to throw off the effects of the recession but gradually the larger sites began to make their contribution and speculative sales recovered strongly in the second half of the decade.

Managerial changes were also taking place in the 1990s as the next generation was introduced into the

3 Ibid.
4 Ibid.

highest offices of the company. Alan Cherry's two sons, Graham and Richard, had both graduated in land management at Reading and joined the graduate intake. Alan Cherry did not regard this as inevitable: 'I did not want my sons to come into this business. My sleeping partner, Bob Bobroff, said "why won't you let Graham come into the business?" It was the only time I have come near to having an argument with Bob. I've seen too many problems with fathers and sons. In the early days of Bairstow Eves, I had also specialised in receivership work and most of the businesses that I dealt with were builders and I saw a lot of this father son problem.'[5] Graham and Richard were appointed to the board in 1984 and 1986 respectively. In 1990 they were described as Managing Directors of commercial and residential and then group joint Managing Directors in 1994. Finally, Graham Cherry was appointed Chief Executive in 1996.

Housing units, 1989-2004

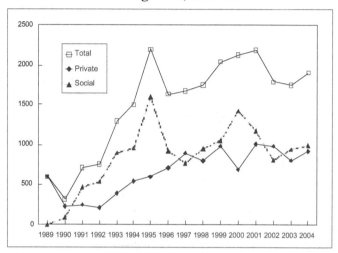

Countryside MBO

Perhaps the most obvious change in strategy that occurred in the 1990s, apart from the growth in social housing, was the geographical expansion: offices were opened in Bristol, Warrington and Middlesbrough. Alan Cherry: 'We felt we should hedge our exposure to the south east. Graham and Richard have some very bold ideas for the future and if they are to achieve them we have to be in more regions than one.'[6] Speculative housing volumes gradually increased and exceeded 1000 for the first time in 2001. However, private sales fell by 20% between 2001 and 2003. Although there was some recovery in 2004, sales were still below target and the firm issued what was described as 'its third negative trading statement in five months,'[7] a contrast to the more positive statements that were coming from its quoted peers. City analysts described Countryside's problems as 'largely self-generated.'[8] The month before, in September 2004, Countryside indicated that a preliminary approach had been received from Alan Cherry for an MBO. When the bid did come, it was rejected by the Rok construction group, controlling 22% of the equity. In January 2005 an increase in the MBO offer of 5p a share to 280p (£222m) secured agreement.

[5] Ibid.
[6] Ibid.
[7] *Building*, 22nd Oct. 2004.
[8] Ibid.

CREST HOMES
Peak units: 2524 (2004)

Crest Homes was formed in 1963 by Cambridge-educated Bryan Skinner, then aged 33, after spending six years in general management and four in management consultancy. With no roots in housebuilding, his introduction to the economics of the business came courtesy of Jim Farrer, an estate agent at Goodman and Mann in Weybridge. 'Bryan came in one day looking for a plot of land, which I found him. Then he asked me to find a builder for him. When the house was built he invited us to it for dinner as a thankyou. During the course of the evening he asked me what the house would be worth and when he realised the difference he asked if I could find him another plot.' Around 1962, Skinner had five such plots, each in a separate company, and it was one of these, Crest Developments, that was expanded into Crest Homes. The name Crest was a typical marketer's choice, based on the expectation that the coming launch of the American Crest toothpaste in the UK would familiarise the name for him.[1]

Skinner's ideas were different from most of the larger groups, in particular his concentration on marketing and not holding stocks of land. 'He was at ease with buying the land and selling the product but he said 'then we get this terrible bit in the middle called building' and he wanted to get on with that as soon as possible.'.[2] Tony Pidgley described Skinner as 'one of the most able men that I have ever met; well-balanced, and very good at motivating people. I think he lacked one ingredient and that was the judgement on people he employed. He was a financier I suppose.'[3] Skinner was the largest shareholder but he did not hold a controlling stake. Just behind him was Geoffrey Fox, a local accountant, who doubled as a part-time Finance Director; Alexander Grant, an insurance broker; and John Haines, a marketing consultant, all of whom contributed to the early finance of Crest. However, the largest single shareholder in the early years was Truscon (The Trussed Concrete Steel Company), for whom Skinner also acted as a consultant. Truscon had its own industrialised system for local authority housing and was interested in the private market; however, the relationship appeared short-lived for Truscon was not on the shareholders' register at the flotation. The working directors arrived in 1964. Jim Farrer joined as commercial manager (becoming a director in 1967) and Michael Wheaton, previously with Truscon, took charge of administration; Wheaton briefly became Managing Director of Crest Homes at the end of the 1960s.

Diversification strategy

In September 1963, a five-year growth target had been established: from a standing start, turnover in the year to July 1968 had grown to £1.1m with pre-tax profits of £200,000; Crest's annual rate of build was believed to be around 200 houses. The 1968 Prospectus emphasised the importance of marketing. 'In many respects Skinner was one of the first of the housing developers who did not come from the construction end of housing and who actually started with: "what does the public want to buy? where do they want to buy it? and what can they afford to pay?"'[4] Skinner had wider ambitions than just housebuilding. Apart from Crest, he founded two of the early conference organising business (later sold into the Slater Walker empire) and was a substantial shareholder in Brent Chemicals. But he also wanted to diversify Crest itself into leisure-related activities, and his definition of leisure was fairly wide ranging. In 1969, Crest bought En-Tout-Cas, the leading (though not well managed) name in tennis court

[1] Ironically, the launch was postponed some 10 years
[2] Interview with Jim Farrer, Jan 2001.
[3] Interview with Tony Pidgley, May 2001.
[4] Interview with Roger Lewis, July 2001.

construction, a move described as 'This week's most unusual bid.'[5]

However, before the next diversification move came a purchase that was more closely connected to the original housebuilding business – P & J Plant Hire and Haulage, bought in June 1971, a demolition and ground works contractor controlled by Tony Pidgley, later the founder of Berkeley. The business was not large (some £325,000 turnover in 1971) but Pidgley had been a sub-contractor for Crest, even sharing the same office building. Looking back on the occasion of his retirement, Jim Farrer recalled his first impressions: '[Tony was] a man we really ought to have on our side. If I ever asked him to do anything, he got it done. I knew that once we got him into our company, he would look after all our building sites and make them work.'[6] Indeed, Skinner put Pidgley in charge of Crest Homes' construction immediately, despite his lack of housebuilding experience: 'They said to me on the first day, "you're in charge of building". They just thought that I had the energy and the management skills to do it, I suppose.'[7]

Acquisition of Camper & Nicholson

In 1972, Crest effected a scheme of arrangement, creating Crest Securities to act as a holding company for three divisions: private housing, property development, and leisure. At the end of that 1972 financial year, Crest made its biggest acquisition to date, Camper & Nicholson, Britain's leading yacht maker (hence the name change to Crest Nicholson) which was expected to reduce housebuilding to only half of group profits. The links between Crest and Nicholson were tenuous. It was suggested that it was no more than 'they were both rather successful and both acquainted with stockbrokers Buckmaster and Moore, who effected the introduction…The logic of the merger lay in Skinner's unconventional view of the role of the housebuilder. He saw housing not as an adjunct of the building industry but of the leisure industry. In that light both houses and boats are places in which leisure time is spent.'[8] Roger Lewis, later Chief Executive, argued that in the late 1960s, early 1970s 'conglomerates were much more acceptable and Bryan believed that the common theme could be in the approach to business as opposed to the industry in which that business was engaged.'[9]

In the event, the recession meant that the property division made only £100,000 profit in 1974, before a £558,000 write-off and it was only doubled profits from the leisure division which gave profits respectability at a group level. Housing profits gradually recovered, though with leisure then taking over as the weak division it was not until 1977 that group profits showed a significant recovery. By that time, there had been a significant change in personnel. Bryan Skinner, although still acting as group Chief Executive, had become seriously ill in 1973 and moved to Jersey; when his health improved he took to visiting the group once or twice a week but never again became a full-time executive. David Donne, then a director of Steetley, Spear & Jackson, Bury & Masco, Williams Lea et al., had been appointed to the board in July 1973 and was made Chairman of Crest in the December. Towards the end of 1975 Tony Pidgley left to form his own housebuilding company (Berkeley Homes) and he was joined by Jim Farrer; other senior Crest Homes personnel were to follow. Roger Lewis took over as Chief Executive of the property division in December 1975. Lewis, a chartered accountant, had first been Crest's auditor and had then joined the company as an accountant in 1972, gaining some operational experience during Skinner's illness. Although Crest lost the men who went on to create a much larger company, and the full time contribution of its founder, there was no discernible impact on Crest itself where, with the help of a

5 *Building*, 9th May 1969.
6 *Housebuilder*, June 1992.
7 Interview Tony Pidgley.
8 *Building*, 1st Feb. 1974.
9 Interview Roger Lewis.

recovery in the housing market, profits reached a new peak of £2.8m in 1978.

Industrial acquisitions

Once Crest had restored profits to acceptable levels, Bryan Skinner wanted the acquisitions to recommence and in this he was supported by Peter Nicholson, the corporate director and Norman Tomlinson, who ran the leisure/industrial division. However, these acquisitions now bore little relation to the original leisure theme. They started with Lamson Engineering in 1975 and included Crofton, one of the country's largest designers and distributors of spectacle frames and lenses, in 1979; the Sharron jewellery wholesalers in 1980; and Greenwood Electronic in 1983. Despite these acquisitions, the leisure/industrial division was unable to raise its profits much above the £2m it had made in 1979; by this time, Crest Homes, though building fewer houses than at its 1973 peak, was contributing £7m profit to the group. Crest Homes had also started to develop geographically. The first regional office was opened at Westerham, Kent in 1977, followed the next year by Ferndown, Dorset, to serve the market from Hampshire to Wiltshire. In the early 1980s an office was opened at King's Langley to cover north London and the northern home counties.

In 1983, Bryan Skinner became terminally ill and Roger Lewis was appointed group Chief Executive. Slowly the emphasis swung back to what had been the core business, partly through the positive expansion of housing (unit sales doubled over three years) and partly by a reduction in the industrial division. At the end of 1985, Crest paid £25m for the west-country building firm **of CH Pearce**, then making pre-tax profits of £3.3m. Pearce was a second-generation general contractor that had diversified into speculative housing around 1960; Pearce was building around 200-250 houses a year by the time of the acquisition and its substantial land bank comprised most of the company's £22m net assets. CH Pearce had strategic advantages for Crest. It took housing into the south-west and the midlands and its three local housebuilders added to the coverage – Harris in Barnstaple, Mogford in Taunton and Cox near Stratford. Pearce also had its own commercial development which dovetailed with Crest Estates. Roger Lewis also thought that the construction business could be used to add value to Crest.

Housing units, 1981-2004

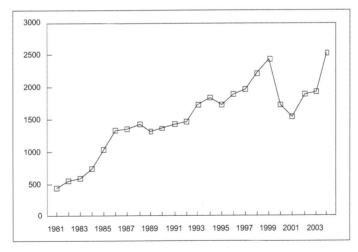

Followed by divestment

Fund raising in 1986 and again in 1987 stressed that the new money was going to increase both residential and the increasingly important commercial property development business; at the same time the industrial division was gradually being dismembered. 'We took the view that we had to become a more focused business. If I was frank about it, the recent businesses that we had bought where not performing very well. So we decided that stage one was to exit from those businesses which had absolutely no relation to a more focused business. The businesses which could be related in some way were those that had something to do with adding value to land, e.g. En-tout-Cas and Camper and Nicholson which by then was concentrating on marinas.'[10]

There had also been a change in Crest's long-standing policy of running the housing division on a minimal land bank, and substantial tracts of strategic land were acquired under option or similar arrangements. There were to be some spectacular successes. In April 1984 Crest Homes acquired a 400 acre farm in the Haydon sector on the outskirts of Swindon for a price 'only marginally in excess of agricultural value plus a further payment to be made on receipt of planning permission…We continue successfully to secure similar land for our longer term programmes by a variety of agreements with landowners.'[11] In all, some 1600 acres of 'white' land was acquired in the mid-1980s and Crest eventually obtained consent for some 5000-6000 units from the Haydon site.

Crest achieved a record £37m profit in 1988/89 before the collapse in the housing and property market reduced this to £8m in 1990. With the predominantly south-east orientation of the housing division, and a speculative commercial property development programme that was largely unlet, Crest had to make provisions of £40m in 1991, and the total pre-tax loss amounted to some £59m. Borrowings peaked at £120m and the banking covenant was breached. Roger Lewis resigned (shortly to join his old colleagues at Berkeley where he went on to become Chairman). Looking back, Roger Lewis thought that 'one of the things which we did wrong was that we bought a couple of big sites at Farnborough and Leatherhead. Until then we had always had a policy of remaining in smaller developments – in market towns which we understood. There were some pressures to buy large sites, and we bought a couple of big commercial sites at Farnborough and Leatherhead – it was a step too far to be honest.'[12]

Callcutt as Chief Executive

Lewis was succeeded by John Callcutt who had joined Crest as an assistant solicitor in 1973, becoming the first regional Managing Director of Crest Homes (at Westerham) in 1977. After a period as group solicitor from 1980, he was appointed Managing Director of Crest Homes in 1984. His first priority as Chief Executive was to reduce bank debt to manageable levels: 'We were in the banks' intensive care section and that period lasted for three or four years.'[13] The debt reduction was dependent on building out the commercial property portfolio and selling it, a task that was largely completed by the mid-1990s. By then, Crest could look to growing the business again. Volumes indeed rose from the 1400 or so that Crest had been doing through the recession to a peak of over 2400 in 1999, coincidentally, the first year that Crest had exceeded the 1989 record.

For this recovery phase, Callcutt believed that Crest needed a new, and more distinctive corporate strategy: He argued that Crest could not compete 'toe to toe with the volume builders' and they needed

---

[10] Interview Roger Lewis.
[11] Group Accounts, 1984.
[12] Interview Roger Lewis.
[13] Interview with John Callcutt, Feb. 2002.

to reposition the group. 'We had to revamp our marketing to get a premium price for a better quality build but quality went further than just build and service. By then, there were the first rumblings on environmental and sustainability concerns. We shifted our entire strategy to achieve and market sustainability. What Crest is emphasising is social sustainability – the community survives in the buildings you provide.'[14] Callcutt argued that this more comprehensive approach helped Crest move land through the planning process – the number of plots with permission increased over 70% between 1997 and 2001.

Where Crest appeared less successful in its strategy was in its regional expansion. Crest had pushed up into the midlands and into Yorkshire (with the purchase of Cowen Homes of Harrogate for £3m in 1994). However, there were losses in the midlands in 1995, the north-east division was sold to Miller Homes in 2001, and Crest withdrew from its embryonic north-west division. Despite this, the repositioning of Crest as an urban developer was feeding through to the profit and loss account. The number of units was reduced (down to 1530 by 2001) but they achieved significantly higher sales values: between 1998 and 2001 housing profits almost doubled. By 2002, Crest was once again increasing its output, achieving higher unit volumes through the large sites, and increasing its social housing target; in 2004 total units reached 2500, exceeding the 1999 peak for the first time.

As a postscript, Gerald Ronson's Heron had declared a holding of 3% in Crest in 2004, gradually increasing to 23% when, in 2005, it made an unsuccessful bid approach. In September 2005, John Callcutt's retired as Chief Executive moving to Deputy Chairman; his successor was Stephen Stone, a chartered architect previously the group's chief operating officer.

---

14 Interview John Callcutt.

CROUCH GROUP
Peak units: c.1000 (late 1930s)

Crouch was one of the more substantial London housebuilders before the war but it never regained its former status, eventually failing as non-family management increased the risk profile of the business. Geoffrey Crouch started building 'in a small way with bungalows' at Walton-on-Thames in 1928, followed by estates at Strawberry Hill and Sutton Common in 1929; he referred to a large number of sites, 'mostly south of the river' being acquired in the 1930s.[1] Like other large developers, Crouch built stations on the railway between Motspur Park and Chessington. Later, Crouch built in north London and the counties to the south of London. The business was incorporated as GT Crouch in 1931, the original directors being Geoffrey Thomas Crouch; his wife Mary; and James Rawlins. Two other companies were formed in the 1930s to hold houses for investment: Kingston Residential Properties in 1935 and Osterley Tudor Estates in 1939. The other name which was to prove significant was Ronald Aris, an accountant who helped form these companies.

No corporate records survive, but the number of estates under construction indicate Crouch was a significant operation. The only numerical references seen have been in *Housebuilder* after the war when it referred to a Kingston estate of 14 houses as 'extremely small for an organisation that used to build hundreds a year.'[2] In a later reference to the Westdene Estate Brighton, begun in 1936, Crouch was 'At that time selling something like 1000 houses a year on various estates in the South of England'[3] The evidence suggests that Geoffrey Crouch died during the war. Ronald Aris appeared on the Crouch Board in 1943 as Managing Director, only relinquishing that role in 1969. There is a service agreement dated 1945 whereby Aris exchanged his rights to commission for 25% of the enlarged equity and this document was signed by Mary Crouch and she continued to sign documents up to 1969.

After the war, the company compensated for the restrictions in private housing by forming an Irish company (which became a subsidiary in 1968) and moving into public sector housing in 1951; Crouch built over 5000 houses for Crawley New Town. As housing controls were relaxed, Crouch set itself a target of 500 houses a year and when the company was floated in 1969, it stated that it had built more than 6000 units since the early 1950s, equivalent to around 400 a year. In the year to March 1968, it recorded 529 sales in the UK and Ireland, including 107 sold to the Ministry of Defence suggesting that sales had built up rapidly to the target level and then remained constant.

John Crouch dies aged 41
By the flotation, John Crouch, the founder's son, had become Managing Director. Aged 37, he had qualified as a barrister, becoming a director in 1957, assistant Managing Director in 1962 and Managing Director on the flotation; Aris continued as Chairman. By the beginning of the 1970s Crouch was building around 500 houses a year, mainly in the home counties and then west through Hampshire to Devon and Herefordshire. In February 1973 John Crouch died suddenly, aged 41. Almost immediately the Stern Group, which had previously bought Dares Estates, approached the trustees to buy their controlling 46% interest. Despite being turned down twice, Metropolitan Property Holdings, a Stern company, made a public bid of £4m in the June; the bid was finally withdrawn in the September.

The new Managing Director was Francis Ryan who had joined the company in 1952 and had been the

---

[1] Jackson, *Semi-Detached London*, p.107.

[2] *Housebuilder*, Sept 1949.

[3] Ibid, Oct 1952.

land director prior to John Crouch's death. Aris resigned at the end of 1977, by then 68, to be replaced by WF Lyons. In March 1978, a private company controlled by Ronald Clempson acquired a substantial shareholding in Crouch Group. The following month Clempson was appointed a director and elected Chairman in place of Lyons. Clempson was previously a director of Buckley Investments, a private property company until resigning in 1978. He had been associated with building and property development since 1962 when he joined Westminster Property Group.

US disaster

Clempson had ambitions for Crouch, particularly in commercial property. In 1980 he actually proposed separating the housing and property and although the break never materialised, there was a determination to limit the importance of private housing: the 'Group's declared objective has been to reduce its dependence on the cyclical house-building and construction industries and to expand its industrial and commercial property interests.'[4] Those ambitions were not confined to this country: 'The goal is to establish Crouch as a major international property and construction group and we are now well down this path.'[5] The first US purchase was a 70,000 sq.ft. office block in New York for refurbishment and this was profitable. However, the 270-acre leisure and residential complex in Florida, purchased with a joint venture partner, rapidly proved a liability and, as is often the way with these joint ventures, the partner proved unwilling to fulfil its commitments. There were also losses on UK property investments. In December 1982 an interim pre-tax loss of £1.2m was declared, after exceptional losses of £1.4m in the development subsidiary, and the dividend was passed. Clempson was removed from the Chair to be replaced by Dante Campailla, a long standing director and the company's legal advisor. 'The directors of the company decided that Mr Clempson's policy of building up the property portfolio thus trying to reduce its dependence on building was the wrong one, hence his dismissal...Mr Bishop, group Managing Director, stated that despite the setback the group was basically sound.'[6]

In the event, the position continued to deteriorate, particularly in Florida, where the parent company had given guarantees. In 1983, the group declared a loss of £3.4m after a write-off of £3.7m. The losses were in both the UK and USA but particularly the latter. The Florida operation had been suspended and in California 'land has been bought which has been found to be valueless, and is being sold at a price less than it was purchased for.' In the UK, Crouch Homes actually made a modest profit. In January 1984, Peter Meyer, then Chairman of Federated Homes, led a rescue attempt, joining the Crouch Board as Chairman. Peter Meyer's private company sold Crouch 1.8m shares in Federated Housing, the consideration being the issue to the Meyer company of 1.8m shares in Crouch. Including shares bought from Clempson and on the open market, this gave Meyer a 43% holding in Crouch. At the same time, an agreement was struck with Federated whereby the latter would develop the bulk of Crouch Group's residential housing interests over a 15-month period. This proved insufficient to save Crouch and a receiver was appointed in July 1984; the estimated deficiency was £7m (revised down to £5m in 1988).

[4] Convertible Loan Issue Circular, May 1981.
[5] Group Accounts, 1982.
[6] Interim statement report in *Daily Telegraph*, 16th December 1982.

CROUDACE
Peak units: 1100 (1988)

Croudace was the creation of Jack Brotherton Ratcliffe, although corporately the company was named after the man who was his partner for the first five years. Jack Ratcliffe was reading physics at Oxford on the outbreak of the Second War, and joined the RAF in 1940 rising to squadron leader. His uncle had a successful chemicals business in Leeds and believed in making funds available to his wider family, giving Jack Ratcliffe the opportunity to select his business interest. After being demobbed in 1946 at the age of 26, Ratcliffe went to live in Kenley, Surrey, where his neighbour Oliver Croudace was doing war repair work, and Ratcliffe was attracted to the opportunities in the building industry. The two joined forces, forming Oliver R Croudace, presumably as the Croudace name was already known. Ratcliffe bought out his partner in 1950 and in 1951 Oliver Croudace took the estate agency and Ratcliffe the building business.

Speculative housebuilding started in 1954 as soon as controls were removed, with a site at Bletchingly, north of Redhill. Alan Wigley, a civil engineer from the local authority, was the first housing Managing Director. In the early days of the business, Jack Ratcliffe was involved in all aspects but his main interest lay in control systems and reporting, being particularly early in the use of computers. The first accounts on file are for 1971 and show turnover of £5m and profit of £470,000; given that the turnover included some general construction, the level of housing output was then relatively modest. Despite the severe recession in the housing market, Croudace achieved remarkable growth in the first half of the 1970s: between 1971 and 1975, turnover quadrupled and profits rose to a peak of £2.7m. A significant contribution to this growth was made by the construction division, then run by David Abel, a quantity surveyor who had become a director in 1968. Abel became a major influence on the Group, viewed at one point as potential Chief Executive before leaving in 1981.

Maybrook Properties
One of Abel's legacies was the purchase of Maybrook Properties, which he identified in 1976. Maybrook had a £21m property portfolio but was unable to service the interest payments. The vacant properties were gradually let, with enhancement to capital values, helping to raise Croudace's net assets from under £5m in 1975 to £23m in 1979. By then, contracting profits were in decline and group profits remained on a plateau through the late 1970s and early 1980s. While contracting profitability was declining, Croudace was steadily expanding its housing volumes, helped by its success in winning planning appeals on white land acquired in Kent. The first numbers on record for unit completions were 470 in 1979 but by 1983 these were approaching 800, and they reached a peak of 1200 in 1988 (of which some 100 were social housing). Croudace was expanding out of its traditional southern home counties market and now had northern, southern and western housing regions based at Bishops Stortford, Caterham and Newbury. Helped by the rise in house prices, profits rose rapidly reaching a peak of £23m in 1988, almost all of which came from private housing.

In 1982, Alan Wigley retired as housing Managing Director, to be succeeded by Tony Timms. Like his predecessor, Timms was a civil engineer, and had joined the engineering department of the housing company back in 1964. He was appointed to the main board in 1987, and in 1988 was made Chief Executive for all divisions except Maybrook. There were some £33m of write-downs between 1990 and 1992, partly residential (including the construction division's foray into bespoke housing as a means of finding replacement work), and partly from a relatively new commercial property joint venture. The scale of the business was sharply reduced; overheads were cut from £12m to under £6m and staff numbers fell from 800 to less than 300. Croudace withdrew from construction in 1992; the regional housing offices were closed and the priority was the reduction of debt which had stood at £45m in 1988. However, the Company had entered the recession with a very strong asset base – shareholder's funds had risen to £94m by 1989 and Croudace emerged from the recession still with net assets of £34m in 1994. This could have been the point when Croudace re-entered the land market. Twenty years earlier, Croudace had used its financial strength to buy property assets at a depressed price; this time it did not repeat the strategy with housing land. One assumes that the owner, by then in his early 70s, had become more risk averse.

Housing volumes decline

Housing volumes had fallen sharply by 1995 – down to 470 units, and 190 of those were social housing. In the latter half of the decade, output ranged between 500-600, compared with the pre-recession peak of 1200. Profits were, of course, steadily recovering as house prices rose and by the end of the decade the group recorded profits of £17m. In the financial year 2001, Jack Ratcliffe retired from the Board aged 81. His four children, two sons and two daughters, had all gone their independent ways. Although Tony Brotherton Ratcliffe, the eldest son, joined the Board as Chairman, it was in a non-executive role, inevitably raising a question over succession, so much a problem for others in the industry. However, from the early stages of the Company's development, Jack Ratcliffe had operated with a professional management team running the business and Tony Ratcliffe's appointment as Chairman suggests that this family/management partnership will continue.

CUSSINS PROPERTY
Peak units: 353 (1996)

Peter Cussins started Lemmington Estates in 1971, aged 22, having graduated in economics. The Cussins family had been involved in property development and contracting in the north east since the 1920s. His father had owned Cussins Contractors and his Uncle, Manny Cussins, had an extensive business career before starting Arncliffe Homes. Lemmington was controlled from the Channel Islands with Peter Cussins having a 65% entitlement; presumably the balance was other family interests. The Board comprised Peter Cussins, Philip Cussins (his father) and his brother-in-law (a Portuguese marine engineer and a director of BOAC). Although entirely separate from the family business, Peter Cussins was able to use staff from his father's Cussins Contractors which had been sold to Hawtin in 1968.

Lemmington suffered an early blow when, in 1973, it had to write £119,000 off land bought with local authority planning permission, later refused by the Department of Environment. It did better in coping with the 1974 recession, making good margins on housing turnover of under £1m. After ten years, Lemmington was building around 150 units a year with a commitment to the top end of the market: 'I see a continued need to adopt a flexible approach to the changing requirements of the housing market. For this reason we do not carry a large land bank…I have always believed that it is better to build high quality houses with good profit margins than feel bound to pursue high volume building with its attendant risks.'[1] By the late 1970s, Lemmington had also started commercial and industrial development property development, partly for sale and partly for retention as an investment portfolio.

In 1981, the Company was floated under the name of Cussins Property (although it was 1988 before Lemmington changed its name to Cussins Homes). The flotation was regarded as 'the prelude to a major growth period for the group'[2] and the residential operation was seen as a source of profit which could be reinvested in commercial property. Immediately after the flotation, Cussins was looking at commercial sites in the south and the 1983 accounts reported that most of the commercial development was now in the south east and the Company had opened a London office. The investment in property kept the housebuilding volumes at around 200 a year through most of the 1980s and profits remained flat at around £1.5m; however, there was a sharp increase in unit sales to 316 in 1988 and profits reached a record £2.7m

Diversification into south east ends in failure

A key element in Cussins' drive to the south-east was the formation in 1985 of a joint company with Throgmorton Trust, linked to the latter's subsidiary R. Green Properties; an associated share placing gave Throgmorton 11% of the Cussins equity. William Waites, senior partner of local solicitors, was appointed to the Board with the intention of playing a major role in the new company. Cussins Green Residential bought its first two sites in 1986 and by 1988 it had 15 sites under development in Sussex, Surrey and Bedfordshire. An additional £4m of equity had been raised in 1987 to support the retention of commercial property, the most important of which was the Aylesham Centre in Peckham, south London, completed the previous year.

When the recession came, profits in the traditional north-east business held up well; in 1990 Cussins Homes still made £2m profit but the over-expansion in the south east threatened the overall viability of the group. The group loss in 1990 totalled £8m: Cussins raised £3.6m through a rescue rights issue and

[1] Prospectus, 1981.
[2] Group accounts, 1981.

announced the separation of the Cussins Green property company. Inter alia, this involved paying £7.5m into the joint company, the sale of Aylesham and of the remaining investment property. Waites, who had become Homes Managing Director in 1987 was appointed group Managing Director, Peter Cussins remaining as Chairman.

A further £7m of losses were incurred in 1991 and 1992 as Cussins completed the withdrawal from the south but despite the severe pressure on group finances, Cussins managed to protect the long term viability of its northern business. Part of the rights issue money allowed Cussins to exercise its option (for £1.6m) to acquire a further 12 acres at its Ashington Farm development in Northumberland, where Cussins Homes had already built over 300 houses. Unit sales recovered from 1990's 200 to over 300 in 1994. The accounts were once again referring to the reinvestment of profits for expansion, this time on regional expansion closer to home. Cussins claimed a market share of 9% of the Tyneside region and the long term objective was given as 500 units from the region; the strategy was to expand by organic growth into adjoining regions, first by establishing a presence in Teesside and Yorkshire. By 1996, 20% of housing profits were coming from Teesside. Cussins was also increasing its involvement in urban regeneration and beginning to move back into commercial development, this time for sale.

Although profitability gradually increased, Cussins seemed unable to increase its volumes beyond the 300-350 range. By the end of the 1990s, Cussins was coming under pressure from institutional shareholders who were becoming increasingly disillusioned with small companies. In response, Peter Cussins raised the funds to finance an MBO but in November 1999, the Company received, and accepted, a higher £23m takeover from the Miller Group. Peter Cussins continued to develop in his own right and in 2001 joined forces with Richard Adamson (ex Leech) under the name of Regent Homes.

DARES ESTATES
Peak units: c.800 (late 1930s)

Dares was a long-established midlands housebuilder with four generations of the Dare family being represented on the Board. The company was possibly the largest housebuilder in the midlands before World War II but its relative importance declined in the post-war period. Ahead of the 1974 property collapse, the group came under the control of the Stern Group and although it escaped the direct effects of its parent's collapse, Dares never again became a force in the housebuilding industry.

According to the 1962 Prospectus:, the business was founded in 1864 by John Dare, the grandfather of the then Chairman, in the Saltney district of Birmingham. He was succeeded by his son, Harry Dare the elder, and after the First World War he was joined by his son, also Harry. During its first sixty years 'the business was confined mainly to the building of houses.' However, such building appeared to be on a contract basis for after the business was incorporated in 1925 (as H Dare & Son) its activities were expanded to include the development of building estates and public works contracts. The only clue to Dares' pre-war size is an article in *Housebuilder* which stated that before the war, Dares completed an average of about 800 private houses a year.[1] This was reinforced by a reference to the company holding land for thousands of houses (2400 at Castle Bromwich; 900 at Stonor Park; 500 at Heath Lodge and 300 at Coventry) which would be entirely consistent with that level of annual production. The probability is that Dare retained some of its production for letting, as this was a characteristic of its post-war operations.

After the Second War, Dare was one of the first companies in the midlands to resume residential development and although they had only built 200 houses by the end of the 1940s, that was more than most of the London builders achieved. No figures are available for volumes or turnover; the profits record shown in the Prospectus is one of unbroken growth, rising to £100,000 by 1958 and £184,000 in 1961, the last year before flotation. If profit margins on the trading income were around 10%, it would imply a turnover of some £1.5m and, using average house prices, sales of around 600. On the 1962 flotation, Harry Dare, then aged 64, was Chairman and Managing Director; his three sons were also directors. The list of sites included the west midlands, Worcestershire, Gloucestershire and Lancashire. No volumes were quoted but in the first public accounts the Chairman reported that the company had sold more houses than in any other year, a comment which probably ignored the pre-war years. The 1965 accounts signalled some change in policy in that the company was seeking larger areas of land to develop; examples were the purchase of the Park Hall Estate in Walsall (600 units), 23 acres at Bamford, Lancashire and 37 acres at Ferndown, Dorset. As well as building for sale, the activities had also included the erection of properties for retention by the property holding and investment companies in the group; the other policy change was a switch in emphasis back towards building for sale, perhaps a consequence of what had been only modest growth in profits.

Rescued by the Stern Group
Dares had been increasing its local authority fixed-price contracting, and the impact of cost inflation, particularly on a housing contract for the Runcorn local authority, took its toll. Losses were incurred in 1969, and in June 1971 Dares suspended dividends following losses of £670,000 (later restated as £1.3m). The shares were the subject of a rescue offer of 8p per share (against the previous market price of 18p) from Metropolitan Property Investments, part of the Stern Group. (Although Stern controlled the company, Dares still retained its Stock Exchange quotation.) William Stern was a US citizen and a

---

[1] *Housebuilder*, January 1950.

Harvard graduate 'a hard working man with his own strong sense of principle.'[2] He joined his father-in-law in the Freshwater Group around 1960 and then set up on his own account. William Stern was later to achieve notoriety as Britain's largest ever personal bankrupt.

William Stern outlined the new strategy: it involved withdrawing from fixed price local authority contracting and ceasing private housebuilding in the north and the midlands. Instead of concentrating on its traditional area, Dares was to develop the housebuilding in Bournemouth and south London 'where we see greater potential and easier management control.' Stern also wanted to enhance the value of the considerable property portfolio. He was increasing the emphasis on Dares as a commercial property company, 'calling on the expertise…[of] the Stern Holdings Group we have now decided to expand commercial property development.' The intention was that by the end of 1972, Dares would be essentially a property investment company with a small housebuilding activity.[3] However, Dares was still buying tenanted houses and in one deal in May 1972 it bought over 700 flats from Ashworth and Steward for £2.8m.

And another rescue

Although Dares made modest profits in 1972 and 1973, the company reverted to losses in 1974 and the collapse of the Stern Group led to Dares' own share quotation being suspended. The 1974 Annual Report said that collapse of Stern had not directly affected Dares except that it has led to pressure for repayments by some banks which lent money both to Dares and to the Stern Group. This pressure was particularly strong from one bank which had advanced short term loans against a block of 500 flats which had to be sold to Birmingham Corporation at a loss of £565,000. William Stern resigned from the Board in June 1975. By then, Dares was probably building no more than one or two hundred houses a year.

In 1976, a new team of Peter Jackson and David Sidi (with Ervin Landau in support as their solicitor) offered 2p a share for the Stern shareholding and began to rebuild Dares. Jackson had started out in banking in the 1950s and Sidi was a Manchester property developer. Dares bought other housing and property assets in the UK, expanded the housing business in Dorset and Hampshire, began building in the north west and even bought land in the south of France. However, the rise in interest rates in 1980 brought disappointing results and in 1981 the midlands housing subsidiary, Dare Developments, was sold to enable Dares to concentrate on commercial developments. From then on, although Dares continued to involve itself in residential development in the South, it was primarily a commercial property company. In 1987 Dares had sold most of what was left of its traditional housing operation to John Maunders, amounting to some six sites, for £3.5m. By 1988 Dares was making profits of £9m. However, it was virtually bankrupted by the recession, with losses of nearly £60m in 1990 and 1991. In 1998 the name was changed to Albermarle Property Investments.

2 Erdman, *People & Property*.
3 Group Accounts, 1971.

DAVID CHARLES
Peak units: 1200 (1974)

David Charles was founded in 1941 by Charles Bennett and a surveyor who contributed his first name of David;[1] Bennett had owned a dairy business which was sold in 1937. David Charles began by doing war damage work although a profile of the company in *Building* suggested that Bennett had formed the company 'largely as a hobby.' After the War, he was joined by two local builders, George Baldwin and William Bromley, when the company switched to general contracting, starting estate development in a small way in 1952. By this time 'David' seems to have left the company. The scale of the business changed with the appointment of Robin Buckingham, Bennett's son-in-law. Buckingham only joined the group because his father-in-law's health was deteriorating. 'At the time he was a serving officer in the Royal Navy and had never seriously contemplated moving into the business into which he had married. But he diligently set about learning the fundamentals, even though for practical reasons (he was on active service in Korea) it had to be by correspondence course. At the end of the Korean war, the young Robin Buckingham…was able to turn theory into practice. He quit the navy and became a builder.'[2]

Buckingham recognised that contracting and housebuilding were conceptually different. 'The two types of business are complementary but need to be separated…for this reason housebuilding activities were put into a separate company in 1957.'[3] Between 1954 and 1963, profits of the David Charles companies increased from £19,000 to £104,000. In 1964 Bennett died and Buckingham assumed full control. He clearly had aspirations to build a large business both by organic growth and by acquisition. Since 1959 it has been the policy 'to acquire old-established building companies and to restore them to profitable working.'[4] Buckingham's approach had two strands. First, there were many local building contractors in the midlands which were not prospering but which traditionally had excellent contacts with both the professions and local authorities, and it made sense to acquire these companies. The second strand was that housebuilding could not be expanded if it was confined to its base in Birmingham.

The acquisitions commence
The first large acquisition, **AH Taylor**, a Nottingham contractor and developer that had been founded by Alec Taylor, was almost as profitable as David Charles and it was combining the two businesses within a new holding company that gave the Company sufficient size to float in 1963. Buckingham, Chairman and joint Managing Director, was then 35 and the somewhat older Bromley (the other joint) and Baldwin remained as directors. In its first year as a quoted company, the enlarged group built around 400 houses. The Taylor acquisition also brought in Malcolm Siddals who soon became Buckingham's right hand man and was appointed Managing Director in 1972. Growth of the housing business was rapid but Buckingham also believed that industry was inherently cyclical and diversification was necessary, but it had to be related. Writing for the 1968 loan stock issue he said: 'In recent years it has been the policy of your board to maintain the private house building activities of the Group at a high rate and to expand the Group's interests in allied activities, principally commercial and industrial development, contracting, plant hire and joinery manufacture.' The diversification started in 1965 with the purchase of Contractors Plant (Birmingham) which formed the nucleus of a building services division. This was followed by David Lewis (Birmingham), Chilwell Brickworks, the AE Symes construction group of Stratford (1971)

---

[1] His surname could not be identified as he used a nominee, a retired dairyman called Norman Summerton, on the shareholders register.

[2] *Building*, 10th May 1974.

[3] Correspondence with Robin Buckingham.

[4] Prospectus, 1963.

and IJ Stocker of St Ives Cambridgeshire (1972). Symes, a public company with an excellent reputation and making a steady £200,000 profit a year, was an important acquisition as it gave David Charles a presence in the City of London. Overseas, the Company developed apartments in Malta.

Housing volumes had increased steadily since the flotation, reaching around 700 by 1967; the acquisition of Gable Construction and **Chansom** helped raise this to some 900 in 1972, with plans for this to rise to 1500 within two years. David Charles was now developing from Kent to Cornwall and Lancashire to Suffolk, growth having come almost entirely from acquisition. Unfortunately, Robin Buckingham's views on the cyclicality of the housebuilding industry seemed to have deserted him just at the point when they were most needed. 'Mr Buckingham does not subscribe to the current pessimism surrounding the housing sector. He believes that this side will continue to expand for a good few years and, as a mark of confidence, he is raising output from 1200 to 1500 houses this year.'[5]

Expansion into the recession

A large part of the growth was being financed by debt. Looking back after the crash, the Chairman rationalised his approach: 'This long term strategy [diversification] required from its inception a high degree of borrowing which, in a happier economic climate, was considered to be commercially acceptable but which, in the past two years, has exposed the company to the problems of some of its lenders in the secondary banking sector and also to the weakness of the property sector.'[6] Some of the developments were financed by merchant banks and interest rates of 5% over base rate were not uncommon. After a fall in volumes to 750 in 1973/74, they bounced back to a record 1200 in 1975; trading profits were a healthy £7m but land write downs of £1m and, most damaging of all, an interest bill of £4.7m reduced the pre-tax figure to £1.4m. David Charles raised £2m from a rights issue at the end of 1975 and set out a very positive programme. This included the expansion of its construction company overseas; a target of 2000 private house sales from its land bank of 7500 prime plots; and expansion of the engineering subsidiary and the travel company. David Charles had even been buying the residual Bacal business from the receiver.

Within months a cash shortage left no option but to cut back the building programme, and the interim dividend for 1975/76 was passed. The most acute problems lay with the commercial side. 'When the recession came we were able to cut back the housing. It was the commercial property side which caused the problem, we couldn't cope with borrowings on half built office blocks – they weren't pre-let.'[7] In October 1976, *Building* carried an article 'The truth about David Charles.' The share price had fallen to around 4p 'and alarmist reports about the health of the company' meant the Chairman sending a progress report to shareholders ahead of the November accounts. He had admitted responsibility for overborrowing and explained that although the profits forecast made at the time of the 1975 rights issue included a substantial contingency margin, 'it did not allow for several major assumptions failing simultaneously'[8] The housebuilding programme was scaled back, reducing cash flow, and some sites needed provisions. The banks provided additional support but in January 1977 the directors placed the company in voluntary liquidation. In Robin Buckingham's own words, 'Its very success had encouraged the company, and its lenders, never to question the future.'[9]

---

5 *Building*, 3rd Nov. 1972.
6 Rights Issue Circular, Dec 1975
7 Interview with Mike Deasley, Jan. 2002.
8 *Building*, 1st Oct. 1976.
9 Correspondence.

DAVIS ESTATES
Peak units: 1200 (late 1930s)

Davis Estates was one of the larger pre-war housebuilders and one of the few to seek a public flotation in the 1930s. Arthur Felix Davis, born in 1896, worked for his father, Abraham Davis, on residential development, primarily flats, but his father did not appear to have been successful. After his father died, Arthur Davis started again and focused on the other end of the residential market – housing estates. The first record of him acting independently is in Kingsbury in 1929 with two estates, and he appears to have been strikingly successful for by 1935 he was advertising as many as twenty different estates in the London area.[1] Davis had also moved outside London and was building in Kent, Sussex and Hampshire.

By 1935, Davis was operating through ten different housing companies, all registered under the Industrial & Provident Societies Acts, and it was these companies that were brought together that year as Davis Estates for the flotation. Profits prior to the issue had averaged £55,000 – about the same as Taylor Woodrow at the time. By the outbreak of war, Davis was building as far north as Birmingham and as far west as Plymouth. There is no official record of unit volumes but articles and books written post war, when AF Davis was still active, indicate that the company was regularly building over 1000 units a year and, by the outbreak of the Second War, over 1200 on more than 30 different estates; on many of these, Davis also built shops.

There is little biographical detail on Arthur Davis and personal recollections are limited, and partially second hand; his wife was of the Fray Bentos family. Descriptions of him include bright, aristocratic, fiercely competitive, 'a very hard nosed man who ruled the company with a rod of iron – a very tough character.'[2] And they were the polite ones. When asked what Davis's qualifications were, the only response was 'money.' Davis was also ultra secretive: the sales department worked through the weekend and had to telephone him with the results using a code where the letters from Davis Estates represented numbers from 1 to 9.

Little wartime activity

The company had a policy of retaining properties for investment and by 1937 had over 700 houses under ownership.[3] Unlike some of its contemporaries, Davis Estates had no construction arm and its wartime activity appeared to be minimal. Some of its land was acquired for agricultural purposes and Arthur Davis concentrated on managing his tenanted properties. Financially, it had left the Company unable to pay the dividends on the preference capital that had been issued as part of the 1935 flotation. In late 1945 and early 1946, Davis formed a subsidiary to undertake a range of local authority housing contracts. Perhaps reflecting the lack of experience in drawing up third party contracts, Davis was unable fully to recoup the cost rises and £120,000 had to be provided over a three-year period. Davis also formed Davis Contractors in Australia in 1949, principally an open cast coal mining business.

The Company appears to have resumed private building in 1953 and the 1954 accounts refer to housing sales doubling again. Building had also resumed on a wide geographical base with estates in London, the southern counties and the midlands. Profits in 1954 reached £383,000 – significantly larger than Ideal Homes was then making. However, just as volumes were accelerating, in 1957 the business was sold to Wood Hall Trust, then run by Michael Richards. The formal reason given by Arthur Davis, then 61, was

[1] Jackson, *Semi-Detached London*, p.107.
[2] Interview with Paul Bliss, June 1999.
[3] *Investors Review*, Dec. 1937.

the need to provide for eventual estate duty liabilities. He had suffered a severe car accident ten years earlier, his health was believed to be poor, and there was no family succession. However, he did sign a five-year service contract and did not formally resign as Chairman and Managing Director until 1962. Wood Hall Trust was a conglomerate with interests in Australian pastoral trading, food, property and building. The housing expansion continued under the new ownership and Davis Estates regained volumes of around 1000 a year by the late 1960s. Some large sites (over 100 acres each) were purchased, e.g. Wantage airfield and Caversham Park at Reading, which were to stand the company in good stead in the early 1970s. Wood Hall installed its own financial control systems but otherwise left the day-to-day management of Davis to its own Managing Director – George Tulip first, then Brian Hewitt through the 1970s, followed by Paul Bliss. However, once the business had reached a certain size, Wood Hall was more interested in sustaining a cash flow than expanding what was inherently a capital hungry business

Sale to Elders

In 1969 Wood Hall bought the general building contractor, Fairweather and formally amalgamated it with Davis in the early 1970s: it did not enjoy the synergies expected. There was a mixed board and it was still run as two companies. The only time Davis used Fairweather for construction 'it was a disaster…You don't apply the same disciplines when you are both part of the same group.'[4] (Fairweather incurred substantial losses in the early 1980s). By the end of the 1970s, Davis was building around 700 units and volumes continued to slip in the succeeding years. In 1982 Wood Hall was taken over by the Australian Elders group primarily for the former's pastoral business. The UK building operations were of little interest and the then Managing Director, Paul Bliss, led an attempted but unsuccessful management buy out with ICFC backing, bidding £8m in March 1983. 'They were a tough but fair bunch and they reckoned – probably rightly – that more cash could be made by winding the company down.'[5] Some of the land was built out but most was sold and Paul Bliss bought the rump of the company, which is still producing revenue from ransom strips to this day.

4 Interview with Brian Hewitt, Oct. 1998.
5 Interview Paul Bliss.

DRURY HOLDINGS
Peak units: 600-800 (mid to late 1930s)

Thomas Albert Drury and his brother-in-law Ralph Grocock started the Leicester-based business in 1934, incorporating it as Drury & Co the following year. The type of work carried out is not known but it was probably local building work including local authority contracts; there was no private housing. After the war, the company concentrated on local authority contracts mainly in the midlands and the London area, but from 1956 work was carried out in Lancashire, Yorkshire, and the south west. Most of the contracts with local authorities were secured through the Gregory Housing subsidiary which specialised in the planning and design of estates for local authorities. Private estate development was started through Drury Estates in 1951 and Drury Estates (Southern) in 1957. Estates were developed over a wide geographical area and by 1964 accounted for half the group's profits.

Grocock was joined after the war by John Smith and Robert Charlton and they became shareholders in the constituent companies that made up the group when it floated in 1964, by which time Drury himself had died.[1] Profits had shown strong growth, rising from £46,000 in 1955 to £471,000 in 1964. No indication was given of the size of the private housing business except that a land bank of 2800 plots with planning permission was disclosed. This suggest a throughput of say, 600-800 houses a year. The estates were spread through Leicestershire and Northants, up to Lancashire and Yorkshire, across to the south midlands and East Anglia, and on the south coast.

The business grew steadily after flotation reaching a peak of £976,000 in 1968. Profits drifted for the next two years and then Drury was hit by fixed price contracts on local authority work begun in 1969 and early 1970; a group loss of £177,000 was incurred in 1971. This left the group vulnerable to predators and at the end of 1971 Orme bought 31% of the company for 100p a share. Drury forecast a recovery in profits to £500,000 but it was not sufficient to keep the company independent. ICFC, which had floated Drury, remained a shareholder and had been thinking Drury would make a good partner for Francis Parker, in which it held 19%. Terms for a merger were agreed valuing Drury at 125p; Orme came back with a bid of 133p but ICFC bought sufficient shares in the market at 130p to support a successful bid by Francis Parker, valuing Drury at £5.4m

---

[1] He may well have died during the war as his name was not on the 1942 register of shareholders.

EDMOND [ALLIED RESIDENTIAL]
Peak units: 360 (1987)

Allied Residential was formed as a holding company in March 1981 to acquire the housebuilding interests of Allied Plant Group (known as Allied Housing Group) and the residential development and financing interests of Thames Investment & Securities; it was Allied Housing which contributed the major part of the active building programme. The stated logic for both companies divesting their residential interests was competition for finance with other group companies, and the need for dedicated management. Two months after the merger, the Company was floated on the Stock Exchange. Several small Humberside companies had come together in this grouping.

FK West Fred West had started as a tradesman in the building industry in 1927, aged 17; he incorporated FK West in 1955. It specialised in industrial buildings and housing development in the Humberside area but was only a small concern when acquired.

Edmond (Builders) Dick Edmond had been a bricklayer before the war. His first company, R Edmond, was formed in the early 1950s and began by building council houses and then gradually moved into speculative housebuilding. Edmond (Builders) was incorporated in 1961 at Willerby, by which time the business was predominantly private housing. Graham Maw, a chartered accountant, joined in 1963 and subsequently became Managing Director. Dick Edmond's only son was senior partner in a firm of solicitors so on his retirement the decision was taken to sell the business. On acquisition, turnover was around £2.5m principally derived from private housebuilding; it was building around 60 units a year.

Westcott Development, based in Hull, was formed in 1959 by Stan Spruit, who described himself as a public works contractor. Spruit bought large sites on a one-at-a-time basis and built around 100 houses a year. The Company was bought by Allied Plant Group in April 1979 and renamed Allied Housing Group in 1980; Stan Spruit stayed on as Chairman but died in the July. Turnover was around £1m when it was acquired.

AE Jenkinson was formed in 1953 at Kingston-upon Hull to acquire the business already being carried out by Arthur Jenkinson; as he was a director of Kingston Plumbers it is assumed that he was a plumber by trade. Arthur Jenkinson had died before 1971 and it is understood that family succession was a problem.

Absila was formed in 1972 by Joseph Benjamin, a chartered surveyor who had founded Thames Investment. It was a small property investment and letting business.

Ermine Securities provided finance to other builders to develop on a joint venture basis.

North Staffordshire Estates was similar to Absila and had some older houses in Manchester for conversion

In the five years to 1980, the constituent companies had built around 1150 houses (including Ermine's joint ventures), suggesting an annual build rate of around 250 at the time of the amalgamation.. Housebuilding was centred on Hull and the surrounding areas of Humberside and Yorkshire, and sites had also been acquired in Cheshire and Devon. The two executive directors were Graham Maw, originally of Edmond, who became the housing Managing Director; and Stuart Crossley, a solicitor who had been responsible for Thames' residential business for the previous six years, who dealt with the rest of the group's activities. Fred West, an executive director of Allied Plant, remained as a consultant. The Prospectus contained a forecast of profits for the year to March 1982 in excess of £1m. The reality was to prove entirely different. The year end was changed to December to avoid stocktaking problems; the shortened trading period produced profits of just £115,000 and the final dividend was passed. In 1982, on turnover of £5.9m (suggesting sales of 200-250) Allied Residential lost £2.2m. as a result of write-offs. The chosen solution was to sell the southern companies to Stuart Crossley [which became Banner] and the Humberside and North Yorkshire business was consolidated under the Edmond name. Allied formally changed its name to Edmond Holdings in 1983 and Graham Maw continued as Managing Director.

Greenwood and Sunguard acquisitions

In 1983 Edmond bought an investment property portfolio valued at £2.8m from Michael Carlton's Taddale Investments; this was accompanied by a capital reduction and rights issue. One of the side-effects was that Taddale was obliged to make a bid under the takeover code, though not pitched at a price that encouraged acceptance, and the Taddale stake was later sold. In 1984, Edmond bought **Greenwood Development Holdings** for £1¼m. The company had been formed in 1976 to buy the south Wales housebuilding business of Cubitt in what was then a secret deal: 'Although most of the old Cubitt property division, including Cubitt Homes, is being disposed of, the operation is veiled in secrecy. Contracts have been exchanged for the sale of Cubitt Homes … but the identity of the buyer has not been revealed.'[1] The business appears to have been named after a past Labour minister and owned by a future Conservative one: 'It is not every day that a former minister runs a successful development company. Greenwood Homes was one of the brainchilds of Lord Greenwood of Rossendale who as Anthony Greenwood, was Minister of Housing and Local Government between 1966-70.'[2] In fact, the shareholders' register shows that the owner was David Young, later Baron Young and a member of the Thatcher Government. The emphasis of the business was switched from south Wales to the midlands and one of its specialities was building houses on Development Corporation sites. Volumes reached 300-400 and by 1983, Greenwood's turnover had exceeded £6m, although it was incurring small losses. It was sold to Edmond in consequence of Lord Young becoming a cabinet minister. The acquisition helped increase Edmond's turnover to £11m in 1985 but profits, having staged some recovery in 1983, barely broke even.

Yet another acquisition was made in 1987, **Sunguard Homes.** Based in Northampton, Sunguard had been formed in 1971 by two civil engineers and two surveyors one of which was Richard Chalcraft. By 1976, Chalcraft had become the largest shareholder and he was to become group Chief Executive in 1990. Sunguard expanded into East Anglia through Drycon Builders in 1986 (there was also an office in Burton-on-Trent): turnover was then approaching £3m on unit sales of around 100, and profits just short of £400,000. On the acquisition, Chalcraft became joint Managing Director of Edmond with Maw, and the enlarged group's turnover rose to £16m in 1987 (360 units) on which profits of £1.6m were earned. Although unit sales eased back the following year, turnover increased to £18m and Edmond made record profits of £4.9m. However, the recession led to profits declining over the next three years before slipping into modest losses in 1992 and 1993, by which time sales had fallen to only 180.

Edmond failed to recover with the market and it became a target for other companies. In November 1994 there was a proposal to use Edmond as the vehicle for a reverse takeover of the then private Linden Homes; this would have left Linden with 61% of the enlarged group but this was voted down by shareholders. In March 1995, Edmond accepted a £13m cash bid from the private property group, Roxylight Properties, an investment company run by Charles Miller and Henry Gwyn-Jones; a separate Roxylight company had previously bought Saxon Homes from Blue Circle Cement for £7m. The Edmond purchase was substantially made with borrowed money, and there was little scope to expand the business. Chalcraft resigned in 1997 and the land was progressively built out. The rump of the business was bought by Saxon Homes in 1999.

[1] *Building*, 10th Oct .1976.
[2] *Housebuilder*, Oct. 1979.

EGERTON TRUST
Peak units: 300 (1989)

Following his high profile career with Bovis, Finlas and Alfred McAlpine, Frank Sanderson took control of the small quoted Caparo Properties in 1985, renaming it Egerton Trust. Caparo had started life as E. Austin and Sons, a general engineering and distribution company. After incurring losses in 1981 and 1982, it recommended a bid from Caparo Industries, controlled by Swraj Paul when it became a 75%-owned subsidiary. The existing businesses were sold and properties were acquired from Caparo Industries; Austin's name was changed to Caparo Properties.

Caparo Properties never made more than modest profits and in December 1985 it bought Beaumont, a nursing home developer and manager owned by Frank Sanderson for £3m in shares; it also bought Dartel, a small private housebuilding company controlled by the Sanderson family for a further £0.5m in shares. Beaumont had commenced trading in April 1983 with Dr Andrew MacDonald and Nick Sanderson (Frank's son) as key executives. Dartel had been formed by Nick Sanderson in 1981 to undertake small developments in the south east but it was relatively inactive until 1985.

Frank Sanderson became Chairman and Chief Executive of the enlarged group, now renamed Egerton Trust, and proceeded to expand it rapidly. Ruskin Homes was formed in 1986 to develop sheltered housing and Dartel was renamed Denehurst. The housing operation was further expanded by the acquisition of the Northampton-based starter homes company, Gayton, in November 1988. Egerton paid £8.5m for Gayton, which had net assets of £0.5m. That year, Egerton also bought McAlpine Homes Scotland, with 11 sites in the Glasgow area, for £3.1m. By 1989, housing output was around 300 units and the residential division had record turnover and profits of £34m and £5.3m. Almost 300 houses were sold in the first half of 1990.

Egerton was expanding on a far wider scale than UK housing. In 1987 it bought the old-established contractor and property developer, Percy Trentham, for £10m, bringing in a £75m turnover. In the US, it bought Peters Hartel Corporation, a housebuilder on Cape Cod which was principally involved in the creation of an 'English Village' of 172 units; and it paid £18m for a US aggregates company. In 1988 the purchase of Foxwood Homes of New Hampshire further increased Egerton's US housing. However, the biggest acquisition was of Reunion Properties in July 1989. Reunion, which had book net assets of £3.5m, cost £25m; there was a large unrealised surplus and Reunion did contribute £7m of Egerton's pre-tax profits in 1989 – but no more.

These acquisitions left Egerton ill-placed to cope with the recession. There had been expectations of £30m profit for 1990 but the first half profits were little more than break-even and the dividend was passed. In a last attempt to achieve a financial reconstruction, Frank Sanderson resigned as Chief Executive in May 1991 and Nick Sanderson took over. However, the following month administrators were appointed. Egerton Homes was subsequently sold to Try.

ENGLISH CHINA CLAYS
Peak units: 1289 (1988)

In 1945, English China Clays acquired Selleck Nicholls & Williams, a quarry operator and building contractor. SNW was soon using the waste sand from the clay pits to produce the Cornish Unit house, a system-built concrete panel construction primarily supplied for local authorities; by 1977 the post-war total was reported as being in excess of 80,000.[1] Whilst demand for public sector housing continued unabated until the early 1970s, fashions changed towards timber frame and SNW designed timber frame systems for local authority estates throughout the UK – the mainstay of ECC's building division throughout this period.

With the cut-back in public sector development in the mid and late 1970s, ECC began to place more emphasis on private sector housebuilding, which until then had been on a relatively small scale in Devon and Cornwall. The 1968 company history described the housing department as 'very much a group enterprise: roads and drains are usually constructed by the Quarries Division, joinery is supplied by one or other of the Building Division's joinery works and mortgages for customers are arranged by another section of the group.'[2] Hudson also stated that 'nearly 1000 houses were started during 1968-69,' but John Reeve, later Managing Director of the private housing operation, suggested the figure was more like 100.[3]

John Reeve creates a focused housebuilding division

John Reeve, who had trained as a quantity surveyor with HC Janes, was recruited in 1972 on the SNW Board's recognition that, they needed more specific speculative housing management experience. Reeve became production director in 1976 and Managing Director in 1980. He led the expansion of SNW's housing, acquiring land in the north west, midlands and the south east. 'During the '70s and '80s there was a belief by a majority of the main board that land for development represented a suitable investment for cash being generated by the mainstream clay business. It was considered that housebuilding was not so diverse from the mainstream business of extraction since their success was all dependent upon land acquisition and planning permissions. The basic difference was that land acquisition for extraction was considered as a long term asset and this approach and that thinking transferred itself in part to housebuilding.'[4] The division also changed during this decade from using local contractors to build its estates to employing its own and sub-contract labour. Completions steadily increased through the 1970s to around 350 by the end of the decade.

Edwin H Bradley

The 1980s saw ECC taking a more positive approach to estate development; indeed, aggressive by the end of the decade. Volumes were increased to almost 700 by 1984, and then at the end of 1984 ECC made an agreed £5m takeover bid for the Swindon firm Edwin H Bradley, a business that was roughly split between building materials (the well-known Bradstone) and Bradley Estates, which had sold some 560 units in its last year. Edwin Henry Bradley was working as a foreman for a Swindon builder when the firm went bankrupt in 1901. With his savings (and his wife's capital) he set up on his own, aged 37, as a housebuilder. He began purchasing land from the Goddard Estate in Swindon where he built over 250 houses up to World War I. All three sons, Hubert, Eddie and Lionel, joined the business in the 1920s, learning their trade at technical college and night school. During the 1930s Bradley began building in the

---

[1] *Building*, 18th March 1977.

[2] Hudson, *The History of the English China Clays*, pp.132-3.

[3] John Reeve correspondence with author.

[4] Ibid.

neighbouring towns, for instance Chippenham and Trowbridge, and by the late 1930s was building more than 300 houses a year. During the Second War, Bradley's main activity was quarrying for defence purposes. Post war, Bradley continued to concentrate on local quarrying and developed its building materials.

On the ending of building controls, Bradley had plenty of white land but not much land with planning permission. Michael Bradley, Edwin's grandson, was Managing Director of Estates and he explained: 'It took us quite a long time to get back to the 300 or so houses we were building before the war... we had a lot of money invested in white land and this reduced our capability to build on a big scale... we must face the fact that there was a time, around the mid-sixties to the mid-seventies, when our holding in white land hampered the growth of the company.'[5] By 1977, sales had reached 450 units but two years later, the number was back down to 300. Large sites were fought through planning enquiries: Haydon Wick, Wootton Bassett and Westlea Down, where 600 acres was granted outline permission in 1978. Gradually housing volumes were increased but, despite the advantageous land holdings, the business was not proving financially successful. From 1982/3 Bradley Estates profits began to fall and the 1984 accounts reported that a 'thorough review of our business... has addressed the current Estates' problems.' However, that did not seem sufficient, and at the end of 1984 the housebuilding subsidiary was sold for £51m to English China Clays.

ECC fails in its bid for Bryant

With Bradley under its control, but concentrating on margin rather than volume, ECC sold over 1000 units in 1985. Its most ambitious move was made in November 1986 with a fiercely contested £137m bid for Bryant. Helped by some enthusiastic profit forecasts, Bryant fought off the bid but ECC was left with a 29% holding (sold in June 1990). John Reeve argues that the bid for Bryant was, 'sadly, very misunderstood! Following the acquisition of Bradley we realised that, as a group, we had considerable expertise in land management and planning and that land was not being maximised in terms of value by a majority of housebuilders. [At] Bradley's ...we cut volumes, the profitability and margin of the combined organisations improved dramatically. We perceived a similar situation would be evident at Bryant and believed that their margin with such a historical land bank was too low.'[6]

ECC continued to increase its volumes, reaching almost 1300 in 1989, generating trading profits of £24m. Helped by the earlier planning successes and its determination to concentrate on margin as opposed to volume, trading margins of 44% were the highest of any large housebuilder.[7] How quickly fortunes change: new management at English China Clays decided that more focus was needed on its core clay business and that private housing did not fit into the mainstream activities; in particular, 'it was considered that our involvement in housing was having a depressive effect on the share price.'[8] Volumes were sharply reduced and controlled land sales were made to other builders over a four-year period; finally, a group of sites was bought by Higgs & Hill in May 1994, and the rump of the business consisting of major land holdings in Devon and Cornwall were acquired in 1995 by Wainhomes. As a postcript, ECC Quarries demerged as Camas (later bought by Aggregate Industries) and then ECC itself succumbed to a bid from the French Imerys.

5 Anon, *Bradley Building on a Name*, p.62.
6 Ibid
7 *PHA*, 1990.
8 John Reeve correspondence.

EROSTIN GROUP
Peak units: 285 (1988)

The Erostin Group was the creation of John Upson and his wife Diane when in 1979 they took control of a largely inactive company based in Milton Keynes. John Upson described himself as 'a working-class lad from the wrong end of Southend-on-Sea';[1] his father had been a local builder and the young Upson went on to become a civil engineer, later construction director of Greenwood Homes. In the early years with Erostin, Upson concentrated on residential development and civil engineering to build up the financial base necessary 'to pursue their primary objective of commercial development.'[2] The Erostin Group was formed in 1984 when the organisation was still of modest size – 52 houses completed, a small civil engineering business and profits of £213,000. Growth from that point was exceptionally rapid: in five years turnover multiplied 12-fold and profits reached a peak of £7.5m.

Geographic coverage had spread to the west midlands taking housing volumes to 285 in 1988. There was also substantial growth from new businesses – building, villa sales, marina development, engineering and plumbing, but it was the commercial property subsidiary that grew fastest, becoming a major contributor to group profits from 1987. In 1987, Erostin raised £4m from the Govett Strategic Investment Trust in a private placing and in June 1988 floated on the Stock Exchange to raise a further £8m. Three months later, Erostin announced its largest development to date, a £67m commercial scheme at Birmingham International Airport. Upson was now actively seeking to move from residential to commercial development and did claim to have anticipated the downturn in the housing market. 'In the Autumn of 1988, Mr Upson decided the housing market had become overheated and promptly sold the group's surplus land. That decision boosted 1989's turnover by more than £20m.'[3] Residential sales fell from 285 to 180 in the year to March 1989 and to only 113 in 1989/90 but further substantial growth in commercial profits enabled Erostin to almost hold group profits (though only by capitalising interest).

Many companies failed in that recession but few can have done so while proclaiming their own immunity so confidently: Upson publicly stated that 'My own view is that housebuilders are now facing a situation like 1974 in which lots of builders will go to the wall…My Company would survive even if sales collapsed immediately.'[4] Writing his Chairman's Statement in June 1990, Upson's confidence had not been dented: 'The policies which have made such results possible are those which the Group has pursued consistently since its foundation and which have distinguished us from most other developer-traders; during the last property boom we kept our expansion under control so that now we are in leaner times we are able to deal with higher interest and lower yields without adversely affecting our ability to continue trading profitably.' The financial position had been deteriorating but £17m of debt against £25m of shareholders' funds did not look threatening. However, Erostin had an extensive commercial construction programme underway including ten completed commercial properties that were not selling. Debt rose rapidly and in March 1991 the Company said it needed a rescheduling of bank debt or an injection of shareholders' funds. The directors said that if they had a year to sell the property in an orderly fashion, then the assets would exceed liabilities. However, Erostin was not given that opportunity and liquidators were appointed in March 1991.

1 *The Times,*16th Dec. 1990.
2 Prospectus, 1988.
3 *The Times,* 22nd June 1990.
4 *Building,* 7th July 1989.

FAIRBRIAR HOMES
Peak units: 280 (1989)

Fairbriar has a place in the contemporary history of British housebuilders that far outweighs the number of houses it built. Remo Dipre arrived in England from Italy at the age of 20, qualified as an accountant and first worked in his father-in-law's restaurant business in Epsom; the existence of three premises on long leases in Epsom was the catalyst for Dipre's subsequent commercial property career. His own investment company, Starwest, was founded in 1960 and concentrated on commercial property development. Much of the finance was provided by the Crown Agents and most of the property was sold just before the 1973/74 crash.

The first residential developments were started in 1970, with the Fairbriar name being adopted in 1972. That year, Dipre was joined by Peter Nesbitt, who had qualified at the London School of Building, as general manager; Nesbitt was made Managing Director in 1976. The first site bought under the Fairbriar name was for 13 units in Cheam; the Company went on to develop imaginative schemes in south London and the neighbouring home counties. Nevertheless, the growth in the business was slow – by the end of the 1970s, Fairbriar Homes was only building around 30 houses a year. However, growth in the 1980s, particularly of profits, was rapid. In 1985, Fairbriar was demerged from Starwest and floated. Unit completions had risen to around 150 and profits were in excess of £2m; four years later, housing completions had not quite doubled but profits had reached £13m.

The 1985 Prospectus had stated that there was no present intention to go into commercial property development but in 1987 Fairbriar began what was to be a substantial development programme. In June that year, Fairbriar also bought a Dorset housebuilder, Ryan of Wimborne; in 1987/88 Ryan contributed profits of £2.5m against £177,000 in its last independent year. Ryan continued to be run by Ray Jessop and it was Ryan that purchased most of the Group's new commercial sites, plus speculative land with hope value. Many of the commercial developments were to be retained as investments, a policy which contributed to high levels of debt. With the onset of recession, Fairbriar's housing sales fell to 170 in 1989/90 and profits collapsed to £2.3m; by then, equity of £41m was supporting £93m of debt plus unquantified joint-venture liabilities. The equity base itself was falling as values came under pressure, especially the Ryan sites bought in 1988 and 1989. In September 1991, Fairbriar was taken into administration. A loss of £64m was declared for the year to March 1991 after write-offs of £52m. Remarkably, the administrators considered that the business could be saved with the agreement of creditors, in particular, the Bank of Scotland. At the end of 1992, Dipre and Nesbitt resigned, and new directors were appointed.

Derek Hankinson, Chief Executive of Bison, became Chairman and provided support out of the Bison office. Despite further losses and a negative net asset value, Fairbriar came out of administration in March 1993 and was trading profitably by 1996. A development programme was restarted and investment properties acquired. However, profits remained at low levels and in February 2004 the Chairman told shareholders that the share price did not reflect the 'underlying value of its activities and the ongoing development work.'[1] A management contract was therefore being given to Managing Director Philip Van Reyk, to take over the residential work and build it out, with the intent of Fairbriar looking for 'suitable opportunities' to reinvest the proceeds. In February 2005, the Chairman led an MBO to take the company private.

---

1 Chairman's statement with 2003 accounts, Feb.2004.

FAIRCLOUGH HOMES
Peak units: 1977 (1994)

During most of its history, Fairclough (later AMEC) was a building and civil engineering business. For little more than a decade it became a national housebuilder, only for Fairclough Homes to be sold into American ownership in 1999. Leonard Fairclough Ltd was the creation of two men: first, Leonard Miller Fairclough and then Oswald Davies. Born in 1890, Leonard Fairclough joined his father's firm at the age of 13. His father had been a monumental mason who had expanded into general construction. By the time the business was incorporated in 1917, Leonard was virtually running it; and he became Chairman in 1927. The emphasis of the firm was on civil engineering rather than building and after World War II it specialised in road building particularly in partnership with Sir Alfred McAlpine. In 1965 Sir Leonard handed over control to Oswald Davies who was to take Fairclough from being a regional contractor to one of the most successful national contractors.

Barton takes Fairclough into private housing

The first move into speculative housing, indeed, the first acquisition of any consequence, came in 1967 with the purchase of **RJ Barton**. Based in Southport, it had been floated on the Stock Exchange only three years previously; private housing accounted then accounted for 12% of turnover and there were plans to build around 100 houses. Eric Barton joined the Fairclough board but stayed only until 1968. Under Oswald Davies, Fairclough purchased a number of well known construction businesses, often when they were in difficulty including CV Buchan, Fram Group and Sir Lindsay Parkinson. Although Sir Lindsay Parkinson was best known for its civil engineering and open-cast coal mining it, too, had an involvement with private housing through a small housebuilder, **Tarrant Builders;** that in turn owned Wentworth Estates, later to become one of the most valuable real estate sites in the home counties, and the golf course.[1] Brian Hewitt, later Managing Director of Costain Homes, joined the firm from school and remembers Tarrant building around 100 units a year, as a separate operation from Parkinson's own housing.

Although Fairclough may have been building three or four hundred houses a year, speculative housing never seemed to play a particularly important role in the group; indeed, it appeared almost peripheral by 1982 when Fairclough merged (though in effect it was a takeover) with the ubiquitous William Press pipeline company under the new name of AMEC. By 1986, some twenty years after the original Barton purchase, Fairclough was admitting to building about 400 units in the south east and East Anglia, with no mention of the north west at all. Moreover, the speculative housing was now contained within Fairclough Building rather than being a free standing entity.

The Hammerfine partnership increases the housing exposure

The occasion for quoting the numbers was the announcement of a 50-50 joint venture with a Blackpool-based housebuilder, Hammerfine, to form Fairclough Homes. Hammerfine was of very recent origin having been formed in 1981 by Malcolm Hawe, best known as the founder of Marc Gregory, which had gone into receivership in 1974; John Crowther, a local lawyer, was the other shareholder. Hammerfine was not particularly large; its 1985 turnover of £4m suggested no more than 150 houses (though press reports referred to 500) with profits of £120,000 and assets of £1/2m. The catalyst for the merger was that Fairclough had been doing joint ventures with Hammerfine and these had been making more money than had its wholly-owned housing operation. AMEC was also being criticised in the City for not having a large housing division like most other contractors. The brief was to create a major housebuilding force

---

[1] The Wentworth Club was sold in 1988 for £18m.

within five years and the contract provided for the Hammerfine shareholders to be bought out by AMEC after that period. Recognising the scale of the opportunities, Malcolm Hawe, as the new Chief Executive of Fairclough Homes, brought in his old Marc Gregory colleague, Mike Ratcliffe, as his deputy. Thus the shareholdings in Fairclough Homes were AMEC 50%, Hawe 30%, Crowther 10% and Ratcliffe 10%.

Volumes were expanded aggressively and Homes achieved nearly 2000 sales in 1988 and made pre-tax profits of £17m. In that year, AMEC elected to buy out the 50% it did not already own for an initial £18½m, with provision for top-up payments. By 1989, Fairclough Homes had been expanded to a 13-region business capable of producing 3000 units a year, but timing was against them and Fairclough Homes became one of the disaster stories of the recession. Rumours in the industry were rife that Fairclough was overpaying for land, although when that very point was put at a results presentation in April 1989 the directors said they could not believe the rumours as their success rate in buying land was only one in 25. What was clearly known in the industry and in the City was either not known or not admitted at the top level of the group. Looking back, Mike Ratcliffe admitted 'We were on a mission. We believed that every site that was for sale was capable of becoming ours.'[2] In the event, provisions against land totalled £107m in the four years to 1992, amounting to £21,000 a plot, one of the largest of any major housebuilder. Volumes fell to under 1000 in 1992, the third year of losses; between 1990 and 1992, Fairclough Homes lost a total of £155m. Malcolm Hawe resigned in 1992: 'Malcolm was brilliant at going forwards but when it came to retreating it is not in his character.'[3] He was succeeded as Managing Director by Mike Ratcliffe who pulled the business back to five regions and increased volumes again to average around 1800 a year but the overhang of old expensive land meant that minimal profits were being earned.

Housing units, 1986-2004

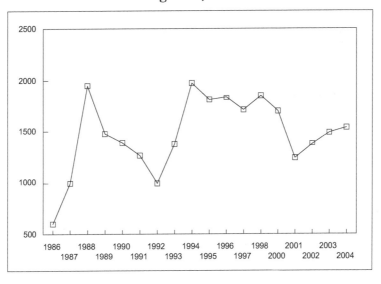

AMEC had also been losing money on commercial property development and construction in general was experiencing low margins. After provisions, AMEC incurred a loss of £88m in 1992; the recovery was slow and by 1995 AMEC was only making profits of £16m on turnover of £3 billion. In November

2 Interview with Mike Ratcliffe, Jan. 2001.
3 Ibid.

1995 the Norwegian Kvaerner launched a £202m bid for AMEC saying that it intended to dispose of Fairclough Homes if successful. After a closely fought battle, AMEC survived. Peter Mason took over from Alan Cockshaw as the new group Chief Executive; housing was one of only two divisions for which Mason took direct responsibility. Mike Ratcliffe had left in the previous December and his place was taken by Steven Devine, previously Homes Finance Director.

Fairclough Homes for sale

In January 1997, Richard Fraser, ex-Chief Executive of Westbury , was appointed Chief Executive of the housing division; the announcement also included the news that there would be a further £25m land write-off in the accounts of the year just ended. Fraser's brief was widely assumed to be to prepare the business for disposal although Fraser himself claimed the instruction was never that clear cut. 'AMEC claimed to me that they had not made their mind up whether to invest more money or to divest. But it was quite clear that the package I was on was designed to get a deal done. We thought about a flotation but every adviser that we talked to said the track record was not good enough. We talked to a couple of companies that we thought we might be able to merge with leaving AMEC with a stake. The presentation I gave to the board was very simple, you haven't got enough capital in the business and without enough capital you can't do the interesting thing and attract the top people. Therefore you have two choices, you either plough some money into it or you sell it.'[4]

In March 1999, AMEC announced the sale of Fairclough Homes to the American housebuilder Centex Corporation. Centex had been interested in the UK market for some years and had previously had a joint venture with Charles Church. Following the acquisition of Charles Church by Beazer, Stewart Baseley, Church's Managing Director, was recruited by Centex to establish a European housebuilding operation and Fairclough provided an ideal entry into the middle rank of the UK industry. The sale price was £109m, a premium of 20% to net assets, plus deferred participation in Homes' profits for a two-year period. AMEC Chief Executive Peter Mason commented: 'The disposal of Fairclough is consistent with our established strategy of focusing on AMEC's core capital projects and service activities.'

And sold again

After the uncertainty surrounding its future, some consolidation was needed at Fairclough Homes: Stewart Baseley's said that 'For seven years it has been clear that AMEC has wanted to exit the market so the firm has not been given any more capital than its basics demanded.'[5] Attitudes, too, needed to change: referring to the Southern division. Alan Burgess, its Chairman, argued that 'We need to change the Fairclough culture from being a builder to being a developer.'[6] Baseley reiterated the commitment to the European theme after the Fairclough acquisition: 'The plan is to build a company which can cross the divide across the whole of Europe. It's not been done before.'[7] However, Fairclough remained confined to the UK. Its volumes declined slightly despite rebranding the south as CDC2000; very modest profits were being made and although they doubled in 2004, trading margins only just reached 10%, well below the industry average. In September 2005, the US parent company announced the sale of its UK housing to the Miller Group for net proceeds of approximately $290m. Centex said no more than the sale was 'consistent with the company's strategic plan to focus on its domestic homebuilding operations.'

---

4 Interview with Richard Fraser, Sep. 2000.
5 *Housebuilder*, Sept 1999.
6 Ibid, April 2000.
7 Ibid, Sept 1999.

FAIRVIEW ESTATES
Peak units: 2287 (1996)

Fairview Estates has undoubtedly been one of the most successful post-war housebuilders. Though confining itself to the London area, it became large enough to be ranked with the volume builders, at which level its profitability has been second to none. The business was powered by estate agents and surveyors rather than builders and for forty years it has been headed by one man, Dennis Cope. But for a broken ankle, Fairview may never have existed. Dennis Cope was born in 1933 and, after leaving school at 15, went to work for the BBC as a messenger; the broken ankle came playing football and it was while he was sitting at home with his leg in plaster that his sister, then working for a surveyor in North London, suggested he filled his time by answering the telephone. The estate agents, Muskett & Co, gradually developed a relationship with a housebuilder, McManus, that had been building houses in Barnet and Potters Bar, to the point that Muskett did all their land buying and selling for them. From general assistant, Cope progressed to personal assistant to the Senior Partner which, as he puts it, 'is how I drifted into land buying and house selling and the new house business.' There was neither plan nor qualification: 'I went to the Balls Pond School of something and they said you're too young.'[1]

When McManus acquired Muskett, Cope did not want to join the enlarged firm and, instead, joined forces with David Maber of McManus; with a little finance of their own and some capital from a lawyer (Harry Howard of Howard Kennedy), they began by doing no more than buy and sell sites. Once they started building houses they brought in Douglas Gordon, previously the construction director at McManus. Almost immediately (August 1963) Fairview Estates (Enfield) was incorporated (taking its name from a site in Fairview Road), with Dennis Cope, David Maber and Douglas Gordon as equal partners. It is doubtful that Fairview could have made the progress that it did without the support of the ubiquitous First National Finance, which arrived at an early stage as a provider of finance and later as a shareholder.

Early support from FNFC

For those that believe that all major business decisions are the result of careful planning, the background to the partnership with FNFC makes salutary reading. Fairview had arranged to buy a site from the Church, financed by a loan from a small building society, but the building society pulled out. Cope remembers going to see his solicitor that day: 'He said a letter that had arrived on his desk that morning from John Black of First National, saying have you got any clients who want to do business with us, we do joint venture financing etc. I can remember saying to Alec, "We've got to exchange contracts in 14 days time – there just isn't time". He said, "No let's ring him up and go and see him", which we did. Black sat there and said "Yes, we'll do the deal". I said "You have to do it in 14 days" and he said "Right, done". I am proud of the fact that I am still doing business with John Black' (later to found Galliard Homes).[2]

Shortly after that first loan agreement, FNFC became an equity shareholder. 'I can remember a couple of days later I had a call from Pat Matthews, "would you come and see me"; I said politely "what do you want?", and he said "I just want to have a look at you". He was a brilliant man in that respect. He got a lot of stick in the secondary banking collapse but he was a man of charm, charisma and very dynamic who did just that, looked at people – "I fancy this chap, he could go places."'[3] In 1964 Cope and Gordon formed a joint company, Cromberdale Properties, with FNFC The two businesses expanded side by side

1 Interview with Dennis Cope, Sept. 1999.
2 Ibid.
3 Ibid.

until a record 750 house sales were completed in 1970, the larger part being flat sales in North London suburbs. By now Fairview's operational style was firmly established. Dennis Cope: 'The philosophy hasn't changed since we started – site assembly, finding situations and taking a view, of course, on planning.'

Fairview floated in 1971 with Cope, Gordon and FNFC as the principal shareholders. Also on the Board were John Bickel and Ken Oliver, later to be Managing Directors of the housing and the property businesses. After the flotation, the strength of the housing market took profits from £0.5m in 1970 to over £3m in 1973; this was achieved while private house sales actually declined from 750 to 550. Fairview's attitude to this unprecedented increase in margins, and the subsequent collapse, was instructive. In the 1971 Annual Report the Chairman specifically warned that 'The vast inflationary tendency in house prices…cannot continue for ever.' Two years later: 'I have previously outlined our resolve not to allow the cyclical nature of the housing business in general to affect the planned growth of your company and accordingly we have increased our housing target for 1974.'[4] While other companies were coming to terms with collapsing sales, between 1973 and 1975 Fairview almost tripled its unit volumes to 1650 with almost half of those coming from bulk sales to housing associations etc.

Doubling output to survive the recession

Cope said that the only way that Fairview could have survived was to liquidate their stock and go for cash, as quickly as possible, selling at whatever price they could. 'At that time I was a great admirer of Jim Slater and I remember him saying "cash is King"; he was too late but I thought he was right. So we doubled our production: we had three or four big sites at the time, we put extra men on and said "You're building that half and you're building the other half." Instead of building 15 a month we would build 30 a month and whatever price we could get for them we would sell them.'[5] Fairview remained in the black and although it wrote £2m of the value of its sites in 1973 and 1974, it was virtually all written back the following year.

Almost from its very beginnings as a private company, Fairview had been a commercial property developer as well as a housebuilder. The 1972 Annual Report stated that the 'intention of creating a major commercial and industrial property content within your company has been pursued diligently.' In that year Douglas Gordon decided to leave the company to pursue his own interests and Ken Oliver took over commercial property. Before too long, Fairview was facing a stock market dilemma: investors did not find it easy to value a hybrid corporate structure wherein commercial property provided an asset base but housebuilding provided the bulk of the trading profits. In his 1979 statement, the Chairman reported that a separation of the two functions was under consideration but it was eventually decided to 'retain the Group in its present form thereby producing income from a controlled housing operation with strict limitation on land stocks…The income earned in housing will continue to be applied to the growth of our Company's property investment portfolio.'

Property demerged

In the end, the split came: 'For several years your Board has been stating its intention to reduce the involvement of Fairview Estates in housebuilding in order to concentrate its resources on commercial property.'[6] Dennis Cope also added a personal note: 'Ken Oliver wanted to run a property company: I wanted to run a housebuilding company.'[7] A variety of options was considered. An outright sale of housebuilding was rejected as it might have been at a significant discount to book values. A controlled

4 Group accounts, 1973.
5 Interview Dennis Cope.
6 *Phased Withdrawal from Housebuilding* Circular, September 1982.
7 Interview Dennis Cope.

run down of the sites may have encountered difficulties as the programme came to a close. The preferred option was a partnership agreement whereby the housebuilding directors managed the housing for a period of four years on a profit-sharing basis. As the housebuilding was reduced in size, so the partnership's capital grew and at the end of the four-year period (when sales were down to an annualised rate of 500-600) the partnership then had a capital base sufficient to re-expand the business. The original Fairview company was renamed Frogmore which, although remaining committed to commercial property, also went on to develop a thriving business in the partnership financing of small housebuilders. The FNFC relationship had turned full circle.

The intention was for Fairview New Homes, the partnership, to remain private. Sadly, Ken Oliver died and, although he had been running Frogmore, a family interest had been retained in the housing partnership. Buying this out on borrowed money concentrated the minds of the remaining six partners and they felt the need to prepare an exit route. Thus started one of the most unlikely relationships – between a food conglomerate and a housebuilder. While plans were being made (in 1987) for a quotation on the USM, Victor Blank of Charterhouse suggested a meeting with Harry Solomon, just taking over as Managing Director of Hillsdown Holdings. 'We met Harry and within seven to ten days we had done a deal. They wanted anything that made money. They were in the business of issuing dear paper for cheap assets but in our case they didn't get cheap assets – they got good management.'[8]

Housing units, 1969-2004

Acquisition by Hillsdown

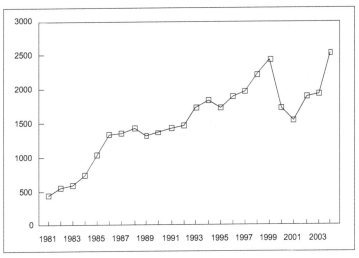

There are two generalisations that can be made about this type of acquisition. First, entrepreneurs taken over by much larger companies tend to resign and start over again. Second, housebuilders controlled by companies that do not understand housebuilding tend to lose their way. It is a tribute to the relationship between Cope and Solomon that neither generalisation proved relevant. Dennis Cope described it: 'It was all about one man, Harry Solomon; he has this ability to make you feel responsible and pleased. I can remember we completed the deal on the Friday and I rang Harry on the Monday morning and I said "Harry, I can't tell you how pleased I am this has gone through, what do you want me to do now, do we need a meeting or something" He said, "it's very simple Dennis, I want you to run it like it's your own." End of conversation. I don't think we could have done it with anyone else. He left us to run it ourselves.

---

8 Ibid.

Having agreed the budget, Harry would then take it to the Hillsdown Board, which really would be a rubber stamping operation and away we go. I just can't speak too highly of the relationship. They didn't come down and look at the sites, they didn't have a man on the Board.'

The first full year under Hillsdown ownership was the climax of the housing boom. Fairview halved its volumes between 1985 and 1988, and at around 650 they were down to levels not seen since 1973; however, soaring house prices meant that profits trebled to £19m. Cope's strategy for combating the subsequent slump was the same as he had successfully adopted in 1974. Volumes more than trebled in just three years, to a short 2000 – a remarkable achievement. Neither did the policy of going for cash preclude Fairview remaining profitable – despite being wholly dependent on the London market, Fairview remained in profit throughout the recession, profits never falling below £5m.

One of the interesting features of Fairview's history is what it did not do: the management refused to expand geographically and at the start of the 1990s, Fairview must have ranked as the most concentrated housebuilder since the London building boom of the 1930s. Dennis Cope never wanted to become a national builder but Hillsdown thought it a natural progression. 'I can remember sitting down with Harry Solomon and him saying "what's the potential for this business, why can't we become major housebuilders." "Well, we can Harry if you want. I'll open a business for you in Glasgow, I'll open a business for you in Bristol and one in Birmingham but I will tell you now, we'll double the size and halve the margins so what's the point. Because once you get into these regional offices you are reluctant to delegate to people at those regions the authority to spend money on sites without planning permission, without this, without that, you are going to have to be extremely lucky to find the number of people you want that have got the skills and the judgements."'

Fairview goes private again
Ten years after buying Fairview, Hillsdown was coming under increasing city pressure to 'focus' its activities. Solomon had gone and under the Chairmanship of Sir John Nott, a structural review of Hillsdown was published in May 1998. Inter alia it provided for the demerger of Fairview, which was effected in October 1998. Fairview once again stood as an independent quoted housebuilder with Dennis Cope as Chairman and Stephen Casey Managing Director. Fairview remained committed to its original planning-led philosophies though now with more expensive London developments leavening the first-time-buyer flats that had previously characterised its product range. Like other small quoted companies at the time, the Fairview directors were not happy with the low rating accorded to them by investors and, after on-off negotiations through 2000, the Company was taken private in January 2001. It was the last of six housebuilding MBOs in a two-year period and the only one not to create substantial goodwill in the purchasing entity, following a £107m surplus on the land revaluation.

In January 2004, Fairview bought the privately-owned Rialto, a Hertfordshire-based firm that had joint ventures with Fairview and Frogmore. Rialto was wholly owned by Jimmy Barham and had started trading as an estate developer in 1978. It built across Essex, Herts. and East Anglia, and concentrated on the first time buyer. In the late 1990s, the emphasis swung to development of large sites in central London, mainly through a series of partnerships with both domestic and international companies. In 2003, Rialto had completed a record 887 units and, after a period of relatively modest profitability, profits had been averaging around £20m. The £60m acquisition by its long-time associate Fairview was a natural retirement solution for Barham.

FEDERATED HOMES
Peak units: c.1000 (1971)

Leo Meyer's principal creation was Ideal Homes but he was also instrumental in the formation of Federated Homes, run successively by his sons James and Peter. Federated Homes was incorporated in 1959; in essence, the new company was created as a vehicle for Leo Meyer's eldest son, James, on his 21st birthday. Prior to that James had worked a full year at Ideal but had no long term intention of working for his father.

Leo Meyer went to Barclays Bank and negotiated a £1m overdraft for Federated but otherwise there was no direct financial support from Ideal. However, there was considerable practical help. In the early stages, if Ideal did not want sites because they were too small, then they were passed over to Federated. Federated staff were often sons of fathers who were working at Ideal, and James Meyer collected a 'super group of youngsters' to work with him. 'There was an incestuous relationship going on, with James down the road receiving professional help which father directed from the Ideal Homes people. As the first development started in Epsom, not only did they need the accounting and legal staff but then they found they needed an architect and an engineer and so they were provided.'[1] Above all, James had as his right hand man Neil Macaulay, an accountant from Ideal's auditors. Tony Harris remembers him as 'a solid counterweight to Jimmy's entrepreneurial instincts. He was a great chap at keeping discipline and quite ruthless.'

Federated started with 14 maisonettes in its first year followed by 60 units the next. The first large site was actually well outside Federated's home area, at Stockwood in Bristol which was being auctioned by the corporation. Federated bought 800 plots which they paid for with a 10% deposit and the rest on completion of the houses. Another large site, closer to home at School Road Ashford, was one most housebuilders would not touch: 'When you went to see it, it was a lake and it frightened everybody. It had been a quarry and we had to survey it by rowing a boat across and dropping a plumb line down – up to 35ft. A committee would never have bought it but Jimmy made the decision.'[2] The company grew strongly in its first decade reaching completions of around 1000 and achieving turnover of £5.7m in 1971 and pre-tax profits of £440,000. Federated had also developed overseas in the mid 1960s in the State of Ohio, without much financial reward, and, more successfully, in South Africa over a period of about seven years. South Africa, of course, was where James had been educated and served his articles as a surveyor.

The business was floated in 1972 as Federated Land and Building Company with Federated Homes as the housebuilding subsidiary. In 1972, there had been a private share placing with Edith Investment Trust, and the Trust recommended that Federated dispose of all the overseas interests prior to flotation to present a 'clean' company. After the flotation, James Meyer still held 66% of the equity. His younger brother Peter, then aged 30, had spent some time with the company in its early years but had moved into merchant banking and was on the board as a non-executive with a 20% shareholding.

Increasing investment in commercial property
Federated had been increasing its commercial property development to provide a more solid base for the company and it was James in particular who wanted to expand this further. Macaulay concentrated on the residential business (he formally became Managing Director of the housing entity in 1970). Regional

[1] Interview Tony Harris.
[2] Ibid.

offices were being opened giving the company coverage of midlands, the south west and south east. Federated coped well with the recession, near doubling its turnover, helped by sales to local authorities; although profits fell, they were no lower than in 1971. However, borrowing levels were a problem (debt was twice shareholders' funds) and the share price fell to 5p at its lowest.

The improvement in trading as the 1970s progressed allayed the banks' concerns on borrowings, allowing Federated to embark on major shopping developments. The largest was at Hempstead Valley near Gillingham, claimed by the Company to be the first greenfield out of town shopping centre. Harris remembered it as 'so revolutionary and so big that no retailer in this country could take it on – something like 140,000 sq. ft.'. Sainsbury and British Home Stores had opened their first Savacentre in Washington and Hempstead became their first store in the south. Hempstead was the first shopping centre to be fully enclosed and air-conditioned; it won the International Council of Shopping Centres European Award in 1979, its opening year. Following that, Federated completed the Leatherhead town centre and was selected for town centre schemes at Stoke and Bristol Docks.

Federated plans withdrawal from housing

Neil McCaulay did not view commercial development in the same way as did James Meyer: 'He saw the amount of money going in to property would constrain the growth of the housing side.'[3] Macaulay stood down as Managing Director of Homes in 1977, in favour of Fergus Coates, and retired from the main board in 1978. Federated was being increasingly driven towards commercial property but found, as others before and since, that stock market investors were ambivalent to companies whose trading profits came from housebuilding but whose asset base rested on commercial property. In 1981, Federated announced a phased withdrawal from housebuilding with the land to be sold over a six-year period to a private company, Tevis, controlled by Peter Meyer, recently appointed as executive vice-Chairman of Federated.

To accelerate the transition to commercial property, Federated proposed a merger with Estates & General, which would have doubled the size of the company but it then received two takeover bids on condition that the merger did not go ahead. Kent launched a full bid in March 1982, firmly rejected by the Federated board. However, this was quickly followed by a cash bid from British Steel Pension Fund, which was duly accepted. James Meyer then left the business. Tevis, which changed its name to Federated Housing in October 1983, was in effect the successor company to the old Federated Homes business and inherited not only the land but most of the senior housing management. This time the Chairman and Managing Director was Peter rather than James Meyer, and he combined both roles while being non-resident. Keith Lovelock joined in 1982 as Managing Director of the main operating subsidiary, Federated Homes, in much the same way as Macaulay had taken that role under James Meyer.

The original Federated Land decision to favour commercial development meant that housing volumes had been reduced significantly – from 985 in 1978 to only 272 in 1981 and the need for the private Tevis/Federated Housing to build up equity did not lend itself to a quick recovery. In 1983, the Federated business again came to the stock market to raise funds for expansion and increase the proportion of land it was buying on the open market.

The abortive Crouch rescue

In December 1983, barely a couple of months after the flotation, Peter Meyer came to the rescue of the ailing Crouch Group. Peter Meyer's first proposal was for Federated to acquire Crouch but he was opposed by the rest of the board. Harris said that 'there was a massive contracting arm – all we knew

3 Ibid.

about was the housing land. They had writs against them and liabilities on past contracts. We said no, much to Peter's annoyance, so he went away and did it himself.' In the event, a deal was done between the two companies on the housing land only, with Peter Meyer using his own shares in Federated to create cross holdings. Federated agreed to develop the bulk of Crouch Group's residential housing interests over a 15-month period. Despite this, a receiver was appointed to Crouch in July 1984.

Keith Lovelock was not finding the working relationship with a non-resident executive Chairman an easy one and resigned in 1985, to be replaced by Keith Palmer from Comben. The company slowly rebuilt its position in the market and by 1987 was selling as far as Bristol, Banbury, Colchester and Dover as well as its traditional area in Surrey. Its land strategy was to acquire sites through option and conditional contracts and in 1988 Federated announced that 'Last year saw a substantial increase in our land holdings...Notably we have contracted to acquire a substantial site in Ashford Kent, on which we expect to get planning permission for in excess of 600 units during 1989';[4] in total it owned or contracted to acquire land for 2000 units or five times its annual output. When the housing market crashed, the terms on which three of those agreements were made proved fatal.

Fixed-price commitments prevent bank support

Tony Harris, who had been with the company from its first house to assisting the receiver, was the land director. 'Cheam was a joint venture bid for £12 million on land which turned out only to be worth £6 million in the recession. Ashford was a fixed-price contract when it was negotiated subject to satisfactory planning consent; it would have been about £25 million to complete and something like £3 million had been invested already, buying up access land, the option consideration etc. The Ashford price was around £400,000 an acre; almost the day after the planning inquiry decision came out, I had people on the telephone offering me £600,000 an acre but we didn't take it. At Erith we were buying along the river and you needed a certain amount before you had a viable package. It was a major commitment for the company on the back of all the hype on Docklands. Disneyland was supposed to be coming across the river at one stage: there was a capital lock up of £10-£12 million with contracts on another £8 million. We were known to be buying everything and we were buying it without planning permission at a figure which was well above its existing use value. Our purchases were getting up to £48m and the available spare funds were just not sufficient to run the mainstream housing business.'[5]

When the banks were approached they looked at the 'time-bombs' and turned the request down. The Ashford deal had not actually been completed but the banks realised that the seller could call on Federated for the money. Federated's other problem was that it had been selling up to half its houses with the assistance of shared equity mortgages, offering Federated the chance of sharing in future house price appreciation. However, as second mortgages, the value of the asset retained by Federated was particularly vulnerable to falling house prices. In September 1988 Federated announced the possibility of taking the company private but in the following January it was decided not to proceed. The Finance DIrector resigned in April 1989 followed by the Managing Director in the November; Peter Meyer took over as Managing Director as well as Chairman. The shares were suspended in April 1990 as the company announced that it had made a substantial loss in 1989 and was in discussions with its principal bankers. Administrative receivers were appointed in July 1990 at the request of the directors and Federated ceased trading; the estimated deficit was £9.5m.

---

[4] Group Accounts, 1988.
[5] Interview Tony Harris.

FELL/BACAL
Peak units: c.1300 (1971)

Fell Construction, later known as Bacal, was incorporated in 1952 as a building and civil engineering contractor by Ronald Fell, then a 32 year old Wakefield builder. Ronald Fell was born in Dewsbury, and spent his early working life as a land surveyor, for some time with the Dewsbury Corporation Engineer's department. Wartime service was with the Royal Artillery Survey section, but after being invalided out Fell joined the Wakefield building firm of Harlow and Milner as a junior director. Fell started his own company with half a dozen employees, and from 1954 the firm (along with its sister company, Lawefield Estates) increasingly concentrated on residential development By 1962 over 2500 houses and bungalows had been built in Lancashire, Yorkshire and Cheshire – an implicit rate of 400 a year which no doubt implies a larger number by the start of the 1960s.

The company went public in 1962 with one of the longest-named chairman in the industry -The Right Honourable Michael William Baron Morris of St John's and Waterford. With Ronald Fell was John Glazier, who had joined in 1955 as assistant Managing Director, and Fell's younger brother Gordon who was in charge of design, although not on the Board. Fell soon showed itself to be acquisitive and scarcely a year after the flotation it bought Adkins & Shaw, a firm that had been founded by Eric Adkins and LW Shaw in 1947. There were already connections as Cyril Choularton was a director of both companies. As with Fell, Adkins & Shaw was originally a building and civil engineering contractor, and from 1954 it also had concentrated on residential development, building estates up to 50 miles around Northampton. The expansion in housing volumes was considerable and in 1964 the enlarged company was claiming that for the first time over 1000 houses would have been built in a single year.

Ronald Fell exits
Around 1964, Ronald Fell sold his shareholding and severed connections with the firm he had founded. It is not known why, but by then he had achieved significant local prominence as a racehorse owner, patron of the Wakefield Trinity Rugby Club and President of various charitable organisations. He went on to form Fell Securities but died in 1967. 'Mr Fell had a meteoric rise to wealth and prominence in his business career, which was characterised by tireless vigour, initiative, shrewd assessment and ability of a high order.'[1]

Following its founder's departure, Fell changed its name to Building and Contracting Associates in 1965 (and to Bacal Construction in 1970) and is referred to as Bacal from here on. Bacal sought to expand its general construction business and in 1968 bid, unsuccessfully, for FPA Construction. In 1970 it succeeded in acquiring Kottler and Heron, a specialist civil engineering business, followed in 1971 by two Northampton housebuilders, Palfreyman and AP Hawtin. The annual report that year stated that not only had Bacal continued to expand in the north but it had opened new subsidiaries in the south and in Scotland. However, the first signs of problems were reported in that they had incurred losses on fixed-price building contracts.

By now Eric Adkins was Chairman, with two Kottlers on the board. Turnover had increased from £6m in 1967 to £24m in 1972 and profits were up from £0.4m to £1.3m. A record number of houses (1300) were registered with the NHBC in 1971, a figure never to be reached again. The downturn in the housing market did not immediately appear to affect profits, which were slightly ahead in 1973 before a £0.4m land provision. Indeed, the 1973 annual report was a confident one. Despite the provision against a few

---

[1] Obituary, *Wakefield Express*, 30th Sept. 1967.

sites, the land holdings overall were thought to have a surplus of several million pounds; house sales were running at a 'very satisfactory level';[2] and civils and building were also doing well – expansion in contracting civil engineering and oil distribution were forecast to provide some 50% of group turnover in 1974.

However, the optimism was misplaced. In the six months to June 1974, Bacal declared a loss of £951,000, attributed to rising interest costs and to £838,000 losses on fixed-price housing contracts. The following March, the shares were suspended: Peat Marwick reported on the company and Adkins was replaced as Chairman by Hugh Fraser, the Conservative MP. The accountants reported that the first half loss had been substantially understated and the group was heavily in debt. Bacal had 17 bankers who met and concluded that they were unable to support the group without the presence of a receiver, and in May 1975 a receiver was duly appointed. As part of the restructuring, Bacal sold its civil engineering subsidiary to Galliford Brindley and David Charles took over most of the housing sites.

2 Group Accounts, 1973.

FIVE OAKS INVESTMENTS
Peak units: c.200 (mid 1960s)

Wilkes Limited became a public company in 1897, quoted on the Birmingham Stock Exchange. Its existence as a manufacturer of nuts and bolts and railway fastenings is of no relevance to this history until the shares were suspended in 1965 prior to the acquisition of the Five Oaks Estates Group. The company had also agreed to purchase Crescent Builders and Estates. Five Oaks Estates, based in Wolverhampton, had been formed in 1954 to acquire the business of builders and developers formed earlier that year by Leslie Pugh and John Canadine. The construction arm specialised in local authority housing and had built some 4000 public sector houses over the previous 11 years. The residential business had sold some 1300 houses since 1954; this averaged over 100 a year and, although annual figures were not quoted, the contemporary figure was probably nearer 200. The prospectus did disclose that 250 houses were under construction with land for a further 1100. Five Oaks had also bought, in 1964, 52% of Thornleigh Building Systems, a quoted company making bricks and sanitary ware.

Crescent was formed in 1944 and was managed by its Chairman Mrs Violet May Hall. Although it also undertook contract building for local authorities its main activity was residential development. No indication was given of its turnover or unit sales, only that it had a very large stock of low-cost building land, sufficient for five years. The renamed Five Oaks Investments had a combined profit of £240,000 for 1964 (of which Crescent was marginally the largest contributor), a substantial increase over the previous record. The profits forecast for 1965 was £450,000 including some £200,000 profit on land sold to its quoted subsidiary, Thornleigh! The outstanding shares in Thornleigh were acquired in 1966 and in the same year the Mark Construction Group (with its "Mark House" industrialised building system) was also bought.

Like many firms with local authority work, the impact of inflation on fixed price contracts caused severe problems. In 1967 these led to a £1.3m loss and although there was a trading profit the following year, there was a further pre-tax loss of £170,000 in 1968, and a deficit of net assets. During 1972 Peter Southall (a Birmingham solicitor with interests in other Midlands housebuilders) and Eric Grove (best known for Canberra, bought by Alfred McAlpine) acquired substantial shareholdings in Five Oaks. There was a wholesale change in the Board and Southall became Chairman and Grove Managing Director. Grove's strategy for rescuing the Company was to sell properties and keep the trading at a minimum. Grove then sold his shares at a considerable profit and resigned as Managing Director in 1974 to be replaced by Kenneth Richardson. There was an increasing concentration on property investment but consistent profits were hard to earn. In 1979, at a contentious EGM, three of the directors were removed by a majority poll of the shareholders and their replacements in turn went a year later when City & Continental purchased 27% of the shares. By now the company was primarily a property company, and it remained as such in the quoted arena until the 1990s when it was acquired by Milner Estates.

FRANCIS PARKER
Peak units: 1400 (1973)

Francis Parker was a creature of the 1970s: following the merger of Bob Francis and the Parker family companies, the enlarged company was almost immediately building 1400 houses a year only to sink just as rapidly into obscurity. By far the oldest of the two companies was **Daniel T Jackson**, founded in 1876 as civil engineering contractors in Barking, Essex, and incorporated in 1928. Until the end of World War II, the business was solely civil engineering. In 1944, the business was purchased by the Parker family, reorganised and moved to Ilford and then Hainault, with the emphasis being on residential development. Thomas Parker had joined the company as an office junior around 1920 and, after the family purchase, continued as Managing Director until 1959. His younger brother James, had joined the firm in 1945, having previously worked at the builders' merchant Page Calnan. James took over as Managing Director and Thomas stayed on as Chairman, retiring through ill health in 1963. Nigel Parker, James' son and a chartered civil engineer working for Robert Douglas, subsequently joined the firm.

The Parker brothers had no operational construction experience. 'Certainly, neither my father nor my uncle would have had any knowledge whatsoever of civil engineering. Thomas was a natural wheeler-dealer.'[1] Probably they steered the firm into private housing from a mixture of default and opportunism. By 1961 Jackson had obtained a Stock Exchange quotation, as a residential developer; no turnover figure was given but the company was making no more than £135,000 profit. The company operated mainly in metropolitan Essex and there were estates in Norwich and Hampshire. There was steady organic growth and by 1971 Jackson's housing volumes were reported as 330 houses with a forecast of 400 in 1972 from 21 estates in East Anglia. Jackson moved back into contracting through the acquisition of two building contractors – Joseph Moss of Colchester in 1963 and the very small John Cracknell of Peterborough in 1966. At the end of the decade it suffered from losses on fixed-price local authority contracts, particularly in 1971 on a GLC contract in Hampshire. Group profits had averaged around £250,000 in the mid 1960s but the contracting losses reduced this to £120,000 in 1971 and £230,000 was written off reserves. Fixed-price contracting for local authorities was extensively cut back.

Bob Francis starts at Butlins
In contrast, the **Francis** group of companies were of more recent creation. RK ['Bob'] Francis, born in 1939, had originally been a clerk at the Butlins holiday camp at Bognor Regis. 'He was shocked at the standard of workmanship involved in erecting the chalets, aired his views to Billy Butlin and was invited to do a better job himself. He did (on borrowed money) and was subsequently offered similar work at Minehead. With the proceeds he bought Littlehampton Contractors in 1962 for £2000 and embarked on subcontracting work for the building industry in the specialised field of structural concrete.'[2] Francis later added other specialist companies – plastering, joinery, electrical contracting, pre-cast concrete; he acquired businesses making building blocks; bought a public works contractor; and moved into residential development. By the start of the 1970s, Francis had nine estates in Sussex, selling around 100 houses in 1970/71 and forecasting 200 for 1972. Residential and commercial development and contracting accounted for around half the £200,000 profit.

Francis and Jackson merge
In 1970, Jackson had announced plans to merge with WA Hills but that came to naught. A year later Jackson was in a weaker position and under pressure from ICFC; in September 1971, the Jackson and

---

[1] Interview with Nigel Parker, March 2001.
[2] *Building*, 20th Sep. 1974.

Francis companies announced their merger. The mechanics were that the quoted Jackson took over Francis although, in effect, it was a reverse takeover. The company was renamed Francis Parker; Bob Francis, still only 32, became Managing Director and in the following year, also Chairman. The enlarged group was forecasting 600 residential units for the year to March 1972; the two housing operations continued to be run separately – Francis's southern business by Colin Loveless and Jackson by James and Nigel Parker. However, there was no intent to confine itself to housing. The acquisition of the quarrying firm John Heaver was negotiated at the time of the merger and Francis Parker then purchased Truscon's pre-cast concrete division. Bob Francis was also determined to use his quoted company status to acquire other public development companies. In December 1971, only two months after dealings in Francis Parker had been resumed, Francis entered a bidding war for control of Drury Holdings, an old-established housebuilder with an excellent land bank, but whose profits had been adversely affected by losses on fixed price local authority contracts. Francis Parker succeeded in buying Drury in February 1972 at a cost of £4.5m; by then, Drury's output had fallen to around 400 units and was trimmed back further to improve profitability.

Housing: acquisitions and then divestment

In 1973, Francis Parker added another quoted housebuilder, the Manchester based Dean Smith, at a cost of £2.6m. A general contracting business had been established in 1962 by Anthony Dean Smith and in 1964 he began to develop residential sites in North Cheshire. The company floated on the stock exchange in 1968. The acquisition of Drury and Dean Smith gave the group a spread of sites from the south coast up to Lancashire and Yorkshire. In his annual statement, published in August 1973, Bob Francis said that the Company intended to raise the number of houses built for the private sector from around 1400 to 2500 by 1975. Exactly one year later, a headline read 'Francis Parker to quit housing';[3] within the next year to 15 months, Francis Parker planned to withdraw entirely from contracting and housebuilding and to concentrate on the supply of aggregates and other building materials. Its 1973-74 profits had fallen from £4.4m to £1.1m after provisions of £4?m on fixed-price local authority contracts.

The contracting side was to be sold to two directors and private housing phased out. The company never really recovered from the collapse in land values. Dividend payments ceased and the 1976 accounts were prepared on a going concern basis on the understanding that finance would continue to be available. In 1980 Tarmac bought the aggregate interests of Francis Parker for £1m plus the assumption of its debt; four years later, Tarmac bought what was left of the company. Bob Francis returned to the construction industry but was later bankrupt and died of a heart attack c.1992/93. Nigel Parker had left the firm in 1972, and his father followed a year or two later. Nigel Parker bought the Cambridgeshire firm of Bennett Homes which is still building some 100 houses a year under Parker family control.

[3] Ibid, 30th Aug. 1974.

GALLIFORD ESTATES
Peak units: 1121 (1989)

Cecil and John Galliford were in partnership in the 1950s building houses in South London and Surrey. John Galliford was a bricklayer by trade and his younger brother Cecil a carpenter; both later described themselves as master builders, but 'Cecil was the driving force.'[1] The first house was built in Cecil's garden in New Malden and the business operated on a small scale for some years. It was incorporated as Galliford Construction in 1959 and was floated in July 1968. The prospectus confirmed that in the early years of the Group 'relatively few houses were built' and, indeed, the first three years of the ten year record disclosed losses. After the flotation, Galliford entered a period of rapid expansion, both organic and by acquisition. Galliford had a small plant hire business and in 1969 it paid just over £1m for Contractors Services, a company actually making slightly more profit than Galliford's £150,000; at the same time it also bought FJG Morgan, an Uxbridge builder. In 1970, the company made a £1m bid for Comben and Wakeling although this failed as the latter's directors sold their controlling shareholding to Carlton at a slightly lower price. Galliford was more successful in late 1971 when it announced the purchase of the southern housebuilder AJ Wait and its associate company EE Reed, for a cash price of £3¹/₄m – almost as much as Galliford's own market capitalisation.

Acquisition of Wait doubles housebuilding
Wait once belonged to Hallmark Securities but passed to Spey Westmoreland Properties when the latter acquired Hallmark. Wait was a larger housebuilder than Galliford: it had 28 estates under development across the south of England with 2100 plots and 530 acres of white land. This compared with Galliford's 21 sites under development and 1370 plots. Their combined building rate was quoted at around 1500 houses a year though this was probably well above the actual build rate. This deal was followed shortly after by the successful bid for the quoted WA Hills & Sons, a smaller housebuilder concentrated in East Anglia. Through its own purchases and the acquisitions, Galliford's land bank rose from £0.7m to £13.3m between 1971 and 1974.

Having gained control of Wait and Hills, Galliford floated a 46% minority in Contractors Services, selling the balance in May 1973. One of the reasons was to generate more capital for commercial property development and in 1973 Galliford actually moved its share listing to the property sector. By the end of 1973 Galliford had built up a property portfolio of £3.2m and was aiming for £10m by 1975. It also moved into Europe by buying Leisure International from Watney Mann; this company was building an £8m 400-bed hotel in the centre of Amsterdam, due to open in 1975, and its Swiss Franc debt was to be a contributor to Galliford's coming problems. The European development programme was quoted as £40m, while the housing side was being kept steady at around 1000 units a year.[2]

Rescue by Sears
In the year to March 1973, turnover and profits had peaked at £16m and £3.7m and, although there was a fall in profits to £2.4m in 1973/74, there appeared little to suggest that the problems affecting some of the other rapidly-expanding housing/property companies were threatening Galliford's existence. In December 1974 Galliford suddenly accepted a £3.2m bid from Sears, a price that was less than its 1973 profits. The link between the two companies was Geoffrey Maitland-Smith of Sears (later to become Chief Executive); Maitland-Smith had been a partner at Thornton Baker, the Galliford auditor and was

---

[1] Interview with Brian Wait, Aug. 2001.
[2] *Building*, 12th Oct. 1973.

familiar with the business. The takeover approach was, however, a shock to shareholders.

The *Investor's Chronicle* spelt out the sudden change in fortunes which followed the reassuring AGM in October: 'Barely four weeks later the same shareholders received notice of a bid from Sears Holdings valuing the company at little more than 20 per cent of its apparent net assets…In his letter explaining the directors' decision to recommend Sears £3.6 million bid, and to accept on behalf of their own 34 per cent holdings, Mr Donaldson performed a sharp about-turn in his view of Galliford's prospects. Gone is the cautiously optimistic talk of continuing growth, and in its place is news that house sales are dismal, with no early prospect of improvement; commercial and industrial developments costing £1.7 million stand unlet; there may no longer be the cash to meet a £2.8m commitment in mid-1975; and the group's bankers are calling in their facilities…The directors saw only two choices open to them, liquidation (which was rejected on the grounds that a forced sale situation would not have been in shareholders' interests) or an immediate sale to a group able to complete the Developments.'[3]

Sears' deputy Chairman, Leonard Sainer, was more tactful, saying that Galliford was not in need of a rescue operation but merely 'a bit strapped for cash.'[4] The reality was disclosed by the first eight-month trading period under Sears' ownership, whereby turnover halved and a loss of £11.3m was incurred. Sears' considerable property expertise and financial strength enabled it to complete the commercial property programme and the housing business was continued as Galliford Sears. John Galliford left on the takeover, although Cecil stayed for a year or two. He was succeeded as Managing Director by Peter Gibson and then David Brill, a carpenter by trade who had worked first for Wates and Costain Homes.

Sears loses interest

Housing was never a central part of Sears' operation and may not even have been the main reason for the acquisition. David Brill said that 'The day I took over as Managing Director from Peter Gibson, Maitland-Smith told me that housing wasn't regarded as a core activity.'[5] Nevertheless, Brill was able to rebuild volumes and move the product mix up-market. By 1988/89 Galliford's sales had reached a record 1121, with turnover of £110m and profits of £31m. Like most other southern housebuilders, the recession hit hard and losses totalled £33m in the three years to 1992/93. Sears was losing confidence in the long term prospects for housing and taking cash out of the business through land sales. Volumes halved and there was no will to replenish land stocks at the bottom of the market.

Eventually, David Brill persuaded Sears to sell Galliford; in 1993 it was bought by the management (backed by venture capital) for £27½m, Sears taking a £27m loss on the sale. Within six months, Prowting successfully bid for Galliford, the timing being influenced by the venture capital articles which allowed the financier to keep the proceeds of sales if made within six months of the original investment (rather than distribute back to its own shareholders).

---

[3] *Investors Chronicle*, December 1974.
[4] *Building* 29th Nov. 1974.
[5] Interview with David Brill, May 2001.

GALLIFORD TRY
Peak units: 899 (2002)

Galliford's roots go back to 1916, when Thomas Galliford moved to the village of Wolvey in Leicestershire and set up business with a threshing machine, going round the local farms. This developed into steamroller hire, but Thomas Galliford died in 1938 and the business was closed down completely during the War. After the War, the business was re-established by Thomas Galliford's widow and the four children, Dick, George, Peter and Peggy, and incorporated as Galliford & Sons in 1952. Galliford was floated in 1965, with Peter Galliford as Managing Director. Peter Galliford, the youngest of Thomas's children, had joined the family partnership after service with the Royal Engineers, and became group Managing Director in 1959 at the age of 30. Galliford developed principally as a civil engineering business, reinforced in 1967 by the merger with Douglas Brindley's Road Surfacing Group; Galliford's name was changed (for a few years) to Gallford Brindley.

Subsequent to the Road Surfacing merger, there was a conscious effort to widen the base of the Group. The building company Wincott was bought in 1968 and Galliford Brindley Properties was formed in 1972. The same year also saw Galliford begin what was to become a long relationship with housing associations. It was not until October 1973 that Galliford entered the private housing market, this time through a £650,000 acquisition – the Coventry company, Crabb Curtis. 'Over the last few years, the Company has changed from being almost exclusively a civil engineering contractor to one with a spread of activities…your Directors consider it appropriate on long term considerations to have a specialist housebuilder amongst its trading companies.'[1]

The first housing acquisition
Crabb Curtis had been formed in 1962 by Ray Crabb, who described himself as a builder's surveyor, and Alan Curtiss, a bricklayer. The business was of a very modest size, probably less than 50 houses a year in the Coventry, Banbury and Oxford area, and the founders stayed on to run it, Curtiss leaving in 1976 and Crabb in 1979. Volumes in 1980 were still less than 100 houses a year and, with the founders' departure, the company was renamed Wincott Homes. There was little further progress in housing until 1983 when Galliford appointed Eric Wood, an ex-Barratt subsidiary Managing Director, to increase the scale of the Wincott Homes operation. Although turnover increased, the company was consistently losing money. Wood resigned at the end of 1986 and Wincott Homes closed its operations. By that time, however, Galliford was conducting a more successful housing business through Stamford Homes.

Stamford was formed as Gilman & Murray in 1946 at Uppingham, by Frank Gilman, a farmer, and Walter Murray, a civil engineer; the name was changed to Stamford Construction the following year when another civil engineer, Timothy Clancy joined. The first speculative houses were built in 1959 but it is believed that housing remained an incidental part of Stamford's business. In 1969, Stamford was bought by Clancy, then Chairman and Managing Director, and Fred Harris, a surveyor. Ken Firman was appointed as building director in 1974, when Stamford restarted speculative housing. Stamford was bought by Galliford in 1976, and the civil engineering side was gradually absorbed into Galliford's construction business leaving Firman to run a housebuilding business which concentrated on affordable houses in the eastern counties, particularly Lincolnshire. The Stamford Homes business was gradually expanded and in 1988 it was actually shown in the group accounts as a separate division rather than part of the general building and development division. That year saw housing completions reach 200 for the first time, built on sites from Skegness down through Lincolnshire, Norfolk and Cambridgeshire. The

---

[1] Annual Report, 1974.

following year, on reduced volumes, housing profits reached a record £3m out of a group total of £10m.

Through the 1970s and 1980s, the strategic direction of the group had been under the control of Peter Galliford and Eric Pugh; Pugh had been involved with the Group as auditor since 1952 and had joined as Finance Director in 1961. They sought to enlarge the coverage of the group, principally by acquisition, and Galliford diversified into distribution, specialist contracting and pipeline cleaning. The 1990 recession inevitably affected all parts of the business, but it was the highly cyclical housebuilding that held up better than most. In contrast, many of the newer activities caused deeper problems; large losses were made in specialist contracting and distribution in 1992 and 1993, and there was a £6m provision against withdrawal from the pipe-relining business in 1994.

Management changes

Eric Pugh had taken over as Managing Director from Peter Galliford in 1987, the latter remaining as Executive Chairman; Pugh retired in 1989 to be succeeded by George Marsh, a civil engineer who had joined the group in 1976. Peter Galliford retired as Chairman in 1993, remaining on the Board until 1999. Ken Firman also reached retirement age during 1996 and Mick Noble, previously with Ideal Homes, had been appointed Stamford Homes' Managing Director the previous year. The early and middle years of the 1990s was a period of rationalisation and disposal, and the private housing business did little more than mark time. However, more investment was eventually committed to Stamford Homes and in 1997 the Annual Report gave its target as 500 houses a year. That 500 target for speculative housing was virtually achieved the following year, as a result of the acquisition of **Midas Homes**. Midas Group had been founded in 1976 by Len Lewis, a civil engineer, and it started housebuilding in the mid-1980s, operating between Weston-super-Mare and Weymouth. Run by Greg Fitzgerald, it achieved private house sales in 1997 of around 150. Midas Homes' other strength was in social housing where it was the market leader in Devon and Cornwall. The social housing element held a particular attraction for Galliford. In 1990, Galliford had bought the Essex contracting business of J Hodgson, which also had a large social housing content and this had proved one of the Group's more successful acquisitions.[2]

In stock market terms, Galliford remained a small company, yet refusing to pursue the focused route then preferred by investors, remaining committed to both construction and speculative housing. The solution adopted was the merger with another quoted company, similarly structured. In 2000, Galliford merged with the **Try Group** to form Galliford Try. Try's Managing Director, David Calverley, became Group Chief Executive with George Marsh his deputy. The two housing operations complemented each other and were headed by Mick Noble. Stamford was a greenfield developer, building lower cost housing in the eastern counties; Try Homes was smaller in numbers (200 in 1999) but concentrated on brownfield sites in the south east. In 2001, the enlarged housing division completed 780 private units contributing some £13m to group trading profits of £19m. However, the three main speculative housing businesses, Stamford, Midas and Try were operating independently and it was not until 2003 that they were merged into one entity under Midas Homes' Greg Fitzgerald; the major part of social housing remained within the construction division. In 2005, Greg Fitzgerald became Chief Executive of the whole group.

[2] The number of social units is not disclosed by the Group.

GLEESON
Peak units: 720 (2000)

The Gleeson family came from farming stock in County Galway. Michael Joseph Gleeson and his younger brother James began visiting England around the 1890s taking agricultural jobs. Michael Gleeson later joined a small building concern in Sheffield run by the Donellan family, also from Galway. Gleeson married Donellan's daughter and, in 1903, effectively took over the management of the business. The Gleeson company dates its foundation from that year although its corporate name was not changed to MJ Gleeson until 1915.

Michael Gleeson built up a successful business in the Sheffield area, both as a contractor and a developer, and he also owned cinemas in Sheffield and a racetrack. Around 1930, Gleeson started taking contracts in the south-east (the Savoy Cinema in Brighton being an example). In 1932, Gleeson Development Company was formed to start housebuilding in south-west London and Michael Gleeson sent his nephew John Patrick ['Jack'] Gleeson, then aged 22, to manage this new operation. Michael Gleeson had no sons of his own and Jack Gleeson, James' eldest son, had left Ireland to join his uncle in Sheffield at the age of 16; the younger son, Pat, followed some years later. The two brothers had both trained as bricklayers and learned to read drawings at nightschool.

The first London housing
With his Sheffield track record behind him, Michael Gleeson was able to secure Midland Bank support for land purchases. The first site was the Park Farm Estate, North Cheam, started in 1933 and comprising some 750 semi-detached houses; it was followed by the Sheephouse Estate, Worcester Park and, in 1936, the Nonsuch Estate in Cheam where 4-bedroom houses ranged in price up to £1350. Other estates were built in Southall and Orpington. A surviving Nonsuch Estate brochure indicates a high level of annual sales was being achieved even from the limited number of sites – and the customer loyalty that had rapidly been acquired: 'out of the five hundred odd houses which they have sold this year, nearly half have been sold to friends of previous purchasers of Gleesons Homes.'[1] The Nonsuch Estate lasted the family some 40 years.

During the war Gleeson engaged in runway construction on a substantial scale, primarily for the US bases in Norfolk alongside such contractors as Taylor Woodrow. Gleeson had already started road construction in the mid-1930s and the aerodrome work reinforced the embryo civil engineering skills, preparing the way for the post-war civils programme. Michael Gleeson retired in 1950; with two married daughters and no sons he decided to split the business. MJ Gleeson (Contractors) was formed in 1950 to acquire the business of its predecessor, leaving the cash, the property and housebuilding land in the old company. The four directors of the new company, with equal shareholdings, were Jack Gleeson, who was to run the business; two doctors, Michael Cleary and Arthur Perren (the sons-in-law) and George Eastwood, Company Secretary of the predecessor company. Pat Gleeson, Jack's younger brother, had been working in the business since before the war but did not become a director until 1957.

Gleeson re-enters private housing market
In 1955, Gleeson re-entered the speculative housing market, firstly in Sheffield and Lincoln but, by the time of the flotation in 1960, the Prospectus was reporting the purchase of several sites 'in the southern and south-western outskirts of London which are in the course of development.' However, private housing remained a secondary activity as Gleeson was now coming into its prime as a civil engineer with

---

1 Contemporary sales brochure.

a strong position in roads and reservoirs. Indeed, until 1982 Gleeson Homes appeared at the back of the accounts merely as one of the 'other subsidiaries.'

The housing volumes in the 1960s and 1970s were modest, perhaps no more than 100 a year. 'In those days we were not at all interested in volume. Jack Gleeson was a great hoarder of land. He used to sit on it and watch it appreciate, often very reluctant to release it for development. If units didn't sell, he wouldn't cut prices – he would stop work and wait until the market caught up with what he felt was the right price.' Despite its relatively smaller size, Jack Gleeson kept the closest control over private housing. 'Various managers came and went but Jack kept a very firm grip on the homes side himself. We had a land buyer but every single bid was vetted by Jack.' [2]

The Group's profits record in the 1970s was flat, fluctuating either side of £1m. The 1980 Annual Report spelt out the problem and the solution: 'As conditions have become increasingly difficult for public works contractors...the Group has pressed on with the policy of extending our residential, commercial and industrial development programmes; and, despite poor market conditions for selling houses, our estates division has again made an important profit contribution....Our present intention is gradually to establish a portfolio of investment properties by retaining the best of our commercial and industrial developments since we regard this as the safest harbour for Group funds during the present years of recession in our industry.'

Reluctance to expand housing

The word 'Contractors' was symbolically dropped from the Group's name but attitudes to housing did not necessarily change. 'We certainly thought of ourselves as, above all else, contractors and in those days people would view the housebuilding arm as a regulator or safety valve, something we turn on and off depending on how the contracting is going.'[3] Greater emphasis was being put on commercial than residential development in the early 1980s. Dermot Gleeson explained that his Uncle's reluctance to significantly expand speculative housing stemmed from the commitment to contracting. 'He was really conscious that contracting was a high risk business. He wasn't one of the people who took the view that contracting is cash generative and you can finance a substantial amount of development activity from the contracting cash flow – he thought it was nonsense.'[4] Clearly, a reluctance to raise fresh capital and dilute family control created a self-imposed financial constraint.

During the 1980s there was a gradual change in leadership – again to a nephew, Dermot Gleeson, Pat Gleeson's son; 'You could say we're the most nepotistic company in the country.'[5] After taking a history degree, Dermot Gleeson determined to make his career outside the Company, working in the Conservative Research Office and the European Commission. He joined the Board as a non-executive director in 1975 but it was not until after the 1979 election that he was persuaded to join the Company. He became deputy Managing Director in 1981 and Chief Executive in 1988, Jack Gleeson remaining Chairman. In practice, housing was the last area where Jack Gleeson relinquished personal control, running it until 1988 with the land buyer and construction director reporting to him. Dermot Gleeson's first move was to appoint Win Bruce, the long-standing Finance Director, as Managing Director of Gleeson Homes. 'We knew that was going to be a transitional measure. Win and I wanted to go for significantly greater growth, to push up-market and to work from a leaner land bank.'[6] That move was

[2] Interview with Dermot Gleeson, Feb. 2002.
[3] Ibid.
[4] Ibid.
[5] *Daily Telegraph* (nepotism is actually the favouring of nephews rather than children).
[6] Interview Dermot Gleeson.

made just as the recession was beginning to bite but it was a period which proved the virtues of family caution. Group profits fell, but by no more than 30% to the trough in 1993.

Colroy brings new housing management

Gleeson used the recession to increase its commitment to private housing, buying **Colroy** in 1991. Colroy brought a land bank at an attractive price; extended housing into the midlands, East Anglia and the north west; and brought in a strong management team. Colroy's Managing Director, Bill Hoggett, became Managing Director of Gleeson Homes in 1993. A further purchase, of **Portman Homes**, the residential business of Portman Building Society, for £12m in 1994, was primarily a land deal. The mid 1990s was a period of consolidation followed by further strong growth. In 1995, Hoggett was replaced by Clive Wilding, a surveyor who had joined the Homes Board in 1987. Housing volumes steadily increased, reaching 720 in year 2000 contributing roughly half group profits. However, trading margins of only 8% at the peak of the housing cycle, were well below the returns achieved by most specialised housebuilders.

'With the benefit of hindsight I think we were too adventurous with respect to the balance between the use of standard house types and concept schemes. We were bolder than most and won a lot of prizes but it is terribly difficult to control costs with large conversions.'[7] In October 2001 Terry Massingham, formerly Managing Director of McAlpine Homes Southern was appointed Managing Director of Gleeson Homes. The following January the Company had to announce that Gleeson Homes profits would be substantially below budget for the year to June 2002 and Gleeson announced plans to shift the emphasis from refurbishment schemes in favour of new-build projects where costs are more predictable. Most of the senior commercial staff in the homes division were replaced. However, for the first time, there was a dedicated housing managing director on the main Board.

Gleeson Homes continues as one of the few housing companies that remain part of an actively managed construction group. At the height of the City debate about focus, Dermot Gleeson argued graphically for the wider base: 'Now that the economic weather is improving, we are in the happy position of having more than one golf club in our bag.'[8] At the heart of his argument lies the diversification of risk and the ability to take a long view but it cannot be separated from Dermot Gleeson's belief that he is accountable to more than narrow, and possibly transitory, shareholder interests. 'What is your test of success? My test is whether I protect the human community that I regard the company to be. I think that we pass that test well; we have survived and we have provided much greater employment security than most. I don't think we could have done that if we hadn't had the wide spread of activities. I do not believe that Gleeson Homes will always be somewhat less efficient than a pure housebuilder. I can't see why it should be so but supposing you persuaded me that up to a point that it must be so, I would still probably for strategic reasons want to keep Gleeson Homes. I don't think that the return on Gleeson Homes compared to its peers is the only consideration.'[9]

In fact, the 'return on Gleeson Homes compared to its peers' has continued to be well below the industry average: its trading margins of 11% in 2004, although better than for many years, compared with 21% for the quoted focused housebuilders.[10] At the time of writing, Gleeson had been notified of a possible offer from the AIM-quoted Castle Acquisitions, a company with a market capitalisation of only £5m. Following the disposal of its building division in 2005, there has also been speculation that Gleeson may dispose of its civil engineering business, leaving it as a more focused development company.

---

[7] Ibid.
[8] *Financial Time*, 17th Oct. 1997.
[9] Interview Dermot Gleeson.
[10] *PHA* 2005.

GOUGH COOPER
Peak units: c.1050 (1972)

Walter Henry ('Harry') Gough-Cooper was born in Newport, Wales in 1907. His father, also Walter, was a university-educated civil engineer working on the Alexandra Docks at the time of Harry's birth. After World War I, Walter began civil engineering on his own account and was working on the Kilkeel Harbour in Ireland in 1923 when he died suddenly, leaving the family penniless. The family moved to Leicestershire to stay with relatives and Harry Gough-Cooper obtained articles with an architect, studying building construction at night school. 'With characteristic determination he set about preparing himself to support his mother, younger brother and sister.'[1]

In the late 1920s, Harry Gough-Cooper gained experience of building private and council houses for Browning Brothers Builders before moving to Dartford in Kent where he worked as a carpenter's labourer while saving to buy his first land – plot by plot. Cooper Estates was formed in 1933 just after Harry Gough-Cooper had launched his first house type called, appropriately enough, the Cooper 1933 houses: 'Until the COOPER £400 house was placed on the market, people were wise in refraining from purchasing, for the advent of this COOPER house saw the introduction of the first and only low-priced house of sound construction and high-grade finish.'[2] Between 1934 and 1938 Cooper Estates built locally at a rate of around 100 a year. The firm was very much a family concern with Harry's younger sister 'Trixie' supporting the office. At the beginning of 1939, Gough Cooper & Co was formed (the hyphen was dropped from the family name as it was thought inappropriate for a company or a site board) to act as a building and civil engineering company; during and after the war it carried out bomb damage work. In 1948, Harry Gough-Cooper formed a South African company, also Gough Cooper, and that business (which was quoted on the Johannesburg Stock Exchange) remained outside the UK company.

With the abolition of building controls, Gough Cooper resumed private housebuilding on a more substantial scale. In the 1950s and early 1960s the Company expanded in the south east and by 1962 had reached a sales level of around 800, probably putting it in the top ten housebuilders at that time. The company gradually pushed further afield as new offices were opened in Leicester and Newbury in 1966 and Diss and Knutsford in 1969. The wider geographical spread did not significantly increase volumes: by the time of Gough Cooper's flotation in 1972, the company was forecasting 1050 sales. Two companies had run side by side since the restart of private housebuilding: Cooper Estates owned the land and Gough Cooper carried out the construction. However, in 1962 Gough Cooper began to acquire its own land as well as drawing from Cooper Estates. Prior to its flotation in 1972, Gough Cooper acquired all the remaining residential land, that had planning permission or was zoned, from Cooper Estates, which remained private.

John Boardman takes control
John Boardman, who had joined in 1939 as a buyer, was playing an increasing role in the direction of the company, and, when Harry Gough-Cooper became non-resident (emigrating to South Africa) in 1967, Boardman was appointed Chief Executive, becoming Chairman in 1969 and leading the company into the public arena. According to Jennifer Gough-Cooper, Harry's daughter, 'No member of the family was involved with running the building company or had any aspirations to manage it.'[3] Moreover, Harry Gough-Cooper's health had been deteriorating and by 1972 he was terminally ill (he was to die three years later); a public flotation was the obvious answer to the succession issue.

[1] *Housebuilder* April 1975.
[2] Contemporary advertisement.
[3] Correspondence with author.

Gough Cooper made an excellent start as a public company as the market boomed and in 1973 turnover rose 70% to £17m and pre-tax profits doubled to £4m. Although profits never reached these levels again, the company avoided the losses that brought other companies down. Whereas some housebuilders tried to expand their way out of the recession, Gough Cooper was selling land to reduce debt. The fall in sales to 850 in 1974 (against a prospectus 'capacity' of 1500) was probably no more than a product of market forces but a couple of years later sales were little more than 400. 'Flexibility and survival are the key words used by Gough Cooper & Co as they search for policy guidelines that will compensate for the decline in building houses for private sale... A developer who a few years ago was opening new sites in the north west and elsewhere north of Watford today seeks business abroad, expands design and build services to housing associations and local authorities.'[4]

The diversification was not a total success and 1978 saw losses of £750,000 in contract housebuilding and, although profits recovered in 1979, further contracting losses meant Gough Cooper incurred a group loss in the first half of 1979/80. This signalled the end of Gough Cooper's independence. In the July, Remo Dipre's Starwest Investment Holdings bought 29^1/$_2$% of Gough Cooper at 95p a share in a dawn raid within only 30 minutes; Starwest said it had no intention of making a bid, although in the September it did make one at 120p. Shortly after, there was an agreed takeover bid from Allied London Properties at 145p valuing Gough Cooper at £11m. Cooper Estates continues as a family controlled investment company.

---

[4] *Housebuilder* March 1977.

GREAVES
Peak units: c1200 (1972)

Greaves was one of the larger Midlands housebuilders in the 1960s but it failed in the aftermath of the 1973-4 recession. John (Jack) Greaves was nominally the founder of the business but it was driven throughout its housebuilding history by Edward Wheatley, Chairman and Managing Director at the time of flotation. Wheatley had left grammar school in 1946, aged 16, following the death of his father and he apprenticed as a plumber. Around 1954, he met the much older Jack Greaves (born 1904), a painter and decorator with a small building business in West Bromwich. Wheatley bought the Greaves business for a nominal sum and from then on Greaves worked for Wheatley. Cyril Rotheroe joined them in 1958 having had his own plumbing business. It was not until 1959 that the partnership began building houses. 'We were doing repairs and improvements and saw others doing well out of housing. It looked an easier way of making money – it was easier to sell a product rather than a service.'[1]

Rapid expansion led to a flotation in 1966. The Prospectus did not indicate housing volumes: Wheatley 'guessed' some 35 years later that it was around 400, a figure that was consistent with turnover; there remained a general contracting business. What the Prospectus did reveal was that 50% of the shares were now owned by Harry Plotnek who had joined the company as a part time finance director. Plotnek, best known as the founder of Allied Carpets, had brought additional capital into the company and 'the three existing shareholders decided it made sense to have a smaller share of a bigger cake.'[2] As a footnote, Harry Plotnek sold Wheatley 20% of Allied Carpets and when it was floated Wheatley bought Plotnek a horse as a present – it turned out to be 'Comedy of Errors' which won the Champion Hurdles twice.

Late 1960s expansion

The company continued to expand rapidly after flotation, concentrating on low-cost homes for the first-time buyer. By the end of the 1960s Greaves was building around 900 houses a year and operated in Leicester, Nottingham, Leighton Buzzard, Chigwell and Southampton.[3] By 1971, the build programme was running at around 1200 a year and peak profits of £1.9m were earned in 1973 on turnover of £10m. During the recession Greaves actually produced a brochure called *Starter Homes* which it sent to over 100 local authority planning offices; the interesting feature was the inclusion of a one-bedroom single-storey 'Studio' home, a concept later used by Barratt to great effect. Greaves went into the recession with high borrowings and other housebuilders remember Greaves buying land 'at astronomical prices.' At first, Greaves seemed to be surviving and, although it lost money in 1975, the losses were not high. Indeed, in 1975/76 the Group broke even and debt was reduced from £13m to £8m. However, when interest rates began to rise sharply in the Autumn of 1976 the banks would support the company no more: on December 1st 1976 receivers were appointed. 'For Greaves the bitter irony is that the end came just as it appeared to be surmounting its difficulties.'[4] Edward Wheatley thought that what finished Greaves was the David Charles collapse: 'all the sub-contractors and suppliers wanted paying quickly and it was like a set of dominoes; they couldn't get their money from Charles so they camped on our doorstep.'[5] The receivers quickly sold the sites and by the end of the month Comben had bought the rump of the business.

---

[1] Interview with Edward Wheatley, June 2000.

[2] Ibid.

[3] *Housebuilder*, Sept. 1969.

[4] *Building*, 10th Dec. 1976.

[5] Interview Edward Wheatley.

HALLMARK HOMES
Peak units: 1250 (1970)

Originally the New Bulawayo Syndicate, the Company saw a complete change in its management and business in 1957, reflected in the change of name to Hallmark Securities. Sidney Bloch, a Brighton solicitor, was Chairman and Managing Director and Herbert Ashworth, a banker, the General Manager. The company acquired a large number of subsidiaries which dealt in or held property plus a group engaged in estate development which had 17 estates in progress. Unusually, the acquisitions were made at below asset value. Hallmark's housing companies had been formed by Alan Draycott of AC Draycott and Partners, estate agents, and he was one of the early Hallmark directors. Private housing was carried out under the name 'Hallmark Homes', and the 1958 accounts claimed that volumes had been around 500 a year since 1955, implying a rapid acceleration after the ending of controls.

The public status enabled Hallmark to expand by acquisition. It bought Hesketh Homes in 1958 and TJ Brabon & Son (Estates) in 1959, the latter owning 'nearly all the remaining undeveloped building land in Brighton & Hove.'[1] There was a clear policy to acquire large tracts of land with long term potential. As well as greenfield land, Hallmark was also aware of the potential in urban redevelopment, and the 1960 accounts reported on the assembly of a team of experts to work with the local authorities; that year, housing sales reached a peak of 536. Diversification started with the purchase of Twentieth Century Banking, a business which was later to cause deep financial problems at Bovis. In 1960, Hallmark formed a relationship with Sun Life Assurance to concentrate on long term investment in commercial property.

Purchase of the quoted A J Wait
In January 1963, Hallmark bought the quoted New Malden housebuilder, AJ Wait, doubling its housing capacity. Draycott had started to do land deals on the south coast for Wait and the relationship developed from there. The much smaller firm of EE Reed (building around 30-40 houses a year) was also bought around that time. It was the Wait management that took control of the enlarged housing division – in the first accounts after the acquisition the Chairman reported that most of the group's estates had already been integrated within the Wait organisation. There was also a change in the construction process, and one which appeared contrary to that taking place elsewhere in the industry. Previously, Hallmark's construction had been carried out by outside contractors 'which gave away some of the profit'; the merger with Wait 'helps vertical integration.'[2] The reality was that Hallmark had been using outside contractors (not subcontractors) to do all the construction. These contractors were not big enough as they were local firms: 'the south coast in those days wasn't very sophisticated as far as building work was concerned. Hallmark had the land but they couldn't produce the goods.'[3] In contrast, Wait used both direct labour and subcontractors.

With a full year from Wait, the number of houses sold was an all time record of 1145 and Hallmark's profits reached £800,000. However, by 1965 housebuilding was down to only 23% of group profit; Hallmark had become a true conglomerate with interests ranging across property, housebuilding, banking and manufacturing – primarily Barking Brassware. Arthur Wait, who had been appointed to the Hallmark main board, left the group after about four years. 'Complete disillusionment; they kept nicking his cash! He was a disillusioned man. He would much rather have been a south of England builder doing

[1] Group Accounts 1959.
[2] Group Accounts 1963.
[3] Interview Brian Wait.

speculative housing than contributing profits on paper to Hallmark.'[4]

Housing cash goes to finance Hallmark property

Arthur's son Brian, who had previously been running shopfitting and then reorganising the Reed acquisition, was put in charge of housebuilding. By then it was building around 900 houses a year and that was gradually increased to around 1250 by 1970. Expansion within the conglomerate structure was not easy. Although there was no direct interference from the main board in the running of housebuilding, financing was difficult. 'The problem was that we were the cash cow of the business; all of the profit, all of it, went out of the window into Hallmark to use for commercial property investment.'[5]

In the Summer of 1970, Bloch resigned as Chairman of Hallmark. 'This errant bearded ex-solicitor…had resigned from Hallmark because he had been served with a summons for the alleged smuggling of a fur coat at London Airport. His recent spouse was a Royal Ballet dancer called Merle Park.'[6] In the October, Hallmark received a £19m bid from the unquoted Spey Westmoreland, run by Bobby Marmor. 'When Marmor came in, he was quite open: he said "I haven't bought it to have a housebuilder. I don't want you."'[7] Kleinwort Benson was employed to find a buyer and in 1971 AJ Wait was duly sold to Galliford Estates for £3¹/₄m. By then, Wait had 28 estates under development across the south of England with 2100 plots plus 530 acres of white land along the south coast. Brian Wait went on to form Clare Homes and Spencer Homes, which he sold on to Berkeley Homes in March 1988.

[4] Ibid.
[5] Ibid.
[6] Gordon, *The Cedar Story*, p.105.
[7] Interview Brian Wait.

HART BROTHERS (EDINBURGH)/CRUDEN
Peak units: 1200 (2004)

Thomas Hart had incorporated his original partnership business in 1954; it started as an excavating and bricklaying subcontractor but by the time it was floated in 1968 it was a main contractor building local authority housing in Edinburgh and Lothian. At the time of the flotation, profits of £350,000 had been forecast for 1969 but Hart fell just short of that and profits declined in each subsequent year. In 1973, the private Cruden paid £2m for Hart.

Harry Cruden was born in Fraserburgh in 1896, the son of a fish curer, and trained as an engineering draughtsman. He served with the Gordon Highlanders in World War I in Kenya, staying on as a coffee planter. He did not return to Scotland until the mid 1930s when he worked as a timber merchant in Musselburgh, in a business owned by his wife. Crudens Ltd was incorporated in 1943 'to acquire the sawmill and joinery business carried out by Mrs Madeline Cruden at Musselburgh' with the couple holding equal shares.[1] 'What catapulted Cruden's career from the mundane to the memorable was the single minded pursuit of an ideal – that essential to the recovery of Scotland at the end of the second world war was the production of houses, and that a satisfactory rate of house production could only be achieved through innovation in the method of house building, and particularly in the use of non-traditional building techniques.'[2]

Control goes to the Cruden Foundation

Thousands of 'The Cruden House' were built in Scotland post war but in the late 1950s the market for low-rise housing began to decline, to be replaced with tower blocks. 'With typical boldness, [Cruden] decided on an almost complete organisational about-turn…the firm was to become an all-round public contractor that could build high blocks and other major projects itself, and embark on property development.'[3] As part of that reorganisation, Harry Cruden stood down as Chairman in 1957, appointing Malcolm Matthews, then a 25-year-old quantity surveyor, as Managing Director. Cruden obtained a licence for the Swedish Skarne industrialised building system using it as the basis for securing substantial contracts throughout Scotland, the north east of England and the London boroughs. Harry Cruden died in 1967, leaving the Cruden Foundation owning all the shares in the building companies, then grouped into Cruden Investments.

Private housing started in the late 1960s through the subsidiary Scottish Residential Estates, and it soon reached volumes of around 200 a year before falling back to only one site. When Cruden bought Hart in 1973 the combined housebuilding volumes did not exceed earlier levels. Cruden continued to be run as a mixed contracting and speculative housing group. The 1976 Accounts had expressed optimism over the private housing market but the directors still decided on a modest reduction in the land bank, and there never seemed the commitment to expand the business. Substantial construction losses in 1980 and again in 1986, combined with ownership by a charity, meant limited generation of funds for expansion. Cruden continued to believe in the advantages of running construction and development together, and the 1999 accounts reported on a Group reorganisation designed 'to enable us to obtain, through our estates development subsidiaries, a reasonable share of the necessary turnover of our building companies.' In the accounts for the year to March 2001 the Company recorded the completion of 276 private housing units; it almost certainly was, and remains, a record. However, social housing had been substantially expanded in 2001 taking total sales above 1000 for the first time.

[1] Articles of Association, 1943.
[2] *Dictionary of Scottish Business Biography.*
[3] *Watters, Mactaggart & Mickel and the Scottish Housebuilding Industry*, p.251.

HERON HOMES
Peak units: c.1000 (late 1970s)

In its heyday, Heron International encompassed motor retailing, service stations, home entertainment, financial services, commercial property both home and abroad, and private housing through Heron Homes. In terms of personalities, Heron has been most closely associated with Gerald Ronson, whose forceful character has attracted many column inches of description: 'a keen sense of humour and no time for superficial culture, making no pretence regarding commercial etiquette of past decades or red tape. Instead, he is keen to get down to the basics of modern trading.'[1] Alternatively, there was 'abrasive, straight-talking, sometimes intimidating…but above all, utterly determined.'[2] The founder of the Heron organisation was Henry Ronson, formerly Aaronson, whose father was an immigrant from Russia at the turn of the last century; he set up a furnishing business in the east end of London. Gerald Ronson went straight into the family business at the age of 15, although he soon developed an interest in property. The first of the Heron businesses (the name being a contraction of <u>Hen</u>ry <u>Ron</u>son) concentrated on petrol retailing, eventually becoming the largest independent petrol retailer in Britain. The other early interest was commercial property, and the 1965 debenture issue refers to Henry and Gerald entering 'property' in 1957. It was from this base that the expansion of Heron Holdings (later Heron International) took place.

Heron Homesteads, as the housing company was originally called, was incorporated in 1958 with Henry Ronson and Gerald Ronson as directors. Despite the incorporation date, Heron's private housing is generally described as having started around 1965 when Henry Ronson bought large tracts of land at Yate, near Bristol, where some 8000 houses were forecast by 1980. Other large land holdings were also acquired in the early 1970s including 160 acres in Gloucester in 1971, the year in which Heron described itself as 'by far the largest private house developer in the West Country.'[3] Sales volumes were increased to around 500 by 1974. Management of the business reflected the diverse interests of Heron International. Gerald Ronson was named as Managing Director in the first (1972) annual return for Heron Homesteads but although he took a close interest, he was actively building up the rest of the group. Henry Ronson had done much of the west-country land buying and Wally Fenwick was in charge of construction. In 1973, Gerald Ronson stood down as housing Managing Director in favour of his younger brother Laurence Ronson. Laurence had joined the family business in 1965 with the service stations division, then spending three years in housebuilding including active on-site experience.

Stanshawe Estates acquired

To expand outside the west country, Heron used a second company which appeared to come into the group by acquisition in 1970. Stanshawe Estates had been formed by Douglas Leonard, a Bristol builder, in 1959. In 1970 the name was changed to Heron Stanshawe Estates and then Heron Garden Estates.[4] As in the west country, Heron purchased large tracts of land by way of option and conditional contracts – a thousand acres were bought in Hampshire and on the south coast in 1973. The combination of rapid physical expansion and house price inflation had a dramatic effect on profits – increasing from £146,000 in 1970 to £2.5m in the year to March 1973, making it by far the largest of the Heron trading companies. Heron even went as far as buying a 23% stake in the quoted Janes, before the latter was bought by Barratt

---

[1] Erdman, *People & Property*.

[2] *Independent*, Oct. 18th 2000.

[3] Heron Holdings accounts, 1971.

[4] Confusingly, Heron Homesteads and Heron Garden Estates later interchanged names before combining as Heron Homes in 1982.

in 1976. The market collapse reduced profits to around £1m in 1974 but this compared favourably with many housebuilders at the time; Heron's land buying had served it well and the group estimated that a surplus of £15m on the land holdings in 1973 had only fallen to £10m in 1974.

Heron achieved breakeven over the next couple of years during which period Laurence Ronson accelerated Heron's housing expansion, increasing volumes from 500 in 1974 to 800 in 1975 and more than 1000 in 1977; there were ambitions to raise this to 1500. Land was bought inter alia in London, Leighton Buzzard and Southampton; 130 acres of land bought in Bristol in 1970 obtained permission. However, the business appeared to lose its impetus, housing volumes began to decline (they reached a low point of under 400 in 1982) and in 1980 the west-country company lost around £800,000. Gerald Ronson came back as Chairman in 1979; within a year Laurence had resigned as Managing Director and was later bought out of Ronson International.

Peter Lewis becomes Managing Director
Housing then had it first externally-appointed Managing Director, Peter Lewis, aged 34, who took control at the start of the 1982 financial year. Lewis was already a successful estate agent in the West Country and he had become a 'guest member' of the Heron Homesteads board in 1975. By 1980 he was the owner of the Corbett Leach estate agency with 22 offices (sold to Hambro Countrywide in 1984). Lewis amalgamated the two housing companies as Heron Homes and rebuilt sales and margins. Although volumes never quite regained the 1000 level, turnover rose from the 1982 low of £13m to £130m in 1989 and pre-tax profits rose from £1.2m to £32m. More striking than even the profits progression was the annual restatement of the surplus on the land bank, which rose from £23m in 1984 to a 'conservatively valued' more than £100m in 1988.

The 1990 housing recession hit Heron Homes far harder than its predecessor had done, leading to pre-tax losses of £11m in 1990/91 and £80m in 1991/92, the latter including provisions of £58m – the comfortable surplus of £100m had rapidly vanished. Heron Homes centralised its operations and withdrew from the south east, reducing its volumes to under 600 in 1992/93. Worse was to befall Gerald Ronson personally; he was caught up in the Guinness share-support prosecution and in August 1990 was sentenced to 12 months in prison, serving half that time. Gerald Ronson has been reported as saying his absence did not affect the company but it is hard to believe that the lengthy trial and the subsequent six months did not severely impede his ability to respond to the pressures developing on all parts of his business.

Heron's wider problems
Heron Corporation (as it had become) had more problems than just UK housing; its international spread of commercial property developments was also in deep trouble. The 1991 final dividend payment of £9m was cancelled and in March 1992 Heron's ultimate parent, Heron International NV, announced that 'continuing adverse conditions in property markets throughout the world has led to a position whereby Heron International NV…may lack sufficient liquidity to meet debt repayments as scheduled.' The group lost £100m in 1991/92 and was on its way to double that loss in 1992/93. The debt negotiations were not concluded until September 1993, and involved a major conversion of debt to equity. In March 1994 the major part of the assets of Heron Homes was sold to Taylor Woodrow for £34m, a premium of £7m over book value. Shortly after, Heron International as a whole was sold to a consortium of business men leaving Gerald Ronson with a 5% equity but still in charge. The business has since successfully been rebuilt and the Heron Homes company, renamed Heron Land Developments, still has some 6000 plots which it continues to bring through the planning process. In 2003, land sales earned the Company some £14m pre-tax profit; Heron has also signalled its interest in returning to housebuilding by the purchase of a 23% stake in Crest

HEY & CROFT
Peak units: 251 (1988)

The business was started in 1956 by Leonard Hey and Bert Croft. Both had begun as carpenters, moving on to subcontracting on housing sites and then building ones and twos in their own name from their base in Southend. They were helped by a local solicitor who introduced them to sites in the area and joined their Board. In particular, a large site bought at Witham was compulsorily acquired shortly after by the GLC and that provided the capital to enlarge the business.

In the late 1970s, the Company diversified into leisure with a development complex that included a hotel, a 36-hole golf course and pubs. However, when the housing market dipped around 1980, the cash flow could no longer finance the leisure losses and the assets were sold. Bert Croft had been concentrating on the leisure side, and after it was sold he wanted to return to housing, then building at the rate of 80 a year. By then, the key positions had been filled and there was a parting of the ways. Leonard Hey bought out the Croft family interests in 1982. The change in control enabled Leonard Hey to install a new management team led by Geoffrey King as Managing Director; King had joined the company in 1965, becoming Finance Director in 1979.

The 1980s saw volumes trebling to a peak of 250 houses in 1988. By then the sites were not only in Essex but also in Suffolk, Buckinghamshire, Cambridgeshire and Norfolk. In June 1987 Hey & Croft floated on the USM, after which the Company enjoyed just one remaining record year. The management stance as the market turned was one of continued optimism, and in February 1989 Leonard Hey wrote: 'The increase in mortgage rates has inevitably led many people to talk about gloom and doom in the housing market. So far as the Group is concerned, activity has continued at a high level. Operating primarily as we do in a part of the country that has seen the largest increase in property values, gives the directors confidence that the improved gross margins secured in 1988 will enable the group to have another good year.'[1]

One of the consequences of the flotation was that the Company started larger projects just before the market fell. In the year to October 1989, profits fell from £2.3m to £1.0m. In 1990 sales fell to only 100; there was a £3.7m loss; debt was twice shareholders' funds, and half the Company's reduced net assets were represented by shared equity mortgages. Not surprisingly, receivers were appointed in September 1992. They reported that it had become clear to the directors 'that cash flow constraints were beginning to prejudice the marketing and maintenance of the assets and so the chances of securing purchasers for houses were further impaired. The loan agreement with its bankers was in default, and the group was unable to pay its debts as they fell due.' The estimated deficiency was £5.5m.

[1] Group accounts, 1988.

HOWARDS OF MITCHAM
Peak units: c.200 (mid 1960s)

Donald G Howard was the grandson of Sir Ebeneezer Howard, the 'apostle of the Garden City Movement' (he created Letchworth and Welwyn Garden City).[1] Donald Howard, who was an FIOB and became a President of the Federation of Registered Housebuilders, started as an estate agent after leaving school and in 1932, at the age of 21, began building houses in Sutton, south London. His activity was on a small scale and the only figures quoted for that period were 150 houses sold between 1937 and Sept 1939 on estates in Bromley and Mitcham.

During the war the Company carried out contract work for government departments and public authorities. After the war, Howard built houses for local authorities and engaged in general building work – schools, hospitals factories etc. In 1954, Howard resumed private housebuilding with estates in Bromley, Banstead and Wimbledon, by far the largest being the 500 unit development at Hayesford Park, Bromley. Little more than nominal profits were earned until 1960, when the Company first exceeded £50,000. It floated at the end of 1962 and in 1964 sold more than 200 private and 300 local authority houses

Howards' volumes came from Hayesford Park and a similar sized estate at Crofton Place, Orpington, both of which were completed by the late 1960s, but it was a development in Wimbledon that was to prove the Company's downfall. Permission had been given for 106 flats and 29 town houses on land which Howards had bought some years earlier. The show flat was opened in 1966 but Sterling devaluation followed a year later and expensive properties were not selling. 'The tower blocks at Wimbledon were superb from the point of view of design and architecture but they weren't necessarily the most commercial thing that one could have put there in terms of the cost of the building. We hung our hats on these twin tower blocks and 29 town houses and they just hadn't sold.'[2]

Four years later, only seven of the flats and four of the houses had been sold. No other large sites were on stream to help cover the costs and Howards fell into losses of £133,000 in 1969 and £217,000 in 1970, by which time shareholders' funds were negative. No attempt had been made to reduce the selling prices at Wimbledon to clear the stock: 'DGH wasn't the sort of chap who was easily panicked. He always believed that the right things would happen in the end. He thought the flats were superb and if you brought the price down you wouldn't sell them any quicker anyway.'[3] In February 1972, the principal operating subsidiary, M Howard (Mitcham) was put into liquidation. After that, the group existed on little more than modest rental income and ground rents and made no more than nominal profits, though debt was repaid.

In the late 1960s, Howards had taken an interest in a proposed redevelopment at Kennington Oval (the Secretary of Surrey Cricket Club was Donald Howard's brother) and this became Donald Howard's main interest. The scheme was assigned to Richard Costain who later abandoned it, causing Donald Howard to criticise the 'Inept handling by Richard Costain of the Kennington Oval re-development' in the 1975 accounts. Proceedings were taken for recovery of substantial damages and some compensation was eventually received. Donald Howard died in 1984. Over the next few years residual properties were sold and in 1988 there was a members voluntary winding up with an estimated surplus of £392,000.

1 *Housebuilder*, Oct. 1984.
2 Interview with Christopher Blyth, June 2002.
3 Ibid.

IDEAL HOMES
Peak units: 5-7000 (late 1930s)

Ideal Homes, or New Ideal Homesteads as it was first known, was by far and away the largest private housebuilder in the 1930s. Its founder, Leo Meyer, was one of the great names in British housebuilding and when he died in 1961 Ideal Homes survived only a few years before being taken over by Trafalgar House, a shadow of its former self. Leo Henry Paul Meyer was born in 1903, educated at Erith County School, served articles as a surveyor with Bexley Council, and became Assistant Surveyor to Erith Urban District Council. He started building at Bexleyheath in the late 1920s, with little experience and capital drawn from private sources, including his Mother. Edward Erdman described him as 'a rugged individualist.'[1] His career began with a company called Blackwell & Meyer (Blackwell being a local bricklayer) which went into voluntary liquidation. 'A man of his word, he swore that, if he ever came into money again, he would pay off all his creditors in full. Within two or three days – following the flotation of Ideal Building – he invited all his creditors to see him and paid them in full.'[2] Meyer's second attempt also began with a partnership and this time the business, although not the relationship, was more successful. New Ideal Homesteads was incorporated in October 1929 'for the purpose of acquiring and developing housing estates'; there does not appear to have been any prior trading. The shares were owned equally between the Meyer family (Leo himself did not appear on the register until 1932) and Philip Edward Shephard and his family. Shephard had been stationmaster at Erith, later London Bridge and then Superintendent at Victoria; he sold Royal Exchange policies as a sideline, acting as an insurance broker. He became a full-time inspector for Royal Exchange about 1920.

The forgotten partner
Although Leo Meyer became the dominant figure in Ideal Homes, and has become synonymous with it, it is by no means clear he had that role from the beginning. Shephard was older than Meyer and there is evidence that Shephard was the early source of land. 'It was largely through Royal Exchange Assurance Co that NIH was formed because Royal Exchange offered him [Philip E Shephard] building land at Dartford Heath. My father over the years had become an expert in property investment; he had no faith in the Stock Market. This knowledge was used to good account when purchasing land for speculative building in the 1930s.'[3] Nothing is known of the early finances of New Ideal Homesteads but it seems likely that Shephard would have had better access to funds than Meyer, particularly in view of the latter's earlier business failure..

The flotation
The pace of expansion from that standing start in 1929 was remarkable. In the next three years over 3000 houses were sold. In 1933, Ideal sold over 4000 houses in that one year, substantially more than its nearest competitor; there were even suggestions that Ideal's capacity was approaching 10,000.[4] Against that background, Meyer and Shephard decided to seek a public flotation in 1934. A new holding company was formed – Ideal Building & Land Development – which acquired New Ideal Homesteads and its associate companies, including Kent and Sussex Building Company which, in a later existence, was to become Rush and Tompkins. The net assets of the companies acquired were £400,000, for which the two shareholders received £400,000 in shares in the holding company plus £300,000 cash. A further 100,000 shares were issued to the public plus £500,000 preference stock – the latter effectively financing the £300,000 cash withdrawal by the original proprietors who still owned 80% of the company. Ideal was then building on

---

[1] Erdman, *People & Property*.
[2] Ibid.
[3] Letter from RD Shephard to Owen Aisher, 6th May 1934.
[4] *Practical Building*, Nov 1933.

16 estates, primarily in south-east London suburbs, down to Sevenoaks and Tonbridge, but also building north into Harrow and east into Ilford. Profits had been rising strongly; the last published figure of £345,000 may now be no more than earned by a housebuilding managing director, but no other housebuilder was then earning as much as £100,000 profit.

After flotation, Ideal's physical expansion continued. There have been suggestions that Ideal reached annual rates of 10,000 but these seem too high and may have been based on extrapolating peak summer sales periods. Certainly, sales in 1935 reached 5500 and the following year Ideal was not only selling off 25 London estates but was also acquiring sites in the midlands and renting houses to tenants to produce extra revenue. By the war, Ideal was building in the home counties, and in Southampton, Birmingham, Gloucester, Crewe and Burton-on-Trent. In the mid 1930s, the company probably built at an annual rate of between 5000 and 7000. To put this in context, Wates was building around 2000 a year at its peak and Davis Estates, Taylor Woodrow and Wimpey no more than 1000-1500. Ideal was thus in a class of its own

Profits collapse – directors' share sales
Unfortunately, not all went smoothly after the flotation. For a start, profits not only fell in its first year as a public company but in the two succeeding years as well and, by 1936, pre-tax profits had fallen to £92,000 compared with the £345,000 historic profit disclosed in the prospectus. The dividend was cut from 15% in 1934 to 10% and then 5%; the shares reached a low point of 6s-3d compared with their £1 issue price and a post flotation high of 52s-6d. An investigation by *The Investors' Review* also disclosed substantial share sales by the directors between the flotation and the first annual return.[5] Shortly after, the company had to deny rumours of 'colossal losses and payment arrears.'[6] Meyer also had to face problems within the company. Philip Shephard resigned without public explanation after only eight months, followed by the resignation of the stockbroker Chairman in August 1935, due to 'ill health.' Meyer and Shephard had been joint Managing Directors for six years and it is clear from surviving board minutes that, whether or not the parting was amicable, it soon became acrimonious with allegations of Shephard breaking his undertakings, attempting to entice away an employee and threats of legal action.

Sir James Dunn had been a shadow promoter of the flotation and his reputation in that area was not of the highest (see Taylor Woodrow). One will never know whether the Ideal flotation was made in the knowledge that profits could not be sustained or if Ideal was simply unfortunate in suffering lower profits at a time when the housing market was booming. When the interim dividend was passed in 1936, one explanation was new building society regulations. It may be that Ideal had achieved its phenomenal sales by offering financial terms or assistance that was not sustainable – like the shared equity that did so much damage half a century later. Whatever the reason, Ideal's finances were clearly strained: in 1936, Meyer had to deposit personal securities with the banks to raise £100,000 and he bought land personally until Ideal could afford to take it up.

As war approached, Ideal expanded into general construction, and during the war built aerodromes, factories and naval bases, although not on the same scale as did Laing, Costain, Taylor Woodrow etc. Neither, when the war ended, did Ideal seek to turn construction into the driving force of the business. In the late 1930s, Ideal had been trying to change its emphasis towards property investment and this strategy was continued by buying and selling blocks of tenanted properties during and after the war; in the late 1940s, Ideal was buying houses four or five hundred at a time. Ideal also worked in partnership with local authorities by building houses to rent on land owned before the war, and selling the houses to

5 *The Investors' Review,* July 1936.
6 Ibid, Oct. 1936.

the local authority. One of the first large schemes was at Park Royal Estate, Sidcup where work began on 500 houses in October 1945 – helped by 50 ex-prisoners of war, all former builders.

Meyer goes to South Africa

Leo Meyer had had three major operations, and after the war was told to go somewhere where there was salt water and sun. His choice was South Africa where he went in 1947; New Ideal Homesteads South Africa was formed the following year. Health was never mentioned publicly: 'In order to give his full attention to the activities of the new company' Meyer resigned as group Managing Director, deploring the fact that capable business men are forced to go abroad. However, he continued to attend UK board meetings. In 1953, Sir Thomas Keens, Ideal's Chairman since 1935, died aged 83 and Leo Meyer, now in better health, returned full time to the UK to become Chairman. Britain was also becoming a friendlier place for housebuilders at that time and Meyer was keen to resume conventional private housebuilding as soon as controls allowed.

Ideal sought an increase in its borrowing powers from £1.2m to £3m to purchase land, stating that 90% of the land owned by the company in 1939 has been compulsorily seized by local councils. Its first land purchases were in 1953 – 511 plots on seven sites in London – and demand was such that on one of these the Company received several thousand replies to a single advertisement offering houses for sale at £1900. Sites were bought in Gloucester and Hampshire in 1954 and by 1955 the land bank reached around 3000 plots. A period of rapid expansion followed, almost entirely concentrated on private housing. By its Silver Jubilee in 1959, Ideal claimed that it had built more than 20,000 houses for sale since the war – again more than any other housebuilder. Exact figures do not survive but at the start of the 1960s Ideal was selling around 2-3000 houses a year, second only to Wimpey which by then was expanding rapidly. The Board meeting of December 1959 was the last which Leo Meyer attended; illness prevented him returning to Ideal and he died in February 1961, to be succeeded as Chairman by Eric Woollard, a long standing colleague of Meyer's. Woollard had been appointed a director in 1942, joint Managing Director in 1946 and sole Managing Director in 1955.

Bought by Trafalgar House

The regional expansion policy was continued with acquisitions in Yorkshire and Scotland (Ailsa Homes). However, the drive had gone from the company and it appeared to drift. Volumes continued around the 2000 level but when the housing market was checked in 1966 by a 7% bank rate, sales fell to only 1150. Ideal's independent days were nearly over and in July 1967, the firm was bought by Nigel Broakes' Trafalgar House for £4.6m. Trafalgar House was to become one of Britain's most high profile conglomerates. Nigel Broakes, a solicitor's son, educated at Stowe, worked first in the Lloyds insurance market before forming a hire purchase company in 1955 and then moving into property redevelopment. One of Broakes' companies, Trafalgar House, was chosen as the lead vehicle, and floated in 1963. It controlled at various times Cementation, Trollope & Colls, John Brown, Express Newspapers, The Ritz, Cunard Line, container ships (Atlantic Conveyor of Falklands fame), North Sea oil wells and, of course, a myriad of property investments.

The catalyst for the purchase of Ideal was the Drayton investment trusts. Harley Drayton had been appointed to the Ideal Board as far back as 1937 and the Drayton investment trusts held around 30% of the Ideal shares. Moreover, the Ideal chair was held on a temporary basis by Drayton's Martin Rich. Nigel Broakes knew this and made tentative approaches. 'Eric Woollard, Meyer's former right-hand man, proved to be less effective on his own as managing director. So when I went to Martin Rich's office one afternoon in April, intending to prepare the ground for a deal in about a year's time, I was taken aback to be told that my visit was welcome...because Drayton's were fed up with the whole situation.'[7] At the time of the Ideal acquisition, Trafalgar House already also owned Prestige Homes, Bridge Walker and Aspect Homes and these were integrated into Ideal as was the luxury housing business of Trollope & Colls, bought in 1968. Volumes quickly recovered to around 2000 and Trafalgar House suggested the enlarged Ideal 'is thought to constitute the second largest private house-building group in the country'[8] (although it was probably no more than number three). The business was structured for an annual level of 3000; however, the drive for volume was at the expense of margins: the Board meeting of November 1967 authorised a reduction in gross margins on future land purchases from 25% to a minimum of 15%.

Housing units, 1966-1995

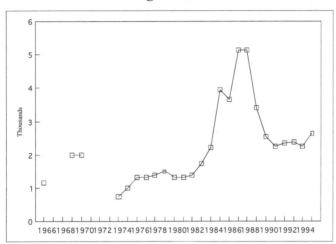

'Gussie' Dear was the Managing Director of New Ideal Homesteads at the time of the Trafalgar House takeover. John Mitchell replaced him as Managing Director in 1969, becoming Chairman of Ideal Building from 1970 to 1975; an engineer by background, he came in from J Arthur Rank, and was seen as bringing an all-round business approach. The longest period of managerial continuity came with David Calverley, an accountant who had joined Trafalgar House as assistant Company Secretary in 1968. He became financial controller of Ideal in 1973 and Managing Director in 1975. He arrived at the tail end of the boom: 'I couldn't believe how much money we were making – we were selling ransom strips for £100,000 – it was very serious money. One transaction was more than we were making in the hotel division, with all their resources. But of course it didn't last. When I took over in 1975, things were pretty dire.'

In fact, sales in 1974 were less than half the rate planned when the budgets were adopted at the beginning of the year, possibly not much more than 500, and in the following year provisions of £4m were made against land values. 'We were losing money at that stage and we needed to stabilise it and then to start growing again, just organic growth; we didn't have a target that we wanted to get to other than to make it a significant contributor to Trafalgar House profits. In 1975-76 there were several problems. Having been out of the land market for two years the network of contacts had gone. It took us time to build them up again though the great thing about that period was inflation baled us out of the problems of 1973.'[9] The remainder of the 1970s was, for Ideal like many other housebuilders, a period of

[7] Broakes, *A Growing Concern.*
[8] Group accounts, 1968.
[9] Interview with David Calverley, Nov. 1998.

consolidation, although they were greatly helped by the Goldsworth Park site, which was selling at a rate of 450 houses per annum at its peak – a third of the company's 1300 sales level at the end of the decade.

Comben and Broseley acquired

From that base, the company was able to rebuild its position as one of the leading housebuilders, helped by two substantial acquisitions – Comben in1984, and Broseley in 1986. These were opportunistic purchases made by a group whose trademark was corporate deal-making. Comben expanded Ideal's regional coverage in the west and the midlands; Broseley gave Ideal the north west (which turned out more useful than they expected), and the London Docklands which had been a 'no go' area while Nigel Broakes had been Chairman of the Docklands Corporation. The acquisitions also provided Ideal with an alternative source of land. By 1987, Ideal was selling in excess of 5000 house a year and ranked number five in the industry. In 1988, housebuilding contributed a peak £78m to Trafalgar's group trading profit of £256m.

However, Trafalgar House was in no shape to withstand what might have been termed a once-in-a-lifetime recession had not Nigel Broakes also been running a business during 1974. The group accounts were overly flattering. Interest was not being charged to the profit and loss account but capitalised; substantial borrowings were being carried off-balance sheet; and there were heavy provisions needed against commercial property. The commitment to commercial property was especially threatening for between 1988 and the first half of 1990, some £750m had been invested. After a £30m loss in 1992, Trafalgar eventually had to face up to reality and massive provisions led to a £347m loss in 1993.

Looking back, David Calverley recognised a lack of flexibility. 'Like all housebuilders, we had a period from 1980 to 1987 when we did extremely well but we were probably slow to respond to changing conditions. We used to roll up interest so we didn't recognise the problem quite as fast as it wasn't hitting our profit and loss account – we were used to land having its intrinsic value. I do think there was huge pressure from the Trafalgar machine that would not accept that profits can go down as well as up. Then the tragedy was that with other parts of Trafalgar also being hit by the recession there weren't the resources to take advantage of the opportunity to replenish the land bank at what by then were historically cheap land prices.

Trafalgar House itself became a takeover target. Hongkong Land had been buying shares and in May 1993, with its holding then up to 25%, it announced that it had consolidated its control of Trafalgar House by taking both the Chairmanship and Financial Director roles. Hongkong Land had no particular commitment to housebuilding and there was a need to reduce debt. Despite the opposition of Beazer, Persimmon was given exclusive negotiating rights, and in February 1996 bought Ideal for £177m, little more than net asset value. Despite itself having acquired two top ten housebuilders in the 1980s, Ideal had declined to be twelfth largest housebuilder with sales of 2644 units in 1995.

JANES
Peak units: 1200 (1975)

HC Janes was a sizeable regional housebuilder both before and after the Second World War. The original building business was founded by Arthur Cole in 1884 but Herbert Janes became the dominant personality in the history of the company, still being Chairman at the age of 74 when the company was floated in 1958; indeed, he was 78 before he resigned the chairmanship. Herbert Janes was an archetypal illustration of self-improvement, a farm labourer's son leaving school aged 12, educating himself, developing a successful business and becoming Lord Mayor of Luton. Janes' first job, in 1896, was as an assistant in a chemist's shop, and it was another five years before he resumed education at evening classes, taking book keeping. In 1905 he joined Arthur Cole as his bookkeeper, taking further classes in woodwork, building construction and builders quantities.

Herbert Janes gradually took over the management and then the ownership of Arthur Cole's business. In 1908, aged 24 and still taking evening courses at Luton College, he was made manager. From 1912 he was paid bonuses that were never drawn out, and, when Arthur Cole was converted into a limited company in 1920, the accountant found that 3/7ths of the assets consisted of Janes' bonuses and therefore he had 3/7ths of the shares. In 1924 a major client, Halden Estates, went bankrupt and Barclays refused to honour Cole's cheques. A deed of arrangement was drawn up with the creditors. Shortly afterwards Cole retired and Janes financed the purchase of Cole's shares by building houses for him; the firm was renamed HC Janes in 1927.

600 units a year by late 1930s
The firm had built houses as a contractor before the First War and had bought some land; in 1923 it began to build houses on its own account in the Luton area. Under Herbert's sole ownership, HC Janes gradually expanded its geographical coverage. In 1927 it was building 300 houses on 12 estates around Luton, there were estates in Aylesbury, Dunstable and Hitchin by the end of the 1920s, and by 1934 Janes was building houses in Bedfordshire, Buckinghamshire and Hertfordshire; by then Janes was admitting to national ambitions.[1] By the end of the 1930s, Janes was building around 600 houses a year from 25 estates. The firm also continued with general contracting work, a contrast with the owner's later views. A significant number of the houses were being bought by investors in the mid 1930s, and in 1933 Janes opened a property department specifically to deal with that market.

On the outbreak of war, Janes had more than 400 houses under construction and a bridging loan from Barclays allowed the firm to complete all the houses by December. As the building societies were forbidden to advance any new loans to buyers, Janes released all the buyers from their contracts and most took that option. Herbert Janes himself bought 200 of the houses, and some of the individual purchasers completed, leaving 172 houses which the firm rented out. During the war, Janes acted as maintenance contractor to the RAF for 58 airfields and camps. In 1943, Herbert's son Clifford was killed in Africa and Herbert appointed his son-in-law Leslie Sell and nephew Harold Janes as directors, with a place being left open for his other son, Robert, after the war.

Janes was immediately active after the war claiming to have built around 120 houses by the end of 1946 on 7 or 8 sites all in different towns. It might not sound much now but, in the conditions of the time, it was probably as large a volume as any housebuilder managed. While many of the pre-war housebuilders had developed substantial contracting businesses, Herbert possessed strong views about the different

---

[1] Kennett, *A Provincial Builder,* p.124.

roles of the housebuilder and the contractor and would not even consider local authority housing. Speaking at the Housebuilders' Federation AGM in 1947 he said that 'the man who built council houses was not a house-builder but a contractor. Contracting required a different mentality, a different technique and a different staff from house-building',[2] advice his company had not followed before the war and which it ignored subsequently, as there was a building and civil engineering division firmly in place some ten years later.

One of the largest housebuilders of its time

The firm expanded rapidly during the 1950s, and by 1958 Janes was building at an annual rate of around 900 houses, making it one of the largest housebuilders at that time, with a geographic spread across the northern home counties. down to Hampshire and across to Suffolk. Although Sir Herbert was Chairman at the flotation, he was described as a consultant and, as he lived in Sussex, presumably had little day-to-day involvement in the business. The rest of the Board was strictly family: the Deputy Chairman was Leslie Sell, Managing Director, Robert Janes, and Harold Janes was the Building Director.

Janes seemed to come through the 1974 recession in remarkable shape. One of Janes' distinguishing features was that it was production-led, employing most of its own tradesmen. A consequence was that it tried to sustain its building programme through the market downturn in 1974. It had built some 1200 units in its last year as an independent company and some of these may have been held for rent – by the time of its acquisition it owned some 1500 rented houses. Profits were also supported by an exceptionally conservative accounting policy – according to the statement of accounting policies, profit was not taken on house construction until the sale of all houses in a scheme had been completed, a policy also followed at the time by Wimpey. Thus, profits in, say, 1974 or 1975 could have reflected whole estates that had been developed over a period of years.

In January 1976, Janes accepted a £12m bid from Barratt. It is suggested that the reason for the sale was friction within the family. The relationship between Leslie Sell, then 76, and Robert Janes had deteriorated to such an extent that they no longer conversed at all, with every communication being by way of memo, through intermediaries. After the sale, Robert Janes became Chairman. He was later voted out over a disagreement over excess overheads; subsequently Robert Janes and his son David formed Janes Builders based in Harpenden.

2 *House-Builder*, Jan. 1947.

JOVIEL PROPERTIES
Peak units: c.500 (1972)

The Company was formed in 1957 as a residential property developer by Stephen Crawford, a chartered accountant, but two years later it became the vehicle for Roy Wright's entry into speculative housebuilding. Roy Wright left school in 1944 at the age of 12; 'no-one bothered much when you left.'[1] His father had run a team of bricklayers and the son followed in his father's footsteps. In 1952 he formed RV Wright Contractors, starting with a few bricklayers and navvies, laying out buildings and constructing roads for housebuilders. It was building at its most basic: 'On Mondays, my first job was to go to the local jail and bail out the navvies.'[2] He later formed Egham Builders and it was this that was sold to Joviel in 1959 to give Wright control.

Financial advice to Wright came from Desmond Byrne, who was also involved in the early days of Crest Homes; Byrne brought in Philip George and John Mattrass, relatives of his wife, as shareholders. The Company operated on a relatively modest scale through the 1960s, concentrating on building houses on a contract basis for other housebuilders though a small amount of speculative housebuilding was also undertaken. The company continued in a modest way until 1969 when the directors decided to accelerate the rate of residential development and to acquire sites for commercial development. From 1970, Joviel also engaged in a number of joint ventures with Marc Gregory Limited and FC Finance. Apart from FC Finance, other secondary bank sources included Edward Bates and First National Finance.

Joviel floated on the Stock Exchange in July 1972 with Roy Wright, then 41, as Managing Director, and Douglas Byrne Chairman. Turnover that year was £3.6m and the company was forecasting housing sales of 480 units. In the boom conditions that prevailed, turnover rose 70% in 1973 (although much of that came from higher house prices and diversification into commercial building) and profits, which had been only £200,000 in 1971, rose to a record £1.4m. Despite the signs of a downturn in the housing market, in August 1973 the Board drew up a five-year growth plan based on a 15-22% growth rate. Like many housebuilders of the time, that growth was based on aggressive financing – the 1973 balance sheet showed debt of £8.4m against equity of £2.3m, and profits were declared after capitalising interest.

The following year, profits were all but eliminated and write-offs created a loss of £1.3m. It was decided to build and sell as rapidly as possible, lowering prices and doing block sales with local authorities. Joviel's own financial strain was compounded by those of its partners. In January 1974, Marc Gregory declared a moratorium on its interest payments and a receiver was appointed in the October. Of its bankers, Bates was one of the first to fail and FNFC needed the support of the Bank of England. The creditors were unable to agree on a refinancing package and Joviel could not obtain the finance to build out its sites. Roy Wright was adamant that he was not prepared to let Joviel continue in that position. 'The banks wouldn't give me the money I wanted to build the stock out so I put the company down – nobody else.'[3] In February 1976 the company filed a winding up petition; further write-offs had created a net asset deficit of £0.7m.

As a footnote, the Monday after the winding up petition, Wright bought the shell company of Gap Crown and developed a successful commercial development business, in the UK, Spain and the USA; it was later sold to P&O for £25m

[1] Interview with Roy Wright, Mar 2003.
[2] Ibid.
[3] Ibid.

MP KENT
Peak units: 658 (1974)

The company was formed in 1959 to acquire the housing development business that Michael Kent had started in the Torbay area only the year before. Michael Kent, the son of a construction plant manager, had been educated at Prior Park public school, Bath, but had no building qualifications; he had been introduced by his father to Eddie Farr of civil engineers AE Farr and was given work on several civil engineering projects in south Devon, where he acquired practical construction experience. He was 23 when he built his first house (which won a House Beautiful Award) but it was one of his next deals that gave him his breakthrough when he acquired land at Brixham for the award-winning Marina Park development. It was purchased with planning permission for 17 houses but the company eventually built 170-180 houses flats and bungalows. Gerald Jiggins, the youngest qualifying chartered accountant in his year, whom Michael Kent had first met at school, joined MP Kent at a very early stage.

The Company moved to Bath in 1963 and by the mid 1960s was building around 150 houses a year. Volumes were increased significantly in the late 1960s, and, by the time the company was floated in 1971, sales had reached 300 a year. By then, Kent had also begun an active commercial development programme, run by director Jeffery Popham. Two significant housing acquisitions followed. The first was the **S Winsley Group**; Maurice Davies was the Managing Director and largest shareholder and he joined the Kent board. Winsley was based to the south of Bath in Radstock and was building around 200 units a year in the Radstock, Midsomer Norton, Frome, Wells and Bridgewater areas. One of its great strengths was its option land. In 1973, Kent bought **FW Davey & Son**, an Exmouth builder formed by Frank Davey in 1930; Davey was also building around 200 units a year, and group sales increased to 645 units in 1973.

The boom years of the early 1970s contributed to a substantial increase in turnover, £10m against £2m in 1971, and profits of £1.8m against £0.2m; a record 658 houses were sold in 1974, a figure that was never again reached. Kent was now more committed to a £20m commercial development programme. In December 1973, Kent announced a deal whereby it was to sell the bulk of its housing to Orme for £4m although, with the housing market deteriorating, that deal was scrapped the following February. The housing operation was then reorganised with the three separate housing business amalgamated in one office for the first time, under Barry Redfearn as its Managing Director. Despite the recession, and the substantial expansion instigated in the years preceding, Kent managed to sustain its profitability through the mid 1970s.

Gradually, the private housing division was run down and by 1980 sales were no more than 250. The nature of the property operation itself was moving away from trading towards retaining completed developments and, as Kent turned itself into an asset-oriented business, the residential trading became even less central to the Company. By 1983, a decision had been taken to withdraw from housing and it was expected that by 1985 the last houses would have been sold. In the event, October 1984 saw an agreed £34m takeover offer from Beazer .

KENTISH HOMES
Peak units: c.200 (late 1980s)

The original Kentish Homes was formed in 1962 as an offshoot of Bromley estate agents Douglas Goodman and Freedman, and was primarily a vehicle for Douglas Goodman to process small development. When he wanted to increase the scale of the business he formed **Cardinal Homes** which probably built around 100-200 houses a year at its peak. As Cardinal grew, Kentish was allowed to decline and it was absorbed by Cardinal in 1973. After a run of losses, Kentish Homes finished 1979 with a deficit on shareholders' funds of some £600,000. Keith Preston, a chartered surveyor, and his wife Kay, acquired the voting shares in 1980 and the balance of the equity in 1986, the attraction probably being the tax losses. Previously, the Prestons had built up a successful property business in East London selling to the first-time buyer. The first of the large property conversions was in 1981 and its planning status marked a turning point: 'Turning an old Metal Box factory into a courtyard development of townhouses and flats in Hackney was a landmark. It was the first Kentish site bought without planning consent and it gave Preston confidence in his ability to negotiate with local authorities.'[1]

Activity remained, however, on a small scale in the early 1980s; profits were modest and there was actually a small loss in 1984. Turnover reached £6m in 1985 and profits passed £1m in 1986 on which basis the company was floated in July 1987. At that time there were just two large projects under construction: the 20-storey Cascades on the Isle of Dogs, where the resale of contracts-to-purchase came to epitomise Docklands euphoria, and Watermint Quay in North London. The Prospectus also listed five other sites to be developed, including Burrell's Wharf, for 310 flats plus commercial space, and the Fairfield Works, Bow for some 670 units. Only one set of accounts was published after flotation. The year to December 1987 saw turnover jump from £6m to £20m and profits quadrupled to £3.9m; net assets of £10m (including £1.7m of capitalised interest) supported £19m of net debt. The Chairman was able to report that 8 floors of the 20-storey Cascades were finished and contracts on all the flats exchanged. 'We have been particularly active during the year acquiring sites for our expanding development programme which has a potential sales value of over £160m.'[2]

On the 19th July 1989 share dealings were suspended. A liquidator was appointed to try to preserve the company as a going concern but the following month a receiver was appointed, first by the Halifax and then Security Pacific. The biggest problem was Burrell's Wharf where little more than 100 units had been sold. The total group shortfall was estimated to be £25m. Robert Fleming, the Company's sponsoring bank, was particularly critical: 'The collapse of Kentish Property Group can be blamed more on lack of financial controls than poor sales at its two major developments in London's Docklands... neither of the two principal projects would have made anything like an acceptable profit.'[3] Not surprisingly, Keith Preston took a different view when speaking at the shareholder meeting: 'The failure of Kentish is a tragedy which could have been avoided. If the Halifax had not taken the course of action it did, then I think things might have turned out better.' Equally unsurprising was the Halifax refutation of 'any suggestion that our action was premature.'[4]

[1] *The Times*, 10th May 1987.
[2] Company accounts, 1987.
[3] Ibid, 20th Aug. 1989.
[4] *Daily Telegraph*, 30th Aug 1989.

KIER RESIDENTIAL
Peak units: 1158 (2004)

The Kier Group, previously known as French Kier, has a tortuous corporate history. French Kier represented the merger of two predominantly construction companies. Speculative housing has not been a continuing entity: there have been old names dating from French's pre-merger history; a period when the group was part of Beazer, and lost all its housing interests; and new acquisitions, each with their own longstanding history, that have been added by the recently independent Kier.

W & C French

French started in the 1860s when Elizabeth French, an Essex farming widow, began construction and gravel extraction around her farm at Leighton. Her two sons, William and Charles, they confined themselves to civil engineering before World War I, and in the inter-war period the business was expanded through the home counties by Charles and John French, William's sons; the business was incorporated in 1931. After building airfields and other defence work in the Second War, development was broadened to include overseas contracting and, for the first time, private housing estates. French went public in 1949. By the 1960s, the French family connection with the business had become tenuous; Charles French, then Life President, died in 1966.

In 1968 French bought the **Homes Group** for £600,000. Homes was a private property group formed in 1964 with French owning 36%; it had land stocks in Essex and adjacent counties and was forecasting profits of £133,000 for the year to December 1967. WJ Braby, a solicitor, was Deputy Chairman of Homes and 'mainly instrumental in the rapid expansion of that company' and became a French director.[1] Homes accounted for 24% of the 1968 profit though its contribution appeared to have diminished, both absolute and relative, in the years immediately following. The development side of French was further enlarged in 1972 when it bought Marrable Holdings and DSB Properties for £2$\frac{1}{2}$m. 'In a major extension of its activities in London and the south east'[2] Marrable concentrated on office and shop developments and DSB Properties on residential estates. Braby was again involved, controlling 61% of Marrable. With further land purchases French was able to report land holdings of 5000 plots in 1972.

JL Kier

Kier dates to when Olaf Kier left Denmark during the early 1920s. He joined forces with Peter Lind in 1928 to form J Lotz and Kier, later simplified to JL Kier; the firm never engaged in speculative development.. In 1973 Kier and French announced their intention to merge. From the Kier viewpoint it was a disaster as French incurred substantial losses on fixed-price motorway contracts. John Mott, a Kier civil engineer, was appointed as the new group Chief Executive and said, with some understatement: 'It is abundantly clear with hindsight that the projections which came from the French side have not been realised.'[3] Braby's land-acquisition strategy also created losses and led to what became a public clash between Mott and Braby. Against the Board's wishes, Braby stood for re-election at the June 1975 AGM but was defeated. Whilst the priority was ensuring the survival of the group, a modest degree of speculative housebuilding continued. Robert Marriott, a 1971 contracting acquisition by Kier, built houses for local authorities and in 1982 a private sector subsidiary, Marriott Homes, was formed. The following year, French Kier completed 230 private houses – a modest figure compared with the land bank.

[1] Group accounts, 1967.
[2] *Building*, 11th Feb.1972.
[3] Ibid, 30th May 1975.

In 1985, French Kier decided to increase materially its involvement in the speculative housing sector by bidding for Abbey, obtaining 34% irrevocable acceptances from some of the Gallagher family, but the bid was ultimately defeated. While the bid for Abbey was in progress, French Kier itself became a bid target. Trafalgar House had acquired a 26% stake in French Kier and it sold its holding to Beazer which then launched a bid for the balance, valuing French Kier at £118m. Although Beazer's initial bid failed in the face of a resolute defence from Mott, Beazer was successful with a £146m bid in January 1986. On completion of the takeover, all French Kier's land and housing operation was put in to Beazer Homes.

Beazer sells Kier

Beazer itself fell to Hanson in 1991, and the last thing Hanson wanted was its construction business. In July 1992 Hanson disposed of Kier Group to a management and employee team led by Colin Busby, an accountant who had joined French in 1969 and become Managing Director of Beazer Construction in 1986. The new Kier Group comprised only construction; there was no speculative housing left. However, from the beginning, Colin Busby emphasised the management's strategy of developing a broadly-based construction group, a clear contrast with many other construction companies, both before and after, that were choosing to focus themselves on either construction or speculative housing. Kier argued for the financial benefits from combining both businesses: 'We remain committed to building both the size and quality of our two business segments, Construction and Homes & Property…Our financial strategy is simple – to generate cash from our construction segment and invest this in Homes & Property and thereby secure a high return on shareholders' funds.'[4]

Within a year of the buyout, May 1993, Kier made its first housebuilding acquisition, **Twigden Homes**, an East Anglian housebuilder founded by Ivan Twigden, for £30m. Twigden had been building as many as 650 houses in 1989 but had cut back to around 200 in the recession, although still remaining profitable. The Twigden family left the business and Bob Stephens was brought in from Beazer as the new housing Managing Director. In the event, he stayed only a year before another Beazer housing man, David Homer, replaced him, joining the main board in 1996. The coverage of Twigden was extended from East Anglia up into Lincolnshire and down into the northern home counties. In May 1996 the southern division of Miller Homes was bought for £16m, giving Kier representation in the southern home counties. At the end of 1996, Kier Group floated with Busby as Chief Executive.

Kier continued to expand its housing by acquisition and in 1998 bought the quoted **Bellwinch**, a regional business represented in the home counties, Hampshire and Swindon. By now, Kier had a wide geographical spread, from East Anglia, pushing into the midlands, across the south of England and into the west country. This regional coverage was further increased in 1998 when Kier Homes was formed to serve the central belt of Scotland. Overall volumes were relatively small in relation to the number of regions. In 1999, unit sales reached 600 for the first time; to put that in perspective, both Twigden and Bellwinch had reached that size in the late 1980s. In September 2001, Kier bought another private housebuilder, this time within its own operating area, **Allison Homes** for £17m. Kier remained committed to expanding a broadly based construction business. Referring to the acquisition of Allison, Colin Busby said 'The acquisition… conforms to our strategy of seeking growth in parallel from homes, construction, support services and PFI investment, which we see as all complementary businesses.'[5] In practice, further infill acquisitions were made and there was a substantial increase in housing volumes, up to over 1100 in 2004, with the housing division being the largest contributor to group profits.

[4] Group accounts, 1999.
[5] Press release, Sep. 2001.

JOHN LAING
Peak units: 3030 (1987)

John Laing & Sons was one of the best known housebuilders of the 1930s, forever associated with the growth of Metroland. The company also developed into a major international contractor and its post-war history illustrates the difficulty of running a speculative housebuilding operation within a construction framework. James Laing (1817-1882) worked as a stonemason in Cumberland, where he gradually began to employ men and take on small contracts. In 1848, the year the company uses to mark the starting date of the firm, he built a house of his own as an investment in spare time between contracts; two more were built on the same strip. James' eldest son, John (1842-1924), moved the family to Carlisle where, in partnership with his brother William, he traded as J & W Laing, eventually undertaking bigger contracts – Sedbergh School extensions, Carlisle electricity works (1898) – but the partnership ended in 1892 as William was reluctant to expand further.

The true architect of the firm was James' grandson, John W Laing (1879-1978), who joined the firm in 1894 aged 14; he was apprenticed to the bricklayer and mason, although backed by a grammar school education. Six years later, the office consisted of John W Laing, his father, sister and one clerk with 50 people employed outside. They were fully capable of carrying out large local contracts which included factories and a reservoir whilst also building houses for investment. In 1904, on John W Laing's 25th birthday, the name of the firm was changed to John Laing & Son and his father gave him control. John senior was then 62, with a portfolio of rented houses to provide him with income.

A World War I contractor

World War I led to contracts on a larger scale than anything Laing had done before – naval armaments testing, a share in the Gretna armaments factory (an enormous 3000-acre township), and even an aerodrome, and by 1917 Laing employed 4000 men. After the war, the young John Laing set in train the expansion that made the firm a national contractor. The business was incorporated in 1920 with a wide range of staff on the share register. Henry Harland, a surveyor (and John Laing's father-in-law), and William Sirey, an estimator, were directors throughout the inter-war period, Sirey becoming John Laing's chief ally. An office was opened in Liverpool and, in 1921, Laing established a presence in London. Laing had local authority housing contracts around the country often using an industrialised building method, Easiform; by 1924, the firm was working on 1500 houses. The centre of the business was soon switched to London. In 1925 Laing bought 18 acres at Mill Hill: 'When I came to Mill Hill the land was on the market. It was everything I wanted. There was the site for the office and some beautiful land nearby where I could build a home.'[1]

Entry into speculative housebuilding

Although there had been isolated examples of speculative housing after the First War (board minutes of June 1923 refer to conveyances in Feltham), the effective start of Laing's private housing was in 1927, with the purchase of the large Colin Park estate near the new Mill Hill headquarters. Asked why he had entered the world of speculative housing after many years as a general contractor, John Laing's response seems today to be surprisingly altruistic. 'We decided to build such houses after carrying out a certain contract for a financial developer. We found the specification was so reduced in order to produce a cheap dwelling that the purchaser received a very poor return for his investment...We therefore decided to carry out developments ourselves, on the principle of giving the purchaser the highest value for money. Instructions were issued to our managers when we started the work that we desired every house to be a

---

[1] Richie, *The Good Builder The John Laing Story,* p.65.

place of which the man who bought it could be proud, and we have sought throughout to keep this in view.'[2] Sir Maurice Laing also suggested that limited opportunities for making money in contracting had a bearing.[3] As will be seen later, the contractor mentality stayed with Laing until the 1980s and it did not make it easy to develop the private housing business after the war.

John Laing's attitude to speculative housing was characteristic of the contractor and Sir Maurice Laing confirmed that his father always regarded himself as a contractor rather than a developer. Although Laing was building around 1000 houses a year, contracting was still described as 'the principal part of our business.'[4] More telling was his belief that only a contractor's profit margin could be expected: 'I understand that after the war people were building houses for sale and making very high profits. But those days are passed. Any person coming into the business now, and desiring success, must be prepared to invest large sums of money in land, bought in bulk, and in materials … he must be satisfied with a small percentage of profit, and trust to a large turnover to make the business successful.'[5] This was again confirmed by Sir Maurice: 'The problem which father had and which I continually complained about was that he never learned what an asset was worth – he always looked at his costs and then added 10% for a margin.' Apart from a small development in Esher, the first estates were in the north-west corner of London – Colindale, Sudbury, Golders Green, and Woodford. Sales from the Colin Park estate began in the Spring of 1929 with a remarkable rate of build for a new venture; in its first full year of speculative housing, Laing built over 1000 units. The minute and sealing books survive and show the pattern of completions below.

Laing housing completions, 1929-39

1929	1930	1931	1932	1933	1934	1935	1936	1937	1938	1939
260	1010	840	680	830	1450	1110	939	801	706	270

At virtually the same time that Laing was launching its speculative housebuilding, it was also forming a new subsidiary to invest in commercial property. This move, which later profoundly altered the shape of the business, had mixed motives. It was to satisfy wider share ownership within the employees, reflecting the strong Christian tradition within the Laing family, and to provide work for the construction company – a questionable logic much adopted by other construction companies after the war. By the mid 1930s Laing was looking further afield and estates were built in the east and south east of London – Shooters Hill, Blackheath and Woodford – and at Purley and Sanderstead in Surrey. However, housing activity appeared to have peaked in 1934. At the time, Laing still appeared committed to growth: in September 1933, *Practical Builder* reported that Laing was building estates in the outer rim of London to a capital cost of £4.5m, representing 5-6000 houses at prices from £685 to £4000. When completed in five years time, this meant that Laing would have built 20-25,000 houses in London. In the event, the growth did not take place and it is not clear why Laing's housing expectations were not realised. There may have been some natural over-optimism but it is possible that the company was finding it difficult to acquire sites – board minutes of March 1933 reported that the company needed to find another large site as early as possible. Sir Maurice has also suggested that the inflow of construction work which began to come in from the Air Ministry in 1935 diverted John Laing's attention back to construction.

---

[2] Betham, *Housebuilding 1934-36*, Interview with Mr J Laing.
[3] Interview with Sir Maurice Laing, April 2000.
[4] Betham, Housebuilding.
[5] Ibid.

The Christian approach to business

John Laing had been brought up within the Brethren and, having been an active member of the Carlisle congregation, formed a new assembly on the move to Mill Hill and went on to found the Covenanter Union. He was closely involved in church charitable organisations and did not exclude his business from the application of his deeply held religious principles. Practical illustrations included the desire to include a wide range of employees within the ownership of the business and the later establishment of charitable trusts in which substantial family shareholdings were vested. For a speculative housebuilder he seemed averse to recognising the essence of the business: 'As a matter of principle he refused to take windfall profits on undeveloped land acquired by the company.'[6] In June 1936 he wrote to *The Times* advocating the national ownership of land. Two years later he was proposing a clause in purchasers' contracts preventing them from indulging in speculation by selling on part of their plot.[7] Even selling enthusiasm had to be restrained: 'It was resolved to remind all estates of the rule regarding Sundays: that no estate office is to be opened, that none of the sales staff is to be on duty but only the watchman should be on the estate and that the watchman can allow show houses to remain open until sunset but show houses are not to be lighted.'[8]

As war approached, housing demand began to weaken, particularly in Carlisle, where Laing had maintained a housebuilding presence. By then, the contracting division was increasing its defence work, particularly for the Air Ministry. The first airfield contracts were secured in 1935 followed by orders for barrage stations. By the end of the war, Laing had built 54 of the country's 480 airfields, a munitions factory at Sellafield; factories; and, finally, ten of the caissons on the Mulberry Harbour. As the balance of the war swung towards the allies, the company tried to determine its post-war strategy. The minutes of October 1943 recorded that 'our first two objects would be town buildings for ourselves and housebuilding for ourselves and local authorities. General buildings for architects would probably come next and civil engineering work after that.' Despite its war time expertise, Laing did not think much of the heavy end of the construction industry.

A new generation leads the post-war recovery

A new generation of the family was active in the business after the war. Maurice Laing had joined in 1935 aged 17, while his elder brother Kirby followed him in 1937, having studied mechanical sciences at Cambridge; they became directors in 1939. When the war ended John was 66: 'Mr Laing reviewed the discussions he had had in recent years that, but for the war, and the absence of Mr Kirby and Mr Maurice in the forces, both he and Mr Harland would have retired from active administration of the business and now they would wish to commence that gradual withdrawal so as to leave the administration more and more in the hands of the younger directors.'[9]

Post-war activity took a different direction than expected. Housing activity was confined to local authority contracts and by 1950 Laing had built more than 14,000 Easiform houses and the annual rate was up to 5000 The first foreign subsidiary was formed in 1947 – Laing and Roberts, in South Africa; there was the first international contract, in Syria for Iraq Petroleum; the Sellafield power station; and the development of the Thermalite lightweight concrete block. By 1951 Laing was earning profits of over £1m and the company was floated on the Stock Exchange with John Laing as non-executive Chairman, Kirby responsible for property and Maurice for building and construction. Ernest Uren, who became the senior non-family figure, ran finance and administration. Although John Laing had agreed to be

---

6 Richie, *The Good Builder*, p.87.
7 Laing minute book, May 1938
8 Ibid.
9 Ibid, Feb. 1946.

Chairman, it was against his better judgement; at the first AGM he faced questions which he had to pass over to his sons. 'He said to us after that if he couldn't answer questions about his own company he wasn't going to be Chairman and resigned.'[10] Unlike Frank Taylor and Godfrey Mitchell, John Laing's retirement was virtually total.

John David Martin

The restart of Laing's private housing was so low key that the company did not even use its own name to sell the houses. 'Everybody thought we were housebuilders and everybody looked down on housebuilders as the bottom end of the market. We were trying to get major civil contracts and the potential clients were saying "you are just housebuilders"'.[11] John and David Martin Ltd (using family Christian names) was incorporated in April 1953 and started with pre-war estates in Purley and Potters Bar. The initial agreement was for the parent company to transfer land to John and David Martin as needed but John Laing still carried out the construction and retained the profit. Over time, full operational responsibility was passed to the housing company and in 1959 it was eventually renamed Laing Housing. The reality of the private housing operation is that it played a smaller role in the group than it had before the war, both in absolute terms and certainly relative to the rest of the group; it was not until 1983 that Laing Homes reached its pre-war peak volumes. Its managing directors were builders rather than developers and the operations remained closely linked with the construction company.

There were no obvious reasons why Laing failed to build on its pre-war housing strength. Maurice Laing conceded that the heart was elsewhere: 'we were just not very interested.' There were early references to poor sales because 'we were not able to use the name Laing to the full.'[12] The attractions of other development opportunities was also relevant; Laing Properties was being actively expanded and, in a family controlled business, capital resources were not limitless. However, the private housing business no longer had the day-to-day presence of the group's leaders. There were frequent discussions as to how the company should best be run. Only the housing managing director, WM Johnson (who had been with Laing since the first war) was on the housing company board and the minute books disclose that those below him did not seem able to work in harmony. Later that year Johnson himself resigned and new plans were made. Housing profits were then running at £70,000 and a target of £250,000 from 1000 completions was set for 1961.

Conflict over housing organisation

The minutes of June 1959 record an extensive debate on the relationship between Laing's regional construction establishments, and John and David Martin as a central co-ordinator. One problem was finding sites and more agents were to be recruited to look at other parts of the country. Where appropriate the contracting company would be asked to undertake construction work on behalf of the Martin company on a contract basis thus providing incentive to the local management of the contracting company to discover suitable sites in their locality. The company's name was changed to 'The Laing Housing Company Ltd' which it was felt could now be adopted without detriment to the civil engineering side of the contracting company's business.

Conflict with the construction arm continued. There were complaints about the decision to permit the construction company to undertake private housing developments in other parts of the country than the north. Land supply also remained a problem and there was even talk of acquiring HC Janes for its land bank.

---

10 Interview Sir Maurice Laing.
11 Ibid.
12 John and David Martin Board minutes, Sep. 1956.

In the event, the problems over land acquisition led to the 1961 target being scaled down to 600 and the actual result fell well short of that. The expansion strategy for private housing was finally laid to rest at the end of 1961 when Uren deleted the reference to 'an expanding business' substituting instead a land policy 'consistent with the amount of the group capital allocated to the business'.[13] There were intermittent attempts in the 1960s and 1970s to revive the previous expansion plans for private housing. In 1964 the Board again agreed that the company should plan to increase up to 1000 starts by 1968 which it almost achieved before falling back to a low point of around 300 in 1972 and 1973. By the early 1970s the growth targets were once more for 1000 completions by 1975 but also with a new target of 2000 by 1978; again, the 1000 target was missed. Housing and property were now under the combined control of John Beavis, but his prime interest lay in commercial property (he went on to head Laing Properties when it was demerged in 1978).

During the 1960s, the Laing family was taking a less hands-on role in the company: 'their involvement in its day-to-day management had undoubtedly been diluted by Kirby and Maurice's devotion to public affairs. In one sense this had been an advantage. It had forced the group to evolve management systems which did not depend on quite the same level of personal vigilance that Sir John had practised with such devastating effect.'[14] Ernest Uren was in effect managing director but ill health forced his retirement at 58. Put at its simplest, the replacements did not work. First the Board decided to go outside for a replacement and Sir Fred Catherwood joined in 1971; he had been Chief Executive of Costain, British Aluminium and NEDO. However, he resigned in 1974 to be replaced by Geoff Parsons, then head of Laing Civil Engineering and, again, his five-year tenure was described in the company history as less than comfortable.

Demerger of Property Division

One of the key events in the Laing history was the legal separation and flotation of Laing Properties in 1978 which, to the embarrassment of the construction company, was soon valued considerably higher than its parent. The housing company was originally going to be included with Laing Properties but it was eventually left with Construction: 'Maurice insisted that housing went in with construction using the argument that construction needed somewhere to put its surplus cash.'[15] The first annual report of the slimmed down John Laing conceded the underperformance of its private housing: 'Although the activities of our Group have expanded dramatically in the post war period we have not achieved a corresponding increase in private housing. We have now taken steps to strengthen and expand our Homes Company and this should be an area of growth for us over the next few years.' When Leslie Holliday took over as group Managing Director in 1979, Laing Homes no longer had to compete with commercial property for capital. New management also brought with it a reassessment of the approach to private housing. 'I looked at it and realised it was not going to develop as it had been. I looked at overseas markets and in searching for the best way forward became certain that brick and block was not the future. We therefore set up Super Homes [a prefabricated timber framed housing system] to be the building source for Homes and we also had visions of it being sold as a system to other housebuilders.'[16]

Ambitious housing targets

The Board once again set ambitious volume targets, only this time they were achieved. The housing company was on its way to becoming a free-standing operation. David Holliday (Leslie's son) was moved into Laing Homes as Managing Director in 1980 (becoming the first housebuilding Managing Director to be appointed to the main board in 1983). He inherited a business that was still closely linked to the

[13] Ibid, Dec 1961.
[14] Richie, *The Good Builder,* p.146.
[15] Interview Leslie Holliday.
[16] Ibid.

construction division. 'The construction company did the work for housebuilding and charged them what they felt like and made a profit, and housing tried to make a profit from development. I said this was not the right way to do it. At that time my appointment was still a construction appointment rather than a developer appointment. I dropped my contractor hat very early on.'[17]

By the late 1980s, private housing sales were over 3000 a year, placing it comfortably in the top ten, and Laing Homes was providing the bulk of the group's profits. Laing was also building houses in California: Leslie Holliday argued for the advantages of offsetting the UK housing cycle and the broadening of perspective. However, the success of the housing business caused its own problems within the group. 'One of the internal difficulties was that you had a contractor who employed 11,000 people and a housebuilder who employed 600 people and you have jealousies – not particularly at the top level but lower down; it is very difficult to weld it into the same culture. What we never achieved was a construction operation that balanced housing. It should have made a choice then; I was advocating selling Homes at that time.'[18] Instead, David Holliday left the group in 1989 to establish his own housing company (Admiral Homes).

Housing units, 1955-2001

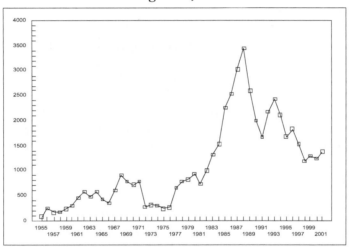

Laing Homes had continued to buy land after David Holliday's departure and the recession brought substantial write-offs. But what was significant about the recession was not the reduction in asset value itself but the reaction to it. Whereas some housebuilders were using the collapse in land prices to restock with cheap land, Laing's policy was to take money out of housing: in June 1992 the directors announced that their policy was to take £70m out of housing world-wide over the succeeding three years. Inevitably volumes declined for most of the decade and by 1998 had fallen to 1180 units – only a third of the level achieved ten years earlier. In the closing years of the 1990s, volumes once again began to increase, retirement home specialist Beechcroft was bought for £10m, and a more healthy level of profits was being earned. Unfortunately, all was not well elsewhere in the group. The construction division lost a staggering £185m in 2000 and 2001 and the private O'Rourke paid a nominal £1 to buy the business. This left a weakened group with two disparate parts – housing and a portfolio of construction related investments. In October 2002, Laing Homes was sold to Wimpey for £297m; the Laing brand name was retained.

---

[17] Interview with David Holliday, Dec. 1998.
[18] Ibid.

LAWDON
Peak units: c.150-200 (early 1970s)

Lawdon was started by Donald Betts in 1961, then aged 39; he was described in the Prospectus as having spent all his working life in the development business. Finishing school at the standard leaving age, his experience of the industry was gained, inter alia, through working in his brother's building business and at Crowborough Brickworks, where he finished in a senior managerial position. Lack of finance meant the first developments had to be carried out in joint venture with public companies but, by 1967, a stronger capital base meant that he was able to develop more of the sites from his own resources.

By 1970, profits had reached £200,00 and in July 1971 Lawdon was floated. Donald Betts was Chairman and Managing Director and his nephew John Betts was works director. The group operated primarily within the London commuter belt with a particular emphasis on the Croydon area and a range of quality homes. No unit sales figures were given but the annual figure was unlikely to have been more than 150. There was also a modest amount of commercial property and Lawdon had started a couple of developments in France: 'the directors considered that certain European countries, particularly France, offered considerable scope for profitable development.'[1]

The 1972 accounts reported the first profits from France plus the start of a holiday development in Menorca which was to prove less successful. The UK market remained strong and although there were the first signs of a slowdown, Donald Betts was able to say that 'I see no break in the growth of the Group...we have every confidence that 1972/73 will show a further substantial increase in profits.'[2] Indeed they did, rising to a record £500,000. By then, however, the market was beginning to deteriorate and although the Chairman emphasised that the majority of land was acquired at pre-boom prices, Lawdon had only just purchased five acres of land without planning permission at Rotherhithe, on the Thames.

In the year to May 1974, Lawdon declared a loss of £524,000 after writing off £732,000 on sites bought in 1972 and 1973 and paying interest which had risen from £237,000 to £767,000. Gross profits were still satisfactory but despite selling land, Lawdon remained highly geared with net debt of £5.3m against shareholders' funds of £0.7m. Receivers were appointed in March 1976.

---

[1] Prospectus, 1971.
[2] Company accounts, 1972.

JOHN LAWRENCE
Peak units: c.1000-1200 (mid-1960s)

Although best known as the Chairman of Glasgow Rangers Football Club in the 1960s, John Lawrence created one of Scotland's largest construction companies of its time. After his death in 1977, control passed to his grandson and the company was placed in receivership in 1997.

John Lawrence was born in Glasgow in 1893, the son of a joiner. He finished school aged 14, and became an office boy at a grain broker; three years later he left to become an apprentice joiner. Technical knowledge was acquired via night school and then the Royal Technical College.[1] In his early 20s he became a foreman with Mactaggart & Mickel before setting up his own business. There appears no unanimity over dates in the various biographical sources, but it would appear that he started on his own with carpentry contracts in the early 1920s, using money borrowed from his aunt; his initial success must have been limited for he emigrated for a brief period to the USA. The original company, John Lawrence (Glasgow) was formed in 1928 and it was shortly after that he built his first private house; Lawrence also began to expand the local authority housing and general construction business.

Private housing in the inter-war period was not easy in Lawrence's home city: 'anyone who wanted to make a living from this sort of enterprise was up against the low-rent tradition in Scotland, Glasgow in particular.'[2] Nevertheless, speculative housing production was gradually increased through the first half of the 1930s. There is no indication of the number of houses built; however, Lawrence has been described as the primary competitor to Mactaggart & Mickel from the mid-1930s.[3] During the war, Lawrence maintained a modest construction output, including air raid shelters and hospitals; it did not appear to be drawn into civil engineering.

The largest private housebuilder in Scotland
After the war, the business appears to have expanded substantially – private housing, local authority housing and contracting. Watters described John Lawrence in the 1950s as 'presiding over the largest private building organisation in Scotland.'[4] He also chaired The Scottish Housing Group 'a cartel of housing contractors...which was built up in the 1940s with [Department of Health for Scotland] and Building Research Station help...to exploit non-traditional construction and resist the incursion of English firms.'[5] Around 1964, the business was divided into two: private housebuilding which built about 1000 to 1200 units a year; and the local authority contract work which represents about 60% of the turnover.[6] If these private housing numbers are correct, it would make Lawrence the largest private housebuilder in Scotland at the time.

As his fortune increased, John Lawrence began to acquire other interests. In particular, he became a shareholder in Rangers FC and its Chairman in 1963, a position which Watters suggests distracted him from his own business: 'John Lawrence's powerful business... was progressively undermined by his own preoccupation as Chairman of Rangers Football Club.'[7] Certainly, it appears that private housing volumes

1 *Glasgow Herald,* Feb.1997; *Dictionary of Scottish Business Biography,* 1986.
2 *Housebuilder,* Dec. 1969.
3 *Watters, Mactaggart & Mickel and the Scottish Housebuilding Industry,* p.14.
4 Ibid, p.160.
5 Ibid, p.120.
6 *Housebuilder,* Feb 1997.
7 *Watters, Mactaggart & Mickel,* p.153.

had fallen by the start of the 1970s – NHBC registrations were down to around 600 a year, and Watters refers to much of its land bank being sold to Wimpey. The first accounts on record are for 1974 and disclosed turnover of £9.4m and pre-tax profits of £547,000, figures which had not increased substantially by the time of John Lawrence's death in 1977. The *Glasgow Herald* said that under John Lawrence's chairmanship, the company had built more than 40,000 private homes and 30,000 council houses throughout Scotland. To put those figures in perspective, if one allows for ten years of pre-war private housebuilding and a good twenty years between the end of building controls and his death, this would give an average of over 1000 private house a year.

On John Lawrence's death, control of the company passed to his grandson, Lawrence Marlborough, who expanded the business in new directions, including garages, full control of Glasgow Rangers and leisure property in Carson City, Nevada. By 1986, turnover had increased to over £75m though profits had changed little. In that year, the private housebuilding business merged with YJ Lovell in Scotland, leaving Lawrence with a 25% interest. By then, Lawrence was building only 150 houses a year with a land bank of around 1000 plots in Glasgow and Ayrshire. The intention was to build the new company up to sales of around 500 a year but in 1991 sales were still only 140 units and the company, by then wholly owned by Lovell, was sold to a new company, Ambion Homes.

As a postscript, John Lawrence incurred losses of over £2m in 1989 and the company began to concentrate more on property development. In February 1997, a receiver was appointed as a result of debts estimated at £15-20m.

WALTER LAWRENCE
Peak units: 1176 (1987)

Lawrence was founded in 1871 but family involvement ceased on the Company's flotation in 1975. The first estate development appeared with the 1965 acquisition of Frederick Coyle, an old-established business based at Weybridge. Coyle, which had been founded by Fred Coyle in 1927, had started residential development on its own account in 1962; by 1975 it accounted for 25% of its business. Subsequently, Lawrence East Anglia, which did some local authority housing, began small scale private development, and by 1975 the group held ten sites for development. Lawrence had also moved into commercial property development in 1971, forming joint companies with two property developers to carry out developments in London. There had even been a development in Malta. In February 1974, John Redgrave, previously with British Plaster Board, joined as group Managing Director; the fact that this was described as a new post exemplified the break from the earlier family management. He took over a predominantly construction business, with profits running at around half a million pounds a year, and its residential and commercial development largely carried out away from the centre of the company. The first strategic move, however, was to direct the construction company to the booming middle-east market. It was not until 1978 that a separate private housing company, Walter Lawrence Homes, was formed, with Barrie Howell joining from Costain Homes.

Housing expansion in the 1980s

A period of rapid growth started in 1981, and by 1985 the group was building some 500 houses a year; housing was the main contributor to group profits of £3m. Redgrave then left Lawrence, to be replaced as Chief Executive by Trevor Mawby, the 36 year old Finance Director. This was the start of more ambitious expansion. Housebuilding was constituted as a separate division for the first time and in 1986 Bob Andrews (from Coyle) was placed in charge of housing. In the September, Lawrence bought Poco Properties, a Lancashire-based housebuilder, for £22m, financed by a share placing; the enlarged group made profits of £7.5m and built nearly 1200 houses, some 700 of which had come from Poco. This profit came after a substantial loss in Lawrence's contracting division, which was then closed.

Profits more than doubled in the next two years, exceeding £19m in 1988. By then, the housebuilding division operated in five regions: the north west (the old Poco base); the southern home counties through Frederick Coyle; the Dorset area (Poco's other region); Kent; and Chiltern (started in the late 1970s and spreading across to Wiltshire). Housing was further expanded in 1988 by two overseas acquisitions as 'The ever increasing cost of development land in the UK has encouraged Walter Lawrence to examine opportunities abroad.'[1] Unfortunately, the overseas markets were to prove every bit as vulnerable as the UK. In March, Lawrence bought a 51% stake in a Californian housebuilder, West Venture Developments for £2.6m; this was expected to sell some 450 units. Then in the October Lawrence made an investment to develop some 400 villas in Majorca. Reflecting the world wide property recession, Lawrence's profits collapsed at home and abroad. After profits of £3.6m in 1990 there was a forecast of little more than breakeven for 1991. That in itself was not the real problem – many in the industry did worse and survived. What did the damage was the rise in debt which 'severely restricts management's ability to maximise the potential of…the existing businesses, or to take advantage of the opportunities which may arise when trading conditions improve.'[2] In March 1992 Raine Industries took advantage of the depressed share price to make an agreed bid, valuing Lawrence at £31m, a premium of 150% on the previous day's price.

[1] Group Accounts, 1987.
[2] Raine Offer Document for Walter Lawrence, 1992.

WILLIAM LEECH
Peak units: 1888 (1973)

William Leech began his working life as a window cleaner; the building business was started in 1932 when he was then aged 31. His organisational talents were developed, so it is said, when he found himself cleaning windows whilst other cleaners worked in overlapping streets. He organised the cleaners into efficient working areas through his own entity 'United Window Cleaners' taking a commission from them. When going into the pubs for a drink he saw that the only people who could afford to buy whisky were builders and so he decided to become a builder. It is also said that he began by building a house for himself, then selling it and building another two.

Based in Newcastle, the company rapidly became one of the largest housebuilders in the north east, and by 1937 was building at a rate of 500 a year,[1] probably putting it in the top three or four housebuilders outside the London area. However, selling the houses proved difficult, and the unfinished houses caused William Leech financial problems. In 1936 John Adamson, an accountant, was brought in by the lenders to provide a control: 'He had to sign everything.' There was an eventual silver lining: 'William Leech built his fortune on not being a very good salesman. There were 2000 unsold houses on the outbreak of the war and these were sold after the war at a substantial profit.'[2]

Agricultural land given to charity

After the War, when Leech was confined to general contracting, the company began building houses for local authorities in the north east and progressively returned to private development during the 1950s, concentrating largely on the first-time buyer. A source of the Company's post-war strength was the tracts of agricultural land in the Newcastle area which gained planning consents. Not all the land was purchased directly. In 1953, William Leech formed William Leech (Investments) for the sole purpose of buying agricultural land and in 1955, he gave the entire share capital of Investments to five evangelical charities. On receiving planning permission, Investments' land was transferred to Builders on favourable terms; the largest site was at Cramlington, used for the New Town developed jointly with Bellway.

William Leech had two daughters, but no sons, and he passed over the role of Managing Director to John Adamson in 1960. Adamson, then 52, had played a pseudo-managerial role since he joined in 1936. Unlike some founders who remain on the Board, William Leech did leave Adamson to run the business which he did as 'a detail man' with operational support from Harry Ross as construction and land director.[3] Adamson's made Leech's first regional diversification in 1968, buying Williamson Construction, a housebuilder operating from Falkirk. Although only building around 20 units a year, Williamson gave Leech a base for a Scottish region that eventually grew to 400-500 units a year. This was followed in 1970 by the purchase of a Humberside building contractor, Wilkinson & Houghton; the contracting was continued and its office was moved to Nottingham in 1973 forming the base for a midlands subsidiary.

William Leech stood down as Chairman in 1973, becoming President. John Adamson became Chairman and his son, Richard, was appointed Managing Director. Richard Adamson, then 31, had joined the company in 1967 (against his wishes, it was sometimes said) having qualified as a chartered accountant. Richard had a more outgoing management style than his father and, along with Peter Milburn, became more involved in the land purchases. Richard Adamson also took a closer interest in the marketing: 'he

[1] Group Accounts, 1982.
[2] Interview Richard Adamson.
[3] Interview John Livingston.

moved the firm from taking orders to getting orders.'[4]

Leech becomes a top ten builder
Leech completed just short of 1900 houses in 1972/73, putting it comfortably into the top ten, although numbers fell to 1500 in 1974. Despite the difficult market conditions, Leech chose that time to diversify across the Pennines. It bought Hugh Owen & Sons of Stockport for £1m to become Leech (North West) and the subsidiary in North Wales became Leech (Wales). The north east was less affected than the south east by the recession but, even so, Leech's profits proved remarkably resilient and in 1975/76 they just edged past their 1974 level. John Livingston, later Finance Director, believes the explanation lay in the low-cost land bank, some of which was in the books at almost zero cost. Leech floated on the Stock Exchange in June 1976 at a time when many of the quoted housebuilders were still trying to recover from the recession.

The strength of the company was its long land bank amounting to some 12,500 plots; in addition, there were some 4000 acres of land without permission. One of the other distinguishing features of the company was that the greater part of the building work was carried out by Leech's own labour force including all the trades, in contrast to most housebuilders where the trades were sub-contracted; Leech employed 2100 people on flotation. The largest shareholder was the charitable trust to which William Leech had given 75% of the shares in 1960; after the flotation, the trust retained a 37% holding. The company's record in just under a decade as a public company proved solid but unexciting. There was an attempt at further regional expansion – a Yorkshire subsidiary was formed during 1979 but it did little. Leech also bought a couple of caravan sites and developed a leisure centre. However, housing volumes showed virtually no change and, although turnover grew, rising interest charges and substantial losses on local authority housing prevented profits from exceeding the £2.8m reported in 1977.

Attempted merger with Bellway
In May 1981 Leech and Bellway announced a possible merger (see Bellway). This was abandoned ostensibly due to incompatible philosophies but the real answer probably lay in an unresolved contest for places on the Board. Leech's finances began to deteriorate: borrowings exceeded equity and 1982's trading profits of £4.6m were almost entirely absorbed by interest of £4.2m. The problem stemmed from the weakness in sales at the end of the 1970s and early 1980s, when Leech had continued to build: 'Work in progress shot up; we were massively overstocked.'[5] Further losses outside the core housebuilding business, this time in leisure held the group back. In June 1984, Beazer bought Poco's 7% holding and launched a full bid. This failed by 3.6% to win control as William Leech, then 84, vetoed the sale of the Trust's 29.7% stake.

In the September, Richard Adamson, was ousted as Chairman and Managing Director by the rest of the Board. The Leech statement referred to 'irreconcilable differences which have emerged between Richard Adamson and other executive directors relating to management style and philosophy.' *Building* said that Adamson's 'personal style was not greatly to the liking of some of his colleagues and the stress filtered to Board level during the Beazer battle undoubtedly did nothing to reduce tensions already in the background.'[6] Former banker Bill Griffiths became Chairman and Peter Milburn, who had been with the company for nearly 30 years, took over as Managing Director. Beazer had been left with 17% of the Leech shares but Richard Adamson sold his own 7% to give Beazer a 24% holding. In January 1985 Beazer returned with another bid and this time the Foundation agreed to sell its shares.

[4] Ibid.
[5] Ibid.
[6] *Building* , 14th Sep. 1984.

LEWSTON DEVELOPMENTS
Peak units: 200-300 (early 1970s)

In 1944 David Stanton, Leonard Somers and Alfred Lewis began acquiring residential property for investment and by 1952 there was a substantial portfolio of residential property in and around London, the majority of which was then rent controlled. From 1953 onwards the original activities were broadened by the acquisition of building land in London and selected provincial centres for developing private housing estates. In the following years a few small developments of houses for sale were carried out but it was not until 1963 that full development of the building land was started.

From 1963, the group concentrated on private estate development in Bletchley, Peterborough, Streetly and Worcester. The Prospectus for the flotation in March 1966 stated that since 1963 over 500 houses had been built; the turnover figure for 1965 suggests sales of around 200. Profits for the year to March 1965 were £246,000 but before 1964 the figures were relatively nominal. After the flotation, profits declined; in 1968 the dividend was cut and by the end of the decade Lewston was barely breaking even.

In 1969, Fordham Investment bought 55% of the Company and announced that it would bid for the balance, although in the event its holding fell below 50%. Fordham's stated intent was to realise the bulk of Lewston's assets but Fordham itself was taken over by Ralli International in 1970. Lewston Developments, which soon became Lewston International, was substantially expanded under Ralli's control. It bought Ralli's own builder Minton, followed by Thomas Vale in January 1972. The acquisition policy was spelt out in the 1972 accounts: 'a policy of acquiring well-established regional companies with good local connections and knowledge and linking them by strong central financial resources and control.' In May that year, Lewston bought the long-established Nottingham contractors, Simms Sons & Cooke at the third attempt.

By 1973, Lewston was going into European development on a substantial scale. By the end of the year it had a £44m development programme in Germany and France, over and above its 60% stake in Lenz-Bau, a German contracting and property business. Profits rose to a peak of £1.7m in 1973 by which time Ralli had become part of the Bowater paper group. Most of the activity was now commercial property; housing turnover was no more than £3.5m suggesting housing completions of 2-300. Profits were maintained in the year to March 1974, but the balance sheet was severely strained with £3m of shareholders' funds supporting £18m of debt. The property obligations were considerable – a £7m office block was bought in Paris after the year end. At the end of 1974, Lewston revealed that it was in financial difficulties and that Bowater and the group's bankers were lending it support. In June 1975, Bowater decided not to extend that support and Lewston was put into liquidation.

LILLEY
Peak units: 486 (1990)

FJC Lilley Ltd was founded in Glasgow by the eponymous FJC Lilley shortly before the First World War. It remained predominantly a Scottish civil engineer until 1955, after which it undertook more work in England and, in the 1960s, abroad. The Company was floated in 1965 with Francis Lilley, the founder's son, as Chairman and Managing Director, and his son also on the board. Gradually, the family hold on the Company declined and in the 1970s, Lilley expanded through a serious of acquisitions, taking on civil engineering work across the UK and abroad.

It was not until 1978 that Lilley first became involved in the speculative housing industry when it acquired the Dumfries builder, **Robison & Davidson**. Robison, a stone mason, and Davidson, an architect, entered partnership in 1922. The business was incorporated in 1948 when Davidson left to buy a farm. At that point, Bob Robison, the founder's nephew, joined as a 15-year-old apprentice bricklayer, eventually becoming its largest shareholder and Managing Director. When Lilley acquired it, the business was (and continued to be) run as a general contractor and housebuilder. In 1981, Lilley entered commercial property development for the first time, buying development land in Aldershot. More development activity came in 1981 and 1982 with the purchase of Melville Dundas & Whitson, another Glasgow-based contractor, and the Cumbrian Eden Construction; like Robison, both these companies had contracting and development businesses and Lilley continued to run them separately. At no time was private housing put under unified control and, indeed, some of the subsidiaries themselves combined both contracting and private housing.

Profits growth of the Group was impressive, rising from £1m in 1974 to £14m in 1984, predominantly from contracting. That year saw the first serious reference to housing in the Annual Report: 'One important feature of this year's trading is the increase in the Group's activity in the private homes market. Sales for the year were 245 and the budget [for 1985] is over 400 units. This is a market that the Group intends to develop over the next few years and a substantial land bank has been acquired.'[1] However, no sooner had the commitment to speculative housing been made than the Group was forced to cut back its commercial development programme: 'major schemes were contracted in the expectation that these would be financed by a re-cycling of available Group funds, in addition to which they would provide alternative work outlets for Group companies....subsequent change in the climate has altered that '.[2]

Bankruptcy averted

By now, profits had come off their peak, but in the year to January 1987 the scale of losses, some £50m, nearly bankrupted the company. UK construction and housing remained in modest profit but there were massive losses in the US construction companies and in international contracting. Under the chairmanship of Lewis Robertson, and a change of top management, Lilley was rescued. In mid 1988, Robertson was approached by Bob Rankin, formerly Chief Executive at Balfour Beatty, with a buy-in proposal; this put £28m into the company. In March 1989, as the housing market was visibly turning down, Lilley paid some £24m for the privately owned **Standen** group, founded in 1959 by Allan Standen; its housing subsidiary built around 250 houses a year in the Nottingham area where it claimed around 10-12% of the local market, raising group volumes close to 500. In July 1989, with group profits heading for a new record, Lilley launched a hotly contested bid for Tilbury Group worth £124m in shares. The bid failed leaving Lilley with 29.99% of Tilbury and financing costs which were a major cause of the fall in profits in 1990.

[1] Group accounts, 1984.
[2] Ibid, 1985.

The recession finally caught up with Lilley in the year to December 1991 when real estate provisions, primarily in housebuilding, totalled £12m. In July 1991 two Spanish construction companies injected further funds by taking a 21 per cent stake in Lilley, a move which seemed to have secured its financial future; however, it proved insufficient and the Group went into receivership in January 1993. 'Lilley's future was sealed, [stockbrokers] say, by the failure to prevent its disastrous plunge into the property market during the boom. When the market slumped Lilley's stated assets of £47m had turned into net liabilities of £13m virtually overnight.'[3] In its article 'What killed the Lilley Group?', *The Scotsman* said that 'in his private moments, Sir Lewis acknowledges that he failed to control Rankin... and attached too much weight for too long to the £28m war chest that accompanied Rankin when he arrived in 1988. According to Lilley's rivals, that money was wasted on over expensive purchases in England, such as Standen, as well as on its abortive bid for Tilbury in 1989. The reality was that Lilley was leaking cash with alarming rapidity because of its involvement in property development.'[4]

The one part of the Group to escape receivership was Robison & Davidson where buy-out proposals had been under discussion since the previous October. In February 1993, Managing Director Bob Robison completed the MBO of what had remained a mixed housing and construction group. Standen was sold by the receivers to the management.

[3] *Sunday Times,* 24th Jan. 1993.
[4] *Scotsman,* 5th April, 1993.

LINDEN
Peak units: 1085 (2002)

In the course of only a decade, Linden was formed, floated, bought itself back, and is now planning for output of some 1500 houses a year. The founder, Philip Davies, had joined Bovis Homes as a management trainee in Frank Sanderson's reign and had later joined him at Finlas, subsequently acquired by Alfred McAlpine. When Frank Sanderson resigned in 1985, Philip Davies succeeded him as Chief Executive of McAlpine Homes where he stayed until 1990. Linden was formed in May 1991 by Davies and Lou Jovic, also ex-McAlpine, who was responsible for administration and finance. Capital was provided by Nash Sells, and Andrew Sells became Chairman.

According to the 1996 Prospectus, the Surrey-based Linden 'established itself by focusing on developing brown land and building quality properties with above average specifications.' It sought sites for no more than 50 houses in the early years and by 1994 was selling almost 200 houses. Unlike Admiral, the high-profile start up that was formed a year or so before Linden, Linden was consistently profitable and established a strong growth record with high capital turnover translating modest trading margins into high returns on capital. In 1994, Linden made its first geographical expansion with the purchase of the Cheshire developer Goldcrescent Land and Estates which had been formed by Colin Muller, also ex-McAlpine, and Peter Howard.

As with most venture-capital companies, Linden was highly geared. However, the flotation in 1996 raised new equity and saw the conversion of venture-capital loans into equity; as a result, gearing fell to a minimal 6%. The flotation facilitated further geographical expansion. A northern home counties subsidiary was formed in 1997 and in September that year Linden bought Amplevine for £7m. Amplevine had been formed in 1987 by Gerard Price, an estate agent, and operated in the Southampton area; Price joined the Linden Board and his land director, Tony Burton, later became group land director. The other significant purchase that year was of the Caterham Barracks at a cost of some £10m – a significant sum in comparison with the Group's then net assets of £22m. The Caterham site totalled 57 acres and involved the conversion of existing buildings and additional new housing. The four main divisions continued their expansion and a further £20m of new capital was raised in 1999, half coming from the Bank of Scotland. A fifth region was formed at Bristol giving the group the capacity to expand sales to 1000 units in 2001 (although it was another year before the target was achieved). However, by then, Linden had left the quoted arena. A potential MBO was announced in June 2000 and in October a cash offer of 290p a share (against a 150p flotation price) was made, valuing Linden at £73m. The management and employee team was led by Philip Davies, Colin Muller, Gerard Price, Lou Jovic and Andrew Sells, with the Bank of Scotland providing loan finance and taking 29.9% of the equity.

Like others, Davies professed disillusionment with the stock market: 'There is very little the stock market can offer a housebuilder… It is difficult to see at the moment how the stock exchange will deal with smaller companies in the old industries.'[1] (In fact, within four years, the stock market had provided Linden a flotation, finance for an acquisition and an equity placing). What the MBO did was to secure a higher percentage of the equity for the management who were willing to accept a higher level of gearing. This did not restrain Linden's growth plans: 'we have a clear vision of growing all five regions to give us the capability of 1500-1750 units per annum in three years time. We will remain a niche brownland developer.[2]

[1] *Building*, 6th Oct. 2000.
[2] Company accounts, 2000.

LOVELL
Peak units: 3101 (1991)

The original jobbing building firm was founded in 1786 at Marlow-on-Thames, coming into the ownership of a Dorset plumber, Young James Lovell, in the 1870s. By 1908 the firm had developed under the control of his son, Clifford Percy Lovell who opened building branches at Gerrards Cross, Beaconsfield, and London. Although Lovell operated primarily as a building contractor, it did some speculative housebuilding, at the upper end of the market, where prices reached £4-5000 and the firm regularly provided a house for the Ideal Home Exhibition. An interview with Clifford Lovell in 1934 disclosed his attitude to housebuilding when asked if it was a side line in his business. 'That is so, as the bulk of our work is contracting... The building of good class speculative houses, however, is an enterprise in which we are greatly interested, and one that is traditional with us.'[1]

At some point Clifford Lovell joined in partnership with an HJ Kay and that partnership ran into difficulties in 1938: 'the subsequent reorganisation into a private company [YJ Lovell & Sons] was of some importance – from it were to emerge the future leaders of the business.'[2] One of those leaders was Ernest Burrows, who became Chairman of the new company and the other was Eric Segrove who had started as the office junior at Gerrards Cross in 1916 aged 13. 'Ernest Burrows steered the company into broader waters during and after the war and charted the expansion on a sound basis and his work has effectively been carried on by Eric Segrove from about 1958.'[3]

Regional expansion in the 1960s
Lovell grew steadily, if unspectacularly, after the war and began to expand regionally during the 1960s. There had also been diversification into timber merchanting (producing some two-thirds of the group profit in the early 1970s), plant hire and property development: 'enterprises which are predominantly outlets for...their main activity, which is building contracting.'[4] However, there was little evidence of any commitment to private housing until 1967, the year before the Company's flotation, when Lovell Developments was formed to engage in estate and commercial development activities. The 1968 Prospectus also mentioned that 'Estate and commercial development on sites owned by the group is a growing feature of the business' although there was little other mention of housing. Ernest Burrows, then aged 77 and Eric Segrove were still controlling the management of the Company at the time of flotation although Burrows had stood down as Chairman in favour of Segrove. Both had sons on the board while Peter Lovell, who maintained the family connection, and Arthur Davies, who had joined the group in 1932, were the joint Managing Directors. The Deputy Chairman was Peter Trench, who had started as a Bovis management trainee in 1946, later becoming director of the National Federation of Building Trades Employers; he replaced Eric Segrove as Chairman in 1972.

The Norman Wakefield era begins
In 1977 Peter Lovell and Arthur Davies were approaching retirement and the three families (Burrows, Seagrove and Lovell) were not in harmony. Norman Wakefield was brought into Lovell as Chief Executive: Wakefield had started in the industry in 1947 as an articled student with Wates, becoming Managing Director of its construction division in 1967 and later Managing Director of Holland Hannen & Cubitts. Wakefield first instituted a financial reorganisation and allowed the housing company to

[1] Betham, *Housebuilding 1934-36.*
[2] Madden, 'Lovell Construction Group', *Building,* 20th June 1969.
[3] Ibid.
[4] Ibid.

rebuild its land bank. A period of expansion followed. The first acquisition was of Farrow Construction in 1978, then the in-house construction subsidiary of ICI; the particular significance of Farrow was that in 1971 it had bought the west-country firm of Rendell. **Rendell** had pioneered the modern form of partnership housing with local authorities just prior to its acquisition by Farrow and, under the ownership of Lovell, was to become the leading force in the partnership housing sector.

Rendell pioneers partnership housing

Rendell has a special place in the history of housebuilders as the pioneer of modern partnership housing. The business was founded by William Rendell (1817-84) who established a business in Devizes as ironmonger, whitesmith and general manufacturer. (He also fathered 20 children, a source of family disputes as later generations assumed control). The business moved through joinery, local authority housing and some speculative housing; several changes of Rendell name; and then cash flow problems in the 1960s. It would have been a story scarcely worth telling were it not for Rendell's involvement in 1970 with the pioneering scheme for low-cost housing for sale to council nominees in Swindon. According to the Rendell history, 'The origins of Partnership housing are to be found in Swindon in 1971, and with the local authority housing project at Area 7 called Eldene.'[5] The Council approached Rendell for a design/build package for 163 houses of which 15 were to be sold privately by Rendell.

There was no suggestion of a prime development role at that stage but the Borough (now called Thamesdown) needed to finance several new schemes. It asked Rendell if it would be interested not only in undertaking a similar project but in financing the scheme and selling the houses to its nominated purchasers. By now, Rendell was part of Farrow, and the decision had to be referred to their Board. Notwithstanding the Borough's offer to buy unsold houses, there was still some concern over a scheme which showed only modest return on capital. Clearly, a further inducement was needed. The Borough guaranteed continuation of development in Swindon, although nothing was ever put in writing. 'On the strength of the word of a trusted partner, the Farrow Board voted in favour.'[6] The specialist department that had been formed to handle partnership housing completed 150 houses in its first year with the Lovell Group (plus 60 private sales) and, by now, Rendell was beginning to talk to other councils that had seen the new schemes in Swindon. Projects were undertaken for Oxford, Gloucester, Wiltshire and by 1980 Rendell had completed its 1000th partnership house. Under Lovell's guidance, partnership housing went from strength to strength and the 2000th house was completed in 1982.

Lovell's profit progression had been steady through the 1970s and it finished the decade with private housing selling a steady 400-500 a year, and partnership housing contributing a further 300. Wakefield's philosophy was to develop Lovell as an integrated contracting and development business and he argued that there is no role in just being a contractor. 'To be a totally viable business now, one has got to be developer, owner and client as well as being builder. And what the recession has done is to take the better organised, more substantial companies further into property development.'[7] He also took Lovell into the USA, where he had previously worked. A regional structure was put in place in the UK capable of doubling the annual production of private housing to over 1000 a year. Additional equity was raised in 1982 to help finance this expansion and a series of housing acquisitions followed. Norman Wakefield was clearly the driving force behind Lovell's expansion. 'He is a man of high profile…In an industry woefully short of willing and articulate spokesmen, Norman Wakefield is often accused of causing an unnecessary stir… he has very clear and sometimes fixed ideas on the way things should be done. And because he has so often been right in the

[5] Salt, *A Good Job Well Done The Story of Rendell,* p.85
[6] Ibid, p.86.
[7] *Building,* 31st July 1981.

past, you tend to go along with him – even if you disagree with what he is saying.'[8]

Private housing acquisitions

In 1983 Lovell Homes acquired the private midlands housebuilder **Birmingham Housing Industries**, then building around 100 houses a year, to provide a base for expansion into the midlands, followed in 1984 by **Essex & Suffolk Properties** for £11.6m. Essex & Suffolk had been founded in 1962 by David Ellman and H Laurence and traded under the name of Laurence Homes; it concentrated on the area to the east and north of London and built around 250 houses a year. The third acquisition came in the at the end of 1984 at a cost of £7m. **Charter Homes** was based in Northants and built around 400 units a year in the east midlands. It had been formed in 1970 by Roy Richards and Ray Wallington, best known for the Richards & Wallington crane hire business. Charter had been run by Wallington, who had made the decision to leave the business in his 60s. Shortly before the Charter acquisition, Andrew Wassall was recruited from Countryside as Managing Director of Lovell Homes to follow Peter Davis who, in the words of the Annual Report, had 'played the leading role in developing Lovell Homes into a major national housebuilder.' Wassall went on to become group Managing Director in April 1987. With these acquisitions under its belt, Lovell's private housing sales reached 1700 in 1985, with partnership housing adding a further 1000. Taking the two together Lovell now ranked eighth by volume in the industry, and housing produced £7m out of the group total £9m profit. As the UK housing market went from strength to strength, so did Lovell's housing. Profits rose substantially on virtually unchanged private housing sales and the partnership housing continued to produce excellent volume growth. Helped also by a buoyant commercial property market, group profits reached a record £33m in 1989. The collapse, however, was around the corner.

Housing units, 1977-2004

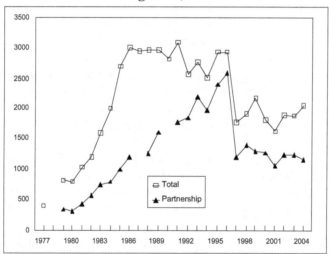

Over-expansion on borrowed money

Lovell had long enjoyed a reputation for conservatism in the City but the risk profile of the group had changed substantially in the second half of the 1980s. It moved into Scotland for the first time in 1987, buying 75% of the housing business of John Lawrence of Glasgow. It bought into the Spanish housing market in 1987 with the purchase of Puebla Aida SA. In the USA, Lovell accelerated its long standing presence buying interests in several major strategic land tracts in 1987. By 1990 it had as many as 38 US projects covering land development, housing and commercial development; the shift from smaller sites

8 'Vision of Reform: Profile of Norman Wakefield', *Building*, 4th Oct. 1985.

was towards large planned communities of 3000-4000 homes. Balance sheet debt went from under £10m in 1986 to £86m in 1990; moreover, all the US business and much of the UK property had its borrowings off-balance sheet – associates had £127m of loans. Perhaps the scale of Lovell's aspirations was epitomised by its flirtation with Germany: 'Lovell is leading a consortium that plans to revolutionise the West German housebuilding industry.'[9] In the UK, Lovell Homes was acquiring pure development land without planning permission in the hope of unlocking development potential. Rendell's partnership experience was also used to establish Lovell Urban Renewal which concentrated on large dockland schemes including Bristol, Swansea, Salford and London Docklands. Finally, as the housing market began to turn down, Lovell launched a fiercely contested, and ultimately abortive, bid for Higgs and Hill, arguing that it felt inadequate at its current size to tackle the problems of the 1990s. The irony was that the management had not realised what the real problems were.

In June 1989, Norman Wakefield moved to a non-executive role (retiring from the Board in March 1990) and Andrew Wassall was appointed Chief Executive. The group had made profits of £33m in the year to September 1989 but the impact of the recession began to be felt in the following year when profits fell to £19m before £11m of extraordinary charges. In November 1990, Wassall resigned as Chief Executive for health reasons and Bob Sellier, late of Wimpey, replaced him. The following month Lovell closed its Urban Renewal and London Housing divisions. An additional £30m was raised from shareholders in April 1991 and Lovell Homes (Scotland) was sold (to Ambion Homes) in the October. The new management stated that their predecessors had 'failed to heed the likely impact on their growth plans of the downturn in general housing demand…They committed the Company to a wide range of ambitious development projects.'

Substantial losses force exit from housing

Despite the rights issue and the asset sales, rising debt and further write-offs meant that Lovell broke its banking covenants, and banking facilities were restructured in February 1992. Lovell had anticipated the losses in Urban Renewal, UK property and Lovell Homes London but had not expected to make provision against the UK land bank and lose money in Washington and Spain. In the three years between 1991 and 1993 trading remained just above breakeven but exceptional and extraordinary losses totalled £137m. After breaking even in 1994 there was a further £32m loss in 1995 and by the end of 1997 there was a deficit on shareholders' funds of £32m. The decision had been made in 1995 to pull out of the private housing market altogether, but the recovery process was still taking too long. David Heppell, who had joined Lovell America as President in 1994, was appointed as chief operating officer in October 1995 and replaced Bob Sellier two months later. Heppell believed that Lovell had been too slow to respond to the problems of the recession: 'When I took over the business, it was clear we were testing the banks' patience to some degree…the company's strategy relied heavily on the market improving rather than the company helping itself.'[10]

The withdrawal from private housing was completed in 1996 and the balance of land transferred to the partnership division. In January 1998 a further financial restructuring was agreed with the banks and shareholders. Finally, as far as the housebuilding story is concerned, Lovell Partnerships was sold for £15m to Morgan Sindall, a contractor with a large refurbishment business. Lovell Partnerships consolidated its position under Morgan Sindall's ownership, selling some 1250 partnership units and 650 speculative houses in 2002. Total housing volumes were sustained at around 2000 a year and, despite its formal name, Lovell gradually increased the speculative content to around 900 in 2004, against 500 in 1999, with a consequent improvement in profitability.

[9] *Building*, 23rd June 1989.
[10] *Building*, 2nd Aug. 1996.

ALFRED McALPINE HOMES
Peak units: 4072 (1998)

McAlpine is one of the great names in British contracting; however, the one name covers two different legal entities. Robert McAlpine's early life is well told in the Saxon Childers biography.[1] He had six sons, the fourth being Alfred, himself knighted in 1931. Alfred was then Chairman of the midlands company; the impact of the depression was such that in 1935 the elder brothers decided to close the midlands company and suggested that Alfred and his son 'Jimmie' move to the south east. Alfred and Jimmie decided to stay, and in 1940 the business of Sir Alfred McAlpine was legally separated. There were no-poaching and territorial agreements, including the common use of a McAlpine sign board which left the casual observer no wiser as to which of the two firms was actually working on the site, and these arrangements lasted until 1983. Indeed, when the firm went public, it used the name Marchwiel, the north Wales village with which Alfred had become linked, as its corporate title, only changing to Alfred McAlpine in 1984. Sir Alfred died in 1944, succeeded as Chairman by Jimmie McAlpine who oversaw the full development of Sir Alfred McAlpine & Sons as a national civil engineer in the post war period. Jimmie McAlpine remained as Chairman for over 40 years, retiring in 1985 and succeeded in turn by his eldest son, 'Bobby.' Bobby had joined the firm in 1950 becoming Managing Director in 1984, and it was he who finally took a McAlpine firm back into private development.

Unsuccessful flirtation with housing in the 1950s
McAlpine did have a brief flirtation with private housing in the late 1950s, first with a block of luxury flats in Birmingham, followed by a housing scheme Wolverhampton. There were problems with design and costing: 'Whereas these two events could have taught a company more oriented towards the speculative side of home-building some useful lessons – namely to employ commercial architects and a competitive construction team – at Alfred McAlpine they caused a distinct loss of nerve on the part of the speculative enthusiasts and a great deal of "I told you so" reaction from those on the board who had been opposed to the company's entry into this field.'[2] Gray went on to say that Edmund Jones and Bobby McAlpine 'lost their nerve when faced with the implacable stance of Jimmie McAlpine, Peter Bell and Alastair Kennedy, who felt it was better to rely on construction contracts where the company's expertise was undisputed and where the element of speculation was not involved. Indeed, private development was regarded by the trio as something akin to gambling on horses.'

It was the mid 1970s before private housing was touched again. Around 1976, Bobby was offered a 450-plot site at Stalybridge; soon after, McAlpine was approached by a private developer, Peter Jones's Emerson Developments, to discuss the possibility of a joint development in Portugal. They decided to develop in the south Manchester area jointly, with McAlpine buying the land and providing the finance and Jones developing – this produced Mottram Homes, later Marchwiel Developments. One or two office developments followed but the partnership ended when the joint venture went into a time share development at Marco Island, Florida, and McAlpine finished as its 100% owner.

McAlpine tries again with Price Brothers
In March 1978 McAlpine bought **Price Brothers**, a Cheshire builder that had been formed by two brothers, Lewis and Geoff Price, although Geoff had left the business well before the takeover. Before the 1974 crash, Price was building around 600 units predominantly in north Wales and Cheshire but this was nearer 500 by the time of the bid. Initially, 75% was acquired and when the remaining 25% was

---

[1] *Childers*, Robert McAlpine.
[2] Gray, *The Road to Success*, p.58.

bought in 1979, Lewis Price left. According to Gray, Owen Rich, then a senior non-family director, was the prime mover whereas Bobby had reservations – he felt it 'was not in the front line of housebuilders', with hindsight, something of an understatement. 'The Price Brothers deal looked very cheap on paper because they had a mass of land in North Wales and the Midlands and they didn't want a great deal of money for it. It was not, to be frank, the best buy around, because although they had plenty of land, their acquisitions included very few prime sites, but at least the deal did get us back into private housing again.'[3]
One industry figure is known to have remarked that if there was a hill Price built on it, and if there was a gap between houses then it was a mineshaft. Lewis Price rationalised his approach on the basis that that if you buy bad land cheaply then it's the same as buying good land on instalment.

Gray's history is revealing in its description of a contractor coming to terms with speculative housing: 'Bobby McAlpine believes that because they were contractors they made a big error in believing that the important element in private housing development was the building of the houses. What they didn't realise, then, was that the real factors are the site and its architectural planning on the one hand, and the marketing of the houses on the other: the least important element is the actual construction of the houses.' There was a frank admission that none of the top management had any professional experience in housing: 'They had not for example, been able to acquire the flair, the ability to size up a site and know instantly the difference between a good and a bad one.'[4]

On Price's departure, Leslie Griffiths of CH Smith, McAlpine's timber subsidiary, became housing Managing Director though that was not his full time activity. The next step was the acquisition of **Macoll Homes,** based at Ashby-de-la-Zouche, and selling around 140 houses a year. It had been founded by John Macadam, who was Managing Director; the Coll part of the name came from the two Collingwood brothers who worked in the firm and who each had a third of the equity along with Macadam. Like Lewis Price before him, Macadam left the business on its acquisition. In 1981, Price and Macoll were amalgamated to form McAlpine Homes but it was not particularly profitable. With many of the sales being in depressed areas of the country, McAlpine decided that it needed both expertise in housing management and access to the south east; the acquisition of Finlas at the end of 1982 satisfied both of these objectives.

Finlas brings in Frank Sanderson
Finlas was the creation of Frank Sanderson. After being forced out of Bovis in 1973, Frank Sanderson formed his own private company, Chailey Securities, and in March 1977 acquired control of Lowe & Brydone, originally a printing business which had not paid a dividend since 1972. Lowe & Brydone, later renamed Finlas, diversified into housing and formed two Ferndale Homes companies building to the east and west of London. Philip Davies joined to run Ferndale West in 1978. In 1979, Finlas bought Procter Homes, operating on Humberside, and the property and construction business of Whyatt Securities, raising housing output to around 350 houses a year. Frank Sanderson and the other directors also bought out the remaining shares in Finlas taking the company out of the public arena.

Bobby McAlpine had been a small shareholder in Finlas for some years and knew Frank Sanderson. This was the professional management that McAlpine had been looking for and, in December 1982, the firm was duly bought for £11m. Frank Sanderson assumed control of the totality of McAlpine's housing and property interests; combined housing output was around 800. Next year, when the agreement with Robert McAlpine was not renewed, McAlpine started to look at Scotland and in 1984 acquired Ambion Homes, a Glasgow company once owned by Frank Sanderson and selling around 75 units a year; and then

[3] Ibid, p.141.
[4] Ibid, pp.141-2.

Whatlings, an old-established Scottish contractor with a £25m turnover, of which £6-7m was in housing. Although Whatlings was bought for its construction, one of its attractions was its relationship with the Glasgow Co-op where it had a joint venture to redevelop the latter's residential properties. Including those, Whatlings produced around 200-300 units a year, though run separately from McAlpine Homes.

US housebuilding

More ambitious plans were being made and the US housing market was targeted, redeploying the proceeds of the sale of McAlpine's South African mining interests. After an unsuccessful bid for the Pinehurst golf courses, Frank Sanderson decided that the best area was the north-east coast from Carolina to New England, and the Boston firm of Moore Homes was bought, closely followed by K & B Construction "What we will basically do" says Philip Davies, now Managing Director of Alfred McAlpine Homes, "is to buy an American company, leave the management intact and let them do it their way."[5] Philip Davies saw America perhaps making 50% of profits by 1990.

Unfortunately, Sanderson was again having difficulties with senior colleagues. 'Frank was getting involved in non-housing things in the States saying they were part of the wider picture and coming into conflict with other Directors. It became inevitable that there would be a parting of the ways. It was his decision to go but I suspect that Bobby did not seek to dissuade him.'[6] Frank Sanderson duly resigned early in 1985 'to concentrate on his family trusts and properties'[7] Philip Davies took over as housing Managing Director and in that year (1985) McAlpine completed a record 1345 houses; as the market strengthened, volumes were consolidated, and the housing company began to make a significant contribution to group profits.

Yet another housebuilder brought in

In 1988, McAlpine purchased another entrepreneurial housebuilder, Eric Grove's **Canberra.** Eric Grove had left school aged 14 and joined Thomas Vale as a trainee site agent before moving to the Stourbridge firm of AH Guest. Finishing national service in 1951, aged 21, he set up on his own as a jobbing builder where his work included house extensions and conversions. This introduction to the housing market drew Grove into the new build market and a year later he bought two plots of land in Kidderminster for £200; in the late 1950s and early 1960s he was building around 30 or 40 houses a year in the west midlands. There was a brief, though unsuccessful, foray into local authority contracting: 'I made the foolish mistake, as we all did.'[8] By the 1974 recession, Grove was building around 50 speculative and 50 local authority houses a year, plus some industrial space. One of his companies, Canberra, was expanded into a more substantial force, developing in both the west midlands and south Wales. Dealing was an integral part of the operation. Eric Grove 'loved buying and selling something that was part built – buying off receivers, buying off someone who was in trouble and had a very wide circle of contacts.'[9] Grove is happy to admit that 'dealing is a great part of my life.'

Despite his obvious pleasure in dealing, Grove decided to structure the company on more conventional lines in the mid 1980s. He had owned the company with a Birmingham solicitor, Peter Southall, and Southall had been bought out on retirement in the early 1980s. Canberra became totally focussed on private housing and Grove brought in as Managing Director Barry Harvey and then Graeme McCallum, an ex-Barratt accountant. Grove's children, Lawrence and Louise, were also active in the business. In its last independent year, Canberra completed 569 houses primarily from the midlands but also with a small

5 Ibid, p.148.
6 Interview with Philip Davies, Feb. 2000.
7 See Egerton Trust.
8 Interview with Eric Grove, May 2001.
9 Interview Philip Davies.

operation on the south coast. The catalyst for the Canberra acquisition was McAlpine's strategic review which had incorporated a potential downsizing in construction, then suffering large losses in the midlands and Scotland, and the possibility of making a £20m acquisition in housing. The initial intent was a 100% acquisition of Canberra, with the Grove family taking all cash at completion plus a future earn-out of profits. However, the discovery of cash flow problems within McAlpine's construction division at the very last moment necessitated a complete rethink on the deal. The revised arrangements led to a new company being created to include all the McAlpine and Canberra housing interests to be owned 60% by the McAlpine parent and 40% by the Grove family. This structure left McAlpine needing to find limited cash to establish a national housing business but with the need to find future cash for the Grove family.

Too many chiefs?

That capital structure was eventually to cause problems as it was written into the documents that from 1990 onwards McAlpine would use its best endeavours to obtain a flotation of the business, allowing the Grove family to realise its investment. However, by 1990 it was clear that because of the housing recession the flotation would not be possible and therefore Eric Grove was not going to get his money out. Without his expected exit route, Eric Grove inevitably became more involved in the day-to-day decision-making. Eventually Philip Davies faced Bobby McAlpine with the conflict: 'You have either got to find a way of buying out the Grove shareholding or I have got to go. The decision was avoided until Graeme Odgers joined as Chief Executive in 1990, but very quickly we then resolved that the structure would remain for the foreseeable future and that I would leave the Group, handing over to Graeme McCallum with both Eric and Graeme joining the PLC Board. It was by far the most logical decision to make at that time.'[10]

That, however, was two years away. On the merger, the enlarged housing operation was forecast to build some 2000 units although, in fact, the total actually fell in 1989. Housing was now beginning to dominate the group profit and loss account, partly as a result of deliberate expansion and partly because the traditional side of the business was making significantly less than five years previous. In 1988, housing profits had risen to £10m out of a group total of £20m; with the inclusion of the more profitable Canberra, the disparity was even more marked in 1989 and Homes contributed £18.6m out of a group total of £23.6m. In contrast to the UK, housing in New England was already suffering a downturn in 1988, compounded by the death of their US President, Colin Wells, and it was not long before McAlpine was withdrawing from this market. Philip Davies considered that the mistake was that 'We bought companies that were too small. We should actually have looked at spending the $10-15m. that we had allocated on one significant company and grown it. Instead we bought two small companies with earn-outs and effectively ended up having to drive the businesses from the UK.'

Bobby McAlpine goes

Rising borrowings and property investment problems put increasing pressure on Bobby McAlpine who brought in a new Chief Executive in 1990 – Graeme Odgers, ex-Tarmac and British Telecom with, in his words, his 'high-wire, bottom up' management style.[11] Extraordinary charges of £40m included a £20m provision against the Warringtons associate. The McAlpine hold on the company was now beginning to fade. Bobby McAlpine found that effective management control had passed to Graeme Odgers, and he announced his decision to retire as Chairman on reaching 60 in 1992 (though staying as a non-executive director until 1994). A rights issue in 1991 reduced the family holding to 19.5% Five years later, a disillusioned family sold its remaining 15% holding to pension fund managers PDFM. Looking back, Bobby McAlpine considered that 'In retrospect I should have realised that building up a substantial

---

10 Ibid.
11 Group accounts, 1990.

housing company demanded more cash than a family company was capable of contributing. Having said that, there is no doubt that the purchase of Canberra laid the foundation for the successful house building company that Alfred McAlpine is today.'[12]

Housing units, 1980-2000

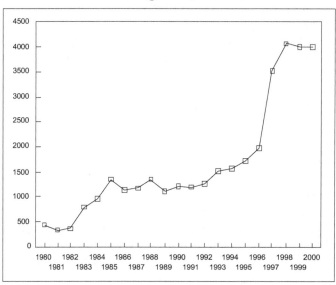

Graeme Odgers did not last long, resigning in April 1993 to become Chairman of the Monopolies and Mergers Commission. He was replaced by Oliver Whitehead, a construction man previously with Babcock International, AMEC and John Laing. The new strategy involved further concentration on housing. The land bank was to be increased, helped by the success in gaining planning consent for a 3300 unit development at Monkfield Park, Cambridgeshire. In January 1996, the group announced the closure of the traditional building business and the asphalt company to concentrate on three core businesses in the UK, civil engineering, homes and special projects, plus US minerals and its slate quarry. In 1997, McAlpine again made a substantial housing acquisition – Raine Industries. In terms of crude numbers, Raine was actually a bigger housebuilder than McAlpine – including partnership housing it had completed 3600 units in 1996 to McAlpine's 2000. However acquisitions and the effects of the recession had left it heavily indebted and it was bought for only £43m. Some of the ancillary businesses were sold and the housing companies integrated into the McAlpine structure. In 1998, McAlpine completed over 4000 units and ranked as number seven in the industry.

From 1998, McAlpine Homes volumes held around the 4000 level, although the closure of the substantial partnership housing business was announced in January 2000. The period was, however, dogged with uncertainty over the future of Homes and, indeed, of the whole group. During 1999, Andrew Goodall's Brunswick Developments acquired a small holding in McAlpine and unsuccessfully tried to bid for the whole company. This was followed by abortive merger talks between McAlpine and Bryant and, at the end of 2000, a reported £244m bid approach from Heron International. In the event, the solution was the sale of Homes to Wimpey, announced in August 2001, for its £411m net asset value plus £50m of goodwill.

[12] Correspondence with author.

McCARTHY & STONE
Peak units: 2596 (1988)

McCarthy & Stone has dominated the sheltered housing market in Britain, becoming the only housebuilder to generate volume sales out of this specialised area. John McCarthy and Bill Stone entered partnership as builders in 1961, trading first as McStone and then McCarthy & Stone Developments (the longer name was thought to give a more substantive image to the elderly purchasers). John McCarthy, the driving force behind the company's growth, left secondary school at the age of 15 and trained as a carpenter before joining forces with Bill Stone at the age of 21. Stone, a couple of years older than McCarthy, was also a carpenter, and the two had met while working on the same building site. John McCarthy's uncles had built caravans and he had worked for them in school holidays; that became the starting point for John McCarthy and Bill Stone. They rented a field and buildings from a farmer for the caravans and also began some general contracting work. After a couple of years they managed to do a deal with the farmer whereby they built bungalows on his land, paying for the land on completion of the houses.

The start of sheltered housing

The business was conducted on a conventional and relatively small scale for some 15 years. In the early 1970s the firm began to buy housing land in larger quantities than previously and high borrowing costs led to small losses in 1974 and 1975. The priority was to reduce debt which had peaked at £1.5m in the August 1974 balance sheet. The Walkford Park estate was sold, some 200 units were built out between 1973 and 1977, after which profits rose to around £100,000 a year. It was then that McCarthy & Stone made its first excursion into sheltered housing with a block of 32 flats in Waverley, New Milton, Hampshire. '[John McCarthy] told me that all the fun began with a paper which the Department of the Environment put round about housing the elderly back in 1976. "Not many people read it ..but we did."'[1] If there was an element of chance about the Company's discovery of the sheltered housing concept, there was an immediate appreciation of the potential such developments offered and the problems that would need to be overcome. 'I knew that if I was to do a sheltered scheme successfully, I would have to change local authority planning attitudes.'[2] In particular, McCarthy managed to reduce the parking requirement from the more conventional one space per flat to one space per three flats, thereby increasing the density and, therefore, the profitability.

In February 1977, before the first development had even been completed, John McCarthy wrote: 'The scheme to develop Waverley with a block of elderly persons' flats will, I am sure, prove most profitable. Following discussions with the Local Authority and the Hampshire Voluntary Housing Association it is clear that there is a need for this type of development all along the south coast and this particular scheme lends itself to repetition on other sites.'[3] The concept of sheltered, or warden-assisted housing, was not original; however, what was new was that these flats were offered for sale, not rented through housing associations or local authorities. The concept of sheltered accommodation for sale to 'the elderly' rapidly came to mean the provision of self-contained accommodation (usually a flat) with a resident warden available in case of emergency; the warden often organised social activities. Each development would also contain communal facilities including guest bedrooms, laundry rooms and residents' lounges. McCarthy and Stone's market was existing home owners, with a minimum age 60 but typically over 70; who wanted smaller accommodation but did not want to rent; and who valued the security of someone on the premises. Typically, about 80 per cent of purchasers were widows with an average age of 74.

[1] *Housebuilder*, August 1984.
[2] Interview with John McCarthy, Sep. 2001.
[3] Group Accounts, 1976.

McCarthy & Stone plans to go national

The Waverley scheme had produced 500 enquiries before the building was complete. 'When the second scheme got the same response – and cost us a lot less because we had learned all the wrinkles – then we were pretty sure that we'd found a market.'[4] From that point, the south coast expansion envisaged by John McCarthy was underway: 'We decided after the success of the first scheme to sell everything else and concentrate on sheltered housing. We had a strategy of covering the country as quickly as possible before others entered the sector.'[5] In 1979, 69 sheltered units were sold and the company began to make substantial profits for the first time. By 1981, output was around 200 and in February 1982 McCarthy & Stone acquired the estate agency business of Peverel & Co from Trevor Foan to provide its own management service. In June 1982, the Company was floated; by then it had completed 15 sheltered developments, with 550 units sold, and a further 12 developments under construction. On the flotation, John McCarthy was both Chairman and Managing Director; although Bill Stone remained on the Board, his shareholding was half that of McCarthy's and his role as projects director responsible for research and after sales service confirmed that the leadership of the Company was coming from McCarthy. In 1984, Bill Stone retired as an executive though he stayed on the Board until 1993.

The growth over the six years following the float was phenomenal. A second south coast office was opened in 1982 at Eastbourne and, in the following year, offices were opened in Glasgow, Altrincham and Worcester, completing its national organisation in 1984; annual sales were now approaching 1000. McCarthy & Stone then sought to broaden its base, both by product and geographically. In October 1985, a Homelife Care Division was launched to provide up-market nursing homes and residential centres with a projected investment of £16m. The Company also looked to take its sheltered concept overseas and began to build on a small scale in France, Majorca and the Channel Islands. In 1988, it paid £15m for France's 5th largest holiday apartment company, Merlin Immobilier (later renamed Quadrant).

Exceptional profits attracts competition

The concept of sheltered housing for sale proved exceptionally profitable. Sales were made to existing house-owners trading down and were not, therefore, as price-conscious as, say, a first-time buyer. McCarthy and Stone also obtained a very high land utilisation (55 – 60 units an acre) because of the small unit size and the limited need for car parking space. In the absence of competition from other sheltered housing providers, they were able to generate an excess land margin compared with a conventional housebuilder, and trading margins consistently averaged 30%. The peak was reached in 1988, when UK unit sales totalled 2600 and profits reached £34m. However, the recession was to test the underlying business model. The potential for disappointment was becoming apparent from the mid 1980s as McCarthy & Stone's success attracted competition. 'There is clearly a profusion of sheltered schemes coming onto the market. Not only are there areas with several projects within a couple of miles radius, but one can even see competing developments being built opposite one another…The problem with a sheltered housing development is that there is no flexibility. If a planned estate of 60 houses sell slowly, the build rate can be reduced or the mix of homes changed. With sheltered developments, it is the whole block or nothing; and once the warden and the first few residents are installed there can be no change of use however slow sales are.'[6]

Once the recession began to affect second-hand house prices, McCarthy & Stone discovered that their

[4] *Housebuilder*, Aug. 1984.
[5] Interview John McCarthy.
[6] PHA, 1987.

customers had developed fixed ideas about what their house was worth and how much profit from its sale they needed to finance future expenses. In short, they became reluctant to move. Combine that with the range of product on offer (there were around 100 builders offering sheltered accommodation, plus the resale of second-hand sheltered units that had been built earlier). Moreover, the overseas diversification failed to make money 'there were too many fingers in the pie on land, and the French employment laws were horrendous.' Neither did the nursing homes have the synergy with the sheltered housing that had once been suggested. 'They seemed a logical development but the management was entirely different – more like the hotel business – and people did not move from the sheltered housing into our nursing homes.'[7]

The banks support McCarthy & Stone recovery

John McCarthy appointed John Gray (previously Finance Director) as joint Managing Director and downsizing began. McCarthy & Stone had begun to sell land as the market peaked; nevertheless, losses were incurred for the four years between 1990 and 1993 and for several years debt averaged 150% of a diminishing shareholder base. The banks were supportive of the company and the management began a long process of working out the assets. Early on in the downturn, the head office and the nursing homes were sold raising £20m and a further £20m was raised from land sales. Work in progress was gradually built out using a wide variety of sales incentives, including taking part-exchange houses that were more expensive than the units McCarthy & Stone were selling, and shared-equity sales. By 1991, sales had fallen from their peak of 2600 to under 1000 units, and they remained at that level for five years.

Housing units and pre-tax profits, 1978-2004

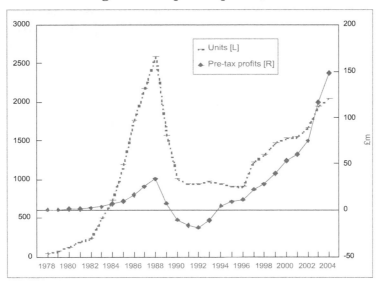

In May 1991 McCarthy & Stone managed to raise £13m through a rights issue. Despite still being in loss and heavily indebted, the banks allowed the company to use some of the money to start building on existing land holdings and even buy some new sites, a decision which was of paramount importance to the eventual recovery of the company. If housing land in general was depressed it was nothing compared to what had happened to sheltered housing sites where no other company was interested in bidding. Early in the 1993/94 financial year, McCarthy & Stone raised £30m from the sale of Peverel and ground rents,

---

[7] Interview John McCarthy.

followed by another £15m equity issue. The company returned to modest profitability and gearing was down to a manageable 40% at the year end. Against considerable odds, the Company had survived and able to think about expanding the business again – some of the land sold earlier was even repurchased at a third of the price.

Record profits and little competition

In March 1993, Keith Lovelock (previously Managing Director of Federated Housing, the international director of McCarthy & Stone since 1989 and operations director in 1992) was appointed joint Managing Director alongside John McCarthy; by the end of the year he was Chief Executive. Lovelock's priority, with John McCarthy's support, continued to be conservation of capital but as the newer sites gradually replaced those bought before the recession, so the profits began to recover; by 1996, with volumes still below 1000, profits had risen to £11m. The number of regions had been reduced to only four to save costs, but within another four years there were eight regions and volumes were once again being increased: by 2000, unit sales were over 1500 and over 2000 by 2004. More important, pre-tax margins once again reached 30% and by 2004 had climbed to a remarkable 44%; pre-tax profits reached £148m compared with the 1988 peak of £34m. This time, there were two important differences from the late 1980s: McCarthy & Stone was cash positive rather than heavily geared; and the revival in profitability had not attracted a flood of new competitors – John McCarthy estimated that the company's market share was back up to 70%.

John McCarthy's stood down as an executive director in December 2000, having reached the age of 60, intending to remain as non-executive Chairman for a further three years. However, in the summer of 2003, the McCarthy family (the two sons had their own sheltered housing business) made unsuccessful bid approaches to the Board and in August 2003, John McCarthy resigned from the Company.

McINERNEY HOMES
Peak units: 640 (1983)

McInerney is one of a number of Irish builders that developed in the English market; unlike, for instance, Abbey and Gleeson, the home market remained the most important and it was the English housing operation that was finally abandoned in the 1990 recession, before being re-entered at the end of the decade. Thomas McInerney started building in a small way in Co. Clare in 1909. An advertisement celebrating the firm's 75th anniversary claimed that 'In 1909 Thomas McInerney built his first house and gave his neighbour a new start', but the firm developed as a general contractor rather than as a housebuilder.[1] His four sons joined the firm after the Second War and it was incorporated as Thomas McInerney & Sons in 1949. The level of activity expanded rapidly, helped by the contract for the new Shannon Airport runway in the early 1950s and the growth in local authority housing. It was not until 1957 that McInerney began general contracting and then local authority housing in England, and not until 1961 that it diversified into private housebuilding in Ireland. In the early 1960s, two of the brothers left to form Park Developments leaving Ambrose and Daniel, a civil engineer, with Irish and English construction.

In 1971, McInerney floated on the Irish Stock Exchange with Ambrose and Daniel McInerney as joint Managing Directors. The Prospectus disclosed that it had increased its speculative housing in Eire from 25 in 1961 to 750 in 1970 with a forecast of over 1000 for 1971. The UK company, originally registered in 1960 as Thomas McInerney & Sons Ltd, had actually been owned separately by Ambrose and Daniel, with Daniel taking managerial responsibility. The ownership was transferred to the Irish Company prior to flotation. McInerney had commenced activities in UK in the early 1960s in light civil engineering work before branching out into local authority housing; since 1967 the business had confined itself to local authority housing.

The first reference to speculative housing in England came in the 1971 accounts: 'A major policy decision taken by your Board since the beginning of the current financial year was to extend the Group's private housing activities to the United Kingdom where the prospects in this activity are attractive.' Two parcels of land were bought in the London area to build 250 houses and further sites were acquired in Derby and Milton Keynes. However, the recession kept UK housing to modest levels, and speculative volumes did not reach 100 a year until the end of the 1970s. This contrasted with local authority work where, for instance, 1000 houses were completed in 1978. Unfortunately, this was not financially successful and the UK Company suffered consistent losses between 1978 and 1980 which led to the balance of activity rapidly switching to the private sector.

By 1982, the UK accounts had private housing as the principal activity, reporting that 'During the year there has been a greater emphasis placed on expanding the private sale sector'; McInerney Homes also entered commercial development with the start in 1983 of a new office in Tunbridge Wells. Private housing, concentrating on affordable homes in the starter and retirement markets, rose rapidly, reaching 640 completions in 1983 over half of which was derived from joint ventures with local authorities. Geographically, Homes was based in Watford, concentrating on the south east; a Bristol office was opened in 1986. Between 1984 and 1988, completions ranged between 500 and 600 but the strong price growth in the market saw turnover rise from £20m to almost £50m and profits from £1m to £7.6m – roughly the same as the Group profit.

---

[1] *Housebuilder*, Sep. 1984.

The reversal in 1989 was dramatic: turnover fell to £18m in the absence of any commercial property sales and a fall in housing completions to 350; a £3.7m loss was recorded. McInerney managed to increase its residential sales modestly in 1990 and it also secured an £18m contract for new housing for the US air force at Bent Water, Suffolk. Turnover increased to £30m but so did the pre-tax loss – to £8.7m. The unaudited 1990 balance sheet showed £1.6m of equity and £17m of net debt and, with the group shareholders' funds also below £2m, the parent was unable to support its UK offshoot. In March 1991 a financial restructuring was agreed with the banks whereby the parent was released from its obligations in respect of McInerney Estates (the UK commercial arm) and the banks received 51% of the equity in McInerney Homes. No cash injection into Homes was forthcoming either from the parent company or external sources and receivers were appointed in September 1991.

The Group as a whole continued to lose substantial sums of money, leading to a deficit of net assets. After lengthy negotiations, a scheme of arrangement was approved in 1996, involving the conversion of debt to equity and raising additional equity finance. Gradually McInerney returned to modest profitability and by the end of the decade was looking to return to the UK. In 1999, McInerney Holdings acquired the Bolton construction company, William Hargreaves, in what was engagingly called 'a first step into the UK market for the Group.'[2] Apart from general construction, Hargreaves did some small commercial development and was moving into private housing. In 2002, McInerney made the more substantial UK purchase of the Charlton House Group, formed by Paul Bolton in 1987, which had been building around 250 houses a year in Cheshire and south Lancashire. Geographical expansion into the north east took place in May 2004 with the purchase of Alex Chaytor's Alexander Developments, which built around 80 units a year, taking the UK total for the year to 500.

[2] Group accounts, 2000.

MCLEAN HOMES/TARMAC
Peak units: 12,165 (1988)

John McLean was already a sizeable midlands housebuilder when it was acquired in 1973 by Tarmac. By the mid 1980s it had become Britain's largest housebuilder and the first housebuilder to make annual profits of £200m. A decade later, it was swapped by Tarmac in return for Wimpey's construction and minerals subsidiaries.

John McLean, born 1888, founded his building business in 1920, incorporating it in 1932. It 'prospered quietly in general contracting, with some house-building, until the early 1950s, by which time the elder sons had entered the business.'[1] This second-generation business was led by Geoffrey McLean with his younger stepbrothers Paul and Larry also in the business in the early years. Geoffrey McLean was born at Coseley near Wolverhampton in 1920 and educated at Birmingham University; he graduated as a civil engineer in 1942 and then joined the REME. By the end of the Second War, his father 'was reaching an age when, to many men, retirement becomes a major aim in life. By then his eldest son Geoffrey was ready to take over the reins, and asked for them firmly – all the reins – and at once!'[2]

Geoffrey McLean drives the business

'The expansion of the McLean organisation began in earnest in 1952 when Mr Geoffrey McLean introduced management consultants into the business.'[3] There is no doubt that Geoffrey McLean was an innovative housebuilder; no-one who spoke or wrote about him said otherwise. One can always argue about firsts, but he was one of the first to use modern techniques in marketing houses. 'They pioneered the application of careful estate layouts …They developed timber framed techniques, initiated after-sales service…and they have even been known to buy a prospective customer's existing house and help sell it for him.'[4] One can, of course, have too much of a good thing: 'He ruled the business completely. He had a remarkable brain, extremely bright and he had boundless energy. The problem with Geoffrey was that he had so many ideas – there were always one or two good ones but the rest were crazy to say the least.'[5]

By the early 1960s, Geoffrey McLean had turned his company into one of the biggest developers in the midlands with a successful subsidiary operation based in Swindon run by Ron King, a later managing director. The company floated in 1963 with private house sales approaching 800 and a significant volume of timber-framed housing for local authorities, the latter business being run by Paul McLean. John McLean, by then aged 75 was still on the Board as Chairman and acting as a counterweight to his son's enthusiasm, but on his death the following year Geoffrey became Chairman as well as Managing Director. Growth after flotation was disappointing and profits were erratic. There was a modest increase in private housing with perhaps an extra 100 units over a five-year period. Although the Swindon operation made good profits, there was an admission that regional expansion had not been easy. 'A number of lessons had to be learned; an important one was that there is a great difference between operating on an ever-widening arc from a central management headquarters and establishing subsidiaries in other regions.'[6] However, the damage was being done by local authority housing contracts, particularly two large specially-designed schemes at Telford and Droitwich.

[1] *Building*, 16th April 1969.
[2] *House Beautiful*, June 1959.
[3] *Housebuilder*, Jan. 1967.
[4] *Building*, 16th April 1967.
[5] Interview with Ron King, Nov. 1999.
[6] *Building*, 16th April 1969.

Enter Eric Pountain

In March 1969 McLean acquired **Midland and General Developments**, a move that was to have far-reaching effects on McLean and later Tarmac, introducing Eric Pountain to the public arena. After a grammar school education, Eric Pountain had joined his father's small building business in 1950, aged 17, before going on to do his national service. 'Coming out of national service in 1956 I thought there was not much future in the family business for me. I picked up the local newspaper when on leave and saw an advertisement in the [Wolverhampton] *Express and Star*. It was from Frank Selwyn [of Maitland Selwyn estate agents]and Frank had been to America to see how they sold houses – it was really marketing new houses rather than conventional estate agency. It quite attracted me; I knew a bit about houses because we had built a few bespoke ones. I got the job as a sales executive, and that's how it started.'[7]

Frank Selwyn had been a copywriter for the *Express and Star* before the war and in 1946 went to work for a local developer before setting up his own sales organisation. He used his American experience to market houses imaginatively, and, although the techniques may have been used on the large London estates in the 1930s, they stood out as original in the midlands in the post-war period. The firm acted for several midlands builders including Bryant, McLean and William Whittingham, and at its peak the agency was marketing several thousand houses a year. Pountain became joint principal of the agency with Frank Selwyn, with McLean being his client. When Geoffrey McLean suddenly decided to do his own direct selling, Pountain's response was robust. 'We had done all of McLean's selling and I was personally responsible for it. I felt slightly aggrieved so I said to Frank, "blow it, let's start housebuilding ourselves" and that was how I started Midland and General in 1961.'[8] There were seven owners of Midland including Frank Selwyn and local businessmen but Eric Pountain was the largest shareholder.

Midland and General thrived on the Maitland Selwyn design and selling techniques and by the late 1960s it was building 200-300 houses a year. By then McLean was experiencing difficult times and in 1969 Geofrey McLean approached Eric Pountain with a view to buying Midland. Asked why he surrendered his independence: 'I don't know, I must have been mad, but it was an opportunity; it seemed a lot of money at the time.' As part of the deal, Eric Pountain secured a seat on the McLean board. That year there were further contract losses, and profits fell to £238,000, lower than at the time of flotation, precipitating a boardroom coup. Four directors resigned and Eric Pountain replaced Geoffrey McLean as Managing Director. Overheads were cut, local authority housing closed and McLean withdrew from California. Helped by the rising housing market, profits rose to over £2m by 1973, on house sales in excess of 1000.

McLean bought by Tarmac

At the end of 1972, McLean had announced an agreed bid for the then privately owned John Maunders but at the last minute Maunders pulled out. A year later (December 1973) Eric Pountain negotiated an agreed £9m bid with Tarmac's Robin Martin, who wanted to buy McLean to strengthen its own private housing business. Ron King remembered Geoffrey McLean saying 'It's my business …but he had to go along with it. The increase in the share price made a lot of money for the McLean family and they said "we will take our money and go".'[9] Eric Pountain was given control of the enlarged housing operation though not then a main board position. Again, he had mixed feelings about surrendering his independence: 'On reflection I don't know why I did it because I could have made a lot more money on my own but I just liked running a bigger company and I couldn't grow McLean fast enough because of

---

[7] Interview with Eric Pountain, Nov. 2000.
[8] Ibid.
[9] Interview Ron King.

the capital constraints.'[10]

Tarmac was a national road surfacing and aggregates business, dating back to its incorporation in 1903 as TarMacadam (Purnell Hooley's Patent Syndicate) Ltd.; during the 1960s and 1970s it also became, largely through acquisition, a national contractor. The construction division contained Tarmac's private housing which had been started in 1962 when Tom McMillan was running the division. Alan Osborne, then development engineer, and colleague Peter Gadsby suggested to Tom that Tarmac Construction should go into private housing: 'We were always doing quite a lot of public housing and the message came back "yes you can go into private housing , providing you don't buy any land"'.[11]

It was not an easy instruction to give to a housebuilder but Tarmac dealt with it by forming a joint venture with Waddington who bought the land, the first site being in Barnsley. Osborne accepted that Waddington also gave Tarmac 'a lot of know-how in pricing a house economically.'[12] The new business was placed in an embryo building subsidiary, TG Construction (later Tarmac Building), run by Bill Cook who had been recruited from Wilson Lovatt. Output rose to around 400-500 houses a year, although without much contribution to profit. Bill Cook died in 1969, and control returned to Alan Osborne, by then running the whole construction division. Over the next five years Osborne increased volumes to around 900 out of three offices – in the midlands, South Yorkshire and Stockton – and steadily improved profits. Helped by rising house prices, Tarmac Homes was making around £800,000 profit in its last independent year and contributed some £1.4m in its first year integrated into John McLean.

Contractor versus developer

There were clear contrasts between McLean and Tarmac's housing in that the former built houses as a developer whereas the latter built them as a contractor. Ron King remembers Tarmac's Bill Francis telling him during the negotiations: 'The way you market and present your houses leaves us standing. That's what we are buying you for.' The McLean team had a poor view of what they found. 'They were just building box type houses, poor quality construction, no design appeal, no selling appeal and nearly a thousand houses built and not sold. Our philosophy was we sell them and then we build them. Whereas they were just totally construction oriented, building houses.'[13] There was some agreement from the old Tarmac team. Tom McMillan frankly admitted that when they started 'they hadn't a clue'[14] and Osborne also conceded that 'when we first were in private housing it was true that we had a more construction-led method of building.' Nevertheless, Osborne did claim that by the time McLean took control, Tarmac's housing was working much more efficiently. On the merger, Tarmac Homes contributed 40% of the combined housing profits.[15]

The amalgamation of the two housebuilding operations immediately produced a 2000 a year housebuilder, putting the business firmly into the top ten. From the beginning, Pountain had ambitions to be a national housebuilder: steady expansion continued until Tarmac was selling nearly 4000 by the end of the 1970s. The growth was primarily organic although there were some modest acquisitions – the old established **Thomas Lowe** of Burton on Trent in 1976 (building around 200 p.a.) and the Scottish firm of **Alexander Turner** in 1977. Thomas Lowe had been a licensee of McLean (as were John Sisk and Carvilles of Northern Ireland) and was bought for its land; Turner gave McLean its entrée into Scotland.

---

10 Interview Eric Pountain.
11 Interview with Alan Osborne, Feb. 2000.
12 Ibid.
13 Interview Ron King.
14 Conversation with the author.
15 Interview Alan Osborne.

However, despite the success of its private housing, all was not well elsewhere in Tarmac. Its profits growth had lagged behind the other large building materials companies and disappointing results overseas had culminated in £16m contract provisions in the Nigerian subsidiary. Following the announcement of the Nigerian losses, Bill Francis, the Deputy Chairman and head of contracting, was dismissed; then the Finance Director resigned. Robin Martin, who had joined Tarmac in 1945, been Chairman for eight years and Managing Director for 16, resigned in turn under pressure from the rest of the board, following a contested appointment of head of international contracting. In April 1979 Eric Pountain emerged as the new group Managing Director having served only two years on the main board. Just as Robin Martin had expanded the roadstone that was close to his heart, so his successor expanded Tarmac's housing. The Pountain management style was more flexible than Martin's: 'Eric Pountain is a man without a plan – but he knows exactly where he is going.'[16] Where he was going was further expansion of housing and taking Tarmac into American quarrying.

Tarmac becomes the largest housebuilder
The regional housing offices had been steadily increased following the acquisition of McLean and totalled 16 at the end of the 1970s giving a potential capacity of 8000 houses a year. Ron King, who had been running the housing division under Pountain became President of the HBF in 1980. It was not a good year for the housing industry; profits came under pressure and stocks of part-exchange houses were absorbing group cash. King returned from his Presidential year only to discover that he was about to be replaced by Sam Pickstock, a long standing McLean man who had originally been the conveyancing manager for Dunham Brindley and Linn, McLean's solicitors, and had been brought in by Pountain as Company Secretary. Pountain considered Pickstock 'very instrumental in building the business up. He was a very good operative; Sam's strengths were organisational, he was a good disciplinarian and he finished up with some incredibly good managers.'[17]

The framework that was in place at the end of the 1970s duly delivered its 8000 units by the mid 1980s. The push for volume was in full swing and by 1987 Tarmac had passed Barratt and Wimpey, both with problems of their own, to become the largest housebuilder in the country. In 1988, unit sales reached a peak of 12,165. Profits surpassed £200m, accounting for half of the group total trading profit and achieving margins of 27%. Even allowing for the boom conditions this was a phenomenal achievement for a volume housebuilder operating off a short land bank. Tarmac was now talking about a long term goal of 15,000 houses a year in the UK, while in the USA its new companies in Virginia and Maryland were building their first houses. Reflecting on the American diversification, Eric Pountain considered it not worth the effort. 'We had got to the stage where we were nearly up to 10% of the UK housing market so we had to do something and we thought America might be OK on the basis that they speak the same language but it wasn't a howling success.'

[16] *Mail on Sunday,* June 1984.
[17] Interview Eric Pountain.

Housing units, 1973-1995

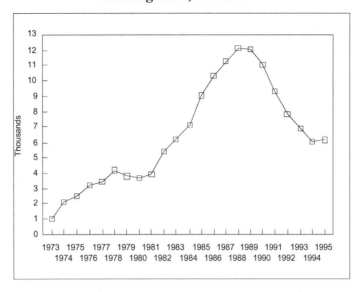

The recession took its full toll on Tarmac, particularly housing and property but there seemed an unwillingness to recognise the reality of the downturn. 'Sam Pickstock's reaction was to carry on regardless. He assumed that the recession would be temporary and encouraged his operating companies to build houses as fast as ever. He also continued to buy land to provide for future building.'[18] Although volumes were held in 1989, they then declined each year to 1994, halving to barely 6000. Trading profits fell to £41m in 1992 and a cumulative total of £132m provisions were to be made against UK housing. Pressure from the City was increasing, as concern was expressed over both strategy and the high levels of debt. In March 1992 Sir Eric Pountain stepped down as group Chief Executive in favour of Neville Simms (previously head of construction) but stayed on as Chairman until retirement age in 1994. Looking back, Eric Pountain thought that one mistake was not to have held more profit back in 1988. He also conceded that he might have cut back more vigorously if they had realised how prolonged the recession was going to be: 'but it is a bit harder when you've built it up yourself; the trouble was that we had two businesses, housebuilding and quarrying, that were massively capital intensive and only construction that was throwing off cash – but not enough.'

Disposal of housing

The appointment of Neville Simms marked the beginning of the end for Tarmac's housing. The 1992 Annual Report referred to the decision to 'reshape' the housing division and reduce its size; the year end capital employed had been reduced from £400m to just over £300m with the promise of another £100m to be released in 1993 (more than achieved in the event). The number of operating subsidiaries was cut from 20 to16. In 1994, Sam Pickstock retired as Managing Director of housing, to be succeeded by Roy Harrison, formerly Managing Director of the building materials division.

On August 2nd 1995, Tarmac announced that it had decided upon a fundamental reshaping of the Group to concentrate on its activities in heavy building products; Tarmac was therefore to divest its private sector housebuilding interests. At the time, no specific proposals were made as to how the housing disposal would be realised; flotation and a trade sale were both being considered. The eventual solution

18 Ritchie, *The Story of Tarmac,* p.110.

was entirely unexpected: in November, Wimpey and Tarmac announced an asset swap. Wimpey was to take all of Tarmac's housing and in return Tarmac would receive all of Wimpey's contracting and minerals. Neville Simms had worked closely with Wimpey's Joe Dwyer at Transmanche. Joe Dwyer said that 'It was more out of curiosity than anything else that I went to see Neville. A figure of £400m was being bandied about for the housing business which I knew we couldn't afford. It became clear, however, during our discussion that Neville wanted to build up assets with cash generated from a sale.'[19] In February 1996, Tarmac's housing division was sold to Wimpey in an assets exchange which brought Wimpey's construction and minerals divisions into Tarmac.

As a footnote, Tarmac continued to come under investor pressure to focus yet more closely on its mineral business. In July 1999 the construction arm was demerged under the new name of Carrillion, leaving Tarmac once again a roadstone and road surfacing business. In the November, Tarmac accepted a takeover bid from Anglo American Mining.

[19] *Building* ,Nov 1996.

MACTAGGART & MICKEL
Peak units: c.1000 (1930s)

John Auld Mactaggart (1867-1956) was born in Anderston Glasgow, the son of a coppersmith: 'His building work was of immense importance to the development of Glasgow and the West of Scotland between 1890 and 1940.'[1] He received a formal education and was 'destined for the civil service' but instead, joined the firm of Robert Mickel, Govan timber merchants. He was described as 'a wizard with figures' and trained as a mercantile clerk. He became chief accountant and dealt increasingly with the property and building side of Mickel. Robert Mickel came from a long-established Glasgow family of tradesmen. He had a substantial business as a timber merchant and diversified into housing: between 1889 and 1898, Mickel built around 1500 units in and around Glasgow [c.150 p.a.] whilst also engaging in land speculation on a substantial scale. In 1909 a branch of the firm was opened in London and several blocks were developed before World War I. Andrew Mickel (1877-1962), Robert's nephew, joined his uncle's firm as a joiner, later becoming a manager, eventually leaving the family business to establish his own firm, concentrating on building for sale and land dealing.

John forms JA Mactaggart

By 1898, John Mactaggart had accumulated enough capital to leave Robert Mickel; 'He used to tell me that he walked three miles to work and back each day to save the tram fare.'[2] He first set up in partnership with an older builder, Robert Pollock, and three years later formed his own firm, JA Mactaggart & Co. In addition to general contracting he began building tenements, largely for middle-class tenants, totalling 2330 houses between 1901 and 1914[c180 p.a.]. 'Through force of character and a gift for publicity, Mactaggart became established in those years as one of the most prominent figures in Scottish housebuilding.'[3] In 1919, John Mactaggart turned the business into a limited company with himself as Managing Director and his son, Jack Mactaggart and Andrew Mickel (very much the smaller shareholder) as the other directors. The post-war period saw a shift away from private development – for sale or rent – towards local authority provision; the firm 'plunged head first into the new world of local authority contracting' including Glasgow's Mosspark scheme, the largest in Scotland with 1510 houses.[4] No doubt he was helped in his understanding of the local authority opportunities by virtue of being 'very much involved in the development of the laws and the schemes that enabled public housing to take place.'[5]

Jack Mactaggart and Andrew Mickel leave to start Mactaggart & Mickel

The opportunities for private development were limited but Mactaggart 'used the depressed conditions of the 1920s as an opportunity to build up a substantial land bank for future developments.'[6] The land was actually bought by the Ladies Syndicate, 'an organisation which Sir John set up specifically to enable his wife and daughters and other members of the fairer sex to benefit from the family's business prosperity, whilst at the same time not acquiring shares in the family holding company which he felt would be disadvantageous to the running of the business in the long term.'[7] In 1925, Jack Mactaggart left his father's firm, taking Andrew Mickel with him to form Mactaggart & Mickel. John Mactaggart's wife had died, leaving all her assets to her son Jack – enough for Jack to start on his own as a controlling shareholder. John Mactaggart

1 *Dictionary of Scottish Business Biography.*
2 Sandy Mactaggart correspondence made available to the author.
3 *Watters, Mactaggart & Mickel and the Scottish Housebuilding Industry*, p.13.
4 Ibid, p.21.
5 Sandy Mactaggart correspondence.
6 *Dictionary of Scottish Business Biography.*
7 Sir John McTaggart correspondence with author.

had no financial interest in the new firm. He wound up JA Mactaggart & Co and purchased a controlling interest in the virtually moribund Western Heritable Investment Company to use as a vehicle for investing in houses to rent. Mactaggart & Mickel built the houses for Western Heritable gradually acquiring 38% of the company in lieu of profit. In 1926 John Mactaggart started construction on land at King's Park owned by the family consortium; by 1930 he had built 1356 homes. In all, the Western Heritable Company built 6038 houses for rent, largely within Glasgow. By 1932, John Mactaggart was 65 and now beginning to take an interest in the London market. Through the London Heritable Investment Company and Grove End Gardens Ltd he built luxury flats in Park Lane and St John's Wood, before and after the Second War. He also assembled land on Park Avenue, New York, but exchange controls during the War prevented the remittance of funds to meet real estate tax obligations and the site was sold.

The largest housebuilder outside the London market

In its early years, Mactaggart & Mickel acted as a contractor to Glasgow Corporation, developed housing estates for sale, and built the houses for Western Heritable. In total, Mactaggart & Mickel built 8260 houses of all tenures between 1926 and 1933 [1180 p.a.]; this was similar in scale to the volumes being achieved in the London area by, say, Taylor Woodrow and Wimpey in the mid-1930s. By the 1930s, housebuilders in the London area were on the brink of an unprecedented boom in private housing. In contrast, Glasgow Corporation still appeared opposed to promoting home ownership on a large scale and its inter-war private housebuilding was only 18 per 1000 population compared with 65 in Edinburgh. The agreement with Western Heritable kept Mactaggart & Mickel out of building for rent in Glasgow, encouraging it to diversify into the Edinburgh market. Another generation, though now only of Mickels, was joining the firm – Andrew's sons Frank (1908-61) and Douglas (1911-2000). In the 1930s, the building of houses to let in Edinburgh (run by Douglas Mickel) accounted for almost half the company's output. The firm was building at an average of just under 1000 houses a year, less than the early 1920s, but this time the figures were not bolstered by contract work for the local authority. These numbers were larger than achieved by Miller, its Edinburgh rival and probably larger than any housebuilder not dependent on the London commuter market.

In the late 1930s, Mactaggart & Mickel faced a taxation problem which created considerable financial and personal pressure. Houses were typically sold with a feu[8] which could be sold for a capitalised value. This capital value had not been taxable until a test case ruled in favour of the Revenue – and the Revenue could go back seven years. 'That was the time when Mactaggart & Mickel was building very, very substantially and, therefore, the tax bite that they were forced to pay was of such a size that [Jack] feared it would bankrupt the company and ruin him…and that may have been the cause of his nervous breakdown.'[9] In the event, Jack Mactaggart went abroad while his father negotiated a settlement with the Inland Revenue. It left a consequent division amongst the directors as to how best the firm should be reorganised. When Jack Mactaggart returned, he settled in Islay, making only occasional visits to the office. In 1938 Mactaggart & Mickel sold its interests in Western Heritable to Jack Mactaggart for £100,000 (since when Western Heritable has been controlled solely by the Mactaggart family) and in the following year Walter Grieve, the only non-family director, resigned to join Sir John Mactaggart.

The Mactaggart family withdraws

The outbreak of war did not produce the immediate cessation of construction seen by other housebuilders and there was some initial attempt to keep the business going. However, Mactaggart & Mickel was soon confined to defence work for local authorities and the principal ministries. Jack Mactaggart, now living in the Bahamas for health reasons, attended only one board meeting during the

[8] Akin to the English ground rent.
[9] Sandy Mactaggart correspondence.

war. In 1947, the Mactaggart family finally withdrew from the firm, selling its controlling shareholding to the Mickel family. Mactaggart & Mickel pressed hard after the war to obtain building licences, but with little success, and continued local authority contracting to keep men occupied. As controls were relaxed from 1951, the firm was fortunate in being allocated bulk licences in both Glasgow and Edinburgh. As private housing activity was restored, the rented housing stock was gradually put on the market. The description of Mactaggart & Mickel's marketing suggests that it was more aware than most of the need to sell houses rather than select from a list of willing buyers, presumably reflecting the traditional Glasgow preference for renting – in 1953 it opened Glasgow's first fully furnished show house since the war, complete with cooking demonstrations.

Central Glasgow was now a diminishing market, and sites were developed over a wider area, including Renfrewshire and Ayrshire. As south of the border, the concentration on a few large sites had been replaced by a greater number of smaller, often infill, sites. By now, the day-to-day control of the business was in the hands of Frank Mickel in Glasgow and Douglas Mickel in Edinburgh. They were achieving steady growth in the business and by the early 1960s, volumes had reached around 500 a year – not far short of the levels achieved solely on the private sale part of the business in the 1930s. Frank Mickel died unexpectedly in 1961 depriving the Glasgow operation of 'his hands-on approach',[10] followed by his father, Andrew, the following year. Apart from the financial impact of death duties which took fifteen years to sort out, this weakened the company at what was about to be a period of increasing competition in the Scottish housebuilding market. Douglas Mickel was Managing Director and James Goold as his deputy – the latter had joined the company in 1961 as assistant company secretary, becoming Chairman in 1993. Frank's son Derek and Douglas's son Bruce, both architects, were yet to join the company. Douglas Mickel remained closely involved with the day-to-day management until his 80s when illness forced him to retire in 1993, and Goold became Chairman and Managing Director. The Lord Goold, as he became, died in 1997 and was replaced as Chairman by an outside accountant, John Craig.

Now a small housebuilder

Watters opens her final chapter on the company. 'In the years since 1960, the orientation of Mactaggart & Mickel's work changed gradually from large-scale housing developments to more selective building activity, especially following the entry of large English-based housebuilders into the Scottish market in the most recent decades.'[11] Mactaggart & Mickel accepted reduced levels of activity, from 1970 onwards, varying between 150 and 300 houses a years. Goold openly admitted to being 'unadventurous' and the directors clearly took the view that their first priority was to maintain their wealth, not risk it buying land when English builders were paying excessive prices.[12] The attitude to wealth preservation was considerably helped by the stock of Edinburgh rental houses the company still retained; there came a point when houses built for £500 could be sold for £50,000. As these were progressively sold during the 1970s and 1980s, there was enormous benefit to the asset base which rose from £2m in 1960 to £62m in year 2000. Mactaggart & Mickel had lost what had been a pre-eminent position in the housing market in the face of competition from more thrusting quoted companies. However, that is to judge by the criteria used in the quoted arena, many of whose participants failed to survive. For a private company to substantially increase its post-war asset base with minimal risk in the way achieved by Mactaggart & Mickel does not necessarily give 'unadventurous' a bad name.

Acknowledgement The author acknowledges the work by Diane Watters cited in the footnotes.

---

[10] *Watters, Mactaggart & Mickel,* p.152.

[11] Ibid, p.152.

[12] Ibid, p.182.

MARC GREGORY
Peak units, c.750? (1973)

Marc Gregory had a particularly short lived existence but the company epitomised the excesses in the banking and property development arena that culminated in the crash of 1974. Moreover, the principal characters were to appear again in other enterprises.

Malcolm Hawe was the driving force behind the company. Originally from Blackpool, he trained as a quantity surveyor and worked in the contracting arms of Marples Ridgeway and Wimpey before becoming general manager at the East Moseley contractor AJ Swann. It was there that Malcolm Hawe first teamed up with Mike Ratcliffe when, aged 22, he joined the firm in 1965. Ratcliffe was a school leaver who trained as a draughtsman and then studied quantity surveying at building college. Swann was mainly involved in contracting for local authorities with a little bit of private development. 'One of the first questions that Malcolm asked me was "can I do houses?" and I said "Yes I can" and he said "Well, we've got a piece of land up the road; would you design some houses to go on it?"'[1] That gave Hawe and Ratcliffe their first experience of estate development but Swann failed in 1969 as a result of cost inflation on fixed-price contracts.

Marc Gregory was formed in 1969 by Hawe and Ratcliffe on the demise of Swann; it took its name from Marc Gregory Hawe, Malcolm's son. The company was formed with no more than £15,000 capital, Ratcliffe borrowing his £3,000 from his grandfather. Unusually for a company founder, Malcolm Hawe vested his shares with a charitable foundation, the Donald Hawe Foundation (named after his father). Thus, the Foundation held 60%, Ratcliffe 20% and the remaining 20% was held by a number of small shareholders.

A handful of houses were sold in 1969, then 49 in 1970; by the end of 1970 there were 250 under construction with another 200 going through the planning stage. The pace of development continued to accelerate, and by 1974 Marc Gregory was on target to reach 1000 units, barely five years after its formation. The financial strain was eased by most of the sites being owned through joint ventures with financial institutions.

Marc Gregory had assumed a particularly high profile at the end of 1972 when Jim Slater sold 24% of the quoted Greencoat Properties to Marc Gregory. Marc Gregory requisitioned an EGM hoping to remove one director and put on four of its own giving it a majority of the seven-man board and effective control. Greencoat Chairman Lord Broughshane described it as 'a barefaced attempt by a minority to seize control.' There were then three months of negotiation about a possible merger and then another attempt to requisition an EGM. During this time, friends of the principals had also bought shares in Greencoat and under the takeover rules, they were deemed to be acting in concert, therefore giving a combined holding in Greencoat of 36%. A plenary session of the Takeover Panel ordered Marc Gregory to bid 32p a share, the highest cash price paid by any of the 'parties'…So ends one of the longest and most bitterly fought running battles in recent City history.' By August 1973, Marc Gregory controlled the quoted Greencoat, although a significant minority shareholding remained.[2] The intention was to reverse Marc Gregory into Greencoat and the prospectus was almost complete when the market turned.

[1] Interview with Mike Ratcliffe, Jan. 2001.
[2] See CALA for Greencoat history.

The rapid expansion of Marc Gregory had been almost entirely financed by bank borrowings and the company was in poor shape to withstand the market collapse and the rise in interest rates. Looking back after a quarter of a century, Ratcliffe regarded it as 'Catastrophic, unbelievable. The accounts were all manual so you didn't have the quality information that you would have today. You took the profit on the units as they were completed without looking at what was going to happen to the balance of the site and on that basis we made £2m in 1973. But by January 1974 we couldn't pay our interest. And that's when we called a moratorium on our five main lenders.'[3]

From February 1974, Marc Gregory operated under a voluntary arrangement but a receiver was appointed in the October when the five main lenders were unable to agree on a joint solution to the firm's cash problems; a compulsory winding up order was made the following month. 'We had some 25 or 26 lenders and they all came and seized their security all within the space of about a fortnight. The total size of the debt was around £40m on a £2m asset base.'[4]

As a footnote, Hawe returned to Blackpool and, after a period farming, resumed to housebuilding with a new company, Hammerfine. Ratcliffe formed his own company, Anns Homes which was later merged in with CALA to form its southern division. Ratcliffe then joined Hawe at Hammerfine when it was merged with AMEC's Fairclough Homes.

[3] Interview Mike Ratcliffe.
[4] Ibid.

JOHN MAUNDERS
Peak units: 1089 (1985)

The Company was founded in 1900[1] in Stretford, Manchester by John Maunders, a bricklayer who first worked with Metropolitan Vickers. He left to set up as a jobbing builder doing extensions, driveways, paths, and plumbing. In the 1920s, the Company began substantial local authority housebuilding as well as more general work; one of the more notable contracts was finishing the refurbishment of the Manchester Midland Hotel, which had been abandoned for some years.

In the late 1920s, Maunders began private estate development and built a number of large estates, examples being 1000 houses at Lostock (Stretford) and at Drolysden (Manchester). The number of houses built in the inter-war period totalled around 10,000 but the majority were contract houses for local authorities; private housing probably averaged no more than 200 a year. The housing market in the north west had started to slow by the mid 1930s and in response Maunders built cinemas, the Derby Baths at Blackpool, and the first swimming pool in the country to be built to Olympic standards. If he could not sell the private houses then they were retained for letting, and when the Company was sold in 1998, there were still a handful of these remaining. On the outbreak of War, the firm was seconded to the Ministry of Public Building and Works doing demolition and war damage work in both Manchester and London.

Shortly before the War, John Maunders became ill and his two sons, John, a bricklayer, and Harold, a carpenter, took over the management of the business; their father died in 1945. With the ending of the war, housebuilding was resumed with over 5000 council houses being built for north-west local authorities in eight years. When building licences were abolished, Maunders re-entered private housebuilding but about the time private housing restarted, the two brothers parted company due to a domestic disagreement and Harold bought out his elder brother.

Young Wendy and John left in control

Harold Maunders continued with the estate development, and in the late 1950s was building around 150-200 houses a year. However, he died suddenly in 1961 leaving a 22-year-old daughter, Wendy, then a secretary at Granada Television, and a 16-year-old schoolboy, John. To make matters worse 'We had problems with estate duty, and various taxes which father hadn't paid. The Company was not really sellable: it was either run it to generate funds to pay the debts or wind it up. It didn't have a lot of assets but what it did have was a very good name.' [2] Wendy Maunders managed the business on her own for the next four years while John attended building college, joining her in 1965 at the age of 20. He took over formally as Chairman and Managing Director in 1967 by which time the business was much reduced in size. 'My sister just had to consolidate the business. We could never get a handle on what the estate duty was going to be. By the time I took it over, it was only building 30 houses plus a little bit of contracting. My strategy at the age of 22 was to get the firm on an even keel, to pay off the estate duty. In 1968 we wound up the old company and formed John Maunders Construction which took over the assets and liabilities of the old company and we withdrew sufficient funds to pay off the estate duty.' [3]

The banks were not that keen to lend money to a 22-year-old, so for the next three of four years John Maunders concentrated on dealing in land, assembling sites and securing planning permission. 'I got myself into gear and went round Lancashire introducing myself to farmers and to estate agents and just

---

[1] The Prospectus said 1910 but family papers discovered later gave the earlier date.
[2] Interview with John Maunders, May 2001.
[3] Ibid.

got involved in deals. It wasn't easy. And that, basically, cleared off the overdraft we had.'[4] The company was now in a position to rebuild its volumes, but the experience had left the young Managing Director with an abiding dislike of high levels of debt. By 1970, Maunders was again building over 100 houses a year. The company was concentrating exclusively on private housing development, predominantly for the first time buyer, and it acquired large land holdings throughout Lancashire, Cheshire and Greater Manchester. Maunders' independent existence nearly came to an end in September 1972 when an agreed £1.2m bid from McLean was announced but personality conflicts led to it being aborted at the last minute. That 1972/73 financial year represented a trading peak for Maunders with turnover of £1.1m (around 150 houses) and pre-tax profits of £350,000. Profits fell back sharply during the recession, but thanks to the earlier land sales and low borrowings, the company remained profitable.

As the housing market climbed slowly out of recession, the 1970s was a period when Maunders developed the infrastructure it needed to grow further. 'In the early 1970s we had no infrastructure at Maunders, no architect's department, no buying systems, no engineering, certainly no legal, so I set about getting these disciplines on board. I felt that if we were going to expand to be a serious building company rather than a small family concern then we needed everything in-house.'[5] Profits were hard to come by and, indeed, there were losses in 1978 as the company had forward sold at fixed prices at a time of rapidly rising build costs.

The expansion begins

It was not until the first half of the 1980s that Maunders changed the scale of its operations but when the change came, it was substantial. Volumes rose from under 200 a year to over 700 by 1985 and, on turnover of £21m, pre-tax profits exceeded £2m. In May 1983, the company went public: 'It was one of the biggest mistakes I ever made. We felt that we had reached a size where, if we were to compete with the large firms, we needed more funding. We convinced ourselves that it was the thing to do but it was probably the worst thing I ever did. We went from 100% ownership down to 60% raising the princely sum of about £2^1/$_2$m. And the next daft thing the we did, in 1987, was to have a placing so our holding went down to 42%.'[6] The flotation also brought a change in the management structure. Bernard Davies, who had joined the Company in 1971 as a surveyor, became joint Managing Director with John Maunders and sole Managing Director the following year. However, no-one familiar with the company would doubt that the forceful John Maunders himself remained very much an executive Chairman.

Once a quoted company, Maunders looked to develop into other regions: 'I consider it essential to expand geographically, in addition to continuing to enlarge our North West operation.'[7] Maunders (South West) was formed with an office in Weston-Super-Mare but that yielded nothing. In 1985, Maunders bought six sites and work in progress in Dorset and Hampshire from Milbury to form the basis of a southern division. This was augmented in January 1987 by the purchase of the major part of Dares Estates' southern region for £3^1/$_2$m. The southern region was contributing around 20% of unit sales and the group was concentrating more on the trade-up market.

Despite the southern acquisitions, housing numbers remained around the 700 level in the second half of the 1980s; with house price inflation trebling profits to £6m by 1989, John Maunders felt no need to chase volumes. The Company was still looking to geographic expansion and in 1988 it opened an office in Bury St Edmunds to form an East Anglia region; the land purchases at the top of the cycle were to

[4] Ibid.
[5] Ibid.
[6] Ibid.
[7] Group Accounts, 1984.

prove expensive. By the standards of the industry, Maunders came through the 1990 recession in good shape. Its land provisions were modest, and pre-tax profits in 1991 did no worse than fall to half the peak level. However, the north-west heartland probably maintained its profits while the south broke even; it was East Anglia that incurred significant losses. Looking back on his regional expansion, John Maunders regretted being drawn away from the north west: 'It was the fashion of the time – why did we grow our hair long and wear flared trousers? If I were starting again, I would just try to be a player in the area I knew well, and where I had the connections – land has always been hard to come by and always will be.'[8]

Consolidation then sale

The early 1990s was a period of consolidation: East Anglia was closed down. Bernard Davies left abruptly to be replaced as Managing Director by Bill Bannister, who had joined in 1980 as sales manager and gone on to run the southern division. By 1994, volumes were in excess of 900 and profits had regained the £6m level. However, the company faced a strategic problem. The north west, which still accounted for 80% of the volume, was operating near its potential and any growth would have to come from further afield. Retentions were insufficient to finance that growth and John Maunders was neither prepared to let gearing rise, nor dilute the family shareholding by issuing new equity. As he put it: 'If you want to have only 2% of a much larger company but all the hassle of running it, then fine. It was almost reaching the stage where we couldn't expand in our own region never mind going to new areas. And that really brought on the position in 1997 when I made the decision to sell the business.'[9] In April 1998, the Company was sold to Westbury for £55m, by which time the family holding was down to 38%.

[8] Interview John Maunders.
[9] Ibid.

METROPOLITAN RAILWAY COUNTRY ESTATES
Peak units: 1800 (1964)

Metropolitan Railway Country Estates must rank as one of Britain's most unusual housebuilders; indeed, in the 1950s, it was one of the country's largest. A similar sounding Metropolitan Railway Surplus Lands was a sister company and both companies feature prominently in the story of Broseley Estates.

Whereas the American railway companies became substantial developers of the lands they opened up, the British companies were more constrained. 'The statutory powers under which they were empowered to buy land also compelled them to sell lands surplus to requirement on completion of the scheme. They were usually given ten years in which to dispose of the land…Only one exception to this is recorded …that allowed by the Metropolitan Inner Circle Completion Act 1874, which allowed the [Metropolitan Railway] to grant building leases and sell ground rents.'[1] The Company began to develop land for 'limited-density high rental' use, but there was a growing concern that Metropolitan might be forced by Parliament to sell its residential property and 'it was deemed discreet to divide the stock into two portions, one representing railway earnings, and the other the rentals and profits of the surplus estate.'[2] This gave rise to the Surplus Lands Committee. Jackson described the Metropolitan Railway Surplus Lands Committee controlling and managing the estates, with the freehold remaining vested in the railway company. Some of the land was sold, but new property was purchased and developed along with the retained land. In the years immediately before 1914, attention was turning to suburban residential development, and two estates were built on 'surplus lands' alongside the railway at Pinner.'[3]

Estates separated from the Metropolitan Railway
The General Manager of the Railway, Robert Selbie, was concerned that the Railway was not obtaining full benefit from the land and suggested forming a separate company to develop estates with the Railway having a controlling interest. In January 1919, the directors approved the formation of the Metropolitan Railway Country Estates Ltd [MRCE], and a 454-acre estate at Rickmansworth and another of 123 acres at Wembley Park were bought by a syndicate for transfer to MRCE. At the last moment, legal opinion suggested that the Railway Company might be deemed to be buying and selling land without statutory authority. 'In the event, it was decided that the railway company would take no direct financial interest in the Estates Company, but would enter into an agreement which would allow the use of the railway's name in the new company's title and provide for all possible assistance through the railway's organisation in the development of the estates to be purchased.'[4]

The Prospectus for MRCE, funded entirely by public subscription, was published in June 1919. It specifically stated that the statutory powers of the Metropolitan Railway Company did not allow the latter to subscribe for shares but it was lending the part-time services of the surveyor to the Company's Surplus Lands Committee. All the other directors were also directors of the Metropolitan Railway Company. The Company was formed to acquire from the Metropolitan Railway Company four freehold estates comprising 627 acres, served by the Metropolitan Railway and the Metropolitan and Grand Central Joint Line 'with a view to their land being laid out in an attractive manner and resold in plots of varying sizes…For many years the development of land in the home county districts served by the Metropolitan Railway has been seriously hindered by reason of the difficulty experienced by purchasers in acquiring sites on which to erect their

---

[1] Kellett, *The Impact of Railways on Victorian Cities,* p.393.

[2] Ibid, pp.396-7.

[3] Jackson, *Semi Detached London*, p.224.

[4] Ibid, p.225.

houses, the available land being for the most part being for sale in large parcels only…The Company's scheme will throw open large areas for development.' In the inter-war period, MRCE went on to buy other estates from the Railway Company and from other vendors. The original 10-year agreement with the Railway Company was extended for a further 10 years in 1929 but on the formation of the London Transport Passenger Board in 1933, 'Country Estates assumed a quite separate existence.'[5]

MRCE more a land developer than a builder

There is some dispute as to how active MRCE was as a house builder rather than just a developer of land. Although the minute books dating back to 1919 survive, they contain no more than the barest formal matters. Rose indicated a substantial level of estate development and a limited building programme, stating that although MRCE sold off some of its land to developers, it went on to develop some ten estates along the main line and the Uxbridge branch. 'It actually built some houses but in the main sold off the land, either to builders or in individual plots.'[6] Bundock's interview notes from 1969 refer to pre-war building levels of 50 to 100 houses a year.[7] Some hard evidence is provided by the annual reports which list the number of acres of land sold, and by the late 1930s these came from eleven different estates. By the outbreak of war, MRCE had sold 536 acres leaving 795 acres undeveloped. These estates were individually very large and suggests that Country Estates was on a par with the larger traditional developers. Unfortunately, there is limited reference to house building numbers. Although the report of the 1938 AGM carried the headline 'Increased Number of Houses Sold' and the text included the words 'the number of houses sold has increased by 50%.', frustratingly, the base number was not disclosed. However, the report of the 1947 AGM contained an interesting reference back to pre-war years, stating that MRCE had built several hundred houses a year. Irrespective of how much building it did carry out itself, it looks as though Country Estates was more a developer along the North American lines acquiring large tracts of land and processing them to a state where they could be subdivided amongst other builders.

During the Second War, MRCE concentrated on using its undeveloped estates for food production to support the war effort; there was no reference to any wartime construction work. Nor did the Company diversify into local authority housing after the War. Instead, it used its capital to purchase agricultural estates, frequently breaking them up and selling farms to sitting tenants. As building controls were gradually removed in the early 1950s, so MRCE began to develop its pre-war estates, first selling serviced sites, and then building houses. MRCE was now less dependent on the old Railway Company areas. The 1956 accounts reported that it was buying land over a wider area and becoming more active than before the War: 'We do not feel justified in stocking up with potential building land on a wholesale view as we did in pre-war days.'

MRCE develops its Whelmar subsidiary

In 1956, MRCE was offered two substantial building estates, one near Manchester comprising 250 acres and the other a group of six smaller sites being sold by the Butterley Brick Company (including ones at Derby, Stoke and Rotherham) with 150 houses at or near completion and several hundred plots. These purchases would have strained MRCE's financial resources, so it invited Metropolitan Railway Surplus Land into partnership. In 1958, MRCE used one of its dormant subsidiaries, Whelmar as a joint company with Surplus Lands, to be managed by Tom Baron, then a partner in surveyors Dunlop Heywood. The change in development strategy was spelt out to shareholders in the 1960 accounts: 'policy with regard to estate development has been to rely increasingly on the full development of building land already

---

[5] Ibid, p.226.

[6] Rose, *Dynamics of Urban Property Development*, pp.120-1.

[7] Bundock, 'Speculative Housebuilding'; interview notes provided to the author.

owned by us…by not only installing the basic services…but building the houses as well.'

The original London base was reducing in importance as MRCE found it hard, by which it presumably meant expensive, to buy land. Instead, in 1960 it was reporting the purchase of sites as far apart as Grimsby, Doncaster, Leicester, Marlow, Fawley and Gosport; and a map with the 1964 accounts showed 47 sites around the country. Volumes had risen rapidly following the land purchases on the late 1950s: in 1961, MRCE reported the sale of 1220 houses (including Whelmar) and in 1962 it considered that the land bank was sufficient to increase the build programme to 2000 a year. Record sales were achieved in 1964, in excess of 1800 of which 800 were in Whelmar; on this basis, it was probably then the second largest housebuilder after Wimpey.

MRCE in decline
In the event, the 2000 target was never achieved and 1964 remained a volume record for the Company; neither did profits ever match the £575,000 earned in 1964, and the dividend was progressively reduced from 15% to 9%. By the late 1960s, volumes had reduced to around 1300 a year at a time when other developers were rapidly increasing their volumes. The reasons for the decline are not obvious. Bernard Docker, Chairman since before the war, retired in 1967; Managing Director Willie Balch (President of the RICS in 1957-58) continued in office but he was then in his mid-60s and presumably considering retirement. A very conservative selling policy may have undermined the Company's ability to replace land in an inflationary era. The 1960 Annual Report referred to the determination of selling prices: 'we have as a matter of policy added to our costs only the normal profit margin necessary to pay our overhead expenses and a reasonable return on the capital employed.' It is little wonder that they went on to complain that 'substantial' profits had been made on resale by customers within twelve months.' If the management was prepared to sell houses at below value it would have difficulty in replacing its land.

In 1968 Metropolitan Railway Surplus Lands was taken over by the property company MEPC, and they agreed with MRCE that Whelmar would be sold to Christian Salvesen. This removed a substantial volume of housing sales from the group and by 1971, volumes were down to around 400 a year. In May 1971 MRCE was taken over by Guardian Royal Exchange for £4.9m and the housebuilding merged in with its Broseley housebuilding subsidiary.

MILBURY
Peak units: 591 (1984)

'This is the story of a dominating and unscrupulous man, [Jim Raper] whose activities were inadequately controlled.'[1] Milbury was originally ARV Holdings, a car and motor cycle dealer. In January 1972 Roy Strudwick and fellow directors of Royco (a housebuilding company that floated shortly after) joined the board and later that year they announced a major reorganisation which included the acquisition of the Milbury Group, a Manchester housebuilder that had experienced financial problems in the mid-1960s, and Regentfield, another building company. Most of the garage activities were sold and the name of the company was changed to Milbury in 1974.

Jim Raper had extensive interests in the UK and the far east and a tendency to gain control of his companies via minority stakes. In November 1972, Raper's Hong Kong company started to acquire shares in St Piran, a mining company and by October 1973 it held 34%. Raper became a director in March 1973 and within a year all the original directors had gone. Raper's policy was to diversify St Piran away from tin mining to UK housebuilding and in July 1973 St Piran bought 45% of Milbury from Royco. St Piran bid for the balance and in September 1973 had 81%, with the quotation remaining.

Milbury was now substantially a north-west housebuilder. Its turnover grew from around £3m in 1975 to £12m in 1980 and profits from £100,000 to £1.8m; it was then selling around 400 houses a year. From 1973 until the appointment of Raper to the Milbury Board in August 1981, St Piran was content to let Milbury manage its own affairs under the direction of Don Smith. However, Milbury eventually became enmeshed in the wider ramifications of Raper's dealings. In 1980, Raper had clashed with the Take-over Panel regarding the manner in which he had taken control of South Crofty: 'The Panel has concluded that Mr Raper, whose conduct in this matter has been deplorable, is unfit to be a director of a public company.' The Stock Exchange suspended dealings in St Piran, and Milbury as well, banning its members from transacting any business with Raper.

In the meantime, Raper was trying to expand Milbury and in 1982 it bought Dare Developments, operating in the Bournemouth and Southampton area. However, the early 1980s was not a profitable period for Milbury. The purchase of Dare had stretched its financial resources and there were three successive declines taking the profit down to only £550,000 in 1983. But Milbury was about to be in even deeper trouble as a result of its acquisition of Westminster Property. In February 1983, St Piran bought 24% of Westminster Property rising to 29.9% as a result of tender offer, raising fresh concerns in the City about Raper's acquisition methods. A 'peace deal' was brokered by the Stock Exchange in the September: Raper bowed to a Panel ruling that he make a full bid for Westminster and offered a comprehensive apology for the way in which he took control of South Crofty in 1980; in return, the Panel agreed to expunge its ruling that Raper 'is a man unfit to be a director of a public company' and the listings were restored to Raper's companies.

The relevance to Milbury was that Raper shifted the obligation to bid from St Piran to Milbury at the original share price – now an excessive £10m. 'Milbury had taken over St Piran's obligation to make an offer for Westminster at a price that was too high. It could not afford to do so from its own resources.'[2] Most shareholders took the cash, the banks refused to lend Milbury the money to finance the bid and therefore Milbury took a £2.6m loan from St Piran, repayable in 15 months. To compound the financial

---

[1] Carlisle and Lickiss, *Milbury plc Westminster Property Group investigation*.
[2] Carlisle and Lickiss, *Milbury plc*.

problems, 'Some of the new management team were inexperienced and unproven in the roles which they had been assigned to play.'[3] All the Westminster directors were replaced.

The March 1984 accounts included Westminster and appeared to present a healthy profits picture, up from £0.55m to £2m, with housing sales reaching almost 600. However, behind these numbers lay a different story. 'The combination of a demanding Chairman, an inexperienced finance director, and a Chief Executive of the housebuilding division who was numerate but imprudent, managed to obscure the true position.'[4] Profits were overstated and to take but one example, sale and leaseback of show homes were treated as normal sales, although incurring future rental payments of £850,000 and contingent capital liabilities.

Despite the financial strains, the management was still trying to expand Milbury and a new division was started in the midlands, based on the purchase of seven sites and work in progress from EGM Cape. Excessive budgets were being prepared to meet profit targets demanded by Raper, which served only to create unsold stock of houses in the northern division. Funds were now being withdrawn out of Milbury into St Piran. The southern housing company, the only one still profitable, was transferred to Westminster and that enlarged company was sold for £1m to an offshore company believed to be controlled by Raper. 'We have concluded that the sale had no commercial substance and was a sham.'[5] Poco's Roy Dixon (see below) said that even before these transfers, the Milbury accounts presented at the 1984 AGM overvalued the company by nearly £7.5m.[6]

In its issue of 9th August 1985, *Building* magazine reported that rumours of trouble at Milbury had been rife and the share price had halved since mid July – not helped either by the departure of the Managing Director and the company secretary during the past year. Two weeks later the shares were suspended. It was following this that Poco bought St Piran's controlling stake for £1, but Roy Dixon was unable to persuade the main banks to agree to a rescue. Poco therefore sought a liquidator for Milbury Homes (North) and subsequently bought its sites from the Receivers. Maunders bought the southern sites from Milbury Homes South' Receivers. In November 1985 liquidators were appointed for Milbury plc. Banks and creditors lost some £15m..

---

[3] Ibid.
[4] Ibid.
[5] Ibid.
[6] *Financial Times*, 11th Sep. 1985.

MILLER HOMES
Peak units: 2871 (2003)

James Miller (1905-77) and his brother John (1907-82) created Edinburgh's largest housebuilder in the inter-war period. In contrast to the Glasgow based Mactaggart & Mickel, the Miller family succeeded in developing the business after the war into a successful British construction and development group, while still retaining family control. James Miller went on to become a leading Edinburgh figure achieving what was a unique double becoming both a Provost of Edinburgh and Lord Mayor of London

James Miller was the son of architect, inheriting his father's Edinburgh practice at the age of 17. He was still only 23 when 'spurred on by a developer's lack of interest, [he]designed and commissioned a scheme in Blackhall, Edinburgh.'[1] He was too young to borrow the money himself so his mother borrowed the money from the Royal Bank of Scotland. The houses were advertised in the *Scotsman* in March 1927: 'It was, I believe, the first time such an advertisement had been put in the paper.'[2] The 16 houses sold almost immediately and the business was under way. The Edinburgh Council was well-disposed towards the speculative builder and, in the period up to 1932, some 75% of the private housing received either loans or subsidies. From its start in 1927 to 1934, Miller built 1922 houses under the subsidy arrangements, almost ten times as many as the next builder.[3] The company's own statistics survive from 1932, when 427 houses were sold; the peak year was 1933 with 705 sales.

Edinburgh's leading housebuilder in the 1930s
Once the housing operation proved successful, John gave up his business in the motor trade to join James. The elder brother, Lawrence Miller (1903-73), was a lawyer and acted as company secretary. There is no doubt that James Miller was the driving force and when the partnership was incorporated, he had 50% of the shares with John owning the other 50%. Output was sustained at around 500 houses a year until the mid 1930s, declining as war approached. By then the firm was clearly established as Edinburgh's leading housebuilder. The company also diversified into small commercial projects – garages, cinemas and dance halls – and general contracting. As with the London housebuilders, war work led to the expansion of what had been a small contracting operation into airfield and factory construction, becoming the forerunner of Miller Civil Engineering. Offices were opened in London and Birmingham, and Miller took over the London contracting firm LJ Speight & Partners in 1942. Open-cast coal mining started in Yorkshire in 1941 in response to a government request.

After the war, Miller took the inevitable route back into housing via local authority work. In 1950 the firm designed its own non-traditional house, the Miller 'No Fines' house, with factories employing around 1000 people; nearly 7000 of these were built by 1955 by which time Miller had been able to restart private housing. By now, there was a natural division of labour, with James continuing with housing and John being responsible for civil engineering and mining. The private housing expansion was rapid once controls were removed. Miller had extensive land holdings from before the war, some of which were still being developed in the 1980s. Miller also expanded into England through offices in Hayes, Middlesex and Wakefield. By the early 1970s, Miller was building 300 p.a. in the South East and 500 p.a. in Scotland. The building and civil engineering business was also expanding and Miller took its civils business international in the 1970s.

For a family business spanning eighty years, Miller is unusual in that it has been controlled by only two

[1] Anon, *Celebrating the Miller Group's Diamond Jubilee,* p.3.
[2] Sir James Miller, quoted in Watters, *Mactaggart & Mickel,* p.219.
[3] Edinburgh Corporation minutes quoted in Watters, *Mactaggart & Mickel,* p.219.

generations. Of the nine children the three brothers produced, only three joined the business – which probably helped the decision making process in contrast to, for instance, Wates where far more of the family joined. Sir James' eldest son, also James, joined the company in 1958, becoming a director in 1960 and Chairman in 1970 on his father's retirement; Roger joined in 1960, became a director in 1965 and from 1970 to his retirement in 1991 was Managing Director of Miller Homes; Sir James' youngest son Malcolm was killed in a car accident in 1966. From the other branch of the family, John's son Keith was some 15 years younger than his cousins and joined the group in 1975, becoming a director the following year and taking charge of the mining division.

Miller experiments with an outsider

The 1970s was a more difficult period for the private housing arm, and the directors were content to let other parts of the group make the running. Volumes averaged around 500 a year, gradually edging up to 700-800 by the end of the 1980s before dropping back to 500-600 in the early 1990s. In the depths of the 1990 recession, the family made the decision to go outside their ranks for a new Chief Executive. The Group faced the retirement of Roger Miller (Chairman of Homes) as well as the Managing Directors of Homes, Ian Mitchell, and Construction, Mike Ballard. James Miller was 57 and thought it time to split roles of Chairman and Chief Executive. In January 1992 David Cawthra, ex-Balfour Beatty, was appointed as the first non-family Chief Executive with trade press commenting that 'When a private company goes outside for a chief executive it is usually taken as a sign of failure, of a board unable to groom an internal candidate.'[4] In the event, the outsider lasted just over two years and the inside candidate, in the person of Keith Miller, replaced him. It was a decade before there was public comment but Keith Miller eventually admitted that 'during the 1980s and start of the 1990s, the company "lost its way". Under its first and last non-family chief executive, it had focused increasingly on low-margin and high-risk contracting, which then accounted for 80% of turnover. When this tipped the group into the red, the family put Mr Miller in charge.'[5]

And back to family management

Keith Miller's strategic thinking is different from most others in the construction industry, certainly different from the housebuilding sector where the current consensus is that the business should be focused. 'At the time, [1994] conventional thinking was that companies such as ourselves should have a narrow focus – in our case this would have meant becoming either a pure housebuilder or contractor. We decided to do the opposite and develop both sides of our business on a deal-driven basis…It is never easy going against the grain – to take the unfashionable route and ignore what others, including your competitors, are doing.'[6] Miller accepts that he cannot replicate the focused housebuilder whose chief executive is living and breathing the business: 'But I can position the business strategically. I get involved in every major land purchase. There is also a degree of overlap with the commercial side where we have a commercial team throughout the UK working on really complicated development deals. There are also big local authority land holdings that you can't unlock just through housing because it does not make enough money – except for down south. If you have the business structured towards client orientation, getting new opportunities, new deals, then you really have to have the whole team working together, so each of our businesses is clearly focused on where it wants to position itself in its particular market.'[7]

Miller succeeded in holding its housing volume steady through the early 1990s. A slightly surprising move

4 *New Civil Engineer,* 28th May 1992.
5 *Financial Times* 29th Aug. 2002.
6 Keith Miller interviewed in the *Glasgow Herald*, 23rd Jan. 1999.
7 Interview with Keith Miller, Feb. 1999.

given its expansion plans was the sale in 1996 of the south of England division of Miller Homes to Kier, although it did bring in £20m. Despite that, sales passed the 1000 a year mark for the first time in 1997, and the 1998 appointment as Managing Director of Miller Homes of Geoff Potton, previously Managing Director of Bryant Homes, signalled the intention to expand further. Keith Miller set out his intentions for the housing business: 'we aim to move into the top ten...Our appetite for further acquisitions in this sector is still strong.'[8] Miller Homes was establishing itself in the midlands, the north west and the north east and reinforced this with acquisitions. After an abortive bid for its Edinburgh rival, Cala, Miller bought the Scottish Lynch Homes (c.200 units) and the quoted Newcastle-based Cussins (330 units) in 1999; these were followed in 2000 by the purchase of the Derby firm, Birch Homes (400 units) and the northern division of Crest Homes (240). These contributed to an increase in total housing volume to over 2000 in year 2001 although trading margins remained well below the levels being achieved by its major competitors.

A top ten housebuilder

Geoff Potton left Miller Homes in 2002, being replaced by Tim Hough. Hough had been in charge of McAlpine Homes' southern region and he took Miller back into the south via a new office in Basingstoke. The intention to make further acquisitions were publicly aired, and in 2004 Hough was quoted as aiming for housing volumes of 4000 a year.[9] At the time of writing, this looks as though it will be just about achieved in 2006 for, in September 2005, Miller agreed the purchase of Fairclough Homes (1500 units) from the US Centex. Apart from increasing Miller's presence in the north of England and the midlands, the acquisition significantly increases Miller's exposure to the south. For the first time, Miller will be in the top ten of British housebuilders.

[8] Group Accounts, 1999.
[9] *Housebuilder*, April 2004.

MORRELL ESTATES
Peak units: c.500? (mid 1930s)

There are few today who will have heard of Morrell Estates. It claimed, though possibly incorrectly, to be 'one of the largest businesses of House Builders in Great Britain.'[1] It was the first, indeed the only, quoted housebuilder to be bankrupt before the War; and through its involvement in the Borders case, it was a contributor to major change in building society legislation.

There were three brothers, Cyril Herbert, Stanley Charles and Frank ('Joe') Morrell, who came from Herne Hill in south London and moved to Bromley. They began building in a small way in 1929, just as the inter-war boom in private housing was starting. It traded as CH Morrell (the oldest brother) and was incorporated as Morrell (Builders) in 1932. By then, the firm was developing large estates at Hayes, West Wickham and Bromley Common (all in the Borough of Bromley). The nearby Coney Hall (to be the subject of the Borders Case) and Petts Wood estates were started in 1933. However, in December that year, tragedy hit the firm as the youngest brother, Joe, then aged only 24, was killed in a road accident, an event which was later suggested as a contributory cause of the firm's failure: 'the firm's management may also have been weakened by the tragic road death of Frank Morrell, the youngest brother, in a head-on collision in December 1933.'[2]

1935 flotation

Within a year or two there is no doubt that Morrell was a substantial London builder and Jackson describes it as 'responsible for launching several ambitious projects in south-east London in the thirties.'[3] On the strength of this, Morrell floated on the Stock Exchange in July 1935, the last of a group of five companies that floated within a 15-month period (Davis Estates, New Ideal, Taylor Woodrow and Wimpey). The flotation vehicle was a new holding company, Morrell Estates & Development which acquired Morrell (Builders). The Board consisted of the two brothers as joint Managing Directors and was augmented by a retired colonial governor as Chairman, an MP and an accountant. The Prospectus listed estates which had been developed or were in the process of being acquired for development; these totalled 14 in the Bromley, Orpington and Herne Hill area, plus one block of flats in Herne Hill and flats at 35 Eccleston Square (where Charles was living) which no doubt gave rise to the claim to be one of the largest housebuilders. Profits had risen from £4000 in 1932 to £100,000 in the year to October 1934: to put that figure in perspective, it was more than either Taylor Woodrow or Wimpey were making in that year.

The price paid to the two Morrell brothers for their business by the new public company was £280,000 satisfied by £111,250 in cash and the balance by the allotment of 675,000 shares (75 per cent of the new company). The issue was not a success and 72% of the shares were left with the underwriters. The proceeds of the public element of the issue was to 'enable the directors to carry out their policy of extensively developing the shopping areas on the estates and letting shops on lease to responsible tenants, thus building up a substantial permanent income.'[4] The company had also bought a 195-acre estate at Chelsfield, adjoining the railway station.

---

[1] Prospectus, 1935.
[2] Blake, *Before the War A Portrait of Bromley & District 1929-1939*.
[3] Jackson, *Semi Detached London*, p.110.
[4] Prospectus, 1935.

Dividends passed

The accounts for the year to June 1936, the first as a quoted company, were not consolidated and the only revenue was a dividend from Morrell (Builders) of £111,000, out of its profits from the year to October 1935, i.e. eight months preceding the holding company year end. It later transpired that Morrell (Builders) had made a profit of only £30,000. No ordinary dividend was paid and at the AGM, in December 1936, the directors reported that the Company was in serious financial difficulty, although they were hopeful that the financial position of Morrell (Builders) would be materially strengthened by the provision of further finance for which negotiations were then pending. However, a circular to shareholders on 6th January 1937 had even worse news: 'Unfortunately however, before these negotiations could be concluded, the cash position of the subsidiary became acute as a result of a sudden and drastic curtailment of overdraft facilities by the Company's bankers… Accordingly, it is proposed to place that company in voluntary liquidation.'

The accounts of Morrell Estates for June 1937 reported considerable progress and substantial economies within its building subsidiary; CH Morrell was now the sole Managing Director. In April 1938 the Chairman's speech referred to 'very critical conditions back in January 1937. There were a large number of unfinished houses, shops and maisonettes on the company's various estates while interest and payments to utilities were in arrears. Since liquidation all the unfinished houses have been completed and many have been sold. Relations with the building societies have been re-established on friendly lines.' It was intended that the company would take over the remaining assets of the subsidiary; there was still a surplus of net assets of £263,000 and creditors would be paid over a period of 18 months. This, too, proved unsuccessful and a letter to shareholders dated 21st December1938 gave notice of an AGM for a voluntary winding up of the parent company. 'Since July last when the assets of Morrell (Builders) in Liquidation passed to your Company the position of the company has been adversely affected by the disturbed international situation as well as by the recent building societies litigation resulting in a falling off in the demand for houses and land of the type owned by your company and the consequent difficulty in arranging finance.' Trading was reported to be 'in an adverse balance' and there was a deficit of net assets. There were no accounts for 1938-39 although the register of defunct companies recorded that the final meeting of Morrell Estates and Development was not until 19 October 1979.

Fraud or naivety?

After the passage of over 60 years, it is impossible to know what caused the collapse. It would appear that the flotation was based on profits that had never been made: the flotation in July 1935 was just 10 weeks before the year end of the only operating company, which was experiencing a major fall in profits at a time when the housing market was booming. The payment of a dividend, far in excess of these profits, to the holding company at a time when the underlying profits appeared to be falling even further, and without any comment by the directors, would be judged harshly in today's regulatory climate. It may also be that the pre-flotation accounting had not been unduly rigorous. An interview with a solicitor's clerk some twenty years ago referred to the desperate lengths that Morrell was going to, to get the houses sold on the Coney Hall estate, where some 800 houses had been built by 1935; this seemed to include letting people move in before they had committed themselves to purchase on a 'suck it and see' basis.[5] If such occupations had been treated as sales, it would have overstated profits and strained liquidity. It may have been that the Morrell Brothers were guilty of no more than overtrading on low profit margins and were financially naïve. However, by the time Morrell needed the support of its lenders, it had become embroiled in the now famous Borders case.

---

[5] I am indebted to Andrew McCulloch for that information.

The Borders case

The Borders case came to Court in January 1938 and finished in the House of Lords in May 1941. Mrs Elsey Borders, the wife of a taxi driver, had borrowed money from the Bradford 3rd Equitable Building Society to buy a house on the Coney Hall estate, which she later named 'Insanity.' Arguing that there were faults in the house, Mrs Borders withheld payments on the mortgage and organised a mortgage strike estimated to be backed by 400 on the Coney Hall estate and 2500 owner-occupiers on other estates around London. The Building Society sued for possession in June 1937 and Mrs Borders conducted her own case in Court taking on Norman Birkett KC. She argued that the mortgage deed was unenforceable because the Society had taken collateral security from the builder[6] and this was illegal under the Building Society Acts; moreover, the deed was not the one that she had signed. She also counterclaimed against the Society stating that, as its name was being freely used in the builder's literature, it had fraudulently represented the house as being well built. The various judgements swayed back and forth between the parties, favouring her in the Court of Appeal but eventually Elsie Borders lost most, although not all, her arguments.

However, her case did lead to the passing of the Building Societies Act 1939 to regularise the taking of additional security, and the Builders' Pool was never used again. Jim Borders was successful in suing Bradford for libel. The Borders case did not cause Morrell's problems but they must have affected the attitude of lenders at the critical stage of the Company's refinancing.

The house in question still stands and was estimated to be worth £250,000 in 2001!

Additional Sources

Stevens, Leslie, *Morrell Builders Ltd of Bromley.*
Wilkes, Roger, 'Inside story Insanity', *Daily Telegraph,* 21st July 2001.
McCulloch, Andrew, 'The Mortgage Strikes', *History Today,* June 2001.

---

[6] These payments made to the building societies were known as 'The Builders' Pool' and performed much the same function as do the insurance indemnity premiums today.

MORRISON HOMES
Peak units: 626 (1999)

Morrison Construction was founded in 1948 by Alexander Morrison in Tain, Ross-shire as a joinery business. It gradually expanded into building and construction work throughout the north of Scotland and was incorporated in 1963 as Alexander Morrison (Builders). In 1974, when the development of North Sea oil was increasing the demand for construction, 80% of the shares were acquired by Selection Trust, and subsequently Morrison became part of Selection Trust's Shand Group. In 1980 Selection Trust was acquired by BP, and in 1981 the Shand Group, including Morrison, was acquired by Charter Consolidated.

In 1989 the Morrison management team purchased the 80% shareholding owned by Charter and at the same time bought the English construction companies, Shand Construction and Biggs Wall. Six years later, in 1995, Morrison was floated. The Company was led by Fraser Morrison, Alexander's son, who had worked in the business since graduating as a civil engineer; had been Managing Director since 1977 and had led the MBO from Charter. One of the Group's objectives, in common with many other construction companies, was to increase the proportion of work won outside the traditional tender system, a strategy which was to be supported by the expansion of the development business. 'To achieve these objectives, Morrison combined its property development and building businesses into a single division in 1991, enabling the property development expertise of the one to complement the construction disciplines of the other.'[1] This solution was different than for most of the quoted companies who were then stressing the need for 'focus.'

Whilst Morrison had built houses throughout its history, initially in the north and then spreading throughout Scotland, by the end of the 1980s Morrison Homes was building no more than 100 houses a year on traditional estates in Scotland. In 1990, Morrison bought the assets of **Lema Homes** in the Scottish Borders for £780,000, more than doubling output in the year to March 1991 to over 200. Lema Homes had been formed in 1977 by Adam Shiels and David Proctor in Jedburgh, and Proctor joined the enlarged housing division for several years. Alastair McDougall, a building graduate who had joined Morrison in 1987, became the housing Managing Director in the late 1980s and, as it entered the 1990s, Morrison Homes changed its strategy: 'Over the last five years, the division has reduced its historic reliance on traditional speculative housebuilding and has concentrated on the low cost sector through developing grant aided homes for private sale into the social housing and rental sector. This change in emphasis has made the Morrison housing business less capital intensive than is the norm for private housebuilders.'[2]

Between 1991 and 1995, the total number of housing completions rose from 211 to 344 but within that there was a decline in speculative housing and the social and rental housing completions rose from 9 to 196. By the end of the decade, Morrison's joint venture with British Linen held a portfolio of 500 rented houses; however, with the housing-for-sale market now more buoyant, Morrison swung back again from social to speculative housing. This time, there was a preponderant concentration on urban development schemes rather than greenfield sites. The integration with other parts of the group had increased following a reorganisation at the end of 1998. Three divisions had been created: property; infrastructure and facilities management with property including building and international activities as well as development. 'A substantial proportion of building turnover flowed from contracts made possible by our

1 Prospectus, 1995.
2 Ibid.

property and residential development activities.'[3] An example given was the consent for 400 homes on the site of the former Edinburgh City Hospital which had been secured through the involvement with the PFI contract to build the new Royal Infirmary.

The late 1990s saw a number of management changes. Norman MacLennan, previously Finance and then Managing Director of the Building and Property Division, became group Managing Director in 1996 but had to step down a year later through ill-health to be replaced by Finance Director Keith Howell. Alistair MacDougall also retired in 1997 and was succeeded by Brian Leith as housing Managing Director. There was further concentration on urban redevelopment schemes, not only in Scotland but in cities in the North of England. Volumes grew to over 600 units and, for the first time, trading margins began to rise to industry comparable levels.

Higher up the organisation, there was further change. Howell resigned in February 2000 and Fraser Morrison resumed the role of Managing Director. In August that year Morrison Construction accepted a £262m bid by AWG plc (ex Anglian Water). Housing development was not a core activity for the water company and Homes was reported to be for sale; there were no buyers, however, and the level of activity was substantially reduced.

[3] Group accounts, 1999.

MOSS
Peak units: c.500? (early 1930s)

Moss is another of the medium-sized inter-war housebuilders that appears to have faded away in the aftermath of the Second War, leaving little trace behind it. There were four Moss firms of which the first was N Moss & Son Builders, Tremorfa, Cardiff, which had been formed by Nathaniel Moss in the late 1890s. He was joined by his son, Frederick Moss, after service in the First War. The second, N Moss and Son, was incorporated in 1931 to acquire the business 'carried on by Nathaniel Moss at the City of Oxford under the style of N Moss & Son'; Frederick Moss was listed as the Managing Director. Moss Estates (Gloucester) was formed in 1939 to acquire from N Moss & Son a 1938 contract for the purchase of a farm in Hucclecote. Lastly, there was a Bridgwater Housing (N Moss & Son Ltd) but no more of this one is known.. These firms between them built over 3000 houses before the war.[1]

No records have survived for the Cardiff Moss but the Oxford firm has left traces and clearly was of substance; it may be that the business migrated from Wales to Oxford in search of better opportunities. It was already being described as 'well known' in 1932,[2] and again as a 'well known Oxford builder' in 1934 when it sold 367 houses to a property company.[3] In 1932 it was developing three estates with a total of 600 houses inside City boundaries, and another at Cowley for 300 houses. It had already sold over 800 houses.[4] For the period 1933 to 1936, the Companies House file lists the mortgages taken out on each individual house by the Bradford Third Equitable Building Society, presumably because Moss was providing guarantees under the Builders' Pool.[5] These total 343 for 1933 and 616 for 1934 before tailing off; the figures suggest a minimum level of sales but take no account of houses that were not recorded in the mortgage register.

Frederick Moss had been a member of the Committee of the National Federation of House Builders in the early 1930s and it must have been some recognition of his firm's position in the industry that he was appointed President of the House Builders Federation in 1946. Nathaniel Moss died at some point during the Second War and it appears that Frederick sold the Oxford firm in 1946; he and his wife had resigned in the May, and new directors were appointed. The firm turned into a commercial property company, passing through various owners, before finishing as a subsidiary of Friends Provident. Neither did the Gloucester firm appear to be active after the War. The Board of Trade queried whether it was carrying on a trade in 1949 and new directors appeared; it was liquidated in 1983 and the land distributed in specie. The explanation of the lack of interest in the UK lies in the formation of New Ideal Homesteads South Africa in 1948, when Frederick Moss joined the directors of Ideal and presumably emigrated permanently.

[1] *Housebuilder*, November 1949.
[2] *Oxford Monthly*, August 1932 p 6.
[3] *Housebuilder*, July 1934.
[4] *Oxford Monthly*, August 1932 p 6.
[5] Companies House No. 00256285.

MUCKLOW
Peak units: 7-800 (late 1960s)

A & J Mucklow & Co was founded by Albert Mucklow and his brother Jothan Mucklow in 1933, primarily as a building contractor and estate developer in the west midlands. From a slow start, the housing numbers had become substantial by the late 1930s. The company estimates that some 2000 private houses were built before the war and the present Chairman, Albert J Mucklow remembers his father (Jothan) saying that prior to the outbreak of war they were building around 1000 houses a year,[1] but this seems inconsistent with the overall pre-war numbers.

During the war and immediately after when housebuilding was restricted, the Company carried out earth-moving contracts and engaged in plant hire. With the exception of building 50 houses in 1947 and 1948, Mucklow did not restart housebuilding until late 1950. It concentrated on estate development in the west midlands until about 1959 when it started in south Lancashire. According to the 1962 Prospectus, Mucklow sold 2712 houses in the ten years to June 1961; the Prospectus gave the contemporary rate of sales at over 400 which would have made the company one of the larger midlands housebuilders at that time. There were large land holdings – some 350 acres with options over a further 300 acres. From an early stage, Mucklow had an interest in retaining residential investments, ground rents at first. An industrial estate company was formed in 1952, and property investment would gradually supersede speculative housebuilding. The first large factory estate was the Waterfall Lane Trading Estate at Old Hill in Staffordshire, which was part complete at the time of the flotation. By then, only Jothan of the two brothers was on the Board, as Chairman and Managing Director, with his two and Albert's two sons as well. All were described as builders though, in practice, none had any trade or professional qualifications other than one of the sons being a chartered secretary.

Through the 1960s and early 1970s, Mucklow averaged a fairly steady 500 house a year with one year in the late 1960s reaching a peak of 700-800. During that time, group profits had increased from £0.2m to £1.25m; however, only £0.4m of the 1973 profit came from housebuilding, with nearly all the rest coming from factory rentals. There was also a substantial residential portfolio: the 1974 accounts referred to Mucklow owning 500 rented flats and ground rents on 7000 flats. Having built up that residential portfolio, the policy was being changed in favour of its gradual realisation.

Housing profits, which were derived largely from the first-time buyer, held up reasonably well in the recession, with what land provisions there were being covered by profits on the sale of other land. However, the attitude to speculative housing development was becoming more cautious as the decade wore on: 'Because of the recurrent problems of the industry, and in view of our concentration on industrial property investment, it is most unlikely that our housebuilding activity will in the future be expanded much beyond present levels.'[2] The reality was that output was being gradually reduced and was down to 200 by 1980. There were further reductions in the first half of the 1980s and by the middle of the decade, the housebuilding division was doing little more than breakeven. A reorganisation followed and the emphasis of the division was moved up market. Helped by the boom, the division actually made some good profits on low volumes – £2.1m in 1989. Although the strength of Mucklow's low-cost land bank again kept housebuilding in the black during the 1990s recession, volumes were reduced yet further and in the mid 1990s the decision was taken to discontinue housebuilding and concentrate entirely on the development of industrial estates.

[1] Albert J Mucklow correspondence with author.
[2] Group Accounts, 1978.

NASH
Peak units: c.750-1000 (1930s)

Tommy Nash was originally a carpenter and probably worked as a tradesman in the early 1920s before forming TF Nash Construction in 1925. For a firm that was one of the larger London housebuilders of the inter-war period, little is known of how he started or what happened to the firm.

His first estate was at Kenton about 1925, 'where there is to-day a whole township of some 2000 houses and shops.'[1] Nash was active in the Harrow area in the 1920s, building much of Rayners Lane and 'more than 4000 houses in the Harrow District.'[2] He was described as 'possibly the largest builder in North-West London'[3] and 'arguably the largest in west London.'[4] Nash's 1933 sales brochure had one page headed 'eight years of progress' and it gives some indication of the scale of the firm. Apart from providing the invaluable information that 'close on 1000 houses are erected and sold in the course of the year', the firm's South Harrow and Rayners Lane estates permanently employed between 800 and 1000 men with a further 3000 to 4000 indirectly employed 'in the various trades.' The two estates described in the booklet cover an area of 320 acres and were planned for some 3500 houses.[5]

Nash was also a major shareholder in George Ball (Ruislip), a neighbouring firm consistently producing over 200 houses a year. Ball built one large estate in Ruislip of around 3300 houses and it was thought to have been responsible for around a quarter of all dwellings built in Ruislip between 1935 and 1939.[6] Nash also appears to have expanded geographically in the closing inter-war years: 'purchasing in 1937-38 large acreages at Collier Row (Romford), Hayes (Middlesex), Sevenoaks, Northolt and St Albans. Much of this ambitious enterprise, on sites often remote from public transport, was rudely interrupted by the outbreak of war.'[7]

What happened to Nash during and after the Second War remains a mystery. The Companies House records are marked as dissolved and destroyed;[8] no NHBC records survive; and none of the long-standing local housebuilders known to the author can provide assistance. The local paper faced the same problem: 'Observer historian Don Walter reviews the meteoric career of builder TF Nash, whose firm carpeted of vast tracts of Harrow with houses and assorted other buildings between the two world wars before both disappeared – apparently into oblivion. For all his high profile as a businessman, little or nothing seemed to have survived locally about Nash the man…it seems that World War II put an end not only to normal building work but also to Nash's truly meteoric career.'[9] His appeal for information was to no avail. The only response to a letter in the *Observer* this author received was from one resident who remembered an estate of police flats being built at North Harrow around 1949-50.

[1] "Nash houses" T F Nash Limited, c.1933; [there is a copy in Harrow Library of this small sales booklet].

[2] [Harrow] *Observer and Gazette*, 23rd February 1934.

[3] Morgan, *A History of the NHBC and Private Home Building*, pp.36-7.

[4] Interview Peter Prowting.

[5] *Nash houses*.

[6] Bundock, 'Speculative Housebuilding', p.317.

[7] Jackson, *Semi-Detached London*, p.107.

[8] No. 318061.

[9] *Harrow Observer*, 23rd April 1992.

NORTHERN DEVELOPMENTS
Peak units: c.4000 (1973)

For a brief period, Northern Developments became one of the largest housebuilders in the country, perhaps second only to Wimpey by 1974, before crashing spectacularly a couple of years later. The company was synonymous with Derek Barnes, often described as an ex-professional footballer with Blackburn, and a man of considerable personal charisma: 'I wasn't prepared for the personal charm and audacity of its young dynamo.'[1]

Derek Barnes was the archetypal self-made business man. He left school aged 15, and the next three years included spells as a boot boy with Blackburn Rovers, bricklaying, and a reported job as a junior surveyor with John Laing in London. Having saved most of his earnings, he returned to Blackburn aged 18 with £500 or £900 (depending on which reports you read) and bought his first land for £10 to build a single house. 'People said I didn't have enough money and didn't know how to build it. I wouldn't be able to sell it.'[2] Three years later, in 1959, Barnes incorporated Northern Developments.

Apart from Blackburn, Northern Developments' first sites were in Liverpool and Barrow, and over the next few years the Company expanded through Lancashire, Yorkshire, Cheshire and Warwickshire. The speed of its growth was such that when Northern came to float in 1968 (which it did in the same week as Greensitt & Barratt) it had to 'agree' a figure for the previous five years' profits with the Inland Revenue. By 1968, Northern was building at a rate of over 500 a year having quadrupled its turnover in two years; profits were £427,000 with a forecast of £600,000. Derek Barnes was still only 31 and although he had the older Thomas Calderbank as Managing Director, it was not for long; Calderbank largely confined himself to the Lake District where he lived. With a young and enthusiastic Board, it was Barnes who was the driving force throughout: 'He was a character who wasn't frightened of tomorrow; he used to do everything on the basis of today.'[3]

Largest housebuilder in the north west

Growth in the next four years was financed from retained funds and bank borrowings. The company stuck to its sector of the market, the low cost house for first time buyers. Although Northern Developments was the parent company, all the building and development was through its principal subsidiary GCT Construction (named after Gerald Conran Townsend who was the group's architect). Land acquisition often involved following in the footsteps of an old-established housebuilder, seeing what land was being negotiated, and then paying a premium to the farmer to secure the site in the knowledge that the investigation process had already been done. Turnover in 1971/72 reached £12m (against £2m in 1968); the company completed over 2600 houses selling off 50 sites in the north of England, Scotland and Northern Ireland.[4] Northern Developments had become the largest housebuilder in the north west and one of the larger companies in the country. There was also some commercial development activity with offices being built in Chester and Sheffield.

There followed two acquisitions, Daleholme and Kelly. Orme had made a contested bid for Daleholme (Holdings), formerly known as Bradley of York, in the February of 1972 but in the following month Orme sold its shares to Northern Developments, which then made an agreed offer for Daleholme,

---

[1] *Investors' Chronicle*, July 1970.

[2] Derek Barnes quoted in *Lancashire Evening Post*, June 1975.

[3] Unattributable interview.

[4] Daleholme offer document, April 1972.

valuing it at £4.1m – 19 times earnings. Daleholme operated mainly in Yorkshire, Lancashire and Scotland and was in a similar sector of the market to Northern Developments. In April 1972, Tony Kelly's housebuilding firm, J Kelly Homes (Stoke-on-Trent), was bought; it was warranting profits of £300,000 and had been considering its own flotation on a forecast of doubled profits. Tony Kelly joined the board and Kelly Homes was used to extend Northern Developments into the midlands. With Daleholme and Kelly Homes on board, the expectation was for housing sales of 3500 in 1972/73. In the event, turnover doubled to £24m and around 4000 houses were completed. Profits more than doubled to a record £7m but the balance sheet was showing the strain of the rapid growth; against an equity base of £11m, there was bank debt of £29m and land creditors of a further £9m.

A 40,000 land bank
Northern Developments claimed that it was developing residential estates in almost every major centre of population from Glasgow to Birmingham involving over 130 sites, with developments in progress in Plymouth and South Wales. As the housing market headed for its peak, Northern Developments had continued with the rapid expansion of its land bank and reported that it controlled land in excess of 35,000 units (a year later it was up to 40,000). The land bank was described as sufficient for three or four years at the current rate of expansion, suggesting that there were plans to increase output to some 10,000 houses a year. Northern Developments' registrations with the NHBC actually averaged 7000 a year in 1972 and 1973 but it seems unlikely that completions reached anything near that figure (registrations virtually ceased in 1974 and 1975 while a significant building programme continued).

Unfortunately, not all the land had appropriate planning permission and in the recession it was the value of undeveloped land that suffered most – there was nothing economic that could be done with it. Barnes had not believed that the rise in land values would come to an end: 'What Barnes did see early on was that the real profit in house building lay not in the building but in the land that it stood on….If you wish to expand rapidly you can generate a certain amount of your finance, but not all of it, from your own profits Barnes figured – and he was not alone in this – that if the money could be borrowed, the rise in the land value would eventually cover the debt and the interest and still leave him a profit.'[5] There was frenetic land buying in the early 1970s 'At the end, he was buying land without even seeing it half the time. Someone would ring him up with the offer of land on the telephone and he would ask 'who are you, where are you, what's your land, are there any roads near, any sewers near, is it flat, how much do you want for it, send me the details.'[6]

The secondary banking crisis
In January 1974, the secondary banking crisis impacted on Northern Developments. In a complicated transaction, the company had borrowed £1$\frac{1}{2}$m from Cornhill Consolidated and deposited bills of exchange; with Cornhill heading for liquidation, Northern had to write off the whole of the amount. Despite this, and the weakening of sales, Derek Barnes was still forecasting an increase in profits from £7m to £10m for the year to March 1974.[7] In the event, turnover did rise significantly, from £24m to £34m but Northern Developments declared a pre-tax loss of over £6m – 'last week's appalling preliminary announcement' as *Building* described it. The company would have made £7m profit but it needed to write off £8.7m from its land bank, £3.1m from work in progress and make a further general contingency provision of £1.5m. Barnes remained positive: 'Your company has undergone a thorough examination of all its operations which has confirmed the directors' view that the company is primarily

[5] *Building*, 25th Jan 1974.
[6] Unattributable interview.
[7] *Building*, 25th Jan 1974.

a victim of economic conditions and that its basic underlying strength remains.'

However, the banks did not share Barnes' optimism. Debt had risen to £41m against a reduced equity of only £6m. In July 1974, the directors and their new financial advisors, Slater Walker, made temporary arrangements with most of the group's bankers under which interest not paid would be 'rolled up.' In October 1974 these temporary arrangements were replaced by a formal agreement to 'roll up' interest. In the middle of this moratorium UDT unilaterally withdrew 16 of its joint sites overnight. 'They didn't tell anybody, and Price Brothers (Somerford) and Poco were given eight sites each. There was a horrendous situation. Poco went on all the sites over the weekend, pulled all the GCT boards down, put all the Poco boards up, and our men went in on the Monday morning to be faced by the Poco men – there were fights, there were bonfires as each burnt the others boards.'[8]

Receivers appointed

In June 1975, receivers were appointed. The *Lancashire Evening Telegraph* cruelly recalled one of Barnes' statements made during an earlier abortive attempt to obtain a seat on the Blackburn Rovers Board: 'To be successful all big business must have an overdraft. Look at it this way – any expanding company must be in the red. If a business isn't making more money than the seven per cent an overdraft costs, then it may as well go out of business.' Northern Developments was attempting to agree the accounts for the year to March when the banks called in the receiver. An overall asset deficiency of £1.6m was reported and the auditors now found they were unable to satisfy themselves that 1974 gave a true and fair view. The receivers formed a new company, Pendle Homes, to continue the housebuilding activities of Northern Developments which was expected to build from 2000 to 2500 houses in the following twelve months on about 80 sites. The Pendle Homes board consisted of directors of Northern Developments, with the exception of Derek Barnes, and representatives of the receivers. In 1979 Poco Group acquired the remaining Pendle Homes sites.

Derek Barnes always claimed that the banks' action in calling in the receivers was premature. The first statement of affairs by the receivers, in June 1975, actually showed a £1.8m surplus; in the end, the Northern Developments creditors were paid in full and there was a nominal payment to shareholders in the early 1980s. In March 1977 Barnes announced that he was suing the company's bankers, Williams & Glyn 'for very substantial damages.' The action concerned the £1.5m loan (above). Bills of exchange to the value of £3m were, in fact, endorsed by Northern which were discounted by City Industrial when that company ran into trouble. It was Barnes' case that he should only have had to pay the first £1.5m until the court decided who was liable for the rest, claiming that he paid the whole sum on the advice of Williams & Glyn. However, 'The judge held that a bank is not liable to the shareholders of a company who suffer loss due to a depreciation in the value of their shares as a result of the bank giving advice to the company which might cause loss to it and which does result in loss to it…the judge [also] held that a bank overdraft or loan is repayable on demand unless it can be shown by the terms of the loan agreement or the nature of the business transaction it was to finance, that the loan …was intended to be available for a fixed period.'[9]

---

8 Unattributable interview.
9 Arora, Ann, 'Williams & Glyn's v Barnes – an overview', *The Company Lawyer,* Vol. 2, No1, 1981, pp. 23-25.

ORME
Peak units: 1357 (1973)

Orme Developments existed as an independent entity for less than a decade but it incorporated constituent companies with somewhat longer histories. Orme itself was nothing more than a holding company formed by two entrepreneurs with no previous involvement in housebuilding. Peter Whitfield and Bob Tanner had previously built up Clubman's Club which they sold to Mecca, becoming directors. Within a few months of the acquisition they had sold the whole of their holding in Mecca, generating significant City displeasure in the process. Still only 34 and 33 respectively, they then looked for a new opportunity. According to Orme's 1971 Prospectus, early in 1970 they had decided that 'there was scope for rationalisation and expansion in the construction industry, property development and allied activities.' Accordingly, they set about assembling a national housebuilding business. The first building block was the privately owned Bruce Fletcher of Leicester, purchased in January 1970, just before the float; two more housebuilders were bought in 1972, Tudor Jenkins and Norman Ashton, and there were failed bids for Drury and Daleholme.

Bruce Fletcher
The Fletcher family were old established housebuilders. Alfred Fletcher owned a brick factory near Bolton, extending his activities into housebuilding in the Lancashire area after World War I, with his son Roy in partnership. A wrongly addressed envelope led to Roy Fletcher being offered Ministry of Defence land near Shrewsbury in 1932 and that purchase was the forerunner of other land deals in Shropshire to the point where the head office was moved to Shrewsbury just before the Second War. Alfred's second marriage produced another son, Bruce, and after reading engineering at Cambridge he joined the family firm in the early 1950s. The age gap of over 20 years between the brothers did not make for a natural partnership and in 1953 the family established Bruce with his own company at Leicester. Alfred and Roy were also directors, with minority shareholdings. Roy Carter, originally a carpenter, became general manager.

By the early 1960s, Bruce Fletcher (Leicester) was building around 100-150 units a year and steadily increasing. However, Bruce Fletcher's health deteriorated and he made the decision to sell, moving to Brighton in 1967. Roy Carter was appointed Managing Director and became a significant minority shareholder; potential buyers thus had a management team. In 1969 Bruce Fletcher, by then living in Malta, resigned from the Board and the company was being looked over by a number of housebuilders, Northern Developments amongst them. In the event, Orme was the successful bidder and Fletcher was bought for £330,000 cash and 130,000 shares in Orme. Bruce Fletcher took all cash with Roy Carter taking most of the shares. Carter stayed on to run Fletcher and was the only other executive director of Orme on its flotation. Fletcher completed 400 units 1970/71 making pre-tax profits of over £400,000. The original Shropshire firm remains active.

Two quoted acquisitions
Tudor Jenkins [q.v.]was a successful, albeit small, quoted company based in South Wales, covering Cardiff, Bridgend and Pontypridd. It was acquired in January 1972 when the company was building around 300 houses a year. **Norman C Ashton** [q.v.] claimed to be one of the largest housebuilders in Yorkshire when it floated in 1964; it too was building around 300 houses a year when the company was bought by Orme in May 1972, although it had been less successful financially than Tudor Jenkins

Not long after the flotation, Roy Carter left the business and Denis Sleath took over as Managing Director with Rod Mitchell becoming the Fletcher Managing Director in 1974. Whitfield and Tanner's interest was in doing the deals, not with the minutiae of housebuilding: 'they would say "We've found this business in south Wales. We've bought most of it. We've done a deal with the management. Can you go down and see if its OK. I hope it is because we have already bought the shares off the directors." They used to turn up about once a month, maybe not that. We used to tell them what was going on. Rightly or wrongly they had confidence in us.[1] To give some idea of the pace of corporate activity in those formative years, in December 1971 Orme bought 31% of Drury for 100p a share only to lose out in a contested bid battle with Francis Parker. The following February, Orme acquired an 18% stake in Daleholme (Holdings) and announced an offer of 68p a share. The next month it sold its shares to Northern Developments which then bid 81p a share. These abortive deals netted Orme a profit of £411,000 – a handy addition to the £1.7m trading profit. There was also a proposal in 1974 to buy most of MP Kent's housebuilding assets but this was aborted as the market deteriorated.

The 1972/73 accounts showed the full effect of the acquisitions and a booming market. Completions totalled 1357; turnover £13m and pre-tax profits almost £3m. That was to prove the peak year for Orme: unit completions drifted down to around 1000 a year and profits declined every year until 1978 when it earned only £0.6m To its credit, Orme avoided the trading losses that afflicted many of its competitors in the recession but it had been deliberately financing a long land bank – over 8000 plots at one point: 'Profits over the last few years have suffered because of the need to finance the very large land bank which the Group has maintained in the belief that land will be very scarce as housebuilding activity improves.'[2] In the long term, of course, the Orme directors were correct; unfortunately, in the short term the firm was taken over.

The search for a buyer

Orme's departure from the public arena was no less colourful than its arrival. The Orme share price had fallen to nominal levels in the recession and Whitfield and Tanner had come close to seeing the value of their investment wiped out. When the market recovered, Whitfield and Tanner began to look for a purchaser. They began discussions with St Piran, a choice that was intensely unpopular with the executive team, who began to look for a white knight. When Comben made its approach it seemed the ideal solution but it precipitated a struggle.

The Comben offer document of August 1978 outlined the background. 'Over recent months we have had lengthy discussions with the Board of Orme and Orme's principal shareholders, Mr Whitfield and Mr Tanner, with the objective of making an offer for the entire share capital of Orme. On 21st July we indicated…that we would be willing to make an offer [of around 56p a share]…On 24th July we were advised that they alone had sold shares equivalent to approximately 22% of [Orme] to Saint Piran for 55p a share. As a further part of the arrangement three nominees of Piran were elected to the Board of Orme and at the same time Piran stated that it was not its intention to make an offer to the other shareholders of Orme.' Although St Piran was refusing to make a full offer to all shareholders, it had bought further shares in Orme, thereby triggering Rule 34 of the Takeover code; the Takeover Panel referred to 'a regrettable lack of care on the part of St Piran.' The Orme board had rejected the first formal offer by Comben but a small increase in price led to an Orme recommendation by majority; six directors had voted for acceptance (including Whitfield and Tanner who had sold most of their shares to St Piran) but the three St Piran director representatives (including the Orme Chairman) dissented.

---

[1] Interview with Rod Mitchell, Jan. 2000.
[2] Group Accounts, 1977.

PAGE-JOHNSON
Peak units: 1250-1500 (late 1960s)

Page-Johnson was developed into a substantial midlands housebuilder by 'Johnnie' Johnson, before being acquired by Bovis in 1971. Herbert Johnson had formed a small building business in 1903. He died in 1939 by which time his eldest son, Frank had joined the firm, incorporated in 1935 as Herbert Johnson (Builders). Victor ('Johnnie') Johnson, some eight years younger, joined the firm in 1944. There was no Page – that part of the name came from Page Street.

There is no indication of the size of the firm before the war, but it was probably very local. The prospectus showed that profits in the early 1950s were only nominal and Page-Johnson was probably typical of those entrepreneurial firms that prospered as controls were dismantled. As well as building for sale, Page-Johnson also built flats to retain as investments, and rental income from these accounted for around a fifth of the £200,000 profit being made when the company floated in 1960. Birmingham was the centre of the private housing business, but the company spread rapidly across the country in the 1960s – from Teeside down to Devon and Hampshire. Further afield, Page-Johnson built flats in Southern Rhodesia and developed in France and Australia.

Johnnie Johnson was an extrovert character: 'He wasn't a qualified architect but he was certainly a good designer. What he was good at was designing houses so they could be built fairly cheaply. Page-Johnson was also good at buying sites that other builders wouldn't touch – quarry bottoms, anything – we could do mountain sides and put houses on them.'[1] What Page-Johnson also had was Mike Robinson, appointed to the board in 1959, aged 32, as contracts manager. Mike Robinson went on to become Managing Director for Wilson Connolly, earning a reputation as one of the most successful post-war housebuilders. For Page-Johnson, he performed the role of an operational managing director, overseeing the UK expansion; by the end of the 1960s, the company was selling around 1250-1500 houses a year in fourteen counties and profits had reached £1m.

Mike Robinson's rigorous approach to the building process was a necessary complement to Johnson's style: 'Johnnie's idea of a board meeting was to roll up at about 5.30 as we were about to leave and get the drinks out. We never had a formal Board meeting all the time I was there; never had any minutes or anything like that. His idea of running a company was – he'd send us a pink 'un and he'd put on the top "I'm thinking of buying this site" and we had to put our replies on that piece of paper.'[2]

Although Johnnie Johnson had sons they were not active in the business and when Frank Sanderson of Bovis approached in 1972, a takeover was soon agreed – again, without too many formalities. 'Johnnie Johnson rang all the senior people to get to Castle Bromwich for a meeting "don't care what you are doing – get to the meeting" and people drove from all over the UK to Castle Bromwich to hear Johnnie recite "If" by Rudyard Kipling and walk out of the door. Then Frank Sanderson introduced Phil Warner and Ray Whatman. [Johnson] wasn't that old – he liked the finer things in life, he'd got to the fun stage, he'd got a boat, property in Australia, farms, an estate in Northumberland. And he got a hell of a price.'[3] Johnson stayed with Bovis for only a few months before leaving to form Escadale Properties, which changed its name to Page-Johnson Homes in 1987.

[1] Interview with John Swift, Nov.1998.
[2] Ibid.
[3] Interview with Bill Gair, Nov. 1998.

PERSIMMON
Peak units: 12,360 (2004)

Persimmon has been one of the success stories of the post-war housebuilding industry. Founded in 1972 by Duncan Davidson, it grew organically under his control to become one of the top ten housebuilders by the end of the 1980s; the takeover of Ideal Homes in 1996 and Beazer in 2001 helped Persimmon to become the largest volume housebuilder in the country in 2001. Few articles about Duncan Davidson omit the fact that he was the grandson of the 15th Duke of Norfolk and a pageboy at the Queen's coronation. He was educated at Ampleforth but left after O-levels: 'I was bored and it didn't help when they discovered I was running the school book.'[1] He signed up for a short service commission in the army, working first for two months as a site labourer on the Blackwall Tunnel – his first exposure to the building industry.

In 1963, after four years in the army, Duncan Davidson joined Wimpey. His brief spell on the Blackwall Tunnel had given him a taste for the building industry and 'I liked the idea of something practical rather than joining the City as a lot my friends were doing. Wimpey seemed to be offering the best opportunities and I joined them on their 18-month commercial training course. After a spell in Abadan as a project manager and then at Billingham, I saw a position advertised on the private housing side and applied for it.' Davidson spent three months there before deciding to form his own housebuilding company. 'I always wanted to be my own boss. I'm not very good in an organisation with people telling me what to do. Looking back, at the age of 24, I probably didn't have the skills that I should have had but I suppose I had the entrepreneurial ability.'[2]

Ryedale is Davidson's first company

Davidson formed Ryedale Homes, in Yorkshire, in 1965. His lineage might have suggested that capital was no problem but that was far from the case: Davidson started the Company with £10,000 capital, half borrowed from his mother and half from his then fiancée, Sarah. A distant cousin, the Hon. Simon Fraser also became in investor as Ryedale grew and needed more capital. One of the early recruits was Tony Fawcett: Davidson remembers joking that 'for the first month he was the joiner; the second month senior joiner; third month site agent; fourth month project manager; and after five months deputy managing director.' He was to be a key partner of Davidson's at Ryedale and again at Persimmon. By 1972, Ryedale was building around 300 houses a year when it was sold to Comben for £600,000. 'Trading had been tough in 1969/70 and when the market picked up in 1971 we thought that if we got a decent offer, we were highly geared, we would sell and start again.'[3] It also gave Davidson the opportunity to liberate surplus cash for the first time.

As was intended, Persimmon was then formed – for those who are curious as to the origin of names: 'We looked at a list of company names in the solicitor's office, they were all boring and then we saw Persimmon, which had been a Derby winner, and we said, that's it.'. This time, Davidson's company was better capitalised and Duncan and Sarah Davidson controlled all the equity between them. The first sites were actually in Durham (through the Aztec Homes subsidiary) and it was not until 1974 that Persimmon started buying sites in York, the Company's base. In effect, Davidson was restarting his business at the onset of the worst housing recession since the War. 'I remember thinking it was lucky we sold Ryedale in 1972.'[4]

---

[1] Interview with Duncan Davidson, Jan. 2002.

[2] Ibid.

[3] Ibid.

[4] Ibid.

The regional network starts in East Anglia

The first step in the creation of a regional network was the formation of Persimmon (Anglia) in 1976. Gray Dawes, early bankers to Persimmon, had a client housebuilder in difficulty and asked Davidson to manage it out for him. Alf Castleton, ex-Comben, was recruited and established Anglia as Persimmon's first region. This was followed by the first midlands company in 1979, notable for the recruitment of John White, later to become Chief Executive, and, also in the same year, the south west. By 1980, Persimmon's output had risen to 300 units; that there were already four regions indicated that Persimmon was laying down the structure for long term growth well in advance.

By 1985, volumes had broken through the 1000 level. As well as growth in the existing companies, new subsidiaries had been established in Wessex (1984) and the north east (1985). Moreover, Duncan Davidson had once again teamed up with Tony Fawcett. After leaving Barratt, Fawcett had started Sketchmead in 1979. By 1984, Sketchmead was selling at a rate of 200 a year and making inroads into Persimmon's home market. In June 1984, Persimmon acquired Sketchmead, and Fawcett once again became Davidson's deputy Managing Director and a 29% shareholder. In March 1985, Persimmon was floated, after the demerger of Davidson's Northumberland estate. The second half of the 1980s was, as for other housebuilders, a period of rapidly rising profitability. The time was used to increase the regional structure, Scotland (1986), the north west (1987) and Thames Valley (1988) in particular; there had also been a modest return to the south east in 1987 after the East Anglian company had made a brief incursion in the early 1980s. Davidson's approach to opening new regions was clear cut and was never done merely for the sake of being in new area. Either he sought out the man he wanted to run it – as with John Millar who started the Scottish company – or he had acquired a strategic site, as in the south west. Most of today's senior operational directors started new regions either in the late 1970s or the 1980s.

John White partners Duncan Davidson

Unit sales broke through the 2000 level in 1988 and profits peaked in the following year at £33m, compared with under £1m at the beginning of the decade. The recession necessitated little in the way of land write-offs but, by 1992, profits were down to £10m, on slightly higher volumes. Profit margins were not going to recover to the excessive levels of the late 1980s, and Davidson recognised that 'Persimmon's future growth in profits…will require us to increase the number of homes that we sell.'[5] A volume target of 4000 units was set and, to cope with this, the management structure was changed at the beginning of 1993. Tony Fawcett had died suddenly in 1990, aged 50 and his role had not been filled immediately. However, John White was now appointed group Chief Executive with Duncan Davidson continuing as Executive Chairman. John White had come up through the industry from grass roots. He left school before completing his 'O' levels to become an apprentice bricklayer, went on to study site management and then worked at Wilcon before joining Persimmon in 1979. The 14 operating companies were controlled by four Regional Chairmen: Mike Allen, who had joined in 1976, John Millar (1986), Mike Farley (1983) and David Bryant (1985).

The Ideal acquisition

By 1995, volumes reached 3600, not far short of the volume target, although profits had only staged a partial recovery. However, at the end of that year, a major opportunity had presented itself. Persimmon's weak area geographically had long been the south east and for some time approaches had been made to Trafalgar House (by then controlled by HongKong Land) about the possible purchase of its housebuilding subsidiary, Ideal Homes. In December 1995 Persimmon was invited to make an offer for

---

5 Group accounts, 1992.

Ideal and in the following February it completed the acquisition at a cost of £176m, little more than net asset value; roughly half the price was paid in cash. Despite itself having acquired two top ten housebuilders in the 1980s, Ideal had declined to be twelfth largest housebuilder with sales of 2644 units in 1995. Although Ideal's operating margins were higher than Persimmon's, its overhead structure was heavy. Ideal's head office and six regional offices were closed and 200 staff left; during the year after the acquisition, rationalisation of land and work in progress enabled Persimmon to reduce debt by £100m. Persimmon was now building over 6000 units a year and was the fourth largest housebuilder. After the consolidation of Ideal, there was further modest growth in volumes, to 7000 a year by the end of the decade. The occasional new subsidiary was formed; others subdivided, and Scotland strengthened by the acquisition of the Scottish businesses of Laing Homes in 1988 and Tilbury Douglas Homes in February 2000. More important, the group's trading margins were recovering and in year 2000, profits exceeded £100m for the first time.

Persimmon recognised that if it wished to achieve significantly higher volumes it had to adapt its organisation to cope with the managerial strains. The 1999 Chairman's statement laid out the new structure. 'The time has now come for us to implement our strategic plans for the continued organic growth of our business…we are therefore splitting our operations into two new Divisions, Persimmon Homes South led by Mike Farley, and Persimmon Homes North led by John Millar. Each Division will consist of ten of our existing operating companies …These two new Divisions, combined with the strength of our existing land bank, place Persimmon in a very strong position to grow our market share.' In effect, it gave Persimmon three managing directors. One of the problems housebuilders face with increasing size is the cost of additional layers of management. Davidson was adamant that Persimmon had avoided this: 'The Divisions were introduced without the addition of any extra people; there was not another layer of bureaucracy.'[6]

Housing units, 1980-2004

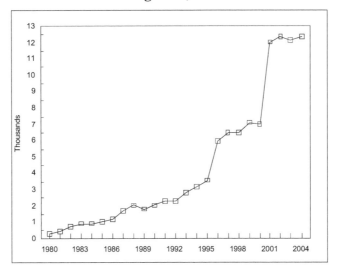

Beazer acquisition takes Persimmon to number one
No sooner was the new structure in place than a fresh opportunity presented itself. In November 2000 Bryant and Beazer announced their 'merger of equals.' To the outside world, neither party was merging

6 Interview Duncan Davidson.

from strength and, in the terminology of the City, they put themselves in play. When Taylor Woodrow announced its bid for Bryant the merger plan was destroyed and Persimmon followed by making its £612m bid for Beazer, completed in February 2001. Beazer was actually slightly larger than Persimmon in volumes – some 8000 plus, albeit around 1000 of these were social housing units; profits of £94m reflected lower operating margins. Persimmon set about integrating Beazer with the same enthusiasm as Ideal. Coincidentally, John Low had been Managing Director of both acquisitions and he left for a second time. Beazer's partnership housing business and its Torwood timber frame factory were sold in October 2001 for £5m. Twelve regional offices were closed and staff reduced by 660. Integration costs were put at £13m and some £33m of annual administration and procurement costs were identified.

Persimmon now had its North and South divisions, the upmarket Charles Church which had also come in with Beazer and the relatively new City Developments, in all, some 30 operating companies. It was building in excess of 12,000 houses a year and, albeit briefly, became the country's largest housebuilder by volume in 2001. The period following the Beazer acquisition was one of consolidation; volumes changed little but operating margins rose from 15% to 23% and pre-tax profits from £175m in 2001 to £470m in 2004. In November 2005 Persimmon announced an agreed bid for Westbury, itself a top ten housebuilder. The combination of the two firms was forecast to produce 16,700 completions in 2006, taking Persimmon back again to number one by volume; if achieved, it would also be the largest volume ever achieved by a British housebuilder, just edging ahead of the 16,500 achieved by Barratt in 1983. Duncan Davidson retired from Persimmon in April 2006, by which time the company he founded had become the first pure housebuilder to enter the FT 100 index.

POCO PROPERTIES
Peak units: 907 (1983)

Poco Properties was a Lancashire-based housebuilder controlled by John Hindle and Roy Dixon. Hindle's father, John Hindle senior, was a property dealer and had formed Poco Properties in 1963. Roy Dixon had joined his father's law practice in 1955 and by the mid 1960s was doing an increasing amount of work for John Hindle Senior and Poco. The first site was at Waddington, near Clitheroe but, before long, Roy Dixon became more closely involved, providing development finance for a site in Barrowford. John Hindle junior returned to the business in 1965, after the Tokyo Olympics where he had played hockey for Britain. John Hindle junior gradually took over the Poco operation, dealing in land and building up to 20 houses a year. The first joint venture between Hindle and Dixon was actually Drindle Properties Limited but, in 1971, Roy Dixon left his law firm and joined forces with John Hindle junior as equal partner in Poco Properties; at the same time Paul Turner joined them as Finance Director.

Almost immediately they made their the first big move with the acquisition of Greenside in August 1971 for £1m cash. It was a fortuitous introduction: 'I met a man on a plane who said Greenside was for sale; I had known Ronnie Williams all my working life. Old Broad Street Securities were very aggressive lenders at that time and they made us an offer of finance with 14 conditions which they thought were unfulfillable but we satisfied them and a fortnight later we told them we had signed the contract. That was really the beginning of it and we just grew from then.'[1] Almost immediately afterwards Poco acquired the Manchester builder, Eric Mercer, whose main asset was one site at Tollemache for about hundred houses.

The organisation was very self-contained. John Hindle bought land and organised the construction, making up in energy and enthusiasm for any lack of direct experience of the building process. Roy Dixon arranged the planning and sales; Paul Turner looked after the finances; and Eric Mercer had returned to look after construction and establish a division in the Bournemouth area. By 1973, Poco was building around 200 houses a year but it had little in the way of reserves to meet the recession; it managed to avoid declaring losses in 1974 by the simple expedient of extending the trading period to 24 months, by the end of which it recorded a £10,000 profit.

Poco still had good access to finance and it took another step forward at the expense of Northern Developments which, from the middle of 1974, was operating under a banking moratorium. In February 1975 UDT unilaterally withdrew 16 of its joint sites overnight, and eight of these were allocated to Poco.[2] Northern Developments' failure also provided Poco with additional key staff, including Jack Kennedy who took charge of sales. By the end of the 1970s, the build rate was up to 500 and profits were in excess of £1m. At the end of 1979, Poco bought a further 11 sites for in excess of £2.75m, this time from Pendle Homes who had purchased them from the receivers of the Northern Developments Group. When Pendle Homes had disposed of all the properties it had bought, Malcolm Kershaw joined Poco as its Managing Director.

In 1983, in its most public move to date, Poco bought 7% of the much larger Leech but later sold the stake on to Beazer which made a successful bid. Poco also appeared again on the public scene when it acquired, for a nominal one pound, 79% of Milbury from Jim Raper's St Piran. Prior to the transaction, Raper had transferred Milbury Homes (South) and the Westminster Property Group to St Piran,

---

[1] Interview with Roy Dixon, Aug. 2001.
[2] See Northern Developments for a description of the ensuing chaos.

transactions which led to a DTI inquiry. Unable to get the banks to agree to a rescue, Poco sought a liquidator for Milbury Homes (North) and subsequently bought its sites from the Receivers.

The Milbury transaction was the last major deal done by Poco. In 1986, it was approached by Walter Lawrence; Poco was then building around 900 units a year and profits in the year to July had reached £2.3m. There had been no intention to sell the business but 'We were offered too much for it. John and I were getting tired and it seemed just the time to do it. We had thought "if you pay double what is worth then you can have it".'[3] In September 1986, Poco Properties was sold to Walter Lawrence for £22m. Its net assets were £11.8m and it was forecasting profits of £3.6m, slightly more than Walter Lawrence.

[3] Interview Roy Dixon.

PROWTING
Peak units: 1718 (1998)

Arthur Prowting commenced his apprenticeship as a carpenter with EA Bance, a Newbury firm of builders, in 1901 aged 14. 'At that time I thought I would like to be a school master but my parents thought otherwise, promising me a bicycle if I would be apprenticed to the building trade.'[1] On completion of his apprenticeship he remained with Bance for four months before moving to London. In 1911, a firm of builders in Ruislip went into liquidation and Arthur Prowting took over the business, presumably for little or no investment. His first venture into property was in 1912 when he bought a piece of land in Ruislip for £600; he built two houses, sold one for £750 and lived in the other.[2]

Arthur Prowting had a simple, but effective, finance model: 'From the start I was most fortunate having no difficulty in obtaining credit from my merchants whose accounts were paid promptly and at that time my cash discounts paid my overheads.' His building work through and after World War I must have been reasonably profitable, for in 1920 Prowting made an important commercial purchase, buying 'the whole of the east side of Ruislip High Street for forty five shillings per foot frontage.' In 1922 he was elected a member of Ruislip-Northwood council and was able to persuade the council to rename the West End Road as the High Street. Land was then sold on at £10 a foot and later at £100.[3] AEA Prowting Limited was formed in 1928, just surviving 'a serious temporary cash flow problem' in 1930. His son Peter remembers having to move house: 'Although he didn't say anything, money was gradually running out and he had to retreat.'[4] Business recovered as the 1930s progressed and the firm was building regularly for the Ministry of Works and for the brewing industry. However, residential development was very limited and Prowting does not appear to have engaged in the large site development typical of the period – a few semi-detached houses at Northwood Hills and detached houses in Ruislip.

Peter Prowting joins the firm

Construction opportunities in the Second War were largely ignored and an army camp in Northumberland was about the only contract the firm took: 'unfortunately, rather than expand, he went back into his shell.'[5] At the end of the war the firm had no more than half a dozen staff: it was left to Arthur's son Peter to create the modern Prowting company. Peter Prowting matriculated from Frays College Uxbridge in 1941, wanting to be a jazz musician rather than a builder. After a spell in a local insurance company he was called up in 1943 and went on a two-year training course with the newly formed Royal Electrical & Mechanical Engineers before being directed to Holland Hannen & Cubitts. It was not until 1948 that he was released from there and joined his father's firm, now taking on more men to do war damage work and local jobbing building.

Their working partnership was not a great success: he clashed with his father and bought a business in Windsor, H Burfoot and Son; Burfoot was sold in 1952 and Peter Prowting moved back to the family firm which, by that time, was building individual houses under licence. Peter Prowting found himself attracted to private housebuilding: in contrast to contract building, it gave him control over the building process without being 'messed about by the architect.' Even so, private housing remained on the most

[1] Prowting, A.E.A., *The East Woodhay Boy who made Good,* unpublished one page memoir, c1971.
[2] Anon,*75 A Family Affair A Brief History of Prowting.*
[3] Ibid.
[4] Interview with Peter Prowting, Dec. 2000.
[5] Ibid.

modest scale when the firm received what Peter Prowting described as 'a lucky approach.'[6]

Another local builder, AV Low, had been buying land from Kings College Cambridge before the war but did not return to the market afterwards. Their architect, Jack Drake and a local estate agent, Arthur North, had then been offered the opportunity of buying a 70-acre tract at Copse Wood, Northwood and approached Prowting as a potential building partner. The proposition appealed personally to Peter Prowting and he mortgaged his house to purchase his 25% of Copse Wood Northwood Estates (the final 25% being taken by a solicitor). Although separate from AEA Prowting Limited, this was Peter Prowting's first large-scale housing development and the one which gave him the confidence to take the family firm down that route. With Arthur North's encouragement, Copse Wood Northwood Estates moved into commercial development, did no more private housing, eventually becoming County and Suburban Investments, a company which re-enters the Prowting story at a later date.

Land acquisitions

In 1953 Arthur Prowting retired and Peter Prowting took over as Managing Director taking the firm into even larger estates than Copse Wood. An early move (1956) was the acquisition of **Leslie Bilsby** which led to Prowting developing the Priory estate at Blackheath. However, the largest volume of land came on the south coast. Peter Prowting was a regular golfing partner of Ernest Burrows, then Chairman of YJ Lovell which had been acquiring options on land along the south coast. 'Ernest decided that he didn't want to develop the Kings Beach Estate in Bognor – 100 acres – and he sold it to me on the drip, and we put over a thousand houses on that site. From there, having established ourselves in that area, I bought 125 acres from Joseph Rank Senior[7] in 1964 and we put up another thousand units. I then did a deal with Jack Webb of Alliance Property on the Beaumont Park Estate, Littlehampton which was another thousand units. In all, we did three thousand units over a period of years along that stretch of coast. Whilst that was happening we were also developing other schemes between Banbury and the south coast. I was helped along the south coast because my father retired there and became a Worthing Borough Councillor and he introduced me to one or two useful agents.'[8]

By the mid 1960s, Prowting was building around 600 houses a year. Peter Prowting was backed by two key people who had joined some ten years earlier, just as the company was starting its large estates – Les Eteson and Tom Whitting in 1955 and 1956 as surveyor and estimator respectively, both later going on to the Board. Eteson was made joint Managing Director along with Peter Prowting around 1960, and the development of the firm owes much to Eteson and Whitting. The division of responsibilities had them handling design and production; Peter Prowting acquired the land and took the responsibility for sales although he regarded himself as more successful at the former and, looking back, views Prowting as having been land driven. By 1973, Prowting was earning record profits of £1.6m and the firm was broadening its horizons. There was an investment in the Turks and Caicos Islands, largely unsuccessful, and property investments back in the UK. Prowting disposed of its own properties to County and Suburban Holdings in exchange for 33% of the shares, then bought a 29.8% holding in Estates & General Investments, a listed property company, for £493,000. Four years later, Estates and General bought the whole of the capital of County and Suburban (see above), raising Prowting's interest in Estates to 37%.

However, the recession was beginning to bite, and by 1976 the company was losing money. The recovery

---

[6] Ibid.

[7] The brother of J Arthur Rank.

[8] Interview Peter Prowting.

was slow and it was not until 1979 that Prowting exceeded the 1973 profits record; housing volumes were only around 400 a year compared with 600 a decade earlier. One important acquisition had been made, in 1977, of **Alford Brothers.** a west-country housebuilder operating in Somerset, Devon and Dorset. Despite the Alford acquisition and the growth in the private housing market, Prowting's volumes remained around 500 a year until the mid 1980s. Looking back in his 1983 annual report at the ten years since the crash, Peter Prowting wrote: 'One of the lessons our Company learned as a result of coming through the above period is that big is not necessarily beautiful and to this end we have pursued a policy of moving away from a vertically integrated administration to give individuals with talent the opportunity of managing their own autonomous sections of the group within the various regions in which we operate.' But there were other reasons why Prowting had not grown.

Diversification failures

Peter Prowting is quite clear that the mainstream business suffered from the group's attempts at diversifying: 'I was getting involved in other things; I wasn't driving the business. In those days conglomerates were the flavour of the month. We bought a Ford main dealer in Croydon; a sock factory in the midlands; a coal mine; I set up a swimming-pool contracting company; we bought a builders merchants in Hereford and Wellington.'[9] Almost all these had been sold by the late 1980s. Prowting also ventured overseas again, buying a block of 198 apartments for refurbishment in Virginia which they hoped would be 'the forerunner of a substantial operation in the USA in due course.' It was not to be.

In 1986, Les Eteson retired after 31 years. Terry Roydon had joined in 1985 following the takeover of Comben, to work alongside Eteson as joint Managing Director before becoming Managing Director under Peter Prowting's chairmanship. Roydon had built Comben into a national housebuilder and he began to expand Prowting's volumes which soon broke through 700 a year; profits peaked at £22m in 1989. The company also took on a more visible profile in the City with a flotation in May 1988. However, with the family still controlling nearly all the equity, Prowting retained the ethos of a private company, as was seen in its attitude to the 1990 recession when volumes were immediately cut back to around 300 a year to conserve the land bank. This was a marked contrast to some of the larger housebuilders who deliberately increased volumes during the early 1990s to trade their way out of the recession.

Acquisitions and management changes

Prowting remained profitable at a trading level, no mean achievement for a purely southern business, although enthusiastic provisioning against land values (some £27m) meant substantial pre-tax losses in 1992 and 1993. Nevertheless, this preceded another period of radical change within the group. In September 1993, Terry Roydon negotiated the acquisition of **Galliford Estates** for £23m in shares and cash. Galliford, which the management had bought from Sears only months before, was building in excess of 500 houses a year and in the first full year of the enlarged group, unit sales reached a new record of 1150. Galliford also brought its Managing Director, David Brill, who became Managing Director of Prowting responsible for operational matters, Terry Roydon becoming Chief Executive concentrating on the strategic development of the group. Galliford formed one of the three principal regions (and trading names) for Prowting, operating from Banstead, Surrey (it also had an office in Worcester); Prowting continued at Ruislip and Alford covered the west of England from Taunton.

There were further acquisitions, the most important being, in early 1997, the west country firm of **Magnus Holdings** for £13m. As well as building some 400 houses in its last year, Magnus also brought with it £22m of tax losses. The much smaller acquisition of **Caspian Homes** the following year gave

---

[9] Ibid.

Prowting a limited exposure to East Anglia. These helped, group volumes reach a new record of 1700 units in 1998 although it was not until 2000 that Prowting managed to exceed its 1989 profits peak. The old trading names of Alford and Galliford were dropped in favour of a universal Prowting name and the midlands regions of Magnus and Prowting were amalgamated.

The end of the decade saw further significant management changes. David Brill became non-executive in 1996 to be replaced as Managing Director by Stephen Rosier, previously of CALA and Alfred McAlpine. Terry Roydon resigned as Chief Executive at the end of 1998 and Peter Prowting retired in 2000 to be replaced as Chairman by Richard Fraser, fresh from resolving AMEC's problems with Fairclough Homes. Despite Peter Prowting's retirement, however, the family still controlled 62% of the company – the last of the large quoted housebuilders to be more than 50% family controlled. In February 2002, Prowting issued a profit warning, accompanied by the resignation of its Chief Executive and Finance Director. The outcome for the year to February 2002 was to be profits of £3.7m compared with £27.5m the previous year. Richard Fraser took over the day-to-day running of the company but it was only a matter of time before a bid came. In May 2002, the Prowting family accepted a an offer from Westbury, valuing the company at £141m.

RAINE/HASSALL
Peak units: 3458 (1995)

Hassall Homes was the speculative housing arm of the one-time engineering company, Raine, later becoming the dominant part of the group. After a reverse takeover in 1986, Raine became acquisition driven until, in the end, it reached too far and itself fell to Alfred McAlpine. Raine was incorporated as the Empire Rib Company in 1946 to acquire the umbrella business ('Fox') of its predecessor company from the liquidator; the company was floated on the stock market in 1961. In 1964, the company acquired Raine & Co, changing its name to Raine Engineering. Raine itself had incorporated in 1957 to acquire the undertaking of the business of steel re-rollers carried on by its predecessor company of the same name on north Tyneside since the late nineteenth century..

Acquisition of Hassall

Raine remained an engineering and umbrella business until 1975 when, seeking diversification, it bought the Sheffield housebuilder **P Hassall**. Hassall had been formed in 1945 by Percy Hassall, a general tradesman, and, with the help of his step-father, Fred Hoole, ran a jobbing building business in south Sheffield where a number of small infill housing sites were developed. In the mid 1950s, Percy was joined by his brother John, then working in hospital administration. John was more committed to acquiring a land bank and the company was successful with several of its land options. By the early 1970s, Hassall was building around 300 houses a year in south Yorkshire and north Derbyshire. At that point, 'Percy took the view that the future for the small local housebuilder did not look too rosy.'[1] Hassall's legal advisor, Michael Taylor, was also Chairman of Raine. He saw the opportunity for Raine to diversify into a more successful business and one with which he was familiar. Hassall was acquired in a cash deal; Percy Hassall retired and John left to form his own business. Graham Thorpe was promoted to Hassall Managing Director and joined the Raine main board. Thorpe had started with Hassall in 1965 as a quantity surveyor, later becoming technical director and he began to expand the new housing side of Raine.

In 1976, **Parkin (Rotherham)** was acquired; it was a well established Rotherham business founded by Oswald Parkin: this was a key acquisition for Hassall. Graham Thorpe explained: 'Parkin had considerable land interests in the Rotherham area through the Duke of Norfolk's estates and the Sitwell estates. Oswald had established an excellent rapport with the estates people over the years and he introduced me to their land agents and that relationship continued.'[2] Parkin provided an excellent land base in the south Yorkshire region and was building around 50 to 70 houses a year, with the potential for much larger volumes. Other small acquisitions gave Hassall toeholds outside its south Yorkshire base. **General Housing (Derby)** in 1981 took Hassall into the east midlands area (reinforced by Derbyshire Builders in 1985), and **Basterfield Kinver** in 1984 provided a base for the west midlands. By the mid 1980s, Hassall was building as far south as Northampton and Worcester and north to Wetherby; however, despite the increased regional spread, overall volumes had grown only slowly, to just short of 400 a year, although profits had doubled from the £400,000 being earned at the time of Hassall's acquisition.

Acquisition of Miller Wheeldon brings in Peter Parkin

Raine's decision to diversify into housebuilding was justified: in 1978 the steel subsidiary began to lose money and for several years housebuilding made most, or even more than all, of the group's profits. 'By

---

[1] Interview with Graham Thorpe, April 2001.

[2] Ibid.

1985, Raine looked distinctly vulnerable.'[3] Neepsend, another local engineering company had sold its 29.9% shareholding and David Abell's acquisitive Suter Industries acquired a strategic holding. Talks were held with a number of companies before Raine was introduced to **Miller Wheeldon**, a Derby based company run by Peter Wheeldon Parkin.[4] Miller Wheeldon, which was building around 100 houses in the year it was bought, had itself been the product of a merger only the year before. JF Miller was a commercial property and housing developer with substantial land holdings, which had been inherited by John Gould from his father. Wheeldon Brothers was a small firm of contractors which had been formed by two brothers in 1867. It was still a small builder when it was bought in 1972 by Peter Parkin, then a 25 year old quantity surveyor. Miller did none of its own construction work, principally using Wheeldon to build its houses; Wheeldon also built a few houses on its own account.

When the proposal to merge Raine and Miller Wheeldon was raised with Nigel Rudd,[5] a friend of Gould, he offered to contribute his company, **C Price & Co.**, a cash shell. Peter Parkin, who became Miller Wheeldon's Managing Director, viewed the three businesses as offering considerable synergy: 'I've got Nigel's money, John's assets, and my building company: two plus two should make five.'[6] Miller Wheeldon was bought in August 1986 but in effect it was a reverse takeover: Raine's Michael Taylor stood down after 21 years; Nigel Rudd replaced him as Executive Chairman; Peter Parkin became Managing Director; and Miller's John Gould, Deputy Chairman. Graham Thorpe remained Managing Director of housing, although he stepped down from the main board a couple of years later.

An aggressive takeover strategy
The first move of Raine's new management's was ambitious, an abortive bid for Tilbury. Raine was more successful in the summer of 1987 buying two privately owned housebuilders, **Millard Holdings**, based in Dudley, building around 100-150 houses a year and **John Twiname** in west Cumbria, building some 200-250 houses. Both of these were retirement sales – Gordon Morrison in the case of Millard, and Alex Twiname. An important diversification also came that year with the acquisition of the Ford & Weston group of shopfitting companies. However, it was in the October that Raine made the acquisition which lifted it into a different league – **Aberdeen Construction**, a quarrying, contracting and housing group which included Eagle Homes and the Hall & Tawse partnership housing business. A few months later, Raine sold Aberdeen's quarrying interests to Evered and in return took in their housing subsidiaries, Fletcher Homes of Stoke-on Trent, West & Sons in Leeds and Fisher on Tyneside – a housing for quarries asset swap (or homes for holes as it was popularly called). The Evered companies were then building around 800 units a year, and after some rationalisation the enlarged Hassall built some 1300 units in 1988. Raine also sold Aberdeen's property portfolio for £41m: 'In effect, we got Hall & Tawse for free.'[7] Another unsuccessful takeover bid was made in 1988, this time a £133m offer for Ruberoid. The 'non-strategic subsidiaries' were sold that year finally converting Raine into a broadly based construction group – private housing, social housing, construction and shopfitting. Turnover was £210m and group profits touched £13.5m compared with £874,000 two years previous. The Hall & Tawse partnership housing was managed within the construction division and it became one of the leaders in its field, second only to Lovell. It was selling around 400 units a year when acquired but by the mid-1990s this had been increased to around 1600 units.

[3] *Housebuilder*, Nov 1990.
[4] Parkin's Wheeldon middle name was pure co-incidence; neither did Peter Parkin have any connection with Parkin (Rotherham).
[5] Best known as Executive Chairman of Williams Holdings.
[6] Interview with Peter Parkin, May 2001.
[7] Ibid.

By 1989, as the housing recession began to bite in the south east, Peter Parkin was becoming more cautious: 'We stopped buying land in January. What I want to do is to run our borrowing down to zero by the end of the year.'[8] The only acquisition that year was the recommended offer for Plumb Holdings in May, substantially enlarging Raine's shopfitting business, but that was soon to become a drain on resources. By the 1990 financial year, group turnover had reached £400m and profits peaked at £25m. Profits inevitably suffered as the recession started to affect all areas of the group but the housing results held up better than most in the industry – having reached a peak of £14.4m in the year to June 1989 (including Hall & Tawse) they fell only to £10.3m in 1993. However, in March 1992 Raine had made the acquisition which probably cost it its independence – the heavily indebted **Walter Lawrence**, which had itself taken over Poco Homes in the late 1980s. Raine thought it had the timing of Walter Lawrence right as the Conservatives had just been re-elected and he believed that the recovery was on the way.

Losses in the USA

Lawrence had within it a Californian subsidiary, West Ventures, with around $70-80m tied up, about half Lawrence's assets. It had never been Parkin's intention to keep the US business: 'We flew out there and instructed merchant bankers. We were actually discussing the sale when Lamont announced that we were withdrawing from the exchange rate mechanism. I had dinner that night with the Wells Fargo Chairman trying to put to bed the deal with our potential purchaser and all he could talk about was that the British had suspended trade in the pound.' Then the local market got progressively worse. West Ventures built around the Antelope Valley, home of McDonnell Douglas which was suffering the short-term consequences of the 'peace dividend' and the problems were compounded by the Northridge earthquake in January 1994. 'And then we couldn't sell the American assets; they became almost unsaleable at any price.'[9]

Back in the UK, although private housing was holding up well, the downturn in consumer spending substantially reduced the amount of shop refitting work available and Plumb's profits collapsed. It was the announcement of the December 1994 interim results that revealed the full scale of the problems, not the least of which was that the banking covenants were likely to be breached. In May 1995 Peter Parkin resigned as Chairman and Roy Barber, one-time Finance Director of AMEC and latterly a company doctor, was appointed non-executive Chairman the following April. Graham Thorpe, still Managing Director of private housing, was appointed back to the main board along with a new finance director. Non-core businesses, including the heavily loss-making shopfitting, were put up for sale; US housing was to be liquidated. (Ironically, no buyer was found for shopfitting and it had to be closed whereas a buyer, the US housebuilder Lennar, was found for West Ventures).[10] Roy Barber took over full executive responsibility and under his contract he was entitled to a £400,000 success fee if Raine was taken over; if he restructured the facility agreements to enable Raine to carry on as a going concern; 'or any other reasonable event.'

Raine announced it was to sell or close all its businesses except Hassall Homes and contractor Hall & Tawse. The full annual results published in November 1995 disclosed a group loss after exceptional charges of £102m. It was then announced that even the southern region of Hassall Homes was to be sold due to the high cost of replacing its depleted land bank. The group managed to return to break even in 1995/96 and executive control was transferred back to David Vincent in December 1996. However, the share price continued to languish and in May 1997 the company accepted a £44m bid from Alfred McAlpine. As a postscript, in January 2000, McAlpine announced that it was closing the partnership housing business.

---

8 *Building*, 23rd June 1989.
9 Interview Peter Parkin.
10 The deal was completed by McAlpine after it bought Raine.

RAWLINGS BROS
Peak units: 240 (1990)

Rawlings was founded in 1886 by JJ and WR Rawlings in the Brompton Road London. The business was mainly that of sanitary and electrical engineering; William Rawlings founded the Electrical Contractors Association though he is best known as the man who patented the ubiquitous Rawlplug. In the early years of the 19th century, Rawlings added building contracting and motor engineering and remained with that range of businesses until its flotation in 1965, under the chairmanship of Ralph Rawlings, JJ's son. There was no housebuilding at the time of flotation but the Prospectus referred to the fact that the Company had acquired properties for development in London and Kent.

Rawlings had enjoyed a decade of steady profits expansion prior to the float and this continued up to 1968 when a record £182,000 profit was made. However, profits halved the following year and a loss was incurred in the year to March 1970. This led to the acquisition of a majority holding by Hawtin Industries (previously known as Dental Manufacturing) in September 1970. Hawtin, which was then in the process of transforming itself into a banking and finance group, disposed of a major part of Rawlings property portfolio and injected a number of its own building and property companies, based in the north-west. Hawtin's ownership was short lived and in February 1972 it sold its 56% holding in Rawlings to D&W Murray,[1] a banking and international trade finance house. Although Murray was obliged to bid for the balance, Rawlings maintained an independent stock exchange quotation.

Helped by the strong housing market, Rawlings made profits of £1.2m in 1973, on turnover of £6m but the recession soon turned profits into little more than nominal levels. No land provisions were being made but cash was draining out of the business, and in 1977 Rawlings faced what it called 'an acute liquidity shortage.'[2] Land write-offs contributed to a £4.6m loss and Rawlings was only saved from bankruptcy by Murray's financial support; following which (in 1978) the minority holding was acquired. Rawlings was reorganised, new management installed, and it operated from two centres, Blackburn and Lenham in Kent. Profits fluctuated in the £500-700,000 range until the tail end of the 1980s boom when they rose to a peak of £2.1m in 1989 on unit sales of 240.

In 1985, management control of Murray, by then Goode Durrant & Murray, passed to the Waring family; Michael Waring was appointed Chief Executive and he began a programme of expansion for Goode Durrant. Although Rawlings prospered in the early years of Waring's stewardship, the recession once again necessitated land provisions (£3.8m in 1992) and housing output was sharply reduced. Rawlings had returned to profit by 1994 but Goode Durrant wanted to concentrate on what it regarded as its core business of commercial vehicle rental. Rawlings' contracting activities were sold in June 1994 and in the August most of the assets of the housebuilding companies were sold to Bowey Group, a private company based in Newcastle. 'I never regretted selling out. I came over like all South Africans do, to start a conglomerate because that's what we knew, but I came to the conclusion that it didn't work because you were always behind with the information.'[3]

[1] Now Northgate plc
[2] Company accounts, 1977.
[3] Interview with Michael Waring, April 2002.

REDROW
Peak units: 4284 (2004)

Redrow was formed by Steve Morgan in 1974 as a small civil engineering company in North Wales; it was not until 1982 that Redrow entered the private housing market on a permanent basis. Steve Morgan had grown up with a civil engineering background as his father, Peter, ran his own plant hire and civils companies. The company's official history spells out a somewhat impetuous and forceful young Steve Morgan, 'revealing a fighting spirit that was to serve him well throughout his school and working life… tough and feisty… Steve and his father were unable to work together.'[1]

The young Morgan left school part-way through his A-level course, before enrolling for an OND course in construction at Liverpool Polytechnic. On completing it in 1972, he had brief periods working for his father and then Northern Developments. There followed two years as a site engineer for Wellington Civil Engineering until, in 1974, the recession encouraged Wellington's parent company to close its civil engineering business. Morgan undertook to complete one of the contracts as an independent sub-contractor with the necessary finance of £5000 being backed by his father. Following his success on that contract, Wellington used Morgan to finish off other contracts.

Formation of Redrow

At that point in 1974, when Morgan was 21, he formed Redrow. The original intention was to use his own name but the obvious Morgan names had been taken. 'Redrow' was concocted out of two previous addresses – <u>Red</u>wood Drive and Har<u>row</u> Drive; a trading name to be used much later, Harwood, was taken from the opposing syllables of the road names. In 1975 Peter Morgan closed Clwyd Contractors to concentrate on the plant hire business and Steve Morgan took over some of Clwyd's contracting relationships. *The Redrow Way* describes difficult trading conditions with Steve Morgan and his wife on the verge of emigrating to the USA.[2] However, new work began to come in from Llandudno council, followed by sub-contracts for Edward Jones Contractors, then the largest construction company in north Wales. It was there that Morgan met Simon Macbryde, a bricklayer he had known at school. Between them they formed a new building company called Mormac Construction (later Redrow Building) which did conventional building work but also entered its first private housing scheme for 18 bungalows at Kinmel Bay. Although the development was moderately successful, there was no more private housing for three years, Redrow preferring to concentrate on the then plentiful construction work.

In 1979/80, Redrow achieved its first significant financial results: turnover quadrupled to £1.7m, earning pre-tax profits of £172,000. By then, Redrow was beginning to expand into Cheshire and the Wirral. In 1980, Redrow Building and Redrow Civil Engineering merged leaving Macbryde with 17 per cent of the enlarged company. By 1982, civil engineering and local authority housing contracts were becoming harder to obtain. 'Redrow decided to take a closer look at how private housebuilders operated and to weigh up the financial implications. An average sized 3-bedroom local authority house cost Redrow in the region of £11,000 to build. Meanwhile, private developers were selling similarly sized houses for approximately £20,000. Even allowing for a land cost of £2-3,000 per plot there was still a huge margin. Redrow decided to chase it.'[3]

---

[1] Burland and Whitehouse, *The Redrow Way*, pp.7-11.

[2] Ibid p.20.

[3] Ibid p.41.

The first housing site

The first site was at Denbigh, with land being bought on deferred terms from the Land Authority of Wales. Sales were achieved simply by virtue of lower prices than the competitors. 'Redrow brought a contractor's no-nonsense approach to housebuilding... to arrive at the selling price, the company simply took the cost of the land, added the build cost and topped it up with a profit margin. It was an unsophisticated formula, but with such low overheads a powerful one.'[4] Morgan's construction expertise was also used to advantage in acquiring the early sites: 'We often bought sites so awful that nobody else would touch them'[5] *The Redrow Way* stressed the benefits of the speedy turnaround to Redrow's cash flow but cash flow was being helped in other ways. Morgan was receiving tax advice from a local accountant, Bill Fedrick, an ex-London tax expert; two company acquisitions were made from receivers providing £3m of tax losses.

Once started in speculative housing, and with favourable market conditions, Redrow's growth was dramatic but it was soon creating organisational and personnel strains. In 1985, the 30-year-old Paul Pedley was recruited from Clarke Securities as Finance Director. One of Pedley's first observations was that financially and administratively 'the situation was virtually out of control.'[6] Apart from introducing more professional systems, there was another important operational change. To begin with, Redrow had run the contracting and speculative housing as one, allowing staff to switch between one and the other. However, 'in time it became apparent that Redrow had begun to outgrow it management structure. With the rest of the industry specialising in one discipline or another it was increasingly difficult to recruit people to fit in with its unique way of working'.[7] Accordingly, Redrow separated the speculative housing from contracting.

Purchase of Whelmar Lancashire

In May 1985, the partnership between Morgan and Macbryde came to an end as disagreements over how Redrow was to be run led to Macbryde's departure. Redrow bought back Macbryde's 17% for around £400,000; even in the light of the company's then profits of £1.2m, let alone what it went on to make in the next two or three years, it was a modest price.[8] A few months later, Redrow bought the construction firm of T Headley; Headley operated from Ashford in Kent and was turned into Redrow's south east housebuilding company. The following year, a midlands housebuilding subsidiary was formed. Although Redrow had made a number of small acquisitions, the companies had never been bought for their operational strength. However, in 1987, Redrow bought an active housebuilder for the first time, Whelmar Lancashire – one of the five parts of Whelmar being sold by Salvesen. The £7m acquisition was building around 400 houses a year; although it was bought for little more than net asset value, the cost was in excess of Redrow's own shareholders' funds at the time. Gearing rose to 150 per cent before a programme of stock reduction cut this to 60 per cent.

Thus, within the space of two years, Redrow had changed from a local builder operating in north Wales and Cheshire with an output of 2-300 to a regional housebuilder with subsidiaries in Lancashire, the midlands and the south east, and unit sales of over 1000. By 1987, profits had risen to almost £4m, and the boom conditions that followed saw profits exceed £16m in the year to June 1989, on volumes that had only increased 20%. Redrow could not help but make money in its new south-east company, but without longstanding relationships to protect it, the company had increasing difficulty retaining its

---

[4] Ibid p.41.
[5] *Building*, 26th June 1992.
[6] Burland, *The Redrow Way*, p.55.
[7] Ibid p.51.
[8] Macbryde went on to form Macbryde Homes.

subcontractors. Morgan became ' increasingly unhappy with the horrendous salary inflation and poor build quality.'[9] At half past nine one morning at the end of April, Morgan found the bricklayers packing up their equipment to go sailing for the day. 'The next morning he called a board meeting and it was unanimously agreed that Redrow should pull out of the South East market.'[10] Redrow Homes (Southern) was closed by the end of the summer of 1988.

Withdrawal from the south east

Although the withdrawal from the south east and sale of most of the remaining south-east land bank protected Redrow from the land write-offs that damaged so many southern companies, Redrow could not escape the effects of the recession. It decided not to compensate for falling prices by increasing production; there was actually a small reduction in volumes and profits gradually declined to £10.5m in 1992 – a healthier position than enjoyed by many competitors. Redrow remained financially strong and prepared for further regional expansion. A south-west company had been formed in 1988, and Yorkshire and south Wales companies were started in 1991. By then there was a clear intent to create a national housebuilder: 'We were looking to see where we wanted to be and picking the regions off one by one.'[11]

In 1992, the 100%-owner of the business decided to take his family on a six-month round the world trip leaving Redrow in the charge of Paul Pedley, newly promoted to Deputy Chairman. 'Steve's decision to take time out was to fundamentally change the way in which Redrow was managed. He had single-handedly started the company from scratch and was the driving force behind its growth.... up to the day he left for his trip, Steve was in charge of the company's day-to-day operations… but on his departure all the responsibility was devolved principally to Paul Pedley.'[12] The adjustment on Morgan's return had to be handled with care by both sides. 'Steve going was straightforward; coming back was much more difficult. It took a year to bed down but Steve accepted the challenge.'[13]

Costain takes Redrow back into the south east

Redrow's decision to withdraw from the south east was described in *The Redrow Way* as based on instinct. The return to the south east was more calculated. In July 1993 Costain Homes was bought for £17m with a further £7m as the tax losses of £93m were utilised. Costain gave Redrow a ready-made organisation building some 400 house a year, a 1400 plot land bank, and a platform for land acquisition in what was still a depressed market. Despite the grave difficulties of its parent, 'The Company was very clean. The historic problems had been sorted out before we bought it.'[14]

With strong signs of a market recovery buoying the housebuilding sector of the stock market, Redrow was floated in May 1994, almost immediately after Beazer and Wainhomes. Pedley was now Managing Director under Morgan as Executive Chairman. On the flotation Redrow raised £50m of new money; in addition, 46m shares were sold by Steve Morgan at 135p, raising him £62m and leaving an additional holding of 132m shares valued at £179m; only twelve years after selling his first house, Morgan was arguably the country's richest housebuilder. The addition of Costain Homes took Redrow's volumes to over 2000 a year in 1994, since when there has been steady organic growth. In 1995, Redrow opened a Scottish subsidiary; that year it also launched its Harwood range of lower cost houses into the north west.

[9] Interview with Steve Morgan, April 2003.
[10] Burland, *The Redrow Way*, p.65.
[11] Interview with Paul Pedley, Oct. 2001.
[12] Burland, *The Redrow Way*, p95.
[13] Interview Paul Pedley.
[14] Ibid.

Steve Morgan withdraws

By 1998, sales were over 3000 and profits reached £48m but by now Steve Morgan was preparing his withdrawal from the company. A further substantial tranche of his shareholding was sold, reducing his holding from 60% to 35%. Morgan had moved to Jersey though still commuting regularly as an unpaid Executive Chairman. In September 2000 Redrow announced that Steve Morgan had decided to leave the company at the AGM the following month. At the same time, the company announced a tender offer to shareholders to buy back 30% of its shares at 170p. Although described (correctly) as earnings enhancing, the buyback also provided Morgan with an exit route for his shareholding. He had underwritten the full amount of the tender offer out of his own shareholding and, on completion of the tender, was left with no more than 14% of the equity. Paul Pedley was well aware of the difficulties experienced by many housebuilders on the transition from founder to managerial control but argued that 'We had already done it in 1992. Steve had always believed in Redrow as a team and many of the key personnel date back to the mid-1980s.'[15]

Redrow made another opportune purchase in January 2002, paying £30m for the troubled Tay Homes. Tay had been building around 1500 units a year in the late 1990s but output had fallen to little more than half that. The acquisition gave Redrow additional coverage in Yorkshire and Scotland and helped to raise group volumes to over 4000 in 2002/03 for the first time. September 2003 also saw the start of further management changes. Finance Director Neil Fitzimmons was promoted to Managing Director and two years later made Chief Executive, with Paul Pedley moving to Executive Deputy Chairman.

[15] Ibid.

REGALIAN PROPERTIES
Peak units: 500+ (late 1980s)

In 1972 the joint venture assets of David Goldstone and FNFC were injected into the quoted Yarm Investments and Finance, by then 'a run-down Midlands based holding company'[1] quoted on the Midlands and Western Stock Exchange. Yarm was originally a Birmingham-based company controlled by David Yarm whose property activities started in the late 1940s. His various interests, including Yarm Developments, car dealing and insurance broking were packaged into Yarm Investments and floated in 1968 with a profits forecast of £200,000.

In January 1971 First National Finance bought 60% of Yarm at 20p a share, little more than half the flotation price, and in October the shares were suspended pending the injection of part of David Goldstone's private property interests. David Goldstone was the Swansea-born son of Polish refugees; he graduated in law at the LSE in 1952 and practised as a solicitor in London. He began to take a more active interest in property and by 1962 he had created a small residential company, Davstone Estates, which was sold to a property company in 1964. From 1967, Goldstone worked closely with FNFC, buying blocks of flats in London to break up for sale to private buyers. Each dealing operation, often for just one block, was handled through a separate joint company in which FNFC had majority control; the joint companies purchased 17 blocks with over 1100 individual flats.

Yarm renamed Regalian
While the Yarm shares were suspended, the car hire and steel stockholding businesses were sold leaving only the property management and hire purchase; there were eleven joint companies in which Regalian held between 15-49% of the equity. On the requotation the Company was renamed Regalian, and the shares rose rapidly to a peak of 134p. In June 1972, Regalian acquired a £22m portfolio of properties from FNFC, with payment deferred until 1980, or the earlier sale of the properties; Regalian was never able to complete this purchase.

Regalian suffered in the recession not only through the direct effects on its own business but also because of FNFC's own problems; by May 1975 the share price had fallen to 7p. The 'lifeboat' allowed FNFC to renegotiate its debt and in May 1976 Regalian was able to restructure its payments to FNFC and postpone the final payment date on its property portfolio to 1982. However, Regalian could not avoid substantial losses. Its record profits in 1973 had been no more than £0.5m; in the following four years, Regalian lost £12m, largely due to interest payments on the deferred purchase portfolio. In 1979, Regalian moved to showing profits on its uncharged subsidiaries only and, on that basis, for the next few years it made profits of a few hundred thousand pounds a year, although the charged subsidiaries were still losing some £4m a year. The charged subsidiaries were finally sold to FNFC in 1982 for a nominal consideration.

Regalian starts urban regeneration
Against the odds, Regalian began to rebuild its operations, and in the 1980s it became one of the pioneers of urban regeneration. The move which set the pattern for the rest of the decade was the purchase of a substantial estate of 450 vacant flats in Battersea Village from the local authority. By the practice of the time it was an unusual transaction but Goldstone thought the risks low: 'We saw a massive chunk of derelict property in what was not a bad area.'[2] In 1982 a new subsidiary was formed to invest in commercial property and, after eight years, Regalian was once again paying a dividend. Equity issues to

---

[1] Hamnett and Randolph, *Cities, Housing and Profits,* p.157.
[2] Interview with David Goldstone, May 2002.

finance this growth raised £3m and £9m respectively in 1984 and 1985. In 1984, Regalian moved into London Docklands, this time with a new-build project for 400 flats at Free Trade Wharf and 100,000 sq. ft. of office space with a potential value of £50m. The 1985 rights document disclosed projects for more than 1000 flats at Lichfield, Cardiff, Washington New Town and Wandsworth, with a further 450 flats in Manchester to follow. Looking back from the 1988 accounts, the Chairman stressed Regalian's role through this period: 'Regalian pioneered the whole urban regeneration movement in 1980, when it broke completely new ground with the refurbishment and launch of its Battersea Village project.'

A further rights issue in 1986 raised £35m additional finance for what was now described as a £325m development programme. The balance sheet at March 1987 showed work in progress rising from £24m to £93m; there were ten sites with a total of 1700 units to be built or refurbished; there were commercial developments including the purchase of the Vauxhall Cross site, which was to be pre-sold in February 1989 for £130m as a 450,000 sq.ft. 'office development' to house MI6. An even larger scheme was proposed at Heron Quay in a £600m joint venture with Canary Wharf, but Regalian sold its interest in the early 1990s..

Commercial property expansion

Profits were coming through at an accelerating rate: from £2m in 1985 they grew to £23m in 1988, on turnover of £57m. In the year to March 1989 turnover doubled to £108m and profits edged ahead to a record £26m. Housing volumes were never quoted but by the late 1980s were in the upper hundreds a year. However, as the recession began to overtake the industry, Regalian assessed its strategy. Writing his annual statement in June 1988, the Chairman said: 'Our confident expectation…is that far from being confronted with a downturn, we are likely to see an appreciable uplift in property prices during the coming year. In the light of this judgement, our response has been to continue with a programme of determined but careful expansion.' A year later there was no escaping the reality of the housing downturn but there was now an explanation of how Regalian had repositioned itself into commercial development. 'Management recognised two years ago that the remarkable escalation in residential house prices would inevitably be followed by a period of quieter performance [and Regalian] embarked on a positive strategy of expanding its activities in the commercial sector, particularly with regard to office development.' More than £250m worth of commercial developments had been pre-let over the previous 18 months, 'an illustration of your Company's foresight in anticipating market trends.' One of the largest purchases was a 50% interest in the 11-acre site at Bishopsbridge Paddington for £16m. The portfolio was now 70% commercial and in the 1991 accounts the Chairman reported that there was only one major residential project under construction and that was in Manchester.

For some while, it looked as though Regalian's strategy had worked. Profits had fallen but it still declared £11m in 1990 and 1991. Although there was £130m of debt in the 1991 balance sheet, there was also some £86m of cash. However, the developments were absorbing cash rapidly. In 1992, debt had risen to £221m despite a £20m rights issue and cash was down to £36m. The auditors qualified their report in case directors' valuations of certain developments were incorrect and further provisions proved necessary. After provisions, Regalian lost £27m and the final dividend was passed; Lee Goldstone, David's son, who had worked for Regalian for 12 years, was made redundant because of constraints on new developments. The full impact of the recession was seen in 1992/93 when extensive provisions increased the loss to £83m: those two years wiped out all the profit that Regalian had ever made. In some respects it is surprising that Regalian, having anticipated the overheating in the residential market, should have reinvested so heavily in commercial property. Like others, Goldstone was critical of the short term demands of the City. 'You are on a treadmill; you have to go somewhere. You might be able to stand still as private company but not as a public company. We were conscious of the problems; we were more cautious but we had to go ahead.'[3]

A revival under the next generation

The good news was that discounted property sales enabled Regalian to substantially reduce its debt levels and, by 1995, Regalian was once again planning new projects, this time with the emphasis reverting to residential. New money was raised via a rights issue in 1997 and in that year Lee Goldstone, who had rejoined Regalian in 1995, was made Managing Director with his father remaining Chairman. By the end of the decade, Regalian was selling some 250-300 flats a year and making modest profits. Regalian was also trying to retain some of its developments to create a stronger asset base but the management became disillusioned by the stock market's then concentration on high technology stocks and the valuation of property companies at substantial discounts to asset values. In year 2000, Regalian sold its Bishopbridge site and announced the sale of its Marble Arch office development with the intention of reverting to its core activity of Central London residential development. In March 2001, Ruskin Properties (controlled by Sir Tom Farmer, Lee Goldstone and development director Roland King) offered 48p a share for the Company (£84m) and its shares were delisted in May 2001.

[3] Ibid.

ROWLINSON CONSTRUCTION
Peak units: 200-300? (late 1960s)

Rowlinson was founded in 1953 by Peter Rowlinson as a Manchester construction business. It initially built houses under contract but within two years was building houses on its own land. In 1957 Rowlinson began building houses for local authorities, later developing the Rowcon industrialised building system. Although the housing stayed within the north west, construction work was carried out across the country. In 1960 Reddish Land was formed to acquire housing land for Rowlinson Construction to build.

Profits grew rapidly after 1960, reaching £147,000 in 1964; the Company was floated in the following year. By then it was developing housing estates in Cheshire, Derbyshire, Lancashire and Anglesey. No housing volumes were stated but the land bank of 680 plots suggests that it was no more than 100-200 a year. The post-flotation performance was disappointing, with profits little more than £50,000 by the end of the 1960s; from then, profits rose rapidly under the stimulus of the inflationary house price boom, exceeding £400,000 in the year to March 1973. Housing output had been increased, Rowlinson had expanded into industrial development, and the construction business had been reduced due to the effect of cost inflation on margins.

Rowlinson came through the recession of the early 1970s in excellent shape, profits reaching a peak of £1.3m in 1977. Housing sales had been reduced during the period but the Company was enjoying considerable success with its newer industrial and commercial development. By the end of the 1970s the policy had changed towards retaining more of the completed properties to create an investment portfolio, but with contracting losses being incurred, profits were little more than breakeven. Residential volumes were substantially reduced and between 1980 and 1983, no new sites were started.

Speculative housing resumed in 1984 and in the following year Rowlinson began purchasing housing in central London for renovation and resale. The initial success with London residential encouraged Rowlinson to undertake London commercial schemes as well, and the favourable market conditions contributed to new peak profits of over £3m. Given the investment that was being made in the London area as the market approached its peak, the breakeven position achieved in 1991 after £1.5m of provisions was a creditable achievement. Profits soon recovered to £3m a year but by now the Company was predominantly a property investment company. In 1997, with Peter Rowlinson approaching 70, the Company was sold to Barlows, a Chester based company.

ROYCO
Peak units: 850 (1973)

Roy Strudwick started a small builders' merchants after finishing national service, financed with the help of his father. That gave him his introduction to the housebuilding sector and in 1962, aged 25, he formed a housebuilding business; the original company was Royco but he soon developed a financial relationship with First National Finance Corporation. Country & Metropolitan Homes was their first joint company, 49% owned by Royco and 51% by FNFC, followed in 1965 by Irkdale Properties, similarly owned. Strudwick was not a builder by training: John Lavers ran the building side from the beginning and others did the land buying; 'He [Strudwick] was an entrepreneur – a risk taker rather than a hands on builder.'[1]

Flotation in 1972

In 1968, the company extended its business to the finance of other developers, and in 1970 it began commercial and industrial development. Profits rose rapidly from 1967, reaching £914,000 in 1971 on £5.3m turnover. At the end of 1971, Irkdale was used to amalgamate the three companies as a prelude to a flotation, leaving Strudwick with two-thirds of the enlarged company, now renamed Royco Group. It was duly floated in March 1972 with Jack Strudwick, Roy's elder brother, also on the Board. The flotation was made in the closing stages of the housing boom, and profits rose from £0.9m in 1971 to £3.0m in 1972. when Royco was probably building around 850 houses a year. The management was also keen to expand its development business and to diversify. In January 1973 it bought C Burley for £3.9m, a privately owned farming concern owning 850 acres of land near Sittingbourne, of which 200 acres were zoned for development. There was also an active banking subsidiary, Queen Street Trust, one of whose ventures was to acquire 43% of motor group ARV (later Milbury). Royco was also looking at development opportunities in Europe and a subsidiary company was formed in France, although nothing came of it.

Profits reached a peak in 1973 at £4.4m with finance and banking contributing over £1m. However. the fall in land values had now begun and there were provisions against land and capitalised interest of £3.6m. Fortunately, Royco had sold a portfolio of commercial properties to a pension fund prior to the downturn in values and that had protected its cash position but, with provisions regularly eating into trading profits, Royco did little more than break even over the next three years. Nevertheless, the management continued to buy attractive sites during this period and this, together with commercial property sales, helped the recovery towards the end of the decade, when profits reached a new peak of £5.3m in 1979. However, Royco was probably building little more than 200 units a year by the end of the 1970s – a more manageable size for Strudwick's impending repurchase of the Company.

The founder buys the company back

Writing his annual statement in March 1979, Roy Strudwick announced that he would be moving abroad shortly and would cease to be Managing Director and Chairman, though remaining a director seeking overseas investment opportunities. David Wilmot, Deputy Chairman for a number of years, became Chairman and Robert Clarke Managing Director. Clarke had been one of the reporting accountants at the time of the flotation and had joined to run the property finance operation; at the time of Strudwick's departure, Clarke was running the Aylesbury region accounting for around half the group's trade. In January 1980, Strudwick increased his holding in Royco, via his private company Bonnerpark, to 40%. He had to make a mandatory offer (fiercely resisted by the independent directors) for the balance at 50p a share and finished up with a 75% holding. This was followed by a partial repayment of 20p a share or

---

[1] Interview with Robert Clarke, March 2002.

£4m to shareholders, capital considered surplus to requirements. In February 1981 there was a scheme of arrangement whereby Bonnerpark bought out the remaining shares at 60p, valuing the company at £12m.

Royco's volumes reduced further and were only running at an annual rate of around 100 by the mid 1980s. Strudwick had taken the company into commercial development in New York and there were two 300,000 sq.ft. schemes financed from the UK. These were beginning to stretch the company financially and they were sold to Strudwick personally. Having done that, Strudwick arranged to sell Royco to the management to raise fresh funds, and in February 1985 Robert Clarke, backed by the Norwich Union, led a management buyout. The first balance sheet under the new structure had shareholders' funds of £0.5m and nearly £8m of debt. However, Royco did have options on Watermead, a development at Aylesbury later described as 'the most innovative of 1988.'[2] The estate was to provide for 800 houses on 80 acres with a 33-acre water-ski lake, dry ski slope, together with retail space, and it became Royco's most prominent development. In the meantime, most of the trading profit was absorbed by interest payments.

A new flotation abandoned

Once profits started to recover, plans to re-float Royco on the Stock Exchange were announced in November 1986. Clarke commented that 'first the City is full of brokers and analysts who won't remember what went before. They are young people who take a current view. Second we are a different company – an experienced management offering an operation very different from before.'[3] However, the float was abandoned amidst doubts that full value could be realised on a public offer; the Company now considered it had adequate finance to process its sites at Watermead and Sittingbourne, its other large development. Through 1987 and 1988, Royco was spending heavily on infrastructure at Watermead and Sittingbourne, giving it a highly geared balance sheet: £4m of equity (net of goodwill) was supporting £14m of debt at the end of 1988 – the year it was named Housebuilder of the Year by *What Housebuilder*. The Chairman's statement for that year, written in March 1989, reported on record sales and profits of £21m and £5.6m; it did not ignore the deterioration in the market but nevertheless remained optimistic of the company's ability to weather the storm. The housing sector was described as 'particularly vulnerable to the current high interest rate policy. However, we are well placed to withstand a downturn in the market…because of the loyalty of our staff, our subcontractors and our professional advisors.'

In 1990, Royco made the first of its losses. New construction was virtually stopped; overheads cut; and joint-venture companies formed in an attempt to secure finance to continue operations. However, it was not sufficient and over a four year period Royco lost some £17m. A winding up order was granted in April 1994. The Watermead site was left partially developed and the options for the remaining land expired with Royco's demise. Clarke formed a joint company with the vendors to complete the project.

[2] *Chartered Surveyor Weekly*, Sep. 1988.
[3] Ibid, Nov. 1986.

RUSH AND TOMPKINS
Peak units: 300+ (early 1970s)

Rush and Tompkins was incorporated as The Kent and Sussex Building Company in 1930 when it was the construction arm of New Ideal Homesteads. Kenneth Rush, a civil engineer, joined in 1938 and Bill Tompkins, a builder, shortly after to implement a policy of expansion into the large construction work then being required by the government. They became executive directors in 1939 and 1941 respectively. 'Kenneth Rush was very much the polished professional, whereas Bill Tompkins was the practical man who understood construction.'[1] George Lovelock, another key figure, joined in 1940. At the end of the war, Messrs Rush and Tompkins bought Kent & Sussex, changing its name in 1951.

Lovelock went to South Africa in 1947 to begin a residential development business using the Rush & Tompkins for the first time. In 1960, Lovelock returned to the UK to lead the Group's UK diversification into property development, where he was supported on the residential side by John Anderson, a surveyor. The 1960s saw a successful rebalancing of the Group's interests. The 1971 Prospectus disclosed that construction was contributing only 23% of profits, 38% coming from commercial property investment and 39% from residential development. Rush and Tompkins had assembled a land bank of some 2200 plots and in 1971 completed over 300 units. The sites were in the south east of England and in Scotland. The plan was for a steady increase of around 100 units a year to an annual rate of 600 by 1974; however, the 300 a year level was never significantly exceeded.

At the time of the flotation, Messrs Rush and Tompkins were 69 and 64 respectively, and had indicated their intention of becoming non-executive; Lovelock was appointed Managing Director. Shortly after, Lovelock became ill and was succeeded by Kenneth O'Brien, the Finance Director. The residential managing directors, first John Anderson and then Tony Watson, never achieved main board representation, a reflection of the construction-driven approach to housebuilding. Housing volumes grew modestly in 1971 and 1972; residential profits multiplied six-fold and accounted for most of the Group's profit. However, housing never again achieved that success. Volumes fell and development activities lost money between 1975 and 1977. The first signs of a retreat from housing came in the 1976 Chairman's statement: 'Action is being taken to streamline our housebuilding operations in the UK and to concentrate on reducing our investment.' By 1980, a year in which the construction division plunged the whole group into loss, unit sales were probably no more than 200 and the view on housing had hardened: 'the results of our housebuilding operations did not justify the large capital investment required [and] we have curtailed our housebuilding in the South of England.'[2] There was still a commitment to housing in Scotland but the following year the talk was all of the costs of 'running down our housebuilding operation.' The valedictory comment on private housing came in 1982 when the Chairman stated that:: 'In spite of the recent upturn in housebuilding we still believe we will get a better return by reinvesting the funds in commercial development in the UK and the USA.'[3]

As a postscript, Rush and Tompkins became exceptionally active in the 1980s as a commercial property developer in the USA as well as at home. In April 1990, receivers were appointed. Touche Ross criticised the Board: 'The Group was going into new ground which, in retrospect, it may not have had the skills to do.'[4] Outstanding debt was reported as £300m.

---

[1] Interview with Keith Lovelock.
[2] Group accounts, 1980.
[3] Ibid, 1982.
[4] *Building*, 11th May 1990.

SECOND CITY PROPERTIES
Peak units: c.1000 (1970s)

Second City Properties (Birmingham viewing itself as the second city after London) was incorporated in 1958 with three equal shareholders, William and Geoffrey Joberns, and Jack Dome, a property developer. The Joberns were father and son partners in Birmingham solicitors, Price Atkins and Price, which had a large house-conveyancing and general property business. In 1962, William Joberns acquired a controlling interest in Ludlow Holdings, a quoted engineering company; Second City Properties was injected into Ludlow Holdings; all of the Ludlow companies were sold and the name of the quoted company changed to Second City Properties. Other property companies partially owned by the Joberns were acquired later.

As reconstituted, Second City was no more than a local investment property company; its move into construction and development came in 1964 with the acquisition of **DB Evans (Bilston),** a company that was already partly owned by William Joberns. Evans was a construction company that had been incorporated in 1929 by Dick Bartlett Evans. By the time of the Second City acquisition, Dick Evans was no longer a director, but still a significant minority shareholder; the largest director shareholder was Howard Wolverston, then William Joberns. Dick Evans also sold his family property company, Bartlett Developments, at the same time. DB Evans had had a chequered history but by the early 1960s it was prospering again, with a workforce of around 600. It had a large civil engineering content and a building division which, amongst other work, was building around 500 contract houses a year for Dudley Council. Evans had also just started a small private housing division which was being run by Peter Pearce, then aged 24, and a marketing man by profession (later a Fellow of the Chartered Institute of Marketing). Pearce was appointed Managing Director of Second City Developments, as the housing subsidiary was renamed, and group Managing Director in 1969.

Marketing drives the housing operation

Evans' construction operation remained successful after its acquisition but it was the housebuilding company that rapidly became the larger part of the group and its driving force. Though by no means the only housebuilder to claim it was one of the leaders in introducing marketing techniques into the housebuilding industry, Second City laid great stress on marketing. Many years later, Peter Pearce set out his philosophy. 'From the beginning its products were based on a design and pricing policy which was truly market driven. Previously in our large construction firm, and throughout the industry, design was architect- and builder-controlled with price simply a function of cost plus a profit percentage. The new and innovative approach was to base production and design on specific professional market research which defined needs and aspirations of potential purchasers.'[1]

Private housing output in the west midlands area increased to around 400-500 a year by the early 1970s. Although Second City's housing grew organically, acquisitions also played a key part in expanding the land bank. They included EG Lester (of Stafford), George Wright (Tipton), and Corah (Loughborough). The only company that was kept on as a separate region was Corah, bought in 1972 from William Shepherd. Second City's most important geographical move was when it decided to start a new region from scratch and based it at Weston-super-Mare to benefit from the growth in the Bristol area. In part, Peter Pearce felt the continuous need for expansion was driven by the requirements of Second City's quoted status: 'which is why running a private company can make much more sense than running a public company! But it was deeply thought through, planned for about 18 months before we made the move. Bristol was tightly constrained by the planners so you had to guess where we could grow by public inquiry and appeal.

---

[1] Interview with Peter Pearce, Nov. 2000.

We got planning permission for a huge area of Weston-super-Mare called Worle which became one of the largest private housing developments in Europe.'[2]

Second City came through the 1974 recession in remarkable shape with profits rising each year: 'we saw the recession coming.'[3] By the late 1970s, Second City was approaching volumes of 1000 a year of which some 300 were coming from the Weston office; profits for the group had reached the £1m level. Beyond then, volumes were held around the 1000 level while management concentrated on improving margins. However, a major distraction for those at the top were the repeated takeover approaches. 'I spent the last three or four years trying to avoid being taken over; very tiring. We had built up a fabulous land bank and that in the end was why we were bought out plus, of course, the fact that the major shareholders were not housebuilders; they naturally wanted to capitalise on their interests. We had very serious talks with Allied London Properties[4] who came very close to buying but I managed to avoid that happening. We also came within a touch of selling out to Barratt; I had a lot of pressure from potential company take-overs.'[5] In May 1983, Beazer became the successful bidder paying £18m for the Group; Peter Pearce left to form First City Ltd..

[2] Ibid.
[3] Ibid.
[4] Allied London had held a 17% stake since the mid-1970s.
[5] Interview Peter Pearce.

SUNLEY HOMES
Peak units: c.400 (early 1970s)

Sunley Homes was part of what became known as the Bernard Sunley Investment Trust [BSIT], a holding company formed by Bernard Sunley in 1944 to group together other private development and investment companies. BSIT was separate from the contracting activity, Bernard Sunley & Sons, which incorporated Bernard Sunley's original business in 1940.

Bernard Sunley himself, born around 1911, has been described as the archetypal rags to riches story: Edward Erdman described a visit to the head office in Berkeley Square: 'There was a powdered footman present in full regalia and I noticed a line up of bottles of crystal champagne...Bernard Sunley was a rumbustious character. Blunt, with little regard for convention...In the late hours, he would often tell you about his early days of hardship, relating how he helped his father to gather muck with a pony and cart.'[1] That picture was a slight exaggeration as his father was gardener on the Harewood estate who moved south when he was headhunted by Carters Seeds to set up a landscape gardening division. After leaving school aged 16 or 17, Bernard Sunley decided he wanted to work in his own right in the landscape garden area. He started buying and selling turf, gradually progressing through landscape work into construction. A family story has him wanting to buy three lorries within a couple of years of starting. As he was under 21, the hire purchase forms needed his father's signature but the parental response was: ' Bernard, I've been meaning to tell you this for some time, carry on the way you're doing and you will ruin the family.'[2]

The post-war period saw the twin development of Bernard Sunley & Sons as a contractor and BSIT as a commercial property company. In 1959, Bernard Sunley & Sons was acquired by BSIT and the enlarged company floated on the stock exchange. Bernard Sunley was Chairman and Managing Director and his son, John Sunley, then aged 23, became a director, having been educated at Harrow and Columbia University. To that point, there had been no speculative housing and the only mention of housing was that the Company owned some 400 houses and flats in the Greater London area.

Sunley Homes, based in Hemel Hempstead, appeared as a separate identity in 1962. It followed the acquisition of Blakes of Beenham, a Berkshire housebuilder selling around 50-60 houses a year, and that provided the basis of the subsequent housing expansion. But of greater import to the group at that time, BSIT embarked on a major property investment programme, and to finance this an agreement was made between the Company, its principal shareholders (Bernard Sunley and his wife) and Eagle Star Insurance to provide £12m over 5 years. In turn, Eagle Star acquired 4m shares, (there was a simultaneous rights issue) and two Eagle Star directors (including their Chairman, Sir Brian Mountain) were appointed to the Sunley Board.

In 1964 Bernard Sunley died and Mountain succeeded him as non-executive Chairman with John Sunley and Bill Shapland as joint Managing Directors. By this time however, it became apparent that the Sunley group lacked sufficient funds to complete the property development programme which had expanded considerably since 1961. Eagle Star was not able to provide additional funds on terms acceptable to Sunley and it was therefore decided to curtail the programme. Thus, between 1965 and 1970, Sunley engaged in little development work, concentrating instead on the expansion of its property investment activities at home and abroad; it also expanded contracting and Sunley Homes.

Sunley Homes was run as a completely separate entity and, although there were a series of managers in

---

1 Erdman, *People & Property*.
2 Interview with John Sunley, March 2001.

the 1960s, John Sunley became increasingly involved with the business, becoming Executive Chairman in 1970, with Colin Shipman as Managing Director. Sunley Homes traded largely in the home counties and Cheshire and, by the early 1970s, sales had risen to around 400 a year and profits were averaging £1 million. *Building* magazine contrasted 'the consistently satisfactory Sunley Homes and the much troubled Bernard Sunley and Sons.'[3] Between 1966 and 1971 the construction company had incurred significant losses on the notorious Horseferry Road [Westminster] site. It was against that background that Eagle Star first showed interest in a merger but the Sunley family was unreceptive. Nevertheless, in 1973 terms for a merger were agreed by means of a scheme of arrangement between Eagle Star, BSIT and a third company, Grovewood Securities; this was referred to the Monopolies and Mergers Commission. By the time the merger was cleared the stock market climate had changed and the original terms needed revising. In 1974-75, BSIT losses were £2.7m, of which Sunley Homes lost £1.3 million. Both sides felt that no offer from Eagle Star was likely to be acceptable until the property market outlook was clearer.

Sunley Homes seemed unable to recover from the effects of the recession and continued to lose money through to 1978. Looking back, John Sunley accepted that the attention of senior management was probably diverted by other challenges within the group. In April 1978 BSIT admitted defeat with its speculative housing subsidiary, announcing that Sunley Homes and Wates Built Homes had reached an agreement whereby the management of the Sunley Homes housing interests was to be undertaken by Wates. In effect, the Sunley land was to be built out by Wates for a percentage of the selling price. Sunley argued at the time that to continue in housebuilding required a further very substantial investment.

In 1979 Eagle Star made another bid for BSIT as the property market had recovered and Sunley had virtually sorted out its problems; in particular, it has agreed to dispose of the loss making Isola 2000 resort for a loss of £7m. Under the terms of the bid, all the construction interests were sold to the Sunley family for £2m and the family almost immediately returned to private housing. 'We bought the Property Estates Development Company from Charlie Ellis. He had a plumbing business called Ellis of Kensington and he put all its profits into the housebuilding company and bought a lot of land particularly in Kent. When he died we bought the housebuilding company and changed the name to Sunley Estates.'[4] Sunley Estates brought in the third generation of the Sunley family, James Sunley, and now builds around 100 houses a year. For the attempt to seize control of Tay Homes in 1999, see the latter's history.

---

[3] *Building*, 14th Jan. 1972.
[4] Interview John Sunley.

SWAN HILL
Peak units: 546 units (1988)

Joseph Hill and William Higgs established their building business at the Crown Works, Vauxhall in 1874, and it became one of the best known building firms in London. It built many prestigious buildings in the 1920s – west end stores like Swan & Edgars, Dickins and Jones and Libertys – and more recent prestige buildings included the Royal Festival Hall. The firm remained largely confined to construction until the 1970s.

In 1971 Higgs bought City & Municipal Properties, which owned a portfolio of flats in London and the south coast. The plans were ambitious: 'Half of the Higgs and Hill profit will come from property development within three years, according to the kingpin of their property division – Mr John Morgan…and plans are now being laid to move into speculative housing in a big way. Within a few years Mr Morgan hopes that the group will be building 500 homes a year for sale, mostly around London.'[1] The *Financial Times* speculated that the enthusiasm for housing may have reflected the poor results from construction in the 1960s (the dividend had been halved in 1968).[2]

Just as the housing recession began to bite, in March 1974 Higgs paid £630,000 for Harry Offer, a small housebuilder based at Kingston, Surrey; it was immediately renamed Higgs and Hill Homes. Over 250 units were built in 1976 but, despite promise of expansion in the annual reports, there was no immediate sign of it reaching the promised 500. Indeed, by the early 1980s, housing volumes were only around the 200 a year range – and this was after opening in Scotland at the beginning of the decade and Bristol in 1984. However, the acquisition of **Southend Estates** in 1986 doubled the size of the housing division to around 500 units a year. Southend had been formed in 1900 to acquire land owned by a local timber merchant and an estate agent, and at the time of acquisition it was still a substantial landowner in the area, helping the group to a total of around 2000 plots.

The benefits of the acquisition lasted but two years before the recession impacted on the group. The Company had argued in its 1988 accounts that 'we are not a volume developer and, by operating in a niche market, we believe that we are less vulnerable than most to any short-term setback.' By 1991, however, volumes had halved and, after peak profits of £15m in 1988, housing lost some £20m in the three years to 1992; construction, however, was also losing money. The last Hill on the board (Brian) retired in 1992 and Finance Director John Theakston took over as Chief Executive. He continued to support the expansion of the housing business and in 1994, Higgs and Hill raised £22m to purchase 932 housing plots in the west country, largely from English China Clays, to form the basis for a new region; volumes rose to 400-450 a year for a brief period. Of more far-reaching importance was Theakston's decision at the end of 1996 to sell the construction division to Hollandsche Beton for £28m: 'one of the simplest strategic decisions I have taken.'[3] This left a renamed and re-focused Swan Hill as a small housebuilder-cum-property developer (including some significant developments in France).

Swan Hill was able to improve housing profitability and raise capital through the disposal of commercial property, but it was unable to sustain housing volumes; these drifted down into the 200-250 unit range, effectively leaving the Company a minnow amongst the quoted housebuilders. There was regular speculation about a possible takeover of Swan Hill, but the pension liabilities retained from the

[1] *Evening News,* 7th Dec. 1971.
[2] *Financial Times,* 14th May 1971.
[3] *Housebuilder,* May 2001.

construction division proved a deterrent. Eventually, in 2003 the bid came. It was from a cash shell company, Raven Mount, listed on the AIM. Raven was controlled by Anton Bilton (the grandson of Percy Bilton), and a new management team was immediately installed at Swan Hill. Bilton's intentions were clear: 'Our game plan is that we've bought into Swan Hill at a good value and we're looking to sell it in its entirety.'[4] Unfortunately for Anton Bilton, the pension fund liabilities meant nobody wanted to buy it, and the losses being incurred in 2004 cannot have helped. The new strategy involved the withdrawal from Swan Hill's traditional business (six sites were sold to Bowmore, for instance) and the redeployment of capital into other development opportunities. These opportunities included the acquisition of Bilton's real estate company, Raven Group. The offer document stated that the intention of the enlarged group was to focus on 'mixed-use, planning gain driven opportunities and the development and management of assisted living centres.' The launch of Raven Russia on AIM in 2005, managed by Raven Mount and with a £10m investment, showed how rapidly the traditional Swan Hill business was changing.

[4] *Housebuilder*, Feb. 2004

TAY HOMES
Peak units: 1599 (1995)

Tay Homes was the third housebuilding venture of Trevor Spencer and Norman Stubbs, both of whom were architects in Trevor Spencer's architectural practice. On the formation of Bracken, founded in 1965 by two builders, Alfred Spencer (Trevor's brother) and Ronnie Bolton, Trevor Spencer and Norman Stubbs had 33% and 16% of the shares respectively. At the beginning of 1972, Bracken was acquired by Barratt Developments; Spencer and Stubbs put up £100,000 and used their Barratt shares as collateral for bank finance to acquire and expand an earlier Tay Developments Ltd. Because of the downturn in the housing market, and Barratt share price in particular, the banks would not extend finance and Tay was placed in voluntary liquidation in 1976 (with full payout to all creditors).

In November 1972, Airedale Devlopments (Leeds) was formed with Alfred Spencer owning 76% of the shares and Trevor Spencer and Norman Stubbs sharing the balance. Airedale's activities were nominal until the end of 1976 when the company was renamed Tay Developments (Airedale); Alfred Spencer resigned, and Trevor Spencer was appointed to the Board as Chairman. Trevor Spencer controlled 60% of the share capital and Norman Stubbs, 40%. John Parlour was also appointed as sales director. Tay initially concentrated on the Yorkshire market from its Leeds base until 1981 when a Scottish subsidiary was formed. Volumes grew steadily until in 1983 they reached 280 and profits exceeded £700,000. Tay was then floated, raising additional funds for the expansion of the business. Spencer was Chairman and joint Managing Director, responsible for the overall running of the business, with a particular brief for design and marketing; Stubbs, the other Managing Director, was responsible for land acquisition and finance.

Regional expansion
Volumes continued to expand albeit Tay had a particularly difficult year in 1984/85 as the prolonged miners' strike affected its home market. It was after this that a steady programme of regional expansion was started as a means of increasing volumes. In 1986, Tay opened up sites on the East Coast and in Cheshire, initially run from the Leeds office, and from the Glasgow office Tay bought its first site in Edinburgh. This prompted managerial changes: George Glover, the Managing Director of Scotland, was appointed to the main board and John Parlour was made Managing Director of the Northern region, allowing Stubbs and Spencer 'more flexibility to deal with group matters.'[1] In 1987, Tay raised new equity to finance growth. An office was opened in Plymouth followed in 1988 by Leighton Buzzard (to cover the midlands and northern home counties) and, in 1989, Knutsford for the north west. Despite this regional expansion, Leeds and Glasgow still accounted for 85% of the turnover and all the profit in 1989. By the onset of the recession, in 1989/90, volumes were over 900 and profits had exceeded £8m.

Tay actually appeared to come through the early years of the recession in good shape. The 1990 Chairman's statement referred to the early warning signs that had emanated from the south east and the consequent prudence in their land buying. Tay had also been successful in obtaining planning consent on two large Scottish sites for 1750 houses on 240 acres. In July 1992, John Swanson, recently the Barratt Chief Executive, was appointed Managing Director of operations, a move intended to strengthen the control systems but which actually left managerial direction shared between the two founders, the operations director and the regional managing directors. It was in 1993, as other companies were beginning to come out of recession, that difficulties began to appear at Tay. The 1993 accounts referred to 'The worst Autumn in the company's history.' Profits for 1992 had to be restated following a changed

---

[1] Group accounts, 1986.

accounting policy relating to its sales to Business Expansion Schemes (where Tay had given guarantees regarding future returns). Although sales reached 1100 in 1993, profits were down to £3m. There was then a short period of recovery and new regions were established in the north midlands (Lichfield) and the west (Stroud); volumes rose to a record 1560 in 1995, and profits of £7m plus almost regained the previous record levels.

However, once again there was a collapse in profits; indeed, they were almost wiped out. 'The housing market during the whole of 1995 and the early part of 1996 has perhaps been the worst experienced in the last 30 years.'[2] Although there had been a definite check in the post-recession recovery, it would be hard to find another housebuilder that viewed 1995/96 as worse than the recessions of the early 1970s or early 1990s. Tay began to retrench, closing the western and north midlands offices. Unit sales and volumes fell and, although there was a partial recovery in profits, the company was perceived as underperforming its peers.

The battle for control

In July 1998 Spencer, then 65, resigned as Chairman, although remaining on the Board. Stubbs became Chairman and Swanson Chief Executive. They launched a strategic review; the board had already decided to release capital by withdrawing from the south west, which had been substantially completed in the year to June 1998, raising £11m. The strategic plan was approved in October 1998, the intention being to close the north west releasing £20m which would be redeployed in the three remaining regions – the north, Scotland and the midlands. As the review was being carried out, Sunley Homes was acquiring an 11% shareholding in Tay, starting what became a three-year struggle for control of the group. After failing to agree appointments to the Board, Sunley called an Extraordinary General Meeting of Tay in February 1999, proposing the dismissal of four Tay directors and the appointment of its own four representatives. In this, they were formally supported by Phillips & Drew, the largest institutional shareholder, holding 17% of the shares. In the event, the Sunley camp lost the vote 49.2% to 50.8%; supporting the Board's own 23% shareholding was John Maunders who had recently bought a 3% holding. At the meeting, Norman Stubbs said that he was stepping down to part-time Deputy Chairman.

A month later, major board changes were announced. Four Tay directors resigned, including Spencer and Swanson. Maunders was appointed the new Chairman: 'I had no intention of ending up in this situation. I took a 3.4% stake in January as an investment because I thought things were happening on the takeover front. After the EGM, I offered to act as a broker between Norman Stubbs and Richard Tice [Sunley] because little companies like ours can't afford wars on this scale.'[3] Maunders brought with him Bill Bannister, late of Maunders Group, as the new Chief Executive; Tice also joined the board as a non-executive director. In June 1999 Maunders announced the findings of the new management's review. They considered that the Company had placed too much emphasis on volumes and had 'suffered a serious lack of management controls and appropriate reporting procedures.'[4] Overheads were being cut and part exchange, which had been used in over 50% of sales, reduced. Provisions of between £10-12m were forecast. Finally, Stubbs left the company leaving the Finance Director as the only link with the old board. Early in 2000, the much smaller housebuilder, Country & Metropolitan, announced a 5% stake. This was gradually increased to 26% and in June 2001 Country & Metropolitan finally proposed a £28m bid for Tay. Talks were terminated in August 2001. In December 2001 the directors agreed a £30m bid from Redrow.

2 Ibid.
3 *The Times*, 13th March 1999.
4 Shareholders' letter, 22nd June 1999.

TAYLOR WOODROW HOMES
Peak units: 9053 (2004)

Frank Taylor, later Sir Frank and then Lord Taylor, was one of the dominant characters of the twentieth-century construction industry. The early story has been told frequently. Born in Hadfield in Derbyshire in 1905, his parents kept a fruit shop in their front room, which Frank helped to run. He left school at the age of 13 but attended night school. When he was 14, the family moved to Blackpool and Frank Taylor took a job with another greengrocer. In 1921, aged 16, Frank Taylor suggested to his father that he build his own home. He had saved £30 and his father lent him another £70. He knew nothing about building but he did have friends. 'I found six young friends that I knew well, a bricklayer, a carpenter, a plasterer, a labourer and a foreman type and they were all young men of integrity who were skilled in their craft.'[1]

The one house became two – one for his parents and one for Uncle Jack Woodrow. Housing was then enjoying a short post war boom; he received unsolicited offers before they were finished and sold them for £1000 each – a 100% profit. With that, he persuaded the manager of the District Bank to lend him £400 and he was on his way with a further 20 houses. Apart from the realisation that there was money to be made in speculative housing, Frank Taylor still had little experience: 'Being naïve, I used the loan to buy materials instead of land! I didn't know any better.'[2] He was then 18, at which point his solicitor discovered that he had been helping a minor to convey land and insisted that he brought in an older man. His uncle Jack Woodrow agreed to lend his name and so Taylor Woodrow was born.

From Blackpool to London
It is possible that Taylor Woodrow would not have become the company it did without the move to London. An engine fitter in AEC, a bus and lorry manufacturer in London, had seen the Taylor Woodrow house advertisements when on holiday in Blackpool. In 1930 he wrote to Frank Taylor out of the blue to tell him that the factory was moving across London to Southall: 'We'll be needing hundreds of houses for our employees like the ones you've been building in the north-west. How about it?'[3] Taylor caught the next train to London and found that the nearest site to the factory was at Grange Park, in Hayes End – 120 acres that other builders had rejected because of a slope and drainage problems. He calculated that the drainage problem could be solved by constructing a pumping station. Midland Bank provided an overdraft of £15,000. When the site opened in 1931, Taylor Woodrow sold 50 houses in the first week and went on to sell 1200 houses in total, plus shops and a cinema. Frank Taylor recognised that it was a tremendous gamble: 'If the simplest thing had gone wrong, or if the bank had got cold feet, I would have gone bust.'[4]

Although housebuilding still appears to have continued in the Blackpool area, Frank Taylor managed to persuade most of his building team to move south, probably not difficult as the depression hit hardest in the manufacturing north. The next site was bought at Perivale in 1932 followed by Kenton, Stanmore and Edgeware, then slightly further afield at Woking and Didcot. The policy of concentrating on large sites continued and in 1935 there were still only six large estates under construction. There were then five separate companies: Taylor Woodrow; F Taylor Jnr.; Wonder Homes; Sudbury Estate; and Ealing Estate. Only in Taylor Woodrow itself did Frank Taylor have a controlling interest and that no more than 51%;

---

[1] Interview with Sir Frank Taylor, 1989.
[2] Jenkins, *On Site 1921-71,* p.15.
[3] Ibid, p.19.
[4] Ibid, p.20.

the probability is that some companies were formed to finance specific sites. The Taylor Woodrow minute book from 1931 (the year the registered office moved from Blackpool to Hayes) survives. His cousin, Miss JE Woodrow was the company secretary (Jack Woodrow had died in 1929) and Frank Taylor senior sometimes attended meetings, signing cheques in his son's absence. The shareholder list began to widen but the names suggest that they were confined to family and employees or co-directors. Key names to appear in the early 1930s were John Hanson and Isaac Rigg, later to be assistant Managing Directors after the flotation, and Tommy Fairclough, the building manager who remained closely associated with private housebuilding after the war.

Flotation in 1935

In 1935, the five separate companies were amalgamated as Taylor Woodrow Estates and floated on the Stock Exchange. As at Ideal and Marley, the flotation was assisted by the Canadian Sir James Dunn, an active promoter of new issues, and British American Tobacco's Dean Finance. Dunn's reputation was such that, on the advice of its lawyer, Taylor Woodrow actually removed his name from the Prospectus. Frank Taylor remembered the conversation: 'Sam Brown said to Jimmy Dunn "I can't imagine anything worse to destroy people's interest than your name on here"; so we removed that.'[5] Arthur Collins, a director of the Abbey Road Building Society, a major source of finance for Taylor Woodrow, was brought in as Chairman. The Prospectus reported that the combined entity had, in the previous four and a half years, sold more than 2000 houses, suggesting an annual average of around 450. In the year to October 1934, 612 house and shops had been sold and a profit of £54,000 made; Taylor Woodrow Estates was forecasting 'not less than 1000 houses to be built over the next nine months.' After the flotation, Taylor Woodrow continued to expand its housebuilding. Numbers do not survive in the Taylor Woodrow archives but an article on Taylor Woodrow Homes in *Housebuilder* stated that it was producing an average of 1500 houses a year before the war on over 20 estates.[6] The probability is, therefore, that volumes rose from an average of 400 a year in the early 1930s, to 1000 in 1935 and around 1200-1500 in the late-1930s.

Dividend cut after flotation

One slight inconsistency in this success story not mentioned in the official history is that in the year to October 1936, Taylor Woodrow's first full year as a public company, profits fell to £29,000 and the dividend was cut from 10% to 5% because of a 'falling off in the demand in the London area for the type of house erected by this company' in turn attributed to larger deposits demanded by Building Societies.[7] This was the second of Jimmy Dunn's housebuilding companies to suffer lower profits and a cut dividend after flotation. Frank Taylor recalled the advice he received: 'In those days, Jimmy was a real tough chap, he said, "Frank, when we form the company, and its all going, make money by all means but don't fritter it away by paying dividends to shareholders"'.[8] Like Leo Meyer at Ideal, Frank Taylor also is believed to have sold the larger part of his shareholding shortly after the flotation, 'Because someone offered me more than I thought they were worth.'[9]

The increase in housing numbers was partly achieved by building further afield. At the first AGM, shareholders were told that apart from small estates in the provinces, the company's sites were all on the west and north-west side of London but 'the directors were taking steps to extend the Company's activities

[5] Interview Sir Frank Taylor.
[6] *Housebuilder*, November 1949.
[7] Quoted in *Investors Review*, Jan 1937.
[8] Interview Sir Frank Taylor.
[9] Quoted in interview with Robin Christie, Oct. 1998.

to the south side of London and possibly to one or two seaside resorts.'[10] Taylor Woodrow went on to develop as far as Plymouth, West Bromwich, Bristol and Scunthorpe. In 1937, Tommy Fairclough, 'a rough-and-tumble man who needed help with the figures'[11] and a carpenter from the early days at Blackpool, became Managing Director of housing. 1937 was also the year when Taylor Woodrow went into general construction and civil engineering; AJ Hill was recruited shortly after and it was he who ran the whole construction operation throughout and after the war. The first contract might only have been for public lavatories in Perivale but Taylor Woodrow was soon building military camps and airfields; like Costain, Laing and Wimpey, it was the war that radically changed the group. 'The war was to raise Taylor Woodrow from a prosperous building firm specialising in housing estates to a place among the giant names in the contracting and civil engineering world.'[12] Taylor Woodrow built dozens of airfields, camps, gunnery emplacements, sea defence works, and aircraft factories; then came the D-Day Mulberry Harbour.

Construction goes overseas

The end of the war saw Taylor Woodrow begin its overseas expansion, recognising the limited opportunities at home. In partnership with Norman Wates, Leo Meyer (Ideal Building) and Godfrey Mitchell (Wimpey), Taylor Woodrow had built houses in partnership in New York State before the war, but contemporary correspondence did not sound encouraging: 'Conditions in the States for the past six months have been most deplorable, especially in the building industry…I have often thought how unfortunate it was that our friend Mr Taylor started his development just at the dawn of this recession.'[13] Work was won in Malta in 1945; the following year the west African partnership was formed with Unilever's United Africa Company, and a South African company formed. Housing land remained in the USA at Virginia (not to mention 120 unsold houses) and New York, and time was spent trying to realise the group's investment. At home, the Arcon prefabricated house was to be one of the backbones of the company, employing 6000 people at one stage, and Taylor Woodrow gradually moved into new markets – power stations, factories and open cast coal mining.

Despite the severity of building controls, Taylor Woodrow tried to keep its private housing organisation active: 'An attempt is being made to start on permanent housing, but this was hampered by Government restriction. Licences were, however, being applied for, and it was hoped that by starting in a small way to build up a team capable of rapidly expanding as and when the time is opportune.'[14] Houses were completed on pre-war sites where possible but there was little success in obtaining licences: in the three years since 1946, the company was allowed to build only 205 houses for private sale.[15] By 1953, the housing outlook was much brighter and the target was an ambitious 1000 private houses; due to a shortage of land, only 500 sales were achieved but the 1000 target was retained for 1954. Land buying accelerated: in April 1953, Tommy Fairclough had described the land position as 'rather hopeless',[16] exactly a year later there was land for 2000 houses.[17] The concentration on London commuter land which characterised so many of the larger pre-war housebuilders was no longer apparent and sites were being sought around the country, including Crawley, Maidenhead, Blackpool. Stowmarket, Windsor, Preston,

---

[10] AGM, April 1935.

[11] Interview with Stan Tribe, June 2000.

[12] *On Site,* p.32.

[13] Letter from Griffin of Ludowici-Celadon to Owen Aisher, 4th Feb. 1938.

[14] Board Minutes, Sept 1945.

[15] *Housebuilder,* Nov 1949.

[16] Taywood Homes Minute Book, April 1953 (Taylor Woodrow Homes name was later contracted to Taywood Homes and that name has been used throughout for consistency).

[17] Ibid, April 1954.

Luton, Bolton and Reading. The target of 1000 houses was formally confirmed: 'as this is considered the maximum number of houses which can be built by the organisation whilst maintaining a high standard of quality, and so enhance the company's reputation.'[18] Taylor Woodrow and Ideal Homes were probably the first housebuilders to get back to building 1000 houses a year after the war. Wimpey directors even minuted their surprise that Taylor Woodrow sold 1400 and completed 1200 houses in 1955.[19] By 1955, Taylor Woodrow had stepped up its target to 1500: 'Constant enquiries are being made with regard to the acquisition of suitable sites, with the exception of the Midlands, which is considered not an ideal place to build houses when there are other areas more attractive.'[20]

UK housing goes into decline

So far, it is easy to understand what had happened; the housing growth of the 1930s, the war-time construction, the post-war diversification and expansion, and the rapid rebuilding of the original business in the early 1950s as housing controls were removed – all under the control of a dynamic and entrepreneurial leader. Housing was once again a significant profit earner. What followed is harder to explain. Housing completions rose to 1258 in 1956 but, while Wimpey was getting into its full stride and a new generation of housebuilders was entering the market, Taylor Woodrow's private housing, though certainly not the group as a whole, went into decline. By 1958 its sales had almost halved to 658; the 1956 level of output was not seen again until forty years later. Taywood Homes' minutes refer to land shortages one time, and lack of sales at the northern sites the next, but there was nothing that did not also affect its rivals. During the 1960s, Homes made profits of only £100-200,000, considerably less than many of the quoted housebuilders were making at the end of the 1960s. In the peak year of 1973 Taywood Homes made profits of £1.6m out of a group total of £9.3m – for comparison the much newer Fairview and Barratt were making over £3m and £5m respectively.

Possibly the management team lost its focus. Frank Taylor 'visited' the housing board but he was running an international construction company. Of course, the same could have been said of Godfrey Mitchell at Wimpey but whereas Mitchell had McLeod driving the housing business for him, Frank Taylor still had Tommy Fairclough, a man who had probably only been an operational manager and who was facing ill health. Frank Taylor had begun to get nervous about the housing market. Following the bank rate increase of 1957 he sent a directive delaying land purchases and referring any 'choice sites' to him.[21] Next year, all land buying in the north of England was halted; the Board was advised that Tommy Fairclough might be away for 6 months. In December Tommy Fairclough was dismissed (he died the following April) and Don Slough took over as Managing Director of housing. Stan Tribe, whose involvement at the centre stretched from audit junior in 1942 to his retirement as Finance Director in 1984, argued that however wide Frank Taylor's responsibilities were, there was no doubt 'above all he had an iron fist in the purchase of sites. That is why they never got back to building 1000 units a year, as Frank Taylor would not buy the sites when they were going up in price.'[22]

Don Slough was a chartered surveyor who had worked for Bexhill Borough Council, joining Taywood Homes in 1953, becoming a director in 1955. The other appointment to the Taywood Homes board that year was a 'Miss C E Hughes'; Christine Hughes was Frank Taylor's secretary, becoming his second wife in September 1956. She wielded considerable influence over the private housing operation becoming its

[18] Ibid, July 1954.
[19] Wimpey Management Board Minute Book, March 1956.
[20] Taywood Homes Minute Book, March 1955.
[21] Ibid, September 1957.
[22] Interview Stan Tribe.

Chairman in 1978. Even before her marriage, the Taywood minutes record her passing on Frank Taylor's instructions. Frank Taylor put it on record: 'People often come and try out ideas on her when I'm not available, and she'll say, "Well. I think Frank will turn that down" or "I think he'd like that."'[23] It was not an arrangement that facilitated decisive action in an entrepreneurial development business and the author has had more than one senior director attributing Taylor Woodrow's inability to capitalise on its successful start in private housing to this relationship. Although Lady Taylor, as she became, was appointed to the Taylor Woodrow main board in 1976, Don Slough never was, although he stayed on as housing Managing Director until the end of 1980; the extensive main board did not, therefore, have a full time housing representative – nor did it until 1998.

International success

There should be no suggestion that Taylor Woodrow as a group was failing: indeed, its success elsewhere probably explained the relative neglect of UK housing. Taylor Woodrow moved from strength to strength on a wide front. Frank Taylor was in his prime: 'Lacking in formal schooling, Taylor relied on his instincts and often appeared to regard business as an exciting adventure. He was a quietly spoken, highly courteous man with deep Methodist convictions...The young Taylor combined an uncanny ability to identify new markets with a natural leadership which enabled him to persuade colleagues, employees and .. financiers of the viability of his vision.'[24] Housing was pursued overseas – a controlling interest was bought in Monarch Investments of Canada in 1953; land bought in Majorca in 1958; the US market re-entered, and investments made in Australia. Taylor Woodrow became one of the country's leading international contractors and overseas profits accounted for two thirds of the group total by the mid 1970s.

At home, one of the most important decisions was to enter the commercial investment market in 1964. Taylor Woodrow built up an investment portfolio that was later to dominate the group; its centrepiece was St Katherine's Dock, the first of the London docks to be redeveloped. It was in commercial property that Taylor Woodrow achieved what other contracting conglomerates achieved in housing. By the beginning of the 1980s, the value of the investment properties was beginning to dominate the valuation of the group: 'Whether Taylor Woodrow is a property company masquerading as a building contractor, or vice versa, is a problem which has been taxing the stock market for some time.'[25] In the 1980s the property investment was translated into dramatic profits growth. Group profits rose from £25m to £117m in the decade and by 1989, almost 60% of that was coming from commercial property – rents, development profits, and the sale of long-term investment properties.

The extended succession to Frank Taylor

The succession to Sir Frank Taylor was long drawn out. In 1974, he resigned as Chairman telling the *Financial Times* 'It is really sad to see older men hanging on at the head of companies after they should have retired.'[26] He was succeeded by Dick Puttick, who had joined the group in 1940, but Sir Frank remained as Managing Director. Brian Trafford, Taylor's son-in-law, was then appointed as deputy Managing Director in 1974 with a clear indication that he would soon succeed as Managing Director. In the event family changes stopped that, and, in 1978, three more assistant Managing Directors were appointed. In 1979, aged 74, Sir Frank finally stood down as Managing Director but remained on the board as an executive director. There was now a Chairman and Chief Executive (Dick Puttick), four Managing Directors, one executive founder and his wife on the board. It was not until 1984, when Frank

[23] Jenkins, *Built on Site,* p.108.
[24] *Financial Times,* 16th February 1995.
[25] *Daily Telegraph,* August 1980
[26] *Financial Times,* Jan 1974

Gibb succeeded Dick Puttick that Taylor Woodrow again had a single Chairman and Chief Executive. Lord Taylor did not step down as a director until late 1990, having seen in his third successor as Chairman (Peter Drew) and as Chief Executive, Tony Palmer.

Those who served through those final years have little doubt that Lord Taylor's presence made decision making more difficult, nowhere more so than at his first love – UK housing. His obituary in the *Financial Times* passed judgement: 'After he retired as Managing Director he continued to have a strong influence on the business…This was not always to the advantage of the company as it sought to reorganise…The self-possession and charisma…were difficult to resist even after he had relinquished an executive role…As Lord Taylor aged, the business appeared to outgrow the man whose management style relied heavily on instinct and a paternalistic loyalty to staff. He was better suited to carving out new markets than day-to-day management.'[27] However, the failure to achieve a smooth succession did not appear to have any immediate effect on Taylor Woodrow as each successive annual profits record made the company stand out amongst its peers. Growth came successively from UK construction, overseas construction and housing and then commercial property development

Housing still the poor relation

Housing still looked the poor relation: whereas those running Taylor Woodrow's commercial property were accorded main board status, Taywood Homes remained without managerial representation. Dick Mooney, originally a carpenter by trade, succeeded Don Slough as Managing Director of Taywood Homes. At the beginning of the 1980s Taywood Homes was only building around 500-600 a year and volumes were gradually moved up to around 1000 a year with good profits being made in the boom years of 1987 and 1988; however, volumes halved again as the recession hit Taywood's heartland. The group had recorded its 29th successive profits increase in 1989 but the composition of profits was not what it had been in earlier recessions. Taylor Woodrow was riding high on the development boom – profits from the sale of its property investment portfolio alone were 35% of the group total – and the traditional construction businesses, so often a store of profit, were also heading for problems of their own.

Over £100m of exceptional write-offs were made in 1991 and 1992 – embarrassing for a group which had prided itself on its stability. The long-overdue reorganisation was in the hands of Colin Parsons, brought back from Canada where he had joined Monarch Investments in 1959, and Tony Palmer, previously Managing Director of Taylor Woodrow Construction. By now, hardly any large contractor was making money and Taylor Woodrow's construction businesses were slimmed down. The axis of the group gradually moved towards housing and property. In the UK, Taywood Homes began to expand regionally; the west country Heron Homes (c.600 units) was bought for £31m in 1994 and the international housing business added further sites. World-wide housing sales exceeded 3000 in 1994 with two-thirds abroad. Indeed, during the 1990s, Taylor Woodrow consistently made more of its housing profits abroad than at home and looks to be a rare example of a UK housebuilder succeeding overseas. North America had been particularly successful. Taylor Woodrow had owned a controlling stake in the Canadian Monarch Investments since 1953 and had re-entered the USA in 1977 with Frank Taylor's purchase of a large tract of land at Sarasota, Florida. Growth in the North American housing owed much to Frank Taylor's personal involvement and to Colin Parsons. Tony Palmer contrasted the UK and the US: 'The problem with UK housing is that it had not been allowed to progress; it was not professionally managed whereas international housing, in contrast, was given the benefit of investment in a geographically diverse base in the US and it profited there through shrewd investment.'[28]

27 Ibid, 16th February 1995.
28 Interview with Tony Palmer, May 2000.

Taylor Woodrow rebuilds itself as an international housing company

By the end of the 1990s Taylor Woodrow had begun to describe itself as an international housing and property group. In the last year of the century, housing and property contributed £108m of the group's £125m profit; and of the £78m housing profit, over 60% was earned overseas. Nevertheless, there still appeared some ambivalence as to its identity. On Tony Palmer's retirement in 1997, John Castle, an ex-Marley Managing Director, was brought in as Chief Executive. He lasted seven months and the radical approach which he recommended for construction was too much for his new colleagues. However, his logic appeared to be accepted, as he was succeeded by Keith Egerton, previously in charge of property, and Paul Phipps, the world-wide housing Managing Director, achieved main board status, with Stephen Brazier acting as Managing Director of UK housing. Construction had been further constrained and to all intents and purposes Taylor Woodrow had become a housing and property company..

Housing units, 1977-2004

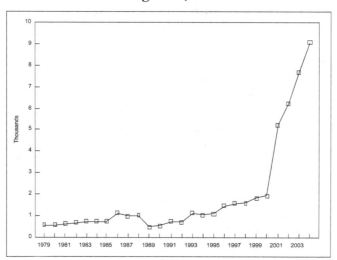

Further substantial changes took place after the turn of the century. Taylor Woodrow intervened in the proposed Bryant-Beazer merger in January 2001, acquiring Bryant in the April for £632m of cash and shares. The latter's 4000 a year output gave Taylor Woodrow a pro-forma volume of 6000, making it the fourth largest private housebuilder in the UK. Paul Phipps was put in charge of the combined housing business and began the process of integrating the two housing businesses. Three months later, and without overmuch explanation, both Phipps and Brazier were jettisoned and Denis McDaid, previously Managing Director of Taylor Woodrow Construction, was put in charge of UK housing. At the top of the Group, Egerton reached retirement age in 2002 to be replaced by Iain Napier, previously Chief Executive of Bass Brewers. The whole of the Taylor Woodrow head office was then moved up from London to Bryant's Solihull, making the acquisition of what had been a weakened Bryant look like a physical, if not a managerial, reverse takeover.

The move to Birmingham saw the Taywood Homes brand name replaced by Bryant and the enlarged housing company also absorbed the London residential business of Taylor Woodrow Developments, run by Tony Wilby. Under the new arrangements, McDaid and Wilby ran the south and the north of the country respectively. In September 2003, Taylor Woodrow agreed a £480m bid for Wilson Connolly giving the enlarged concern a pro-forma annual output of over 10,000 units a year. Graeme McCallum, who had been responsible for much of the recovery at Wilcon, joined as the third operations director of UK housing. Both McDaid and McCallum were main board directors, but there did not appear to be a specific managing director of UK housing.

TILBURY HOMES
Peak units: 762 (1988)

Tilbury's history stretches back for well over a century; within that, speculative housebuilding only started in the 1960s and finished in the 1990s. The business was first incorporated as the London and Tilbury Lighterage in 1884, re-formed as Tilbury Dredging and Contracting in 1906 on the merger with founder Edmund Hughes' other trading interests. The business remained concentrated on lighterage until 1938 when the principal customer decided to take over its own transport and purchased the major part of Tilbury's fleet. Almost immediately, World War II curtailed most of Tilbury's residual activity, and some of its remaining vessels were requisitioned. After the war, Tilbury decided to diversify and, in 1947, formed Tilbury Construction. As the remaining dredging work for the Port of London Authority became increasingly vulnerable (it ceased in 1964) Tilbury began to purchase private civil engineering and building companies from 1957. To these were added roadstone, mechanical service plant hire and speculative development.

Reflecting the boom conditions in the 1960s, Tilbury formed TBC Developments to carry out residential development in Kent. and by 1972 was also building in Sussex, Suffolk, Dorset, Somerset and Oxfordshire. In that year, Tilbury took the opportunity of selling land surplus to its immediate requirements and exceptional trading profits of over £500,000 contributed to an increase in group profits from £678,000 to a record £1.95m. No credit was taken for anticipating the coming collapse but, fortuitous or not, the sale left the group in a stronger position than many of its competitors. During the recession, the building programme was maintained and this time, in the 1974 accounts, the Chairman was able to claim that sales 'fully justified our decision made earlier in the year to maintain our building programme despite the fact that at the time the forward market was not generally considered to be promising.' Output, however was never more than 200.

In 1976, Tilbury purchased **AE Whichello**, a Sussex developer. However, that was the year in which high interest rates belatedly caught up with TBC and the new Chairman's attitude to housebuilding was more pessimistic. High interest rates and planning delays 'rendered uneconomic housebuilding at the lower end of the market where this division's activity conventionally lies.' Difficulties persisted through to 1979 when actual unit numbers were quoted for the first time – 94, and well below the division's potential. It was also the year that provisions against a Nigerian contract took the group into loss.

Housing continued in a relatively quiet way through the first half of the 1980s, the peak output being 200 units in 1984. By then, Tilbury was taking a distinctly cautious approach to its traditional area: '[It is] likely that fewer houses will be built due to a reduction in land available for immediate development in the South East where the cost of replacement land has been at prohibitive levels. This state of affairs has been an important factor in the decision to expand housebuilding to other areas of the United Kingdom.'[1] The chosen area for diversification, in April 1985, was as far away as central Scotland. However, Tilbury had the opportunity of substantially expanding its embryonic Scottish business when Salvesen began to dismantle its Whelmar housing company. In September 1986 Tilbury bought Salvesen Homes (Scotland) for £7m cash; the new business had achieved sales of 362 units in its last year.

Scottish acquisition substantially enlarges housing
The Scottish housing business began to dominate, partly through its own success and partly because of Tilbury's growing difficulty in coping with the explosion in land prices in the south east of England: in

---

[1] Group accounts, 1984.

1988, Tilbury sold 520 units in Scotland compared with 240 in England. The acquisition of Robert Douglas in 1991 (leading to a name change to Tilbury Douglas) brought in the small Douglas Homes, formed in 1989 and with five operational sites in the Birmingham area. The key housing decisions, however, were further south: 'having seen the dangers of an over-buoyant housing market, the company has been repositioned over the past two years resulting in a smaller land bank.'[2] When the land market duly collapsed, Tilbury declined to reinvest: 'Following a careful review of strategy, the decision has been taken to close English Housebuilding, where we are a relatively small player over a large geographical area. In Scotland, however, we are a major player in a restricted area with positive cash flow.'[3] The Scottish housing business continued to run successfully but was increasingly looking out of place in what was now a major construction company. In February 2000, Tilbury announced the sale of Scottish housing to Persimmon for £23m. 'A key part of our strategy is to increase shareholder value by developing our business as a service provider. Scottish housebuilding clearly did not fit in with this approach.'[4] In March 2001, Tilbury Douglas renamed itself Interserve, emphasising its concentration on integrated support services.

[2] Ibid, 1989.
[3] Ibid, 1992.
[4] Ibid, 2000.

TRENCHERWOOD
Peak units: 529 (1988)

Trencherwood Estates was established by John Norgate and started trading in 1971. Norgate, born in 1942, was a chartered surveyor who had worked on land acquisition for a number of developers, latterly with Gough Cooper. Norgate spent his first few years building 8-10 units a year in the Newbury area; his big breakthrough came when he managed to obtain two large schemes on phased payments. The first was a 180-unit site in Newbury, owned by FNFC as a result of one of its clients failing, which was started in 1978. Then Norgate persuaded a large local landowner to take deferred payments on the sale of the 300-plot Thatcham farm. A substantial part of Trencherwood's sales in the early 1980s were from these two sites. From this base, Trencherwood secured a strong presence in West Berkshire through extensive options, many of which achieved planning success in the structure plan at the end of the 1980s.

Trencherwood was floated in 1984 when virtually 90% of its sales were still in West Berkshire. However, new projects were starting in Gloucestershire, Oxfordshire and Hampshire and there was an active commercial programme. The regional expansion accelerated, spearheaded by Brian Eighteen, who had moved up from his role as Finance Director to Managing Director under John Norgate. In 1987, a regional structure appeared for the first time: central region from Newbury; southern from Southampton; western from Gloucester; midlands to be operational 1988/89 and a proposed eastern region to be operational 1989/90. By 1988, site purchases had stretched as far as south Wales. Trencherwood was also active in the retirement home market.

Unit sales had increased from 100 at the beginning of the 1980s to over 500 in 1988 with a budget of 675 units for 1989 and 1000 the target for 1990. In the event, sales reached only 400, offices were closed and staff cut. The planning consents were coming through on the option land but. with the purchase terms being at market value at a time of falling sales, it was too late to be of much help. By 1990, Trencherwood was financially stretched. Provisions were made against both residential and commercial land and some of the joint-venture partners failed to fulfil their financial commitments. By and large it was the newer areas that had caused the problems. John Norgate returned as Managing Director in 1991, and by 1992 the business had been scaled back to a level where housing volumes were only 165. Shareholders' equity was negative and in January 1993 the banks agreed a refinancing package whereby £35m of debt was swapped for ordinary and preference shares.

In October 1995, John Norgate died aged only 53. Richard Brooke stepped up from Finance Director to Chief Executive but it was only a matter of time before Trencherwood would lose its independence. In March the following year Wilson Bowden announced that it had bought the firm for £10m. Wilson Bowden was not the only firm expressing an interest but David Wilson gave John Norwood's widow an undertaking that he would make no employee redundant. Indeed, Richard Brooke later became Managing Director of David Wilson Homes.

TRY HOMES
Peak units: 201 (1992)

William Sydney Try founded the business in 1907 as a builder and decorator. He was soon building single houses as a contractor and records show the price of a house in Derby Road Uxbridge was £308 and a detached house in Station Road Cowley as £641. After World War I, Try began developing detached houses on his own account, leading on to some small estates in Cowley and Uxbridge. The Second War saw a succession of small military projects under the direction of the Ministry of Works but after the War and the ending of building controls, there was no early return to private housing – only local authority housing. Indeed, private housing did not start again until the 1970s. In the early part of that decade, WS Try Southeast had been formed at Banstead, Surrey and that began both local authority and speculative housing, the view then being that cash generated from contracting could be reinvested in the higher margin housebuilding. As the investment increased, it was decided to separate the building and housing operations and in 1976 Mike Deasley was recruited from David Charles when the latter failed.

Under Deasley, Try Homes moved to Dorking and began to expand – helped in the early stages by the purchase of land from the David Charles receiver. However, activity remained on a small scale and by 1988 Try Homes was building no more than 100 units. In that year it bought Ellis Homes, a company building some 50 houses a year in East Anglia, followed in 1991 by Egerton Homes from the receivers of Egerton Trust, then building around 150 houses a year in the south east and Scotland. Despite these acquisitions, output peaked at only 200 in 1992.

Hugh Try, the founder's grandson and a chartered builder was Managing Director from 1968 to 1986; in that year, Try became Chairman and Peter Howell (previously a Trafalgar House director) was appointed as the first non-family Managing Director. The Try Group was floated in April 1989, partly to raise money for what was then perceived to be expansion, and partly to raise money for the family. The reality was that the recession had already started by the time of the float. Land provisions contributed to housing losses approaching £6m in 1990 with further housing losses over the next three years. Mike Deasley left in 1993 and volumes were sharply reduced.

In 1994, David Calverley (previously Managing Director of Trafalgar's Ideal Homes) joined as Managing Director; the operations in East Anglia and Scotland were closed and Try Homes was repositioned as a specialist regional housebuilder concentrating on brownfield land in the south east. By 1996, sales were below 100 but the housing division was back in profit. Amey Homes, building around 80 units in the southern home counties, was bought in 1997; benefiting from this acquisition, the effect of the reorganisation and the strong market, unit sales recovered to over 200 by 1999 and housing profits approached £4m.

Peter Howell retired in 1985 and Calverley succeeded him as Chief Executive. The plant company was sold, property development ceased, and Try confined itself to construction and housing. By 1999 group profits had risen to £5.4m, a new record, but in stock market terms the company remained small. The solution adopted in 2000 was a merger with the similarly-sized Galliford to form Galliford Try, Calverley becoming Chief Executive of the enlarged company.

UNIT CONSTRUCTION/MOWLEM HOMES
Peak units: 1200 (1988)

Unit Construction, one of the oldest names in the housebuilding industry, never had an independent existence. For most of its life it was owned by a Liverpool merchant house before being bought by John Mowlem and finally vanishing into the Beazer organisation. Unit Construction was founded in early 1919 by the metal window company Crittall Manufacturing Company. 'The original intention was to build houses for the company's employees.'[1] It was a short-lived ambition and in September 1919, Crittall decided to sell Unit; the majority of shares were acquired by Alfred Booth, the Liverpool merchants.

By the end of 1920, Unit was beginning to undertake substantial contracts for local authorities around the country. 'Under its new ownership, the Unit Construction Company set out from the first to be a large scale contracting firm.'[2] It had its own cement and aggregates subsidiaries for some years. In 1923 a branch office was opened in Liverpool, to handle northern contracts; the Booth history claims that Unit 'built up a remarkably efficient house-building organisation in Liverpool over many years.'[3] One of the Liverpool housing contracts enabled the company to experiment in the building of 'no-fines' housing well before Wimpey appropriated the expression for its own building system. As a result of problem contracts in 1925, the company withdrew from civil engineering and concentrated solely on large scale housing contracts. Unit worked primarily in London and Liverpool (with the occasional exception of Brighton and Cambridge) and completed contracts worth £10m between 1925 and 1939. No overall housing numbers have been reported but an average price of £500 a house would suggest volumes of around 20,000 over this period making Unit one of the larger housebuilders during the inter war years. However, by far the larger part of the turnover was with the local authorities on a contract basis rather than the speculative housing; nevertheless 'it was inevitably drawn into the boom for privately owned houses.'[4]

Speculative housing in London and Liverpool
The first speculative housing was developed by the London operation with sites at Hayes (88) and Uxbridge (48) in 1929. The depression which followed postponed further speculative schemes – as many as 30 out of the 88 at Hayes had to be re-purchased. Unit started private estate development again in 1933 with two small schemes – 44 houses in Liverpool and 8 larger houses at Cobham. There followed larger schemes in Liverpool: Unit bought 60 acres of land at Bowring Park Liverpool from the Marquis of Salisbury to build 700 houses and these were all built by 1935;[5] another 64 acres were bought at Speke in 1936 at £500 an acre and by the outbreak of war, some 659 houses had been sold. Thus, in the inter-war period, Unit was a substantial builder of houses and although the majority were under local authority contract, Unit was capable of developing large private estates. Unusually for the period, Unit operated from two geographically distant centres. The other difference from the typical pre-war housebuilder was that Unit did not appear to have a single dominant individual driving it forward.- the Booth history mentions a number of names responsible for the management of the company operating under a Booth Chairman.

---

[1] John, *A Liverpool Merchant House Being the History of Alfred Booth*, p.146.

[2] Ibid, p.146.

[3] Ibid, p.147.

[4] Ibid, p.149.

[5] *Practical Building* Oct 1934.

During the war Unit Construction worked on military camps for the army, navy and air force and then the inevitable war repair work in Liverpool and London. Less is known of Unit's early post war existence: their work appeared to be housing contracts for the London County Council, large re-housing schemes in Liverpool, and houses and roads in Northern Ireland. Booth's traditional interests were gradually sold or declined in importance and by the early 1960s the building activities, which included more than just Unit, was responsible for nearly all the profits. As the shareholdings gradually passed down the generations, there was clearly disagreement over the direction of Alfred Booth. The AGM minute book contains continued references to disputes within the extended Booth family and to attempts to take the company public. Annual accounts have not survived but Unit's profitability in the 1960s was mixed.

Unit returns to speculative housing in 1965

Belatedly, Booth had decided to take Unit back into private estate development. There is no indication in the minute book of what, if any, estate development Unit did until it acquired the Redhill firm of Tickner & Emmerton in 1965. **Tickner & Emmerton** was formed by Douglas and Percival Emmerton, and their uncle Fred Tickner, and commenced trading in 1955. Fred Tickner had traded before the war as Tickner & Sons in the business started by his father, building around 50 houses a year. Douglas Emmerton was a chartered quantity surveyor and his brother described himself as a builder. Over a ten-year period the firm built some 2500 houses and was building at a rate of 400-500 a year by the time of its acquisition. The Emmertons had intended to float the business but the election of a Labour Government in 1964 and the impending introduction of capital gains tax led to its sale to Unit. The founders left on the sale and Denis Harrington was recruited from Ideal Homes. Harrington, President of the Federation of Registered House-Builders in 1966, was described as the person who 'built up this branch of our business which was just a sideline of Unit',[6] which seemed unfair to the founders. Harrington stayed as Managing Director of estate development until 1974, aged 70, when Anthony Vincent succeeded him.

In 1974 the Tickner sales budget was 327, less than had been achieved a decade earlier. However, the company was beginning to expand its geographic coverage. Unit Construction as a whole enjoyed peak profits of £1.6m in 1974 before the recession contributed to a steady decline in profitability. Nevertheless, the business continued to expand: by the mid 1970s Tickner & Emmerton was building in the Cambridge area, and in 1977 went into the north west with a site at Aigburth, and into Glasgow in 1979. Roger Clark, a chartered surveyor, became Chief Executive of Unit Construction in 1978, a position he held until the final disposal of the business to Beazer. Profits recovered in the early 1980s, averaging around one and a half to two million pounds a year. Housing volumes had reached around 1000 a year including design and build work. Nevertheless, the Alfred Booth shareholders remained unhappy. The 1985 AGM saw more shareholder complaints about unmarketability of the shares, and perhaps it was inevitable that the business was sold. In 1986 Mowlem bought Unit Construction to give its construction business a meaningful presence in speculative development.

Mowlem buys Unit

Mowlem was one of the oldest established contractors in the country with a national and international civil engineering and building business. Mowlem had been late in coming to the speculative end of the housing industry although it had a long standing presence in local authority housing. It began speculative commercial property development around 1970 which it continued in a reasonably active way. At the same time, Mowlem formed Mowbridge as a residential operation and it built flats for sale in Glasgow and Edinburgh; however, residential development was conducted on a very low key basis and was not

6 AGM Minute Book, 1968.

overly successful: 'The contracting people were always interfering and although the houses were good quality, we were unable to make money.'[7]

When Mowlem did buy Unit, they were determined not to interfere and left the management team intact. 'Diversification was the way of the world at the time. Contracting was highly volatile and we thought housing and construction would be both complementary and counter cyclical; for substantial periods they did work together. However, none of us recognised the inability of housebuilding to spin off cash when it really matters.'[8] In some respects, Mowlem's timing was excellent: profits of the renamed John Mowlem Homes in the first year were £4.7m rising to a peak of £13.5m in 1988 on turnover of £82m and volumes of 1200 (these included design and build and partnership schemes with local authorities). The recession took its inevitable toll. Volumes fell to around 700 a year of which a good part was in Northern Ireland and local authority schemes. The company moved into losses, albeit not large by the standards of some of the construction companies that had expanded their private housing during the latter part of the 1980s. After a £46m rights issue in 1991, there was an initial intention to commit some of these funds to land acquisition. However, as group finances deteriorated, Mowlem was soon seeking to extract capital from speculative housing and refocus the business to design and build. No land at all was bought in 1992, a year that offered considerable opportunities to companies with both cash and nerve.

By 1993, Mowlem's finances were under even greater pressure. After losses totalling £58m in the previous two years, 1993 recorded a £124m loss, primarily in construction and the recently acquired SGB scaffolding business, and the banking covenants were threatened. John Mowlem Homes was deemed to be 'no longer a core activity'[9] and was sold to Beazer in July 1994 for £31m.where it lost its independent identity. The Northern Ireland subsidiary was bought by the management.

---

[7] Interview with Brian Watkins, Oct. 2001.
[8] Ibid.
[9] Group Accounts, 1993.

WAINHOMES
Peak units: 1300 (1995)

Wainhomes was one of the five successor companies to the Whelmar business, broken up by Salvesen, and the only one to emerge with an independent existence, the other four having been sold to trade buyers. In December 1986, Whelmar (Chester) was the subject of a £10m management buy out led by Ron Smith. Ron Smith worked first for the Manchester Ship Canal and had joined Christian Salvesen in 1974, moving to Whelmar (Chester) in 1980. At the time of the buyout, Whelmar (Chester) was building around 300 houses a year in the Cheshire and north Wales area, concentrating on the medium to upper price range. In the next couple of years, volumes moved ahead modestly until, in February 1989, a three-way merger was agreed with Bill Ainscough's Lancashire business of Wainhomes, and Trevor Hemmings' Lanley Builders, also based in Lancashire. The enlarged group's name was subsequently changed to Wainhomes to avoid confusion with the Whelmar (Lancashire) name owned by Redrow.

Bill Ainscough had founded the original **Wainhomes** in 1972 at the age of 24. Ainscough's firm was building 300-400 houses a year in Lancashire, with a product orientation towards the lower to medium price bands. **Lanley**, also based in Lancashire, had a smaller building operation, some 100 houses a year in the trade up market, but its principal asset was a substantial land bank, much of which was used in the early days of the enlarged group. In total, the group was building around 800 houses with pre-tax profits of over £7m. Trevor Hemmings (who developed extensive leisure interests including Littlewoods Pools, Blackpool Tower, and a near 50% holding in Arena Leisure) had formed his first building company in 1959, Hemmings and Kent, which, ironically, was later sold to Whelmar. He left Whelmar in 1974 and, inter alia, formed Lanley (Builders).

Ron Smith continued as Chief Executive of the enlarged group with Trevor Hemmings as Chairman; Bill Ainscough took over as Chairman the following year With its northerly bias, Wainhomes withstood the recession well. Volumes fell to around 550 in 1991 and the profits low point of £5.3m, in 1993, was only 40% below the 1990 peak. After consolidating the enlarged operation in the north-west, the group began a programme of regional expansion opening a south-coast and a Yorkshire region in 1990, although the first meaningful sales did not come in until 1992. A midlands region was started in 1993. Volumes rose rapidly to 1300 in 1995 and profits reached a peak £10m.

The Company floated in March 1994. Although Ainscough was Chairman of the group from June 1990 to January 1994, it was felt more appropriate to bring in an outsider as Chairman of the quoted entity. At the time of the float, there had been plans to increase volumes to 1800 units out of the existing regions but, in the event, volumes stayed around the 1300 level for the rest of the decade. 1996 proved a very difficult year for Wainhomes. Profits fell from £10m to £2m primarily due to problems in the north west, both market related and internal. In the January, Ron Smith was summarily dismissed as Chief Executive amidst claims and counterclaims. At the same time, police were asked to investigate alleged valuation irregularities at its Northern Division (Ainscough's original company). All concerned were at pains to stress (as does this author) that Smith had not been involved in the irregularities.[1] The detail is not relevant to a short history; suffice it to say that there had been a breakdown in Boardroom relationships. Ainscough was appointed Chief Executive and the only good news he had to report that year was the purchase of over 2000 plots from English China Clays for £24m, to be paid over ten years.

After 1995 there was no significant change in Wainhomes' volumes although one more new division was

---

[1] Wainhomes subsequently paid Smith compensation of £225,000; *Financial Times*, 21st December 1996.

opened (in the south west). Profits soon recovered from the problems encountered in the northern division and by 1998 were heading for £14m. In March 1999 Bill Ainscough led an £88m management buyout for Wainhomes; the offer price was 140p a share against the flotation price of 170p. In fact, 'management' was overstretching the concept as it was only Ainscough himself who participated, with 71% of the new equity, the Bank of Scotland holding the balance. The larger portion of the bid was financed with bank debt; the equity commitment by the two partners was £18.6m, Ainscough's contribution coming from the sale of his existing shareholding. Thus, the sale of his original business in 1989 had translated into 71% ownership of the enlarged group.

In April 2001, Wilson Connolly agreed the acquisition of Wainhomes, paying £62m for the equity compared with revalued net assets of £29m. Ainscough received £44m and joined the Wilson Connolly board as a non-executive director; he also retained both the south-west assets and the Wainhomes name. That gave the new Wain an annual output of over 300 units and the company followed this by acquiring land in the north west, where Ainscough had founded his original business.

AJ WAIT
Peak units: 400-500 (early 1960s)

Arthur Wait may now be best remembered by football supporters for the AJ Wait stand at Crystal Palace, but he was a substantial home-counties housebuilder in the post-war period; when its business was integrated with the housebuilding business of Hallmark Securities in 1963, the enlarged entity was building some 1000 houses a year. Arthur Wait, born in 1910, attended John Ruskin School in Croydon and then technical school until 16, when he started work in a joinery firm. There was a period where he worked as a joiner on building sites after which he returned to joinery manufacture, this time at the Mitcham firm of SC Williams, which specialised in shop fitting, blinds and shutters. Arthur Wait was progressively promoted to foreman, manager and, in 1944, Managing Director. During World War II, the firm specialised in the manufacture of ammunition boxes and also worked on shuttering for the Mulberry Harbour.

Almost immediately after the War, Arthur Wait bought SC Williams. Brian Wait, his son, does not know where the finance came from, except that one month after its purchase, his father had to go to Lloyds' head office for further capital. Arthur Wait also formed AJ Wait which was to become the building and development company. He had already been rebuilding war-damaged properties and in 1946 he began the development of a 28-house estate at Woodmansterne, Surrey, which was to take him three years to complete. What prompted him to try housebuilding? 'Money – I think my father was motivated by cash. He was familiar with the housing market as he had worked for Wates on their estates.'[1]

Further speculative housebuilding activity was restricted by building controls and Wait switched to contracting for local authorities. The shopfitting activities of Williams were also moved across to AJ Wait which, by 1950, was producing profits of almost £50,000. On the change of Government in 1951, and the first steps to the removal of controls, Arthur Wait returned to speculative building although it was not until 1953 that substantial building began. Working with him were his older brothers, Ernest, a significant minority shareholder and a director, and Bert, who was not a director. Ernest was an expert in joinery and wood working machinery and was responsible for that part of the business. Bert, previously a salesman with the Gas Light & Coke Co., ran small contracts, post-sales house maintenance and started Wren Craft, the flat-pack furniture subsidiary.

By 1956, the company was large enough to seek a public flotation; indeed, it could be regarded as the first housebuilding flotation to take place since before the war.[2] The Prospectus description of its activities showed that a substantial organisation had been built up in only a short space of time. Estates at Tonbridge, Leatherhead, Horley, Kenley, Reigate and Woking had been completed. Five other estates comprising over 700 houses were under development. In total, the company claimed to have built over 2000 houses 'of various types' since it was formed but this must have included local authority housing as well as private. Other building work included office blocks in the City of London, factories, shops, flats and farm buildings.

The objective of the issue was to secure the family's personal financial position: 'Until we went public we never had any money. We had our day-to-day living expenses and we didn't do too badly. He went public so that he could realise cash on a personal basis; the money didn't go back into the company.'[3] The

---

[1] Interview Brian Wait.

[2] John Laing had floated in 1951 but it was then primarily a construction company.

[3] Interview Brian Wait.

company continued to expand after flotation, helped by two new equity issues, and it probably increased its speculative housing output to 400-500 a year; by 1962, profits had reached just short of £200,000. One of those equity issues had been to provide the capital to retain shops and flats that were being built as part of its housing estates.

Arthur Wait had 'set up an organisation that was able to take advantage of the housing boom that was to come.' He had a commercial manager for land buying, a building director who organised the sites and a co-ordinator to deal with architects and design. Nevertheless, throughout this period, the company remained dominated by Arthur Wait. 'He was the driving force – all the others were very nice people but they wouldn't have done it on their own. He was very strong willed, though he never lost his temper. We never lost sub-contractors and the staff were extremely loyal to him – and they were not the best paid.'[4]

In 1963 Wait received a takeover approach from Hallmark Securities, which had an equivalent sized housing organisation, although on the south coast where Wait was now beginning to take an interest, and using the same estate agents. 'The family had the major holding and the old man said "It's got to go." I think he regretted it but equally he didn't like the pressure that was put on him as a public figure in the City when he really wanted to be left alone in Surrey.'[5] Although it was Wait that was taken over, Arthur Wait was given the enlarged housing operation to run, all under the AJ Wait name. See Hallmark for continuation.

[4] Ibid.
[5] Ibid.

WARD HOLDINGS
Peak units: 528 (1987)

George Hartwell Ward made his way into housebuilding via estate agency – a route more common in the post-war than the pre-war period. He came from a poor family in Carlisle and joined the railways aged 14. After World War I he returned to Chatham Barracks, married a local farmer's daughter and settled in the area. He found work as an office boy in a Tunbridge Wells estate agency, cycling the round trip of 50 miles each day, returning in the evening to tend his allotment. He borrowed £500 from his mother-in-law and went into partnership in the Medway towns. By 1922 he was trading as Mr GH Ward, Auctioneer, Valuer, Estate and Shipping Agent, Rent and Debt Collector. Having built his first house for himself in the late 1920s, he started to build houses for sale but not on any scale.

In 1935, George Ward formed GH Ward Ltd, trading in the beginning as Ward Ideal Homes; his brother Albert was to help with the administration over a long period. By 1938 the firm was trading 'in a very substantial way'[1] though Denis Ward thought the figures were probably no more than 40 a year. Most of the houses were built at Rainham on the outskirts of Gillingham. On the outbreak of war, housebuilding stopped, leaving only the house repair and the estate agency. George Ward joined up again as a Lieutenant in the Royal Engineers and the firm switched to war damage clearance, building radar stations and the production of lifeboats. On the cessation of hostilities, Ward built large numbers of council houses over the succeeding five years and became general contractors; building work came under the direction of Robert Partridge, his son-in-law who had joined the company in 1948. George Ward's son Denis had joined in 1946 after war service and spent several years on sites learning the bricklayer's trade.

Innovative post-war development
Although building controls were still a considerable limitation, in 1949 Ward 'Seized the first opportunity to get back into private development';[2] like other pre-war builders, it already had the land and roads on the uncompleted developments. By 1950, Ward was building at an annual rate of around 100 units; by the mid 1960s, volumes were around 250 a year. It could be argued that Ward was decades ahead of its time with its marketing: in the 1950s it started building bungalows for the elderly and, in the 1960s, flats for single people. Adverts were 'Of Special Interest to Old Folk, Widows, Widowers' and 'A Block of Luxury Furnished Bachelor Flats...specially designed for the needs of single people.'[3] By the mid-1950s, Ward had ceased general contracting and concentrated solely on residential development, on estates ranging from 20 to 1000 mainly in the North Kent area. The Company's strength was an unrivalled knowledge of the land market in its home area and a willingness to experiment with new house designs.

Ward floated in 1972; sales in the 1971 financial year had been a record 344 units and profits, not quite a record, £274,000. George Ward, the founder, resigned ahead of the float; Denis Ward was Chairman and Managing Director, and had effectively been running the firm for many years before that. Once quoted, Ward began to broaden its coverage. Anvil Plant Hire was formed in 1972 providing the base for what was to prove a somewhat troublesome manufacturing division. Of greater long term success was the property subsidiary formed in 1973.

Ward had begun its expansion just ahead of the property crash. However, commercial property construction had not commenced and housing volumes were broadly maintained. Although profits did

---

[1] Anon, *The Ward Holdings Story*, p.4.

[2] Ibid, p.10

[3] Ibid, p.14.

fall, down from £930,000 in 1973 to £230,000 in 1975, Ward must have been the only housebuilder in that period to have exceptional profits exceeding land write-downs. It was not until the 1980s that volumes began to move significantly higher, rising to a peak of 528 in 1987. Up to 1980, Ward's policy had been to build within one hour's commuting distance from its base but Ward gradually extended its coverage to 'one-off' developments in other south-east counties. Its long term land holdings and a rising market produced excellent returns for the housing operation – pre-tax margins in excess of 25% between 1986 and 1988, and group profits peaked at over £14m in that latter year, virtually all generated out of that localised north Kent market.

Heavy London losses

Denis Ward had long resisted regional expansion: 'All the time I wanted to be able to control everything; that gave me the work satisfaction.'[4] By the mid-1980s, he had decided to move further afield, to the London market – geographically adjacent but operationally far removed. By 1986, ten sites had been bought in London and construction had started. Writing in the Annual Report in February 1988, Denis Ward took the optimistic view that 'the recent Stock Market correction will have little direct effect on sales'; the completion of the first London developments was expected to bring substantial profits in the coming year. In the event, London demand collapsed in 1989: 'It caught us on the hop.'[5] The property division repaid its earlier investment with profits up from £0.8m to £6.8m, partially offsetting the fall in housing profits from £13m to £1m. Within that £1m housing profit were £4m losses in London. Ward had also started an East Anglia division in 1989 and that incurred small losses.

The London operation was little short of a disaster for Ward. In 1990 it sold only 13 units, yet accounted for £20m of the group's £35m debt. Still supported by commercial property sales the group continued profitable in 1990 but eventually it was realised that the recession was no temporary phenomenon. Although the directors claimed that there was an overall surplus on the totality of its land bank, some £12.5m provisions were made against land bought at the top of the market. It proved insufficient and a further £10m of provisions were made over the next two years. Operations were again centralised at the Kent head office. Finance director David Pead was made Managing Director, Denis Ward remaining as Executive Chairman. Succession was now becoming an issue. Denis Ward was 70; his only son had been killed in a road accident and his son-in-law, Graham Wall, had been in the Company five years but only in the sales department.

Housing volumes had fallen to below 200 a year in the mid 1990s and in 1996 the Company was hit by an unexpected £6m loss from a fire in an uninsured commercial development. At the end of 1997 David Pead resigned and the following February David Holliday, whose Admiral Homes had been acquired by Bryant, joined as Chief Executive. Almost immediately, a further £12.5m was written off land values, giving a £10m loss for the year. Not surprisingly the kitchen-sink approach facilitated better profits in the succeeding years. By 2000, volumes were comfortably over 300 and profits had staged a partial recovery to £7m. There had been extensive takeover speculation over Ward, but in July 2000 Holliday led a £34m management buy out. Helped by favourable market conditions, the new management increased volumes to over 400 in 2003 and profits trebled to £21m, At the end of that year, Wilson Bowden acquired Ward for a total consideration of £74m.

---

4 Interview with Denis Ward, Dec. 1998.
5 Contemporary interview with Denis Ward.

ARTHUR WARDLE
Peak units: c.800 (1981)

Although the Wardle business could just trace its roots back to the 19th century, the company enjoyed little more than a decade as a private housebuilder before being acquired by Barratt Developments in 1972. Its particular place in history may lie not so much in its own achievements as a north-west housebuilder but in the number of senior Barratt directors that were to emerge from this Manchester business. Arthur Wardle (the individual) started a painting business in the Manchester area in 1897; his son Ronnie, born around 1903, joined the business and Peter represented the third generation. Painting remained the sole activity until the early 1930s when they formed an electrical contracting business, then general contracting and, finally, shopfitting. Ronnie Wardle took over the management of the company in 1946 on the retirement of his father and continued to run the business as a specialist sub-contractor. In 1953 Wardle acquired a plumbing business, S Cookson, and it was this subsidiary that made Wardle's first move into private housing in 1959.

Ronnie Wardle had also been a director since the Second War of a neighbouring firm, Alex Wigan, another company with roots back to Victorian times, and which had also made a recent entry (1956) into private housing. Arthur Wardle then bought Alex Wigan, merging the two housebuilding operations as Cookson Wigan, the only part of the Group not to trade under a Wardle banner. 'Ronnie explained to me that as he saw it, people still retained this idea of housebuilders from the 'thirties as a bit of a nasty type of trade – we don't want people to know we are involved in this one.'[1] The housebuilding side expanded rapidly under the leadership of Alex Wigan's Bob Pope and, helped by a couple of anchor sites in Bury and Bolton, it was selling some 500-600 houses a year by the mid-1960s making it a significant regional housebuilder.

The Arthur Wardle Group was floated in 1965, with historic profits being £135,000. As the story goes, Ronnie Wardle had read in the Financial Times that a lot of small housebuilders were going public in anticipation of a Labour victory; he thought he might as well do the same and within six weeks it was a quoted company. In 1966, Wardle took over another building contractor, John Lawlor, to merge with Arthur Wardle Builders. It was not a successful move. 'The management teams didn't really get on, things went completely wrong. At that time they didn't have any management accounts, the auditors came in every six months and produced a set of accounts – it was a surprise. The reaction was to bring in a firm of accountants to do a report – they recommended recruiting a chartered accountant to implement it, which is where I came in.'[2]

Profitability gradually improved, volumes increased to around 800 a year and in 1971 profits exceeded £400,000. In March 1972, the then Greensitt & Barratt made a bid for the company on a price earnings ratio of 22. Ronnie Wardle had died two years earlier. Peter Wardle was offered a seat on the Barratt Board (though he only lasted two years) and he wanted to diversify the family's assets. Thus, Barratt had made its first regional acquisition. Two of Wardle's non-family directors went on to become senior directors at Barratt. Alan Rawson and John Cassidy, who became Finance Director (bringing with him his financial controls) and Deputy Chairman; the Manchester office also had Terry Van Ree, Harold Walker (later Chairman of Barratt's central region), and it recruited Frank Eaton, later to become Barratt Chairman after Sir Lawrie's second retirement.

---

[1] Interview with John Cassidy, March 1999.
[2] Ibid.

R T WARREN
Peak units: c.750 (late 1930s)

The firm of RT Warren was a substantial inter-war housebuilder that was sold to Bovis in 1967 to provide one of the cornerstones of that firm's subsequent expansion. Tom Warren was born in Devon in 1885, left school aged 12, had two years as a farm labourer and four working in a slaughterhouse, before leaving for London at the age of 17. He took up the plastering trade, although with no training, building up a small business as a subcontractor on housing estates. In 1906, at the age of 21 he started building houses on his own account, probably on a relatively small scale. After service in the First War he returned to housebuilding and for most of the 1920s it appears as if he was developing one site at a time; the accounts for 1927 survive and all the £68,000 turnover was derived from the Orchard Estate at Heston (the average price was a little over £400, suggesting annual sales of around 150).

By the early 1930s the scale of operations increased substantially, as it did with many other London builders; he employed a direct labour force of some 400 and one other indication that he was recognised as one of the industry leaders was his election in 1938 as President of the House Building Association of Great Britain. Warren was building a number of relatively large estates in north-west London and Middlesex, following the underground lines to Ealing and Uxbridge. There are no accurate figures to indicate Warren's size. Jackson[1] has no mention of the firm but, based on a 1969 interview, Bundock identified over a dozen estates and had the firm building some 10,000 houses before the war.[2] This might be slightly on the high side, but not excessively so, and the 1930s could have contributed some 7-8000 of these suggesting a best guess annual rate of around 750 house a year.[3]

Warren confined itself to war damage repair work during the Second War, and after the long period of building controls the business never regained its pre-war scale. Tom Warren was 60 at the end of the War and nearly 70 when controls were finally abolished. There were four daughters and no sons by his first marriage so Tom Warren brought in his nephew, Wyn Hurst, to help him run it. There were two sons by a second marriage and with the business being passed down a generation, that meant seven family groups controlling the business (described as 'internecine strife' by one descendant). There were still sizeable estates: a site at High Wycombe had over 500 houses and there were a number of other sites of between 50 and 100 units being built at the same time. Tom Warren died in 1964 and his obituary referred to a lifetime building 12,000 houses.[4] However, by the time of his death it has been suggested that output was then being set by the directors to produce only as much profit as the family wanted to take as dividends. The building companies were sold to Bovis three years after Warren's death when they were producing around 100 units a year, although the land bank of 1000 plots was a particular attraction for Bovis. The investment company, owning some 500 properties built by Warren, was retained by the family.

[1] Jackson, *Semi-Detached London*.
[2] Bundock, 'Speculative Housebuilding'.
[3] The approximate magnitudes were confirmed in conversation with RT Warren, Junior, Nov. 2001.
[4] *The Dorset Year Book*, 1964.

WATES
Peak units: 1500-2000 (late 1930s)

Wates is one of the great family names in British housebuilding: brilliantly led in the inter-war period when it was one of the largest in the industry and with a fine post-war record of technical and marketing innovation. Yet despite the successes of the Wates business elsewhere, by the end of the century the housing arm was building no more than a tenth of its pre-war achievements.

The dominant figure in the Wates history was Norman Wates (1905-1969), a second generation housebuilder. The first generation comprised four brothers; Edward (Norman's father), Arthur, William and Herbert. Arthur and Edward had a furniture shop in Croydon and in 1901 joined with the other brothers (both carpenters) to build a couple of houses in Purley. From the beginning the houses concentrated on design: 'They wanted to replace the antiquated, badly designed Victorian house with what was then a more modest concept, placing maximum emphasis on light, hygiene and labour saving.'[1] By 1909 the partners were building 50 houses in Streatham followed by a similar estate in Norbury. This was also the time that cheap land was bought in Purley in the slump of the late 1900s, to be used in the 1920s, and by the middle of the decade sales were running at around 400 a year.[2]

It was about then that Edward's three sons came into the business – Norman in 1923, Ronald 1928 and Allan in 1930. By now, the first generation had largely withdrawn from the business. Norman went to Emmanuel School in Wandsworth and also received some training in accountancy before going to work on the Norbury development. 'He rapidly and easily learned building and marketing techniques, the latter being of increasing importance as the company grew.'[3] The company's financial resources were strengthening and it appears to have been Norman who took Wates into its first major London site, 1000 houses at Streatham Vale built over five years from 1926 in 'what was then an enormous speculation.'[4] It was the scale of that purchase that presumably led to the incorporation of Wates Ltd at the end of 1924 – the Articles specifically mention the purchase of a freehold estate of 56 acres in Streatham.

Rapid expansion in south London makes Wates one of the largest housebuilders

There followed a period of rapid expansion all the more remarkable for its very narrow geographical concentration, 'almost exclusively in one area embracing Sidcup, Catford, Lewisham, New Malden, Streatham and Croydon. Wates' philosophy was that by concentrating the development it undertook in one area only, it could keep a permanent work force and need not rely upon casual labour. Moreover, the company recruited its work force from the locality in which it developed and generally took on its payroll only those who were within cycling distance of the area.'[5] The financial policy regarding profit and land prices was also refreshingly simple. 'As little as £30 [profit] per house was deemed sufficient, because that represented the price that was paid for the plot, and Wates worked on the principle that if it could get the money out of a completed house quickly by selling cheaply, it would buy the next plot that much quicker.'[6]

Within ten years of joining his family business, Norman Wates had turned it into one of the biggest

---

[1] *Building*, 12th December 1969.
[2] Unpublished typescript history.
[3] *Dictionary of Business Biography, 1984-86.*
[4] Unpublished typescript history.
[5] Rose, *Dynamics of Urban Property Development*, p.98.
[6] Ibid,pp.98-9.

housebuilders in the country. By World War II, Wates is believed to have built some 30,000 houses and is widely quoted as regularly building around 2000 a year during the 1930s. Unpublished interviews in 1970 with senior executives all confirmed their own memories of a steady 2000 a year in the mid 1930s,[7] although the main sales ledger showed a smaller 1500 a year. In the early part of the decade, the sales were achieved off 10 or 12 sites but the larger sites became more difficult to find and by 1938 Wates was operating off 26 sites. These was still largely confined to south-east London although there were also sites in Oxford and Coventry.

Move into general construction

Norman Wates became a leading figure in the housebuilding industry and was one of the small group instrumental in establishing the National House Builders Council in 1935. Shortly after the war he was to become President of the Federation of Housebuilders. He became close friends with Godfrey Mitchell [Wimpey], Frank Taylor [Taylor Woodrow] and Owen Aisher [Marley], and the four became partners in housing development in the New York State in the mid 1930s. That was also about the time (1936) that Wates moved into general contracting (under Allan Wates) which proved to be a major contributor to the wartime effort. Its work included aerodromes, factories, docks and it was one of the leading contractors on the Mulberry Harbour. A testament to Wates' standing came immediately after the war. 'Before the war the name of Wates stood for all that is best in the production of houses by individual enterprise. It still does, but it is now much more. The firm of Wates Ltd. have been builders of good houses for nearly half a century… They were "master builders" in the best sense of the term. They initiated their own enterprise, selected admirable sites, laying them out in the most attractive manner and using their competent architectural staff in their ever-improving designs and increasing amenities, and in devising the most effective fittings and equipment to ensure comfort and ease of working in every house.[8]

The private housing work after the war was confined to filling in undeveloped portions of pre-war estates and, although small scale, the 300 houses completed by 1950 may have been more than many achieved. However, like Taylor Woodrow and Wimpey, Wates' wartime construction work had given it an expertise in concrete technology; in Wates' case it came in the person of Charles Mitchell, the senior non-family member of the firm, who had previously worked for the Trussed Concrete Steel Company, one of the pioneers in the concrete industry. This was Wates entrée to the local authority housing market, and as early as the summer of 1945 it built its first pair of non-traditional houses at Sutton; by 1951 it had built 10,000 for the Ministry of Works. Important though local authority housing was, Wates emphasis was increasingly on construction and overseas where businesses were opened in the USA, Morocco, France, Holland and Sweden, frequently licensing their high rise housing system. One of the largest contracts was the joint venture with the Rouse Corporation to build the Columbia new town between Baltimore and Washington.

The restart of active private housing as controls were lifted was perhaps a little slower than it might have been; even in the mid-1950s Wates was still tidying up old sites and it was not until 1957 that it started buying land again, building around 100 units a year. In 1958 Wates Built Homes was formed with the executive home as its target and a fresh wave of expansion and innovation then began. At this point, the Wates Built Homes board consisted solely of family members with Neil Wates, if not formally managing director, very much in charge. To avoid confusion, we now need to refer to the third generation of Wates. Both Norman and Ronald Wates had three sons: Neil was Norman Wates' eldest son and a charismatic figure, and a later description outlined the relevant roles. 'We now find Neil Wates, articulate and incisive,

[7] Bundock, 'Speculative Housebuilding'.
[8] *The Housebuilder,* June 1946.

disconcertingly direct at times, as primus inter pares, Michael looking after marketing and communications, Christopher responsible for finance matters and Paul concerned with commercial developments other than housing.[9]

Early emphasis on marketing

Wates was clear which part of the housing market it was targeting. Allan Holland, who later became sales director, remembers the discussions with Norman Wates when Wates Built Homes was started. 'Norman Wates sat down and drew a pyramid. The top part are the very wealthy. They are well served by the smaller builders. The bottom part are people in council houses. The block above that are the volume builders. What we want is the bit above the volume builders – what today would be called the executive market. We went into that specifically, and in areas that other builders would not touch. At one time we had $12\frac{1}{2}\%$ of what I would call the work in the London Boroughs. No other builder had as much as 1% – because they would not touch urban renewal. East Croydon was the largest private urban renewal project in Britain.'[10]

One of the features of Wates housing at the time was that its designs were more imaginative, quicker to recognise contemporary living patterns (e.g. the family room off the kitchen), backed up by an emphasis on marketing which was rare in an industry which had been operating in a sellers' market since the end of controls. The author remembers attending a conference in the mid-1960s where Neil Wates literally shocked the housebuilders in the audience by announcing that he would sub-contract anything from the foundations to the roof but the one operation he would never sub-contract was marketing. It is probably fair to say that Wates' emphasis on marketing pre-dated Barratt by a decade.

Wates became known for its large schemes often based on partnerships with large landowners. The Church Commissioners supplied land in East Croydon and the Hyde Park Estate in Bayswater, while land in Dulwich came from the College. Gradually Wates' volumes were rebuilt and, helped by a midlands division, probably reached 1000 to 1250 by 1972-73, and these volumes would have been at substantially higher than average selling prices. When the recession came, Wates significantly scaled down the level of its private development, perhaps to as low as 200-250 a year, not wanting to deplete its land stock in poor market conditions. Instead, there was an emphasis on joint venture deals with local authorities; in total, Wates post-recession volumes might have been around 700-800.

Death of Norman Wates leads to family split

Perhaps of more fundamental impact than the recession were the changes in family management. Norman Wates, the driving force behind the company for forty years, died in the Summer of 1969. His brother Ronald Wates succeeded him as Chairman, standing down in favour of Neil Wates in March 1973. Barely two years later Neil Wates resigned as Chairman and Managing Director after a celebrated boardroom row, to be succeeded by his brother Christopher. *Building* magazine contrasted the resignation to the way in which Norman Wates handed over 2 years previously when it was presented as a logical generational succession. However, the article suggested that both events were evidence of boardroom splits brought about by family strains and by the strong personality of Neil Wates and that the death of Norman Wates had removed the one man who could hold the disparate family members together. 'Neil Wates had been Managing Director since 1964 and the strong and intensely felt opinions and ambitions he held about and for the group made it increasingly difficult to accept the chairmanship of his uncle Ronald …Now Ronald's son Michael is to become Chairman and there is to be no new chief executive.'

[9] *Building*, 18th July 1969.
[10] Interview with Allan Holland, May 1999.

No explanation of the change was forthcoming from the company, but it probably reflected both policy and personality differences. Neil Wates was described as 'a demanding man with an impatience for the superfluous. He has never been afraid to voice strong opinions as when he shocked the business community in1970 by launching a well publicised attack on South Africa's apartheid and refusing to do business there.'[11]

Partly because Neil Wates had been withdrawing from housing in favour of a wider involvement in the group, Wates Built Homes experienced a number of top level changes, some involving family, some not, and one Managing Director even came from a background of the Sudanese political service and Kleenex. It was not until 1976, when Bill Gair joined as Managing Director, that Wates Built Homes had a continuity of direction. It was also constructed as a proper company rather than just a brand name operating within Wates Limited. For the second time, volumes were rebuilt and housing returned to profit. Apart from Wates Built Homes itself, Blakes of Oxford was bought in 1978, Marc Gregory's land was built out for the banks and Sunley Homes' land was similarly developed for Eagle Star following the latter's acquisition of Bernard Sunley Investment Trust. The company is unwilling to provide information but, including the joint ventures, it is thought that Wates was selling over 1500 units a year by the late 1980s. With profits peaking at £16m in 1988 there was even consideration of a flotation for the housing company (Wates' commercial property business had been successfully floated in 1984, raising £41m).

The decline in housing

As before, the recession produced fundamental change in the positioning of the housing company. The family appeared to want to run for cash and sold land in a falling market but, unlike others that did the same, did not reverse that policy when the land market bottomed out. Bill Gair left in 1991; the role of managing director oscillated between Christopher Wates and outsiders, none staying in the role for long. Losses were incurred every year from 1990 to 1994 reaching almost £50 million in total. By the end of the 1990s, Wates was building little more than 100 houses a year, and only 50-60 some years after that, a pale shadow of its former self. It is difficult to know why the decline has been so pronounced. Certainly, the succession from the dominant family figure was not handled to the company's benefit and perhaps there were too many family members in the business at one time. On the other hand, the family has had a wide range of interests in the construction and development area and one part should not necessarily be judged in isolation – Wates City of London Properties has made substantial sums for the family as did other ventures such as Pinnacle Leisure, sold for a family profit of £25m. Perhaps that has created an equivocal attitude to role of the private housing company.

[11] *Building,* 11th April 1975.

WESTBURY
Peak units: 4538 (2003)

Westbury was established by the Joiner family in Gloucestershire and formally dates its formation to 1964; prior to that, Stanley Joiner had a civil engineering business. There were three sons, John, Jim and Bob, and a daughter Margaret, each of whom was entitled to a quarter share in the combined business assets. The next family venture was actually in the unconnected television rental sector; this was sold on to the American ITT. It was only then that John and Bob Joiner looked for another venture, the favoured candidates being package holidays and housebuilding. Allegedly, a toss of the coin determined it would be housebuilding and the Joiners duly bought some land and started building houses.[1] Although the father had some building background, the sons had no direct experience; rather they were a family that were owners of businesses rather than operators. The Westbury name came from the first site that the Joiners investigated (although never bought) in Westbury-on-Severn in the Forest of Dean.

Geoff Hester develops Westbury for the Joiner family

Westbury probably built no more than 100 houses between 1964 and 1971. What enabled the Joiners to expand was the recruitment of Geoff Hester in 1971. Hester, a one-time county council surveyor, had worked for the Joiners on a part-time basis as a land surveyor. 'Geoff was a dynamo and he had a way of motivating people. Eventually they must have hit a little bit of a purple patch and sold a few houses quickly and took him on full time. He moved on to arranging the contractors and doing the selling; effectively he was self-taught. He was the real catalyst for the Joiners to develop the business. They had the grand ideas but Geoff was the person who could actually put it into practice.'[2] Geoff Hester was appointed operations director in 1971 and Chief Executive in 1973. By this time, Westbury had raised its annual output to around 250-300. Throughout its existence, Westbury was managed by professionals rather than the founding family. 'The Joiners could think things through; they had great clarity of objective but they were not hands-on managers.'[3]

Westbury began making meaningful profits at a time of very high rates of tax and exchange controls and the family felt the need of a bolt hole from the UK. Jim Joiner lived in Canada, and finance was provided for him to start a new business. Around the same time, Bob Joiner also emigrated; he moved to the Bahamas and established what was to be Westbury's ultimate holding company. Thus, from 1973 to 1976, John Joiner became the titular head of Westbury. With Geoff Hester running the business operationally, Westbury began its first regional expansion, into South Wales, although the recession saw its temporary closure the following year. That brief period of expansion brought in two future managing directors. Richard Fraser, Managing Director from 1981 to 1995, joined the South Wales operation as accountant in November 1973 (having previously been a management accountant with Avon Rubber). Martin Donohue, who succeeded Fraser, joined in 1972 from John Laing where he had been a surveyor. The other key member of the team was the Finance Director John Caines who, although only there for a short while, 'had the tremendous ability to get the secondary and tertiary banks to fund developments from a very weak balance sheet. We were highly geared, never mind 50% we were geared something like 10-1. You wonder how the banks ever lent these sums of money to the company.'[4] At that point Westbury was building perhaps 100 units a year in South Wales and 200-300 in the Gloucester area.

[1] Interview with Martin Donohue, Jan. 2001.
[2] Interview with Richard Fraser, Sep. 2000.
[3] Geoff Hester correspondence with author.
[4] Interview Richard Fraser.

The first family split

In 1975 there was the first of the family splits that put pressure on the Westbury equity base. Under the family agreement, Jim was entitled to a quarter of the family's business assets even though his Canadian company had actually lost money. He withdrew his equity and Westbury assumed control of the Canadian business. Richard Fraser spent a year there followed by Martin Donohue, but it was decided to close the company in 1977. With the recession over, Westbury resumed its expansion plans. Wales was re-opened around 1976, a Bristol region was formed and the central region was based in Gloucester. By the early 1980s there were three regions, each capable of building around 500 units; Westbury actually reached 1600 completions in 1984 compared with less than 700 in 1977. Although the UK business was growing rapidly, the Joiners still wanted an overseas business and this time focused on the USA. Richard Fraser remembers going with Geoff Hester to the housebuilders' conventions: 'we talked to companies about buying them but in the end we just took some money over to Houston and started from scratch.' In 1981 Martin Donohue moved out to take operational control and it quickly became a profitable business. Meanwhile, there were more personality conflicts brewing. Geoff Hester parted company with John Joiner in 1981; he was compensated with 10% of the estimated value of Westbury, and was succeeded as Managing Director by Richard Fraser. Then John and Bob Joiner parted. John Joiner took the Houston business, which was then making almost as much money in late 1982 as the UK, and some cash; unfortunately, in the aftermath of the oil crisis, the Houston business began to lose money and failed shortly after. Bob Joiner was then left at the head of the UK business having spent the previous ten years in the Bahamas. In effect, the two brothers reversed their roles.

Regional expansion follows Joiners' departure

By 1984, Bob Joiner wanted to realise his now considerable investment in Westbury. A flotation was arranged but, just two days before the underwriting date, interest rates were raised by two points and the issue was pulled. Westbury was then put up for sale and the successful £11.8m bid was from the management team led by Richard Fraser. In April 1986 the company again arranged a flotation, this time successfully, with a valuation of £39m. A few months later, in the October, Westbury made its first acquisition, the Midlands division of Whelmar for £13m. This provided the impetus for an internal restructuring. Although Westbury had been building in three different regions, they were not truly self sufficient operations. 'At that point we were doing 1600 units very much from a centralised operation. After Whelmar, we opened offices in what had become the four separate regions. We could never really get our volumes above the 1600 level and we came to the conclusion that it was because we were so centralised.'[5] After 1986, Westbury did indeed accelerate its production reaching a peak of 2400 in 1988, and it opened two further regions in the south and the west midlands.

One of the consequences of the family ownership arrangements was the continual drain of capital from the business which limited the opportunities for acquiring a long land bank. Westbury's new-found public status gave it the opportunity to change that, and between 1987 and 1990 the land bank trebled – with hindsight, not the ideal timing. Richard Fraser: 'We had access to capital, we had always felt that we had been starved of land because of the Joiner spending habits, always around the 18-22 months supply; we didn't have any longer term options and we had always said that if we ever got the chance to run this ourselves we would lengthen the land bank. We had had two or three good years after the Whelmar acquisition and we all began to believe we could walk on water. Anybody else knew it was partly because of inflation but we thought it was because we could manage the business.' When things go wrong in the housing business, it tends to be the areas most distant from home that cause most problems. Westbury had two divisions with the traditional Westbury area run by Donohue, and there were no land write-offs

5 Ibid.

in Wales or Gloucestershire. However, the southern region was still expanding and it opened an office in Fareham and started buying at exactly the wrong time. Richard Fraser: 'So, it was a couple of things. It was not just us expanding the land bank for the sake of it, it was trying to get into different territory – giving the Northampton team a bit more cash and setting up the Fareham office.'

Westbury held its volumes well through the recession of the early 1990s largely through substantial sales to housing associations – as many as 700 in 1993. However, provisions against land values totalled £38m over the period and pre-tax losses were incurred in the three years to 1993. From then, Westbury steadily restored its profitability as the older high-cost land was worked out. Housing association sales were replaced by private sales and then Westbury's geographical expansion was resumed. In May 1993, Westbury formally set itself a target of 3500 sales a year by 1998 (Westbury actually beat it by 24 units). However, before that period expired, Richard Fraser announced his resignation, in October 1995: 'I just didn't fancy sticking it out for another five or six years. It got a bit too bureaucratic; I was too distant from the people; I felt it was time for someone else to do it.'[6]

More acquisitions but little growth in volumes

In 1995, Westbury made the first of a series of regional acquisitions. Clarke Homes, a substantial loss-maker during the recession, was bought from BICC; Fraser had made approaches a year earlier without success so when Clarke Homes was formally put up for sale in mid-1995, Westbury was able to move quickly. The £61m acquisition was completed by Martin Donohue in December 1995; in part, Clarke Homes was a means of acquiring land in Westbury's existing regions but it also strengthened the business in the midlands and took the company further into the south. In 1998, Westbury acquired a readymade north-west. region; Maunders, which was building over 1000 units a year was purchased for £55m. These two acquisitions helped lift Westbury's completions to 4300 in 1998/99, making it the seventh largest housebuilder in the country. The third acquisition was of Prowting for £141m in June 2002, which strengthened Westbury's position in the western home counties. By then, group volumes had fallen back to 3800 and the acquisition of Prowting did little more than return volumes to their 1998/99 peak.

By the end of the 1990s, Donohue was taking Westbury into territory which, if not entirely new, was different from traditional housebuilder strategy: 'We have also set out to differentiate ourselves by developing from a traditional housebuilder to a more innovative retailer of both new homes and home-related products and services.'[7] Most housebuilders would claim to differentiate their product but a key part of Westbury's strategy was to pursue vertical integration. A factory was purchased at Castle Bromwich and £13m invested capable of producing 5000 prefabricated housing units a year; 'Space4' was to supply a substantial part of Westbury's requirements, and generate sales to third parties. Space4 was instrumental in Westbury winning the 'Best building efficiency initiative' in the *Building Homes* Quality Awards in 2001. Parallel with a move towards vertical integration was the launch of Westbury Direct in 1999 with the aim of providing a wide range of home-related products and services to existing Westbury homeowners and to new customers, including financial services, white goods and removals. Although management remained positive about both ventures, they were still losing money in 2004.

Quoted companies are vulnerable to comparison with their peers, and there was increasing speculation about Westbury's future as an independent entity. Although profits had shown strong growth as house prices rose, volumes had shown no change since 1999 and operating margins were lower than the average for the sector. In November 2005 Persimmon announced an agreed bid for Westbury worth £643m.

[6] Ibid.
[7] Group Accounts, 2000.

WHELMAR
Peak units: 3200 (1973)

Through the 1970s and 1980s, Tom Baron was one of those housebuilders whose name was almost better known than that of his company. A Lancastrian, whose accent deepened the further south he came, he was a chartered surveyor who strayed into housebuilding almost by accident. He was a founder member and Secretary of the Volume Housebuilders Group; an original thinker whose speeches where as humorous as they were thought provoking; and, in 1979, special advisor to Michael Heseltine, then Secretary of State for Environment. For the industry he was 'Incisive, imaginative and a brilliant if at times voluble advocate'[1]

Tom Baron was a grammar school boy who joined Dunlop Heywood, probably Manchester's largest surveying practice, in 1941, aged 16, becoming a chartered surveyor. In the early 1950s he realised that housebuilding for sale would expand rapidly when a Conservative Government came into power and persuaded various clients to buy potential building land in the north west at prices averaging £200 per acre; he put in roads and sewers and sold land in blocks to a variety of housebuilders. By 1958 he was becoming disenchanted with the quality of the housing they built which in his view did nothing to enhance the value and saleability of his remaining land. As he succinctly put it: 'I realised how often they made a balls of it and I used to think "I could do better than this." By 1962 I was probably the biggest spec builder outside Wimpeys though nobody had heard of me, because I was working for seven companies. The involvement was total but I couldn't take an equity stake in any of my clients under the rules of the RICS.'[2]

Readers who have approached these company histories in alphabetical order will have realised the overlap with Broseley and Metropolitan Railway Country Estates. The relationship between Whelmar and Broseley was more a personal one between two entrepreneurs (although Baron did have options in Broseley) but the work with the railway offshoots was fundamental to the creation of the Whelmar business. In 1958, William Balch, Managing Director of Metropolitan Railway Surplus Lands, and Metropolitan Railway Country Estates agreed to set up a joint venture between the two public companies with Tom Baron, aged 33, running it. Whelmar was then a dormant subsidiary of MRCE and was chosen as the vehicle. Expansion was rapid and in 1965, the MRCE Chairman was telling shareholders that the Whelmar associate had a target of 1000 houses for the year.

Whelmar moves to Christian Salvesen
In 1968 Metropolitan Railway Surplus Lands was taken over by MEPC and they agreed with MRCE to sell Whelmar to Christian Salvesen, the ex-whaling group that had moved into transport, food and refrigeration. Salvesen, another important client of Dunlop Heywood, merged its housing into Whelmar. Salvesen also bought a stake in Tom Baron's management company (Dunlop Heywood Housing Limited); Tom Baron then closed down all the other housing activities and concentrated on the enlarged Whelmar. In 1972, Baron was appointed Dunlop Heywood senior partner, a promotion that would normally have been regarded as the pinnacle of a professional career. By then, Whelmar was building 2500 units a year and Salvesen was concerned at its size relative to the rest of the group, given that they did not control Whelmar's management. Within a year, Salvesen persuaded Tom Baron to retire from the senior partnership, bought out the balance of Dunlop Heywood Housing and Baron joined the Christian Salvesen board.[3]

---

[1] *Building*, April 1982.
[2] *Housebuilder*, August 1986.
[3] Correspondence with Tom Baron.

Salvesen bought a number of housing companies in the early 1970s including the quoted Eldon Gorst in North Wales; Hawker Homes in north-east Scotland; Kenton Homes in Doncaster (200-300 units in 1971/72); Hemmings and Kent in Leyland (500-600); Ashton and McCaul in Leigh (c.500); and J & A Jackson Limited. These acquisitions were made to expand Whelmar geographically and to acquire land banks; all were absorbed into Salvesen Homes. In 1972/73, the last financial year before the recession, Whelmar sold 3200 houses, vying with Northern Developments for second place behind Wimpey, by then in a different league to everybody else. Those volumes were never achieved again. After the recession it was decided to let sales settle at around 2000-2500, to 'avoid the risks of over exposure in the volatile market which existed between 1974 and the mid eighties.'[4]

Christian Salvesen floated as a public company in 1985 and Tom Baron retired the following year, not wanting to be part of a public company – 'a pet aversion of mine.'[5] With the founder and guiding light of the business departing, Christian Salvesen decided on a sale of Whelmar and offered it in five regional slices. By February 1987 the last of these had been sold raising a total of £50m. These comprised the Midlands division to Westbury; Scotland to Tilbury; Yorkshire to Beazer; Lancashire to Redrow while Whelmar (Chester) was the subject of a management buy out led by Ron Smith, eventually turning into Wainhomes.

[4] Ibid.
[5] Ibid.

WILLIAM WHITTINGHAM
Peak units: c.1000 (1972)

William Whittingham was a substantial midlands developer whose independent existence was cut short by the premature death of the third-generation managing director. The business was founded in 1930 by William Whittingham, who started as a subcontract painter in 1908 and was also a pub landlord and a bookmaker. His son William David was working as a carpenter for a local builder and in 1933 joined his father; as specialists in two of the key trades, they gradually expanded into housebuilding. William finally retired in 1950 and his son 'who was fortunate to still have some building land they had possessed before the war, gave rein to his adventurous entrepreneurial gifts and built on this land bank.'[1] The third generation was represented by Tom Whittingham; after spending two years at the Brixton School of Building and a further two years as a quantity surveyor; he joined the firm around 1960.

When the Company floated in February 1964, it was still only developing housing estates within a 35 mile radius of Wolverhampton. Volumes were not disclosed but Whittingham did hold residentially-zoned land for 3000 houses. A year after going public William David Whittingham fell ill; Tom was then aged 26. 'A serious problem faced the company when WD Whittingham became seriously ill and Tom Whittingham had to take on discussions about a possible take-over. Characteristically, he handled the crisis firmly and successfully manoeuvred himself into the managing director's position and rejected the take-over advances.'[2] Two years later his father died and Tom became Chairman.

Tom expanded the firm rapidly, spreading the business across the midlands. He also became actively involved in the HBF particularly in marketing; he became Chairman of the marketing committee on its formation in the late 1960s, introducing marketing courses based on the experience gained in USA and Europe. In 1971, he became the youngest HBF President, aged 32. By 1970, Whittingham was building 600 private houses a year, increasing to almost 1000 by 1972. There was also a property development division, an environmental engineering subsidiary, and a photographic processing company (Colortrend). Turnover rose to £10m in 1973 and pre-tax profits £2m. Whittingham entered the recession highly geared, and although its losses in the next couple of years totalled no more than one million pounds, its future was not guaranteed. Whittingham in turn added to the troubles of others. In November 1973 the secondary bank Vavasseur bought 18% of the shares at a cost of £1.9m and by the June of 1974 was showing a loss of £1.3m

Profits slowly recovered and then the Company was struck again in January 1977 when Tom died aged only 38. Geoff Sharples joined the Board as joint Managing Director teaming up with PJ Howells; midlands businessman John Wardle came in as Chairman. The business consolidated and, helped by an exceptional contribution from Colortrend, group profits reached £3m by 1981. Unfortunately, 'an orgy of price cutting' in the processing industry completely eliminated Colortrend's profits in 1982;[3] housing profits were difficult to earn; and interest charges remained high. Housing sales were now down to only 400 a year; group profits fell to £600,000 and Whittingham was vulnerable. In July 1983 Milbury announced that it had acquired a 9% shareholding and bid 83p for sufficient additional shares to take it to 29.9% (the maximum that could be acquired without making a full bid). John Wardle was also on the board of Barclays Merchant Bank and was instrumental in arranging an agreed bid from Comben at 130p a share, valuing the company at £8m.

[1] *Housebuilder*, Jan 1971.
[2] Ibid.
[3] Group Accounts, 1982.

WILSON CONNOLLY
Peak units: 4700 (1999)

Thomas Wilson, a shoemaker, left Northampton in the early 1890s, to seek his fortune in America, walking to Liverpool en route. He remained in the New England states for a decade before finding work on a new building. While there he married Elizabeth Connolly of Lynn, Massachusetts – thereby explaining the future name of both the company and its directors. He returned to England in 1904 and started his own small building company. In that year, Connolly Thomas Wilson was born and Thomas Wilson also built his first house, for his brother-in-law.

After the First War, Thomas Wilson continued his general construction business, and work for Northampton Corporation included some contract housing. Con Wilson, the only child, joined his father in 1920 aged 15 and played an increasing part in the inter-war growth of the business (later known as T Wilson & Son). Ancillary activities included a small brickworks and Mix Concrete, later a public company in its own right. Wilcon did not appear to begin speculative housing until 1932 when it was advertising three-bedroom 'Villa Residences' in the Northampton area for £550; at that time private housing was seen as just another way to make money in a widely-based construction business. For the rest of the 1930s, Wilcon maintained an active housing programme, although largely confined to the Northampton area, averaging around 150 units a year. Con Wilson, now taking a larger role in running the business, also decided that the company should also have a property base and in 1934 Newilton was formed to build a block of flats; commercial property development later followed.

Wartime construction

Construction became the dominant activity during the war, and the firm was engaged in aerodrome maintenance contracts, particularly at the USAAF bases. Thomas Wilson had died in 1942 and the company was under the sole control of Con Wilson after the war. Reconstruction work and housebuilding for Northampton Corporation were the Company's mainstay and during the 1950s it was building some 200 houses a year for the Northampton Corporation. There was no serious attempt to restart private housing until the end of controls in 1954. A need to relocate the plant depot from the centre of Northampton led to an increased commitment to property development and, indirectly, the start of regional expansion. A 16-acre site was purchased outside Northampton, far bigger than the company needed, and an industrial estate was started. One of the early client relationships was with Plessey, and Wilcon built factories for the company in Northampton, Hampshire and Swindon, the latter leading to the formation of Wilsons Swindon. This was at first a construction business but later moved into estate development. Otherwise, the only other area where Wilcon build speculative houses in the 1950s was Rugby.

A third generation of Wilsons joined the company in the 1950s. Con Wilson's elder son, FCT Wilson (known as 'young Con') trained as a bricklayer and although active in the management of the company into the 1960s, eventually decided that he preferred to work on his own. It was the younger Lynn Wilson who was eventually to play the dominant family role. Lynn Wilson was educated at Oakham School (his father could only afford one private education) joining Wilson Builders (Northampton) in 1957. Surveying skills were acquired at technical college while 'I went through every department in the business and on various management training courses but I was almost chucked in at the deep end – at age 26 I found myself joint Managing Director of a plc.'[1]

---

[1] Interview with Lynn Wilson, Sep. 2000.

Lynn Wilson becomes joint Managing Director

Lynn Wilson became joint Managing Director of the group with his father, (whose health by then was failing) in 1966, on the flotation of what then became Wilson (Connolly). Although at the time of the float the company was operating on a very localised basis, the Prospectus revealed sizeable speculative volumes, 5100 over the ten years to 1964, with the annual average being over 600 in the most recent three; in 1965, some 750 houses were sold, 550 by the Northampton parent and 200 by Wilsons Swindon. Pre-tax profits were disclosed at £350,000 having risen from £86,000 over the ten year period; this included £62,000 from the substantial property portfolio. The profits forecast of £325,000 was slightly lower than the last historic figure, but that forecast was not met; indeed it was not reached until 1970. Looking back in better times, Lynn Wilson referred to the Prospectus forecast as being 'not entirely justified…What matters is that we have now developed management attitudes and controls which should stand us in good stead when conditions in our industry change once again and the going gets much harder.'[2] Helped by price inflation, profits increased in 1972, to £1.2m, a level which the company held through the recession.

Mike Robinson arrives

Lynn Wilson became sole Managing Director in 1970 on the death of his father. In that same year, Mike Robinson joined as Chief Executive of the construction and housing division. The company's history some ten years later said that the appointment 'Provided additional flair and leadership at a moment in the company's and the industry's history which was singularly well timed.' *Housebuilder* was later to write of him 'He was a man of immense size, of power, of strength, of presence. He had a directness of approach that was astonishing in its honesty and simplicity. With an acute sense of humour that was never far from the surface.'[3] The reality was a symbiotic relationship with the Wilson family in which Robinson transformed the company into one of the most highly regarded national housebuilders.

The decision to bring in an outsider at such a senior level is always a bold one for a family controlled company and showed shrewd judgement on the part of the young managing director. Lynn Wilson: 'What I realised was that the executives my father had, merely took his instructions and were not capable of running the thing without his direction. I realised that if you are a public company then you have to perform. I wanted to be first division so you have to get first division management. I don't know that I ever said to myself I can't do this but what I did say was that I definitely need some help. When we interviewed Mike there was almost electricity between us within five minutes. He knew exactly what he wanted; he had a very analytic mind, although there were times that one had to pour oil on troubled waters. He was a fantastic operator and ahead of his time by miles.'[4]

Regional expansion

Mike Robinson was educated at Whitgift School Croydon, taking a first in civil engineering at London University; his early career was with ICI, Tarmac and then Page Johnson. In 1972 he was appointed joint Managing Director with Lynn Wilson, and sole Managing Director in 1982 following Lynn Wilson's year as President of the HBF. In that year's annual report, Lynn Wilson, now Chairman, wrote: 'Mike Robinson's arrival with us in 1970 proved to be a milestone marking the start of an era of accelerating profits to which his contribution, particularly in housing, has been literally invaluable. Now the impact of his standards and his personality are felt everywhere within the Group and respected everywhere outside it.' Robinson's first priorities were to revamp the designs and layout and make the business more functional and cost effective. Most of the employee tradesmen were turned into sub-contractors and the

---

2 Group accounts, 1971.
3 *Housebuilder*, Oct. 1990.
4 Interview Lynn Wilson

construction and housebuilding operations were formally separated. Once that had been done, Wilcon was able to pursue volume growth and a period of regional expansion followed, first into Wales, then Yorkshire, Nottinghamshire, and a south coast office in Southampton. By 1978, unit volumes were comfortably through the 1000 mark; combined with an improvement in operating margins, this took profits from £0.7m in 1971 to £5.5m in 1979.

Significantly, the 1973/4 housing collapse made barely a dent in the annual profits progression. One of the remarkable features of Wilcon was its ability to control volumes to smooth out the housing cycle. Thus, at the tail end of the 1970s, when the industry was enjoying a strong increase in demand, volumes were reduced from 1221 to 1016 – the author remembers Mike Robinson explaining that they just took the salesmen off site. Conversely, in the more difficult period that followed, Wilcon doubled its sales in four years. The equally simplistic explanation that 'we made the salesmen work harder' belied the fact that Wilcon had a lower cost product than most in the industry, produced economically at prices that would always attract buyers.

Mike Robinson dies

Wilcon continued to extend its geographical coverage during the 1980s, primarily from its existing operational centres, although the Scottish market was entered in 1986. Volumes increased to 2600 by 1987 but as the boom became yet more frenetic Wilcon again behaved in counter-cyclical manner and reduced its sales by 30% in two years while profits climbed to a record £54m, albeit that owed more to the property division than had previously been the case. During the 1980s the company had disposed of its old investment portfolio and turned itself into an active developer of property parks; helped by investment sales, the property contribution to group profits reached £17m in 1989 against only £2m in 1987.

In June 1990 Mike Robinson died in a swimming accident. His commanding presence and control over all aspects of the business made succession difficult at short notice. Ian Black, previously Finance Director and then Commercial Director, succeeded Robinson. He had been the intended successor but was thrown into the managing director's role at the worst possible time. Looking back some years later Ian Black said 'Mike had been a guiding light and in some ways the guru of the industry, so it would have been nice to have had him round to advise during the recession but, as it was, we faced situations that we had never faced before.'[5] Once again, volumes were doubled in the face of an industry recession, reaching a new peak of 4200 in 1994, well over double the 1989 level. This time it was insufficient to hold profits. By the standards of the industry, land provisions in 1990 and 1991 were relatively modest; the low point for profits was the £17m in 1992 – again, more than most of its competitors were earning. Perhaps the disappointment was that Wilcon was unable to ride out the smaller market setback in 1995 and profits fell once more.

Lynn Wilson conceded two fundamental mistakes. The first was not to have sold everything that they could at the top of the market. 'We would have made over £70m but we would have been cash rich at the right moment – and then have come to the City and said we are not going to repeat this next year. The other mistake that we made was not to make large provisions against land values. We traded the land out over a period of time so you died a death by a thousand cuts. If I had my time again the two things that I would do would be to take the market when it was in flood and I would have written values down. So Ian did inherit a difficult situation but unfortunately we didn't climb out of it with flying colours in 1995.'[6] However, what the mid 1990s did see was a greater focusing of the business on private housing.

5 *Building Homes*, Nov. 1996.
6 Interview Lynn Wilson.

The group supported management buyouts in both construction (1994), where it recognised that its presence was no more than a historical accident, and property (1996) to effect a controlled withdrawal from those markets. It also began to move the product range more up market. Ian Black described Wilcon as 'the Ford of housebuilding selling one, two, three and four beds. The new four and five beds will be our Jaguars.'[7] Wilcon also made its first acquisition in 1995 – the Glasgow based London & Clydeside, a small quoted company building around 250 units a year. Nevertheless, despite these changes, and despite its long land bank, volumes did not increase again until 1998, and it was not until the following year that Wilcon finally exceeded its 1989 profits peak.

Housing Units, 1971-2002

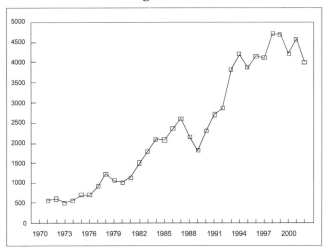

New management – the beginning of the end

The end of the decade saw a new management team emerge. Ian Black retired in 1999 to be succeeded by John Tutte, and Lynn Wilson announced the appointment of Allan Leighton, Chief Executive of Wal-Mart Europe, as Deputy Chairman with the intent of Leighton succeeding him as Chairman in 2001. Leighton arrived with some challenging views for the housebuilding industry: 'I think this industry is about to explode; it will just get completely reinvented. I am a change agent, and I have an intuitive feeling that we can lead this change. We will develop the most efficient supply chain in the world for the housebuilding industry.'[8] There are those who might have argued that Mike Robinson had achieved that once before but Leighton's vision went further than mere building efficiency. 'Behind the rhetoric, Leighton has a sound plan of action: razor-sharp supply-chain management, research and development of faster construction methods, buying up suppliers to achieve vertical integration and selling 10% of homes over the internet.'[9]

The new management had volume ambitions and, in April 2001, bought Wainhomes paying a generous £65m for £11m of net assets.[10] The attempt to apply retailing philosophy to the housebuilding was also leading to changes in operational methods, including rationalisation of the supply chain and the purchase of the Prestoplan timber frame business in January 2001: in the *Building Homes* Quality Awards in October

7   *Building Homes,* Nov. 1996.
8   *Building,* 11th Feb. 2000.
9   Ibid.
10 *PHA,* 2002, p.12.

2001, Wilcon won the award for 'Best company-wide sustainability strategy'; second prize for 'Best approach to partnering/supply chain management' and third prize for 'Best options and choices initiative.' The impact on the actual business was less flattering. A profits warning. in October 2001 (at the height of the boom, profits were to fall from £71m. to £43m.) led to the resignation of the Managing Director, and the architect of the change, Allan Leighton, assumed executive control.

Comments were critical: 'Allan Leighton has had a tremendous impact on Wilson Connolly...but the results are quite unexpected...Unfortunately, the similarities between housebuilding and retailing only go so far. Retailers sell goods, housebuilders buy land';[11] and 'The management fiasco at Wilcon has come home to roost.'[12] In March 2002, Graeme McCallum, formerly Managing Director of Alfred McAlpine Homes, was appointed Chief Executive and began a reorganisation which he described as no more than going back to basics: 'It doesn't require rocket science to put it right.'[13] The profits recovery was, indeed, rapid and, with expectations of a full recovery in 2003, the Wilson family, who still controlled 26% of the shares, lost little time in agreeing a £480m bid from Taylor Woodrow in September 2003.

[11] *Daily Telegraph,* 27th Oct. 2001.
[12] Credit Lyonnais Securities, *Mid-Cap Monitor,* Nov. 2001.
[13] Building, Mar .2002.

DAVID WILSON HOMES
Peak units: 5558 (2004)

David Wilson Homes originated from a partnership between David Wilson and his father Albert, although the reality is that the housebuilding business was the creation of the son, not the father. Albert was a carpenter by trade and employed four or five people and had a small joinery workshop, when he was joined by his son in 1960. David Wilson had a childhood ambition to be a dentist but around the age of 17 he abandoned that and decided that, somehow, he wanted to get into the building industry. He took the National Diploma in Building full-time at Leicester for two years but then his training was interrupted. 'At the end of that two years I was intending to do the HND but my father had his first heart attack during the summer holidays and I never went back.' The next few years included everything from driving the lorry to small building works. 'I was quite good at the architectural drawings and quite good at surveying and estimating. I could do a bungalow plan in about three or four hours. Someone would say "I would like a bungalow" and you asked them how much they wanted to spend; if you couldn't design it accordingly and leave a profit then it was a bit pathetic. I very quickly realised that the only way to make money in construction was to be in charge of the project; it was pretty obvious that there was more money in private housing than there was in contracting unless you were doing design and build.'[1]

A financial lesson
His first land deal gave David Wilson a rude insight into the world of finance. The land cost was £9000 compared with the overdraft limit of £11,000 but the bank stopped the cheque because he had not warned them he intended to spend so much money! 'I changed banks the next day from Midland to Lloyds: I suppose these are experiences that managers can never have.'[2] In retrospect, the business probably grew more slowly in the 1960s than David Wilson had hoped. The first large site was not bought until 1966 – for 36 detached houses in Packington, Leicestershire. However, it was not until 1971 that turnover exceeded a million pounds and 1972 when the first significant profits were made. By 1973, the onset of the recession, AH Wilson & Sons was building around 150 houses in its own name; there was also a joint company with First National Finance Corporation, Bowden Park Holdings and when First National got into difficulty, its 51 per cent was bought out.

AH Wilson (later David Wilson Homes) appeared to ride through the 1973/74 recession without a problem. 'I suppose our build costs were low and the midlands was a good place to be at the time. Also, I think we were quite innovative in those days; we had our Home Centres where buyers could choose and customise their homes. Borrowings were not high and we have always been fairly cautious and aware of what can happen in this industry.' At this point, David Wilson becomes quite reflective on the subject of caution and his comments could serve as a text for dealing with a highly cyclical industry. 'On the one hand you've got to be dynamic and ambitious but on the other hand you've got to be very aware of what can happen. Saying no is hard to do; I don't know why. It takes a lot of courage and intuition – and intuitive management can be very irritating for the people around you who like to have decisions explained clearly.'[3]

The first geographical expansion
Turnover and profits rose every year through the 1970s, finishing with unit sales of around 300, turnover of £13m and pre-tax profits of £1.6m. There had been modest geographic expansion in the midlands –

1 Interview David Wilson.
2 Ibid.
3 Ibid.

Rutland in 1969, Lincolnshire in 1974 – but the first real break from the midlands was a somewhat fortuitous move to the south coast where a Bournemouth office was opened in 1978. 'We had a business in Oakham called Tyres Brothers and one of the brothers said that Bournemouth was the place to be and he went there every year on his holidays. He managed to persuade a local firm of estate agents to let him use their boardroom and stayed there free of rent for two years. I suppose lots of businesses develop for the wrong reasons rather than sitting down logically and deciding 'where shall we expand.' We would like to think it is all an incredible plan but it isn't really.'[4]

Housing Units, 1980-2004

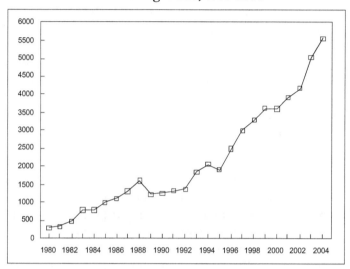

David Wilson was not a believer in large acquisitions but there were a number of small ones in the midlands. **William Corah** was bought in 1977, mainly for its land. **J G Parker**, bought in 1982 for £840,000, gave Wilson its entrée to the Nottingham area; the firm was then building around 50 houses per year. Parker retired, the Managing Director went to South Africa and Wilson installed its own management. **The French House Limited**, based in Coventry, and bought in 1983, had the most interesting background. It was owned, not surprisingly, by a French housebuilder that had decided it wanted to expand and came into the UK. 'They looked for a housebuilder who could speak French: they found one man but he cost them an absolute arm and a leg: they hadn't a clue what they were doing and they were building French chalets all around the Midlands. They gave us about eight or ten sites and that got us into the west midlands. It also gave us huge tax losses.'[5] Although these acquisitions are worth mentioning, the expansion was primarily home grown. David Wilson's preference in starting up a new region was to find a local man who knew the area well and exercise close supervision from the centre, particularly over land buying.

Diversification into property
The building contracting business had, by the mid-1970s, diversified into industrial development (helped by the Corah acquisition) and, in the early 1980s, into retail property. 'The thought process was that having a rental income would help out in times of difficulty and for many years the property business

[4] Ibid.
[5] Ibid.

had its overheads completely covered by rental income. We gradually dismantled [the investment portfolio] after the float because of the slight confusion as to why we owned property.'[6] Although the third-party contracting was gradually reduced, property development for sale continued to expand. Wilson's property operation was not the single site, city centre development but rather out-of-town (usually near motorway junctions) industrial estates/business parks, often a hundred acres or more. The economics of these commercial developments were more akin to those of the housebuilding business than of urban property development: large sites would be acquired on option with development taking place in phases as demand warranted.

The 1980s was the decade that marked Wilson's transition from a local housebuilder into a more serious force in the industry, with sales rising from 300 in 1980 to 1600 in 1988. Group profits reached a peak of £40m in 1989, against £2m, helped by an £8m contribution from property. The Group had been floated in March 1987 as Wilson Bowden, the second part of the name coming from the Bowden Park Holdings which had been used for the commercial property side of the business. The float secured David Wilson's personal position and provided a platform for further growth without stretching the balance sheet. By the time the 1990 recession arrived, David Wilson was too large to be unaffected but the company came through that difficult period in better shape than most other housebuilders. The same caution that had protected David Wilson some 15 years earlier, prevented the company paying excessive prices for land at the top of the market. Moreover, David Wilson also argued against the practice that some companies had adopted of holding back volumes at the top of the market; in contrast, he tried to push through as many sales as possible in 1988 and 1989, using those profits to make early (and undisclosed) write-downs on land.

The move to national coverage

Wilson was still heavily dependent on the midlands at the start of the 1990s (perhaps 80% of output) but that decade saw the company's transition to a near-national housebuilder with volumes approaching 4000. While many in the industry were still concentrating on survival, 1992 saw Wilson establish new operational areas including Hereford and Worcester, Hertfordshire and Kent. A clear strategy was set out for 1993 and 1994 to increase market share through expanded site coverage. A new office was opened in Leeds in 1993; in 1997 Wilson extended into the north west (Cheshire) and the first site was acquired in Wales; Glasgow followed in 1999. During this period (1996), Wilson had also made one strategic acquisition, the Berkshire firm of Trencherwood, which had a dominant position in the West Berkshire land market, but had been financially strained by the recession. In 2003, Wilson also bought the old-established housing business of Henry Boot, again largely for its land holdings, particularly in Yorkshire and Cheshire.

By the time of the Henry Boot acquisition, Wilson was building over 4000 units a year as against only 1200 at the beginning of the 1990s and had established itself as one of the most consistently successful of the quoted housebuilders. David Wilson himself had reached 60; his son James had joined the business in 1996 and was running one of the midlands housing subsidiaries but, at that stage, family succession could be no more than a theoretical possibility. Ian Robertson, the Finance Director, was appointed group Deputy Chief Executive at the beginning of 2001 and Chief Executive in 2003, thereby laying the basis for a transition to managerial succession in a business which had being controlled and run by one man for 40 years.

---

[6] Ibid.

WIMPEY HOMES
Peak units: 13,480 (2002)

Wimpey has been the pre-eminent British housebuilder of the twentieth century. Indeed, in the 1970s it became Europe's largest building contractor, although that aspect of its business only concerns us peripherally, insofar as it explains the Wimpey Homes' philosophy. The roots of the Company go back to 1880 when the 25-year-old George Wimpey established a stone-working business in Hammersmith but by 1919 the business had been substantially run down. It is at this point that the history of Wimpey really begins. The modern Wimpey was the creation of one man, Godfrey Way Mitchell, who dominated the company for sixty years. Godfrey Mitchell was born in Peckham in 1891; his uncle was joint Managing Director of Limmer & Trinidad Asphalt, and his father had a business in London, shipping granite from Alderney for sale to the London boroughs for road surfacing. Godfrey Mitchell attended Haberdashers' Aske's School until 1907 ('He shone at mathematics and science but his inability to spell caused many a dire report') leaving aged 16 to join his father at the London Bridge office. He learnt accounting and office management, the structure of the London market for roadstone and 'the intricacies of tendering and chartering.' He gained a commission in the Royal Engineers in 1916, and spent most of his war running quarries in the Pas de Calais.[1]

Godfrey Mitchell buys Wimpey

After the First War, the family firm was sold, leaving Godfrey Mitchell to search for a new business. On the advice of his uncle, he settled on George Wimpey, which he bought in June 1919 for £3000, raised from his post-war gratuity and the sale of 1000 shares in the Limmer & Trinidad; his father lent him £3000 for working capital. For most of the 1920s, Godfrey Mitchell developed Wimpey's previous activities, chiefly paving and roadworks, benefiting from the growth of suburban London. In particular, he used his wartime contacts to develop the use of clinker-based asphalt; this brought in Lionel Daniel Lewis who later took over the asphalt side of the business, becoming Godfrey Mitchell's right hand man and, most important of all, giving him the time to experiment with private housebuilding.

Private housing started in 1928

Amongst Wimpey's routine work was the construction of roads on other firms' housing estates, and at some point Godfrey Mitchell decided that he could do the development process more efficiently himself. He invested privately on a 50-50 basis with another individual and developed 12 plots of land. Once that worked, he took Wimpey into private housing and started the Greenford Park estate in 1928. Lionel Lewis then took over all Wimpey's work other than housing and left Godfrey Mitchell to concentrate on housing. Surviving ledgers covering some part-years suggest that Wimpey was building at the rate of around 500 a year around 1930. That soon accelerated and sales rose to 1290 in 1933 and 1370 in 1934.[2] After 1935 Wimpey sales started to decline – attributed to the 'dearth of land purchased on which Artisan houses could be erected. We were forced into a higher price market with a more restricted demand.'[3] Wimpey operated on a limited number of large estates, no more than eight in the early 1930s, all in the Ealing, Harrow and Hayes area. The incidence of large sites was typical of the London housebuilders but Wimpey perhaps had a greater concentration for its size than others. Having come into housebuilding as a contractor laying out estates in the most efficient way possible, the contractor influence in housing development was strong and would remain so in Wimpey's post-war history.

[1] *Dictionary of Business Biography*, Vol.7, p.256.
[2] Minute Book No, 2.
[3] Godfrey Mitchell memo, May 1945.

Wimpey remained active in construction and road building and was also moving into civil engineering. The ownership of the business was still largely shared between Godfrey Mitchell and his father, with Lionel Lewis also having a small shareholding; these three were the directors when the firm floated on the stock exchange in 1934. Turnover was around £2m and pre-tax profits had risen from £53,000 in 1929 to £81,000 in 1933. No public issue of shares was made and an explanation for the flotation emerged later: 'Some twenty years ago when he had been away with appendix trouble, there had been some trouble with staff which had made him pause and reflect, and rather than see the company fall down he decided to make it a Public Company.'[4]

Control passes to charitable trust

Wimpey stressed in its 1936 annual statement that it had 'always been our aim to spread our activities widely' and referred to housing as 'somewhat aside from our main business.' In this, Wimpey was already different from the other large housebuilders. Although some like Wates and Taylor Woodrow were moving into contracting, no other housebuilder had such a large contracting business, and, except John Laing, no other large contractor was building over 1000 houses a year It was probably this broad spread of business which kept profitability on a strong upwards trend, doubling between flotation and 1938, when it made profits of £188,000. Flotation made little difference to Godfrey Mitchell's control of the company. Rather than the company itself raise money directly by the issue of shares, Godfrey Mitchell sold some of his own holding so that 'he will have additional personal funds available for financing the Company. The Board then had a discussion of what happens if the Chairman dies',[5] a discussion that was nearly half a century premature, but which led in 1955 to the divestment of family shares into a Charitable Trust which maintained a controlling interest in the company until its first disposal of shares in 1986.

The outbreak of the Second War led to an immediate decision to complete work on houses in the course of construction and then let them. By then, Wimpey's wartime construction work was in full swing. Defence contracts had been a major feature of the workload since 1936. Contracting turnover increased from £2.4m in 1938 to a wartime peak of £16.6m in 1943. During the war Wimpey was responsible for 93 aerodromes of the 577 built for the RAF and the USAAF, plus factories, army camps and civil defence work. By 1943, Wimpey was employing 16,000 men and the foundations had been laid for Wimpey to become Europe's largest contractor.

An extensive range of wartime internal memos from Godfrey Mitchell have survived, vividly illustrating the extent to which Godfrey Mitchell and his colleagues, while immersed in rapidly-increasing defence work, were planning for the housing needs after the war. In 1943 the directors set out plans to build up immediately the nucleus of a House-building Department. RH Pilkington, the pre-war land surveyor, was nominated to run the department with a head office staff 'who could carry through all negotiations in connection with the location and ultimate purchase of land, layouts, designing, contact with local authorities, selling and conveying houses.'[6] Wimpey's own architect 'would control the selling organisation throughout the country. The department would be concerned only with the estate development and the ultimate sale of houses. The building of houses, roads and sewers would be undertaken by the contracting departments and no separate building department would be set up at first. By this method we should be able to develop in areas other than London and our regional offices would be called on to play a part.'[7] Therein lay the blueprint for a national housebuilder integrated into a construction company; it

---

[4] Board of Management Minute Book, Jan 1955.
[5] Wimpey Minute Book, Dec.1934.
[6] Board of Management Minute Book, Oct. 1943.
[7] Collins memo, April 1944.

was to be the basis both for Wimpey's post-war housing success and its later failure.

Local authority housing

For all that Wimpey had prepared for the resumption of private housebuilding, controls did not permit it. Instead, Wimpey developed in two entirely new areas – municipal housing and international contracting. In his annual address to the Management Board in January 1946, Godfrey Mitchell recognised that 'speculative housebuilding, which in pre-war years was one of the mainstays of the Company, could no longer be counted on. We must, therefore, cast our minds into the future and completely forget the past.' Local authority housing was a natural market for Wimpey's building skills. The Management Board minutes of February 1942 recorded that 'the regional offices should take any favourable opportunity of securing contracts for building houses for the Government or Municipal Authorities, thus getting a small staff who could be employed on Municipal Housing schemes after the war, and who could be available if and when conditions render speculative house building a remunerative proposition.' Godfrey Mitchell memos the next year showed that, if he did not anticipate the bar on private development, he did recognise that local authorities would be playing a far larger part than before the war. 'The sites cleared by blitz are not likely to be rebuilt by speculative builders; it is much more likely that Local Authorities…will clear them.'[8]

By 1947, Wimpey was working on over 50 local authority sites and had built or had under construction 4000 units. Godfrey Mitchell realised he needed a building system and sent Collins, the chief architect, to find one. The answer, Wimpey's No-Fines system, came from Norway and was first used in Middlesex. By the early 1950s Wimpey was building 18,000 local authority houses a year, with profit margins reaching a remarkable 15% – a figure more in keeping with returns on speculative development. The numbers eventually peaked in 1967 at 21,600 and stayed a significant part of Wimpey's domestic business until the mid-1970s.

The regional strategy

Thus, in the post-war period, while Wimpey was prevented from resuming what had been its most profitable pre-war activity, it was developing its general UK contracting business, open-cast coal mining, overseas construction and municipal housing. Organisationally, the decision that was to have the most far-reaching effect on Wimpey, and on the way in which its private housebuilding was to be run, was the introduction of the regional structure. The official story is that the regions were formed as a philanthropic gesture to provide jobs for returning servicemen. Godfrey Mitchell: 'When the war ended, there would be absolute disaster, because you couldn't start enough work around London for the floods of people coming back…so I started the Regions …Initially, it was with no other purpose than to find work for our people who came off the aerodromes and back from France.'[9] In fact, there had been a move to regionalisation early in the war. Again in Godfrey Mitchell's words: 'Regional development had somewhat tended to slow down, but we would go ahead and build up these organisations principally along the same lines as Scotland was developed, taking the smaller jobs for the regional offices and leaving the more complicated contracts to be managed by the head office.'[10]

Despite all the wartime planning and the opportunities which existed for modest levels of private estate development, Wimpey did not resume private housebuilding until 1954, the year that the remaining controls were lifted. Probably piecemeal activity was no longer appropriate to the Wimpey machine which

8   Godfrey Mitchell memo, Sep. 1943.
9   White, *Wimpey*, p.22.
10 Board of Management Minute Book, Jan.1943.

then had more than enough to occupy itself.. 'As to speculative building, Sir Godfrey said we should for the moment not bother about entering this market. We could use all the staff we have got at present on building remunerative 'No Fines' work for Councils... but we must all watch what was happening while the smaller firms were trying it out and be prepared to switch into it when there was real money in the proposition.'[11]

The restart of private housing and the role of FW McLeod

In the Summer of 1953, a paper was circulated to the Board suggesting that private housing would be 'a Regional responsibility and each Regional manager would therefore be expected to initiate the first investigation as to possibilities in his region...searching for suitable land. W Barr said that only by this method could we hope to extend this branch of the business in an economic commercial manner.'[12] By the end of 1953 around 500 plots had been acquired but there was now more confidence in Macmillan's intentions to encourage speculative building and the directors recommended 'more forthright action to acquire land.... it was very necessary that each Region should now have a man detached from all other work solely engaged in hunting through the Region searching for suitable sites...a man with knowledge of estate agency or similar outlook was the obvious choice but we should not waste time and each region should therefore make its own plans forthwith.' There followed what may be the first recorded complaint about land supply: 'Fundamentally, this country was short of building land for semi-detached houses.'[13]

Housing Units 1955-1972

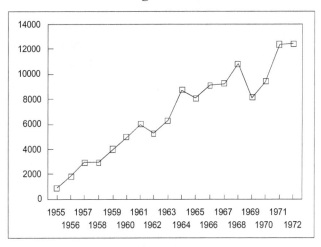

Once the Wimpey machine did swing into action, it moved with remarkable speed. By September 1954 almost 5000 plots had been purchased and the directors were confident of reaching 6000 by the year end towards an ultimate target of 10,000, implying an annual production of around 3000 houses. By 1957, annual sales had almost reached that 3000 (probably making Wimpey the largest housebuilder in the country). The growth in Wimpey's private housing continued at a remorseless rate, all achieved through organic expansion and reached a peak in 1972 of 12,500. By then Wimpey Homes was some three times the size of its nearest competitor: to the man in the street, Wimpey was housing. The man responsible for this remarkable achievement was FW McLeod, a bricklayer by background: 'He was a very direct man,

[11] Ibid, Jan. 1952.
[12] Ibid, June 1953.
[13] Ibid, Feb. 1954.

he was very tough but when you got to know him he was a man who thought very clearly and had an awareness of peoples' ability.'[14] When he died in 1969, the Chairman paid tribute to him in his next Annual Statement: 'The Company suffered a great loss by the death of Mr FW McLeod after 32 years' outstanding service. He was the driving force behind our private house building activities and his experience and judgment will be sorely missed.' David Penton, later Company Secretary, started his Wimpey career as a sales office manager for private housing and has a clear memory of FW, as he was always known. 'He was responsible for the post-war drive in private housing; while it was left to the regions, it was very tightly controlled by McLeod. I have no question that the big peak was due to him driving these people and also the seeds of what went wrong. He was such a dominant individual and he would impose his way of doing things – all his processing and land buying. Every land bid was approved by his team, it was a tremendous control. Probably the design of these things was done in his department, but I never got the impression he took much interest in it.'[15]

Placing private housing in a group context, Wimpey still had a substantial local authority housing business; housing subsidiaries in France, Canada and Australia; it was a significant international contractor; its traditional road surfacing business had been augmented by a string of stone quarries around the UK; and it had some exceptionally profitable commercial property partnerships with Harry Hyams (Oldham Estates) and Joe Levy (Euston Centre). In 1973, as the world recession was breaking, Wimpey's world-wide turnover reached £321m and the group earned pre-tax profits of £32m, up from £8m two years earlier. This dramatic increase, albeit after a period of profits stagnation, must have owed much to house price inflation in the UK. Yet the paradox is that private housing appeared to be regarded as a poor relation in a group where the 'real' men were contractors running exciting multi-million pound civil engineering projects. During the 1960s the company published a 122-page illustrated book, *George Wimpey & Co*, of which only one half page was devoted to private housing. Annual reports displayed the same bias towards construction which usually enjoyed several pages in the Chairman's statement, compared to but a few lines on housing – indeed, sometimes less than the space given to Wimpey Laboratories.

The Wimpey 'barons'

By industry standards, even including housebuilders that were part of larger contracting groups, Wimpey's housing was an anachronism. It was unfocused, dispersed amongst regions so powerful in their own right that their heads were referred to as 'barons', and it had no centralised management. Ironically, this structural weakness was identified by Wimpey's own management almost from the beginning. The Management Board minutes are unusual in the detail they record of the discussion, and those of July 1956 reveal the conflict between the contractor, Barr, then Chairman of the Management Board, and Collins, the group architect, when it was suggested that other housebuilders were making more profit per unit than Wimpey. Barr argued for the regions: Collins said that the smaller firms of speculative builders were not involved in so many other types of work. 'In our case it was difficult to expect managers to control contracts as well as the many complications of selling houses.'[16] Collins clearly lost the battle, if not the argument; those comments should have been made fifteen years later, when the market was about to become more competitive, prone to sharp setbacks and, in short, needing flexibility and focus from dedicated top management.

Private housing lost its momentum in the 1970s. Sales fell by a third, from 12,500 in 1972 to 8000 in 1974.

---

[14] Interview with Sir Cliff Chetwood, April 2000.
[15] Interview with David Penton, Oct. 1999.
[16] Board of Management Minute Book, July 1956.

There was a partial recovery to 11,500 in 1979, helped by the inclusion of Donald Moody's Essex business in that year, but by 1981 sales were down to 7000. Barratt Developments, far more in tune with what had become a buyer's market, had overtaken Wimpey as the largest housebuilder. Cliff Chetwood put it down to people: 'You had two exceptional men and McLeod died and Sir Godfrey began to get frail.'[17] The structural weakness that was emerging in Wimpey's housing was masked by a strong profits performance at a group level. While the specialist housebuilders were experiencing a collapse in published profits, or even worse, Wimpey's group turnover more than doubled between 1973 and 1978 and profits rose from £32m to £57m; this was entirely due to Wimpey's overseas construction, particularly in the Middle East where the leading British contractors were making exceptional profits.

A separate housing company at last

Although turnover was to more than double again, group profits did not regain that 1978 performance for almost a decade. Significantly, 1978 also marked the first public attempt by Wimpey to break the regional structure. A Scheme of Arrangement in January 1978 created a new holding company with separate subsidiaries covering the principal activities. For the first time there was a Wimpey Homes company but even then its degree of independence was questionable. The new group structure was explained: 'The UK construction division carries out building and civil engineering work from a network of 20 regional offices throughout the United Kingdom; it includes the Group's private housing operation in the UK.'.[18]

Although there was pressure for change, the old management still held sway. Mitchell had retired as Chairman in 1973 but he remained a director and, by all accounts, still a dominant figure within the group. His successors RH Gane and, in 1976, RB Smith had worked all their lives under Mitchell's shadow, and ruled under his influence; operational control was shared amongst four joint managing directors. Sir Godfrey, as he had then become, finally retired in November 1981, following his 90th birthday although he remained as President and continued to come into the office until his death in December 1982, some 63 years after he had bought the company. Sir Godfrey was a remarkable figure but there is little doubt that he stayed too long, was unwilling to change what had been a highly successful formula, and did not adequately prepare for the succession.

The month after Mitchell's retirement, two significant appointments were announced. Cliff Chetwood was appointed Chairman of Wimpey Homes with Nelson Oliver, a tough Scot, as its Managing Director. Their arrival coincided with the start of an inflationary bull market which makes it hard to distinguish between internal and external influences but at the least, they ensured that Wimpey was able to profit from that boom. By 1988, UK housing was still building around 9000 houses but these were contributing almost 80% of group trading profits on less than a third of the turnover. Cliff Chetwood became Chief Executive in 1981 but he was still surrounded by an old guard of directors – the 'barons.' It was not until he was also made Chairman, in 1984, that he could make substantial changes at the top and introduce more modern management structures. By 1991, with Chetwood now non-executive Chairman and Joe Dwyer appointed as Chief Executive, Wimpey finally had a slimmed down, conventionally structured board and head office; only then could one really argue that the post-Mitchell era had arrived. Much had been done to restructure Wimpey in the 1980s and it is perhaps contentious to argue that more would have been possible. In the event, when the recession came, Wimpey was still hit hard. For its size, Wimpey Homes' £52m provisions were by no means excessive. To some extent the management had anticipated the downturn in 1987 and had been trimming volumes back. However, in 1992, there were heavy

[17] Interview Sir Cliff Chetwood.
[18] Group accounts, 1979.

provisions elsewhere in the group, particularly commercial property and US housing. In total, Wimpey disclosed losses of £112m that year.

The Tarmac assets swap
Joe Dwyer, who had joined Wimpey aged 16 as a junior engineer, instituted a major disposal programme. However, the area selected for new investment was Wimpey Minerals, with the housing land bank to be contained. Richard Andrew, a career banker, was recruited in 1992 to run housing by which time sales had fallen to only 5500, a figure not seen since 1960. Andrew was soon criticising housing as 'too large, too inflexible and too unresponsive.' Despite all the changes, he was arguing that housing had remained contractor-dominated in the 1980s.[19] It was still proving difficult to turn the Group around and, after an earlier recovery, 1995 saw pre-tax profits fall to £16m. In November that year, Wimpey and Tarmac surprised the industry by announcing its asset swap. Wimpey would take all of Tarmac's housing, principally McLean, and in return Tarmac would receive all of Wimpey's contracting and minerals. 'A figure of £400m was being bandied about for the housing business which I knew we couldn't afford. It became clear, however, during our discussion that Neville [Sims] wanted to build up assets with cash generated from a sale.' Renowned as a lateral thinker, Dwyer reasoned, why not short-circuit the process and give Tarmac Wimpey's mineral assets in return for its housing arm? 'We put the idea to our boards and…the deal was done. Ultimately, the contracting division became part of the discussions as well.'[20]

With the inclusion of McLean Homes, the Wimpey Group was selling over 12,000 houses a year – once again, substantially more than its nearest rival and, ironically, back to the level it had achieved in its own right at the start of the 1970s. McLean brought with it a higher level of profitability, surplus assets (some overseas housing, property) were sold and, in a rising market, trading profits from UK housing were approaching £100m by 1998, with little change in volumes. However, although Wimpey was now solely committed to speculative housing, in the UK and USA, the Board structure remained construction-led with Joe Dwyer as Chairman and Chief Executive and Denis Brant, previously in charge of Wimpey Construction, as deputy Chief Executive; the operational heads of Wimpey Homes, McLean and Morrison in the US were not on the Group Board.

Housing Units, 1972-2004

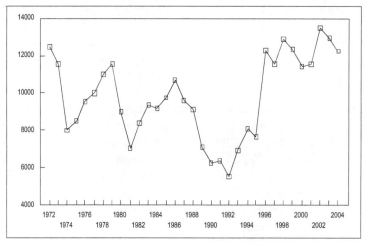

---

[19] Speech at Credit Lyonnais housing conference May 1993.
[20] *Building*, Nov 1996.

Joe Dwyer retired in 1999 to be succeeded by Denis Brant but he took early retirement in October 2000. A new Chief Executive was recruited from outside the Group, Peter Johnson, previously Chief Executive of Rugby, the cement group. Keith Cushen, Managing Director of McLean, was appointed to the Board and immediately set about merging the separate Wimpey Homes and McLean organisations under the Wimpey name. Although cost saving was an important objective, there was a philosophical change intended finally to break with the old Wimpey centrist approach. Wimpey closed its central design, procurement and strategic land departments in favour of 'a more localised McLean-style approach. Wimpey was a national housebuilder with regional offices. McLean is a series of local businesses with a managed centre.'[21]

Wimpey was also prepared to be acquisitive buying McAlpine Homes (4000 units) in October 2001, for £463m, largely as a land transaction, followed by Laing Homes (1230 units) in November 2002, for £297m. In contrast to McAlpine Homes, Laing Homes was retained as separate premium brand. UK housing volumes were allowed to drift a little over the next two years and at 12,232 in 2004 were almost identical with the volumes of 1996, the year of the asset swap. However, there had been a greater concentration on operating margins in the latter years, raising them close to that of the quoted company average. At the same time, Wimpey has been expanding its US housing. Between 2000 and 2004, Morrison Homes had increased its unit volumes from 2600 to 4400 and operating profits more than trebled. In its 2004 accounts, Wimpey argued that 'We benefit greatly from having the ability to balance investment between our UK and US businesses and will continue to do so.'

Additional Sources
Files of Wimpey correspondence and early minute books are held in the CIRCA+WICCAD archive at Kimmins Mill, Stroud.

---

[21] Keith Cushen interviewed in *Building Homes*, April 2001.

AND THE REMAINING SMALL QUOTED COMPANIES

ALLISON HOMES

The Company was formed by CD Allison in the 1940s and it built in the east midlands, primarily to people moving from more expensive property in the south east. In 1985, Allison sold his company to Messrs Hayklan and Silverton who sold it on in turn to the quoted **Wiggins** in 1987. Wiggins had its own acute financial problems during the subsequent recession and extracted some £6m of cash from Allison. The housing subsidiary had a different bank than the parent and Allison was put into receivership in 1992. Allison was then bought out by David Mee, (who had been made development director in 1987) and Karl Hick who was Wiggins' Finance Director. The customer-orientation of the business was changed to produce a greater reliance on the local market. Unit sales increased to around 200 a year although it was not until the year 2000 that profits reached the £1m mark. In September 2001, Allison was sold for £17m to Kier, where it continued to trade under its own name.

ASHWORTH & STEWART

Ashworth & Steward was founded by Arthur Jordan in 1946 as builders and fireplace manufacturers; Jordan was joined the following year by George Bates and the two families became equal partners in the venture. By the time of the flotation in 1964 it was primarily a developer of houses for sale and blocks of flats for retention as investments in the Birmingham area. Wesleyan & General, which had owned 18% of the company on flotation, supported a switch to commercial development in 1968, and in 1970 there were large sales of housing land and the level of housebuilding activity was reduced. The Wesleyan gradually increased its shareholding to a controlling 51% and, in 1972, put its shares up for sale by tender. Ashworth was acquired by Ron Shuck's Cornwall Property Holdings and almost immediately Ashworth sold 712 flats and 33 mews houses to Dares Estates for £2.8m. Cornwall's residential arm then included Alliance Property, building in central London; E & L Berg , building in the suburban south east of London; and Ashworth & Steward with a combined residential turnover of £5m. By 1974, Ron Shuck had left and the companies became part of Argyle Securities. When the renamed Ash Homes was acquired for £1.9m by Barratt in 1978, it was building around 150 houses a year in the better residential areas of Birmingham.

ASHTON

Norman Ashton, born in 1908, founded his Leeds housebuilding business in 1933 when he was joined by his younger brother Edwin. On the cessation of private development during the war, Ashton was restricted to small local authority contracts but he set up a coach building and motor repair business. Private housebuilding resumed in the 1950s and on flotation in 1964, the Company claimed to be one of the largest housebuilders in Yorkshire, with land holdings of around 2000 plots. However, its profits showed only modest growth thereafter, and it was building around 300 houses a year when the company was bought by Orme in May 1972 for £3.2m, the directors having sold their 63% holding.

BARTON

The Southport firm of RJ Barton was founded in Southport in 1944 by Richard Barton and his sons, William and Eric, as a general contractor. Local authority housing became its speciality and at the time of its flotation in 1964 accounted for 70% of turnover. There had been a move into private housing and the prospectus disclosed that it then represented some 12% of turnover; the land bank had increased to 300 plots and there were plans to build 100 units that year. When the company was acquired by Fairclough in 1967, it gave the latter an entrée into the private housing market for the first time. Eric Barton joined the Fairclough board.

BIRSE

As far as housing is concerned, the Birse story is one of timing: a contractor entering the development market at the top and exiting at the bottom. The Company had been founded in 1970 by Peter Birse, initially working for the petrochemical industry on Humberside and then gradually spreading into conventional building work across the north east. In 1980 Birse established an office in the south east, which accounted for the major portion of the group's sales by the end of the decade. Further regional offices were opened in Manchester in 1983 and Northampton in 1987 and a branch in Birmingham in 1988. Birse Properties had been formed in 1982 doing a modest amount of commercial development and it was not until 1987 that a housebuilding subsidiary, Birse Homes, was established in Bristol, followed by a central London housing company.

The company was floated in August 1989, and was five times oversubscribed despite the signs of imminent danger in the industry. Substantial sums were invested in the new development activities: residential and commercial work-in-progress rose from £4m in 1988 to £48m in 1991. Start-up costs on housing were followed by trading losses and then write-downs. Housing sales reached no more than 125 units at their peak (1993). Because of changing bases of disclosure and restatements it is not easy to see the exact losses from development but they probably approached £20m from what was inherently a sideline to the main business. In 1995, Birse withdrew from the housing market, at a further £5m loss on the written down values. One of the subsidiaries was bought by Persimmon in April 1985 and Admiral Homes bought 17 sites in the June to form the basis for its Western region. Perhaps the last word should belong to Peter Birse, quoted in *Building* at the time of the Company's maiden results as a quoted company: 'House Building was one of the worst mistakes of my life.'

CHANSOM

WJ Channing and WR Osmond founded a building business in the south west of England in the mid-1920s. The partnership was dissolved in 1936 but Channing continued to trade on his own account until 1947 when the business was transferred to W J Channing and Sons. The son of the title was Hubert, who had begun his working career with his father and become a director in 1951. There is no evidence of any housebuilding until the formation of Chansom Estates in 1954 by Hubert Channing and Kenneth Sloper, who had joined the Channing business in 1948. Chansom become the dominant company and acquired WJ Channing in 1958.

By the time Chansom was floated in 1968, it was developing in Berkshire, Surrey, Hampshire and the south west of England, and was forecasting some 230 units for that year. However, profits collapsed in

1970, from £273,000 to £100,000, and in March 1971 the Channing family offered to buy back the shares at 33p compared with the original 58³/₄p issue price. However, this was overtaken by a higher offer from David Charles.

COLROY

Colroy was formed in 1966 by Phil Jacobs, then aged 60, his son-in-law, the actor David Swift[1] and Coleman Jeffreys. Phil Jacobs' first venture was a garment manufacturing business which became Northgate Group, a quoted company and major supplier to Marks & Spencer; he had also been a director of Granada Television, Chairman of Lambert Howarth and director of many other companies. The business grew rapidly until a £1.2m profit was earned in 1973, but losses followed in the recession and profits never approached that record figure until the late 1980s. Bill Hoggett, a regional Managing Director of Ideal Homes, joined as Managing Director in 1986 in readiness for Colroy's flotation in 1988, by which time Colroy was building in the north west, the midlands and East Anglia. Sales reached a record 300 units in 1989 and profits peaked at £4.4m. However, profits began to fall sharply as the recession deepened, by which time Jacobs, still the controlling shareholder, was in his mid-80s. In January 1991, Colroy was bought by Gleeson and Hoggett later became Managing Director of Gleeson Homes.

CROSBY HOMES

James Crosby established his business in 1925, building houses in north Cheshire. During the war, the firm turned to civil engineering and contracting but 'The buoyant economy of the late 1950s encouraged a return to traditional housebuilding activities and from this time James Crosby specialised in building executive homes.'[2] By the 1980s, Crosby was controlled by four families, among them descendants of the original Crosbys, but they took little part in day-to-day activities. In 1986, Eric Crosby sold out to the senior management, led by Michael Burgess, for £4m. Crosby had completed only 29 units in the year to March 1983 and incurred a loss of £120,000. Burgess, who had joined Crosby in 1974, became Managing Director in December 1982 and gradually increased output (by 1986/87 it was up to 171 units) and restored Crosby to profitability. In July 1987, the company was floated; pre-tax profits reached a peak of £4.1m in 1988/89 but volumes fell sharply in the recession. Following substantial land write-downs, the interim dividend was cut in December 1990, and the Berkeley takeover was agreed the following March. Michael Burgess joined the Berkeley main board but resigned soon after. Crosby was kept as a separate entity within Berkeley and in 1993 Geoff Hutchinson, previously Managing Director of Beazer Central, was appointed its Chief Executive. As with its parent, the emphasis was gradually changed towards city centre development, ranging from Birmingham up to Newcastle. As part of Berkeley's restructuring, the Company was sold on deferred terms to the management in 2003. Crosby was then sold to the Australian Lend Lease in 2005.

---

[1] Played Harry in Drop the Dead Donkey
[2] Crosby Prospectus, 1987.

DEAN SMITH

The Manchester-based Dean Smith Construction was established in 1962 by Anthony Dean Smith as general building contractors. In 1964 Dean Smith (Investments) was formed to develop residential sites for sale in North Cheshire, followed in 1965 by Weydove for commercial development. These companies were brought together in 1968, and the group floated on the Stock Exchange, when it was described as 'one of the most successful of the housebuilders that came to the market in 1968.'[3] Its residential turnover suggested housing volumes of not much more than 50 a year.

Profits rose from £73,000 in 1968 to £183,000 in 1971 with the property subsidiary providing nearly half the turnover. Birmingham Estates, described as 'originally engaged in certain speculative ventures which were not suitable for a public company',[4] and controlled by the directors, was acquired early in 1972. Three-quarters of the shares in Birmingham Estates were owned by the Dean Smith directors with the balance owned by Paul Holland who, in turn, owned 10% of Dean Smith; the transaction took the directors' interests in Dean Smith up from 38% to 46%. In July 1972, Francis Parker and ICFC each purchased 12% of Dean Smith with the intention to sell Anglia Commercial Developments, a joint company of Francis Parker and ICFC, to Dean Smith for shares to the extent that a controlling interest would be acquired. This transaction fell through and in May 1973 there was an agreed bid of £2.6m from Francis Parker.

GORST

Eldon R Gorst & Son was founded by Eldon Roy Gorst in 1958; he was then aged 47 and had been in the building industry since the early 1930s; the 'Son' was Tony Gorst, a quantity surveyor. From 1961, substantially all the Company's activity lay in developing its own estates along the North Wales coast. The Company floated in 1965 although only making profits of £120,000; housing volumes were not stated but the land bank statistics suggested between 100 and 150 units. Profits rose to a peak of £230,000 in 1968 but within two years they had fallen back to under £100,000. In August 1971, Gorst accepted a £900,000 takeover bid from Christian Salvesen.

GREENSQUARE PROPERTIES

The Company was formed for the purpose of acquiring two development companies, Silverdale and Fordstow, prior to a flotation in 1972. The principals, based in Manchester, were John Harrison, a solicitor, and Howard Goodie, a chartered surveyor and senior partner of Lancashire and Cook. The Silverdale Building Co. was incorporated in 1955 and, in 1968, sold to Land Securities (North West), a private investment company; its management was taken over by Harrison. Fordstow, which was much the smaller of the two companies, was incorporated in 1963 to develop a commercial property in Handforth, Cheshire and it acquired other investment properties after that date. Goodie became a director and major shareholder in 1967.

The housebuilding was centred on Lancashire, Cheshire, Westmoreland and north Wales at the time of the flotation but it was the stated intention to spread to the south of England, and a site had been bought in Caterham. No unit volumes were quoted in the 1972 Prospectus but a six-year land bank of 655 units implied an annual rate of around 110. The profits record had been erratic due to what the Prospectus

3 *Building*, 26th June 1971.
4 Acquisition circular, Feb. 1971.

described as 'problems inherited by the present management'; the forecast for the group for the year to September 1972 was £250,000. However, the stock market was falling by the time the flotation took place and 73% of the shares were left with the underwriters; in the event, profits exceeded the forecast at £283,000. The Accounts reported the purchase of several sites for development in the executive market, plus two commercial sites in Knutsford and, in line with plans for expanding in London and the home counties, four apartment blocks in Chelsea.

In February 1973 Harrison sold a 28% holding to merchant bankers Eldridge Stableford and DJ Eldridge joined the Board. Despite the weakening of the housing market, the management continued to take a positive view: profits in 1972/73 exceeded £300,000 and the holding in Langstone Estates was increased from 50% to 100%; 150 completions were planned for the year. However, the Company was highly geared and £1.3m of the £1.8m asset value was represented by goodwill. After a half year loss of £75,000, a receiver was appointed in April 1975.

JAMES HARRISON

James Harrison founded his company in 1953 to undertake joinery contracts, and expanded into public works contracting specialising in houses and schools. The 1968 Prospectus disclosed that over 800 local authority houses had been completed that year. Subsequent expansion into western Scotland was heavily loss-making and in 1971 it was decided to diversify into private housebuilding to lessen the dependence on the public sector. Through the Perdovan Property Development Company, Harrison acquired around 250 plots and was soon building over 100 houses per annum; Perdovan's legacy was the start it gave to John Swanson, the eventual successor to Lawrie Barratt. Barratt made its first bid for Harrison in 1972, subject to its Chairman buying back the construction operation, which turned out impossible to achieve. Perdovan was later sold on to Bradley of York. The construction losses in the west were eliminated and private housebuilding expanded again. James Harrison retired in 1975 to devote more time to his other interests, although remaining as Chairman. Barratt returned with a second, successful, offer in 1978 valued at £3.2m.

HILLS

WA Hills & Co was incorporated in 1936 to acquire the building business founded in 1920 by William Ambrose Hills. The company was a small contractor based in Colchester, working in East Anglia until after the war. Hills began residential development in 1946 and over the next twenty years developed residential estates around Colchester totalling some 1250 houses. In the early 1960s it was averaging no more than 90 houses a year. The company was bought by the quoted City and Country Properties (part of the Freshwater group) in 1960; Stanley and Ernest Hills, the founder's sons, and Alan Hills, the grandson, continued to run the business.

In 1965, the company was floated on the Stock Exchange to raise funds for the parent's property investment plans; the Hills continued to run the business, and City and Country Properties retained 46% of the shares. Hills changed little during its public life, although in 1969 it purchased the **Larter** group of builders and estate developers, operating from Norfolk. In 1970 a merger with Daniel T Jackson was proposed with both parties to have equal shares in a new company, but in the end it fell through: 'I think that the Hills bid was very much a takeover by Jackson and at the end of the day Hills wouldn't do it.'[5]

5 Interview with Nigel Parker, Mar. 2001.

In April 1972 City and Country sold its controlling stake to Galliford Estates and the full bid followed.

TUDOR JENKINS

The business was founded by Tudor Jenkins in 1936 as general building and civil engineering contractors. On incorporation in 1948, he was joined by David Jenkins[6] then aged 21 and fresh from Cambridge University. David was made Managing Director in 1954. He was joined by Bram Davies, a quantity surveyor, in 1962 and the company was floated on the Stock Exchange in 1964 (by which time Tudor was deceased). The Company was then building private and council houses, factories and civil engineering though 'in the past few years the company has devoted an increasing part of its total effort towards building houses.'[7] The business remained very local, being confined to a 20-mile radius of Pontyclun – covering Cardiff, Bridgend and Pontypridd – and its profits were no more than £45,000. Its subsequent record as a public company led *Building* to refer to 'the astonishing success story of Tudor Jenkins'[8] and by 1971 the company was building around 300 houses a year and making profits of £531,000 – still within only a 40-mile radius of Pontyclun. However, when the offer came from Orme the documentation referred to a need to expand geographical coverage, and the directors argued that this could best be achieved as part of a larger organisation.

KAY-BEVAN/GRA PROPERTY

The Kay referred to Hermann Kay, born in Vienna in 1901, a civil and structural engineer with a degree from Vienna Technical University. Kay was described as the founder of H Kay (Buildings) and, according to the 1963 prospectus, had been with the company since 1943. The Company was actually incorporated in that year as R Watson (Birmingham) with Richard Watson owning 7% and Julius Lunzer, an engineer, owning 93%. Watson resigned in 1944, but Hermann Kay did not become a director until 1956 and the Company did not change its name to H Kay until 1963, prior to the flotation. The Prospectus stated that no building work was carried out between 1945 and 1956 but from 1956 the company built houses for sale in the Birmingham area. From 1960, the firm concentrated on building for its investment subsidiaries. Profits in the first year as a public company were only £50,000.

In 1966, Kay bought Leslie Bevan's **Bevan Homes**, hence the change of name, and by 1968 profits had risen to a record £240,000. The Company then began to diversify, buying a car dealer in 1969 (which was losing money the following year) and then a steel stockholder and a plumbing and heating contractor. In March 1972 Kay-Bevan accepted a bid of £3.3m from **GRA Property** Trust by which time it was building around 100-200 houses a year. GRA had been formed in 1927 as the Greyhound Racing Association Trust. In 1970 it merged with White City (Manchester) Associated; both companies had recently begun to rationalise their greyhound racing interests in order to release land for development, and the merger was specifically intended to accelerate this process. A substantial commercial property development programme was instituted in the early 1970s and the acquisition of a housebuilding company was intended to complement this. The addition of property development to the original sporting interests was 'likened … to fitting stabilisers to a ship.'[9] Come the property recession and the

---

[6] Presumably his son.
[7] Tudor Jenkins Prospectus, 1964.
[8] *Building*, 29th Nov. 1968.
[9] Group accounts, 1973.

stabiliser had the opposite effect. All the housing and property was then grouped within the Kay-Bevan subsidiary and that was placed in receivership in October 1975. GRA entered a scheme of arrangement in July 1976 to secure its own future. Leslie Bevan refused to resign and was voted off the Board at the next annual general meeting.

LONDON & CLYDESIDE

London & Clydeside was formed in 1972 by John McIntyre, a one time local authority land surveyor and land negotiator for Bellway. Although McIntyre had a shareholding, the company was originally a subsidiary of a Newcastle building company. In 1978 a management buyout saw McIntyre and his fellow executives assume complete ownership. At that time, the business was based in Glasgow where it had a couple of small sites, plus one major site near Aberdeen; it was building a little under 100 houses a year. By the time L&C was floated in 1984, it had sites across the central lowlands and in Aberdeen (a total of 232 units in 1983) and was active in the commercial property market.

Volumes changed little in the succeeding years and by 1994 were still around the level achieved in the flotation year. The 1994 Chairman's statement reported three executive directors over 60, including McIntyre himself who was going to remain only until 1996 or when a new managing director was found. Following a deterioration in interim profits, a £12m offer from Wilson (Connolly) was agreed in May 1995.

SCOTTISH HOMES INVESTMENT COMPANY

Scottish Homes had interesting antecedents. It was incorporated in 1924 by David Oppenheim as a finance and trading business. His son, Meyer, bought the company in 1963 when it was no longer active, introduced fresh capital the following year, and bought James Laidlaw & Sons and 42% of Argyle Securities, both quoted companies. Laidlaw had started in joinery a century previous and at the time of acquisition was active in local authority housing, with its own high and low rise systems. When Scottish Homes was floated in 1968, Laidlaw had significant land holdings and was undertaking part of the development of the new town being built at Dalgety Bay, where Argyle controlled the land. Laidlaw was then expecting to complete significantly more than the previous year's 70 units. In the event, Laidlaw lost money on private housing in 1970 and 1971 and decided to withdraw from the market. When Barratt bid £2.6m for Scottish Homes in 1980, it was primarily buying a large land holding at Dalgety Bay plus some commercial property.

TERN GROUP

The Tern Group was founded in South Wales in 1971 by Roger Wisenden, an ex-Wimpey civil engineer, who acted as Chairman and Chief Executive, and Alan Edwards. It was not until 1980 that Tern moved into development and at first this was commercial property, a move which was thought to provide further work for the construction companies. Tern Residential was started in Southampton in 1984 'to create high quality, low density housing schemes and sheltered accommodation.'[10] By the time of the 1985 flotation, Tern was operating off just two sites. Tern Residential was sold to CALA in April 1986 for £1.4m; it then had four sites.

---

[10] Placing document, 1985.

VARNEY HOLDINGS

Harry Hobdell (born 1914) and Samuel Varney (1899) formed a partnership in 1945 as jobbing builders trading in London. They were later joined by Harry's two brothers, Fred and John, and further companies were formed, principally to develop residential estates; Varney retired in 1964. The company was floated on the Stock Exchange in 1968 by which time it had offices in Manchester, Birmingham, London, Erith and Falmouth. Residential development was begun in England in 1957, principally Hampshire and Sussex, and two yeas later John Hobdell started a Scottish subsidiary that was to become one of the larger developers in the lowland belt, building almost 300 units a year by the time of the flotation; this compared with around 130 south of the border. Varney had an inauspicious start as a public company with almost three-quarters of the shares left with the underwriters. The subsequent profits record was erratic and the plant hire subsidiary had periods of loss. In June 1973, Bovis bid for Varney, but wanting only 65% so that it would retain a public quotation. Bovis's intention had been to keep Varney as a Scottish quoted company and put all of its own Scottish interests into Varney, with Bovis holding the majority stake. However, this was never done and, at the end of the year, the outstanding minority shareholding was acquired.

BIBLIOGRAPHY
General

A full bibliography can be found in the companion volume *British Housebuilders: History & Analysis*. The general works below are those specifically cited in the text.

Betham, E., [ed.]	*House-building 1934-36,* (London, 1934).
Bundock J. D.	'Speculative Housebuilding and Some Aspects of the Activities of the Suburban Housebuilder within the Greater London Outer Suburban Area 1919-1939', M. Phil., University of Kent, 1974.
Cox, R.C.W.	'Urban Development and Redevelopment in Croydon 1830–1940', PhD thesis, University of Leicester, 1970.
Erdman, Edward L.	*People & Property,* (London, 1982).
Hamnett, Chris and Randolph, Bill	*Cities, Housing and Profits*, (London, 1988).
Jackson, Alan	*Semi Detached London*, (London, 1973); 2nd.rev.ed., (Didcot, 1991).
Jeremy, D.J. and Shaw, C. (eds)	*Dictionary of Business Biography*, 6 Vols (London, 1984–86).
Kellett, John R.	*The Impact of Railways on Victorian Cities,* (London, 1969).
Marriott, Oliver	*The Property Boom,* (London, 1967).
Merrett, Stephen	*Owner Occupation in Britain,* (London, 1982).
Morgan, Nicholas	*A History of the NHBC and Private Home Building,* (Carnforth, 1987).
Nicholls, C.S. (ed.)	*Dictionary of National Biography 1986-1990, (Oxford, 1996).*
Rose, Jack	*Dynamics of Urban Property Development,* (London, 1985).
Slaven, A. and Checkland, S. (eds)	*Dictionary of Scottish Business Biography* (Aberdeen, 1986).
Supple, Barry	*The Royal Exchange Assurance A History of British Insurance 1720-1970*, (Cambridge, 1970).
Wellings, Fred	*Private Housebuilding Annual* (London, 1980-2005)*
Wellings, Fred..	'The Rise of the National House builder: a History of British Housebuilders through the Twentieth Century', PhD thesis, University of Liverpool, 2005.

*The *Private Housebuilding Annual* [PHA] was a stockbroking publication between 1980 and 2002; in 2003 and 2004 the *PHA* was published by *Building* magazine and in 2005 by the author.

Companies

Balfour Beatty

Anon	*Balfour Beatty 1909-1984,* (London, 1984).

Beazer

Beazer, Cyril H. G.	*Random Reflections of a West Country Master Craftsman,* (Bath, 1981).

Henry Boot

Anon	*Henry Boot A Brief History*, (Sheffield, 1986).
Baines, Ron	*The Boot Family* 2nd ed (Sheepbridge, 1998).
Boot, Charles	*Post-war Houses,* (Sheffield, 1944).
Gent John B., [ed.]	*Croydon, the Story of a Hundred Years,* Croydon Natural History and Scientific Society, (Croydon, 1970).
Perry, George	*Movies from the Mansions A History of Pinewood Studios,* (London, 1986).

Bellway
Anon   *Bellway 50 years of housing Britain*, in 1996 Annual Report
Bradley
Anon   *Bradley Building on a Name,* (n/p, c.1983).
Bovis
Anon   *Bovis Centenary 1885-1985,* (n/p, c.1985).
Cooper, Peter   *Building Relationships The History of Bovis 1885-2000,* (London, 2000).
Bryant
Anon   *1885-1985 One Hundred Years of Building,* in 1985 Annual Report
Comben
Anon   *Comben Homes Celebrate their 75th Anniversary,* (Bristol, c.1975).
Costain
Anon   'Richard Costain Centenary 1865-1965' *Bulletin, Staff Journal of the Costain Group,* June 1965.
Costain, Sir Albert   *Reflections,* (Cirencester, 1987).
Catherwood, H. F. R.   'Development and Organisation of Richard Costain Ltd' in Edwards, Ronald S and Townsend, Harry, [eds], *Business Growth,* (London, 1966), pp.271-83.
Catherwood, Fred   *At the Cutting Edge,* (London, 1995).
English China Clays
Hudson, Kenneth   *The History of the English China Clays,* (Newton Abbot, c.1968).
Higgs and Hill
Anon   'Higgs and Hill 1874-1974', *The Crown Journal,* Centenary Issue No. 178, 1974.
Laing
Coad, Roy   *Laing The Biography of Sir John W Laing (1879-1978),* (London, 1979).
Anon   *Team Work The Story of John Laing and Son,* (n/p, 1950).
Harrison, Godfrey   *Life and Belief in the Experience of John W Laing,* (London, 1954).
Ritchie, Berry   *The Good Builder The John Laing Story,* (London, 1997).
Walter Lawrence
Anon   *Walter Lawrence 1871-1971 A History of the Family Firm of Walter Lawrence,* (n/p 1971).
Lovell
Anon   *Howard Farrow: A Story of 50 Years 1908-58,* (London, 1958).
Salt, Richard   *A Good Job Well Done The Story of Rendell A West Country Builder,* (Amersham, 1983).
Janes
Kennett, David   *A Provincial Builder,* Unpublished typescript, Luton Library, c.1970.
Ideal Homes
Furnell, Michael   *The Diamond Jubilee of Ideal Homes,* (West Byfleet, 1989).
Broakes, Nigel   *A Growing Concern,* (London, 1979).
Mactaggart & Mickel
Watters, Diane   *Mactaggart & Mickel and the Scottish Housebuilding Industry,* (Edinburgh, 1999).
McAlpine
Gray, Tony   *The Road to Success Alfred McAlpine 1935-1985,* (London, 1987).
Anon   *McAlpine The First Hundred Years,* (London, c.1969).
Childers, J. Saxon   *Robert McAlpine A Biography,* (Oxford, 1926).
McLean/Tarmac
Anon   *Tarmac 50 Years of Progress 1903-1953* (n/p, 1953).
L.W. Madden   'Builders and their Businesses 7: John McLean & Sons Ltd. of

	Wolverhampton', *Building* 18th April 1969.
Ritchie, Berry	*The Story of Tarmac,* (London, 1999).
Milbury	
Carlisle, Hugh and Lickiss, Michael	*Milbury plc Westminster Property Group investigation under…the Companies Act,* (London, 1988).
Miller	
Anon	*Miller Celebrating the Miller Group's Diamond Jubilee,* (Edinburgh, 1994).
T,F.Nash	
Anon	'Initiative and Progress shown by Private Enterprise in attempting to solve Oxford's Housing Problem', *Oxford Monthly,* Aug.1932, p.6.
Anon	*Nash houses T F Nash Limited,* (London, c.1933).
Prowting	
Anon	*Prowting 75,* (Uxbridge?, 1987).
Redrow	
Burland, M. and Whitehouse, J.	*The Redrow Group,* (Flintshire, 1999).
Taylor Woodrow	
Jenkins, Alan	*On Site 1921-71,* (London, 1971).
Jenkins, Alan	*Built on Site,* (London, 1980).
Beaverbrook, Lord	*Courage: The Story of Sir James Dunn,* (London, 1962).
Tilbury	
Anon	*Tilbury 100 Years Onward Tilbury Centenary 1884-1984,* (Horsham, 1984).
Unit Construction	
John, A. H.	*A Liverpool Merchant House Being the History of Alfred Booth and Company 1863-1958,* (London, 1959).
Ward	
Anon	*Work is Fun the Ward Holdings Story,* (Chatham, c.1990).
A.J.Wait	
Anon	*The AJ Wait Group,* (n/p, c.1960).
Wates	
Anon	*Wates Have a Way with them,* (London, !963).
Anon	*Wates Build,* (London, 1963).
Wilson Connolly	
Anon	*Wilson (Connolly) Holdings Ltd the first 75 years,* (Northampton, c.1980).
Wimpey	
White, Valerie	*Wimpey The First Hundred Years,* (London, 1980).

Index

Companies

People

If there are two family members in same company, both are identified in same line; if more, then et al. is used as in Gallaghers and Laings. Brief mentions excluded and where name are synonymous with the company, the reference can be found by checking in the company index, e.g. Geo Bainbridge

Abel, David 102

Adams, Eric 89

Adamson, John and Richard 105, 174-5

Adkins, Eric

Ainscough, Bill 278-9

Al-Fayed, Mohammed 90

Allen, Mike 232

Anderson, Alan 75

Anderson, Dudley 92-3

Andrews, Bob 173

Aris, Ronald 100-101

Ashworth, Herbert 22, 145

Bailey, Ben and Richard 17-18

Baird, Brian 59, 60

Balch, Billy 67, 211, 293

Baldwin, George 108

Ball, Geoff 76-7

Bannister, Bill 208, 263

Barber, Roy 243

Barham, Jimmy 126

Barnes, Derek 225-7

Baron, Tom 25, 66-7, 92, 210, 293-4

Barratt, Lawrie 23, 25-29

Bartholomew, John 20-1

Barton, Richard et al. 120, 312-3

Baseley, Stewart 80, 122

Bates, George 312

Beazer, Brian et al. 30, 32, 34-5

Bell, John et al. 36-9

Benjamin, Joseph 113

Bennett, Charles 108

Bett, Iain et al. 47, 49

Betts, Donald 170

Berg, Ellis and Lewis 41

Benzecry, Cecil 7

Berry, Leslie 51

Bevan, Leslie 317

Bickel, John 124

Bilton, Percy 50, 261

Bilton, Anton 261

Black, Ian 298-9

Black, Ivor 75

Black, John 123

Bliss, Paul 111

Bloch, Sidney 145-6

Bloor, John 51

Boardman, John 142

Bobroff, Ben et al. 89

Bobroff, Solomon 92-4

Bolton, Paul 194

Bolton, Ronnie 24, 262

Boot, Charles et al. 52-5

Borders, Elsey 219

Bovis, Charles 57

Bradley, Edwin et al. 116-7

Bradley, Jack 63-4

Brant, Denis 310

Brazier, Stephen 270

Brill, David 136, 239-40

Brooke, Richard 273

Brooks, Derek 7, 8

Brown, Norman 64

Bryant, Chris et al. 69-71

Buckingham, Robin 108-9

Burgess, Alan 122

Burgess, Michael 314

Burns, William 75

Burnett, Peter 11

Burrows, Ernest 180, 238

Burton, Tony 179

Broakes, Nigel 154, 156

Bruce, Bill et al 24, 26

Busby, Colin 163

Byrne, Desmond 159

Calderbank, Thomas 225

Callcutt, John 98-99

Calverley, David 138, 155-6, 274

Canadine, John 132

Carey, Tony 44

Carter, Roy 228-9

Casey, Stephen 126

Cassidy, John 24, 26, 28, 284

Castleton, Alf 232

Catherwood, Fred 88, 168

Cawthra, David 215

Chalcraft, Richard 114

Chapman, Michael 70, 71

Chapple, Alan 30, 32, 34

CPSIA information can be obtained
at www.ICGtesting.com
Printed in the USA
LVHW101511151218
600597LV00006B/37/P